American Foreign Policy in the 21st Century

Series Editor

Thomas Henriksen
Stanford University
Palo Alto, California, USA

This series seeks to provide serious books on the U.S. response to contemporary global challenges. The collapse of the Soviet Union in 1991 marked a new and altered stage in U.S. foreign relations. The United States now confronts a very broad spectrum of problems in the post-Cold War period. These include issues such as environmental degradation, climate change, humanitarian disasters, piracy, globalization, ethnic civil wars, sustainable economic development, non-state terrorism, and the role of international law in global affairs. Even more familiar troubles such as state-to-state relations have taken on new trappings with the threats from rogue nations and the return of great power rivalries with a rising China, a resurgent Russia, and a self-reliant European Union. Nuclear weapons, energy dependence, democracy promotion, regional problems in the Middle East or Africa, along with ascendant China and India are now viewed differently than in the previous era. Additionally, there are important and troubled bilateral relationships. Today, these state-to-state difficulties include Pakistan, Venezuela, and Mexico, to name just a few that scarcely appeared on State Department radar two decades ago. This series publishes monographs on topics across these foreign policy issues, and new ones as they emerge. The series editor is Thomas H. Henriksen, a Senior Fellow at the Hoover Institution, Stanford University, USA.

More information about this series at
http://www.springer.com/series/14764

Thomas H. Henriksen

Cycles in US Foreign Policy since the Cold War

palgrave
macmillan

Thomas H. Henriksen
Hoover Institution
Stanford University
Palo Alto, California, USA

American Foreign Policy in the 21st Century
ISBN 978-3-319-48639-0 (hardcover) ISBN 978-3-319-48640-6 (eBook)
ISBN 978-3-319-74852-8 (softcover)
DOI 10.1007/978-3-319-48640-6

Library of Congress Control Number: 2017930173

Printed on acid-free paper

This Palgrave Macmillan imprint is published by Springer Nature
The registered company is Springer International Publishing AG
The registered company address is: Gewerbestrasse 11, 6330 Cham, Switzerland

Acknowledgments

Once again, I must express my gratitude to the Hoover Institution for its generous support for this book as for the others researched and written under its auspices. Its renowned archives, attentive administrative staff, and stimulating intellectual atmosphere make for an ideal scholarly oasis. The Hoover Institution's director, Thomas Gilligan, and his administrative associates underpin the structure that enables its scholars and visitors to engage in academic endeavors free from so many routines that distract from scholarship. My colleagues, once more, furnished thought-provoking insights, often in Hoover's Senior Common Room.

On this book, I have been blessed with many first-rate assistants who have helped research, fact-check, and catch errors. Led by Nicholas Siekierski, they included Robyn Teruel and Griffin Bovée.

A special note of thanks for their love and encouragement is due to my wife, Margaret Mary, and our family—Heather, Damien, Liv, and Lucy.

Contents

Note from the Editor

As the decades slip by since the Berlin Wall's collapse, international observers have gleaned a clearer view of America's post-Cold War role and of the conduct of US foreign policy in the absence of the bipolar standoff with the Soviet Union. During the past three decades, Washington administrations have had to face a variety of international crises. The global scene has witnessed a host of failed and failing states, some marked by appalling human tragedies. Civil wars in the former Yugoslavia yielded mass death and huge flows of refugees before producing a handful of new sovereign states. Worse still, the Arab Spring upheaval tossed the Middle East into catastrophic violence. Terrorism and warfare have become prevalent in the aftermath of the September 11 attack within the United States. Terrorist movements have plagued not only Middle Eastern states but also North and sub-Saharan African countries along with the Philippines and Indonesia. Geopolitically, the world has been transformed by the resurgence of Russia and the emergence of China as great powers. America has not been a bystander in this changing environment and its varied reactions more than deserve our attention.

This current volume falls within the Palgrave series American Foreign Policy in the Twenty-first Century, which has as its goal to narrate, analyze, and comprehend US global involvement in the still-new era since the Soviet Union vanished, ending the Cold War. Interested readers and students, it is hoped, will gain knowledge and insights about America's foreign policy in the unfolding global order from reading volumes in the series. As the United States becomes more enmeshed in international affairs, it behooves American and foreign audiences to develop awareness and understanding about Washington's policies from different perspectives. This series strives to contribute to the clarification and, perhaps, even the illumination of how the United States confronts a host of world issues.

The first volume in the series was Howard J. Wiarda's valuable book, *American Foreign Policy in Regions of Conflict.* Professor Wiarda concentrated on the familiar basics of international relations by focusing on the history, geography, culture, and economics of the global regions. He eschewed the mathematical modeling techniques embraced by many contemporary political scientists. A reliance on the fundamentals, he advocated, will more likely lead to a sounder American policy and a clearer understanding of the international landscape.

The second book, *America and the Rogue States*, was my own addition to the series. It deals with US policy toward a small number of belligerent powers, which depart from the norms of international relations by their sponsorship of terrorism and pursuit of weapons of mass destruction, chiefly nuclear arms. The origins of these international pariahs date from the Cold War but they emerged menacingly on the world stage with the end of the Soviet Union. Countries such as North Korea, Iran, Syria, Sudan, Cuba, and pre-US invasion Iraq preoccupied Washington for decades because of their threats to their neighbors as well as regional peace and stability. Washington tended to treat the rogue regime differently from one another, just as it characteristically approached other problems in varied ways. The rogue-state phenomenon still persists but it has been joined by other growing threats to American interests, such as terrorism and great power rivalries.

How and why American responses fluctuate toward overseas challenges is the subject of this current volume. *Cycles in U.S. Foreign Policy since the Cold War* is the third volume in the series. It addresses the proposition that American foreign policy cycles alternated between bouts of engagement and disengagement in global affairs. Scholars, philosophers, and enlightened commentators have observed the pendulum-like swings of political activity and inactivity since Classical antiquity. As recently as the 1980s, an eminent historian and several political scientists have described these political cycles. My study concentrates on the post-1989 era by analyzing international policies of the four US presidential administrations that governed after the Soviet Union fell. The book aspires to make the study of cycles an enlightening factor in appreciating the past and in offering an expectation for the future.

Thomas H. Henriksen
Senior Fellow
Stanford University's
Hoover Institution

CHAPTER 1

Introduction: The Cycler Nature of US Foreign Policy

"Full knowledge of the past helps us in dealing with the future." —Theodore Roosevelt[1]

This book hypothesizes that pendulum-like cycles took place in US foreign policy alternating broadly from engagement to disengagement and back again in the four American presidencies since the Cold War. These cycles of international extroversion and introversion reflected political sentiments of the presidents, major parties, and the voters themselves. Engagement-cycle presidents resorted to military power and diplomatic pressure against other powers, whereas disengagement-cycle presidents retrenched from international entanglements, while relying on normal economic and political interaction. These cyclical arcs reflected public sentiments, as mirrored in national elections and public opinion polls. But the policies carried out by the White House occupants must take into account presidential decisions made to secure US interests or to nail down historical legacies, which could run counter to the national mood.

Much has happened to America and the world since scholars wrote in the 1980s about political cycles in the American past. The Iron Curtain fell, and with it the former bipolar standoff between the United States and the Soviet Union, which bifurcated the planet into two armed camps. Communism's expansion no longer frightens Western democracies. The United States, in fact, emerged after the Soviet Union's demise as the sole remaining superpower, although today, it faces a more multipower world.

T.H. Henriksen, *Cycles in US Foreign Policy since the Cold War*,
DOI 10.1007/978-3-319-48640-6_1

When the Cold War still seemed permanent, American scholars wrote convincingly about interpreting America's past through a prism of cycler ebbs and flows of international activism and in-activism. The renowned US historian Arthur M. Schlesinger Jr. called attention to the cycles between liberalism and conservatism in US domestic annals in his book, *The Cycles of American History*.[2] The Harvard professor drew for theoretical guidance on the writings of Ralph Waldo Emerson, Henry Adams, and his own father, who was also a prominent academician. Another scholar, Frank L. Klingberg, identified what he termed "mood cycles" in American society, which impacted foreign policy pendulum swings as described in his book, *Cyclical Trends in American Foreign Policy Moods*. Professor Klingberg paid close attention, over many years, to pendular alterations between "extroversion" and "introversion" in America's foreign policy dating from the founding of the Republic to beyond World War II.[3] Neither of these scholars were the first to comment on the patterns or recurrence in history. Famed illuminati such as Niccolò Machiavelli, Giambattista Vico, Arnold Toynbee, and others have posited some form of historical repetition.[4] The two American advocates, nonetheless, were among the most recent and precise observers of the cycler alterations in US policies.

Professors Schlesinger and Klingberg perceived cyclical arcs spanning different time spans. For Schlesinger, the "model of a thirty-year alternation between public purpose and private interest" fit the political history of the United States.[5] During "public purpose" times, according to Schlesinger, the country moved toward the expansion of federal government programs for the general welfare of its citizens. But in the years of "private interest," the nation's "public problems are turned over to the invisible hand of the market" in a reference to Adam Smith's metaphor of the economic market bestowing unintended social benefits.[6] For Klingberg, who wrote about the shifts from "introversion" and "extroversion" in "international mood phases," the "average length of the introvert phase was 21 years, and of the extrovert phase about 27 years" dating from 1776 to 1983.[7] Extroversion denoted "a willingness to use direct political or military pressure on other nations." Introversion, on the other hand, "stressed domestic concerns as well as normal economic, humanitarian, and cultural relations abroad."[8]

These definitions suffice for this current book about the post-Cold War's engagement–disengagement alternations. The use of military force or strong diplomatic pressure defines an engagement strategy, while emphasis on domestic concerns and routine diplomacy identifies a disengagement game plan. This study found that the back-and-forth cycles in the post-1989 timeframe were much briefer than the observations advanced by Schlesinger or Klingberg of an earlier period. The post-Cold War cycles roughly conformed to the presidential terms. Writing in the *American Political Science Review*, three additional scholars examined cycles in electoral politics from 1854 to 2006 by using statistical evidence. In their analysis of "realignment cyclicity," they posited that the "partisan seat share of the Democratic and Republican parties has not varied randomly over time." Rather, it has "oscillated back and forth in a fairly regular pattern for the past 160 years." The period of "oscillation … is approximately 25 to 30 years."[9] This political science article pertains to political party dominance but its relevance here points to the cycler nature of American politics.

Yet another political scientist assessed the pendulum shifts in the American mood, or political opinion, as a factor related to governance. Commenting on "liberalism and conservatism in public preference," this professor wrote about "the public changing its attitude toward government action" as a reaction to its approaches. The academician concluded that "this common national mood we know responds thermostatically to government policy. Mood becomes more conservative under liberal governments and more liberal under conservative regimes."[10] The same factors impacting the public mood, domestic political parties, and their programs also influences public opinion on international engagement and disengagement cycles. Fatigue, weariness, fear, disenchantment with the status quo can sway the public mood. Professor Schlesinger wrote about how "disappointment is the universal modern malady" and how it might drive political cycles:

> People can never be fulfilled for long either in the public or the private sphere. We try one, then the other, and frustration compels a change in course. Moreover, however effective a particular course may be in meeting one set of troubles, it generally falters and fails when new troubles arise. And many troubles are inherently insoluble. As political eras, whether dominated by public purpose or private interest, run their course, they infallibly generate the desire for something different.[11]

Arthur Schlesinger and Frank Klingberg concluded that a cycler theory offered insights into history and even about the possibility of what was to come. About the future, Schlesinger wrote: "The dialectic between past and the future continue to form our lives."[12] And the other proponent of historical cycles, Frank Klingberg argued that cyclical trends were not only an "important element in the interpretation of past events" but also "the prediction of likely directions for the future."[13]

Such strong convictions in the forecasting power of historical analysis might be less than 100 percent on the mark. But they are one reason—not the only one—to look again at the hypothesis of rhythmic patterns in the most recent period of US foreign policy. Did cycler fluctuations occur in the post-Cold War era? Where the historical cycles just a fluke before Berlin Wall toppled? Or, can we divine cycles in the contemporary time-frame? Finally, why did these purported oscillations take place at all?

The hypothesis of this work is that post-Cold War US foreign policy, indeed, has swung between the poles of active international involvement and disengagement, or at least detachment. Cycles of international engagement coincide with the use of direct military power or diplomatic pressure against other nations or entities. But cycles of international disengagement reflect a strong domestic orientation and dissociation from risky overseas problems. A sub-hypothesis centers on the observation that both engagement-orientated presidents—George H.W. Bush and George W. Bush—modified their initial pronounced internationalism prior to leaving office in recognition of growing domestic opposition to engagement actions. On the other hand, the two disengagement-orientated presidents—William Clinton and Barack Obama—largely maintained their inward-looking focus to the end of their terms. These two theses are confirmed by abundant empirical evidence, which will be presented in subsequent chapters. But first a little historical perspective about the search for cycles in the past is necessary.

Searching for Cycles in the Past

Seeking historical patterns is a time-honored practice. Notable figures have examined the past as a means to divine the outcome of present-day events. Cycles or reoccurring patterns in the past seemed to offer a way of prognosticating what lay beyond the horizon. Among the first Western references to the notion of cycles came from a Greek historian, Polybius (circa 200 to circa 118 B.C.), who asserted that governments cycle through different forms starting with primitive monarchy, includes kingship, tyranny, aristocracy, as well as oligarchy, and concludes with ochlocracy (or mob rule).[14] The comings and endings of governmental types were taken up by other thinkers. The Italian philosopher and Enlightenment thinker Giambattista Vico wrote about recurring cycles in what he saw as the three epochs in history: the divine, heroic, and human in his influential book, *The New Science*, published in 1744.[15] The notion of cycles in the rise and decline of civilizations was touched upon by the eminent British historian Herbert Butterfield in his treatment of the Classical Greek and Roman historians.[16]

The idea took root that history could be studied so as to foresee what lies ahead. In the Middle Ages, as Paul Johnson wrote, wise men counseled: "History is the school of princes."[17] A counselor to men of power, Machiavelli, the Florentine Renaissance political thinker held that a prince must look to the past for guidance:

> Whoever considers present and ancient things, easily knows that in all cities and in all peoples there are the same desires and the same humors, and there always have been. So it is an easy thing for whoever examines past things diligently to foresee future things in every republic and to take remedies for them that were used by the ancients, or, if they do not find any that were used, to think up new ones through the similarity of accidents.[18]

Perhaps the most incomparable expression of this repetitive proposition flowed from the pen of the Spanish philosopher George Santayana. He admonished humanity to learn and apply the lessons of history in his oft-quoted aphorism: "Those who cannot remember the past are condemned to repeat it."[19]

Others have dismissed the whole notion of deriving eternal truths or even insights from studying times long past. The renowned British historian A.J.P. Taylor, insisted: "The only lesson of history is that there is no lesson of history."[20] More succinctly, Henry Ford, the American automotive titan, thought history was "bunk."[21]

The utmost that can be derived from the study of history is that exact prediction is unwarranted but it may be possible to develop a foresight so as to pinpoint factors that are starting to influence the direction of events. Lewis Namier, another eminent British historian, held that the "enduring achievement of historical study is a historical sense, an intuitive understanding—of how things do not work."[22] Intuitively perceiving how things might work out—or won't work out—quite possibly is as near as professional scholars, statesmen, or political figures should venture about forecasting coming events. Forebodings and premonitions about writings on the wall can at least temper the enthusiasm for a possible catastrophe; if not totally alter the course of a misadventure.

This author shares the skepticism about historians or politicians having crystal balls or clairvoyant powers. The complexities of major events, with a multitude of variables, make for vagaries, not replications. Even taking up analogies can result in misleading conclusions, because the analogies mostly rest on superficial understanding of events and debatable premises. In brief, this author makes no claims to the prediction of specific events. Yet, a circumspect review of the ebb and flow of tides encompassing American foreign policy offers a way to understand the past and to anticipate probable behavior ahead. Seeing cycles in US foreign policy since the fall of the Berlin Wall is the case this book sets out to make.

Cycles do abound in human activity. Fatigue follows exertion. Economic busts trail financial booms. Retreats come after crusades. Ying and yang alternate. The precise characteristics of each of these cycles can be distinct but their yawing phenomenon is expected, just as ebbing precedes flowing tides. Moods, or public sentiments, have fluctuated as America's past indicates. The changes, in part, account for bouts of America's engaged internationalism oscillating with periods of disengaged insularity toward the outside world. Internationalist lurches reflect a willingness to employ direct military power or diplomatic pressure against other states. Insular swings, on the other hand, exhibit strong domestic concerns and dissociation from overseas problems.

Cycles Before the End of the Cold War

Cyclical swings between international engagement and disengagement appeared before the post-Cold War era. There were, in fact, cycler movements dating from founding of the Republic. In the early history of the United States, a turn outward was characterized by an expansion of territory to the south or west. Inward turns, by contrast, were "years of consolidation" in preparation for renewed territorial aggrandizement.[23] As the United States rose to be a world power, the pendulum phenomenon materialized most dramatically in the twentieth century. America's strategic withdrawal from international affairs followed its military involvement in World War I. The interwar years are considered a decidedly isolationist chapter in American history. The next global conflict dragged the United States back into world affairs. Following World War II, Washington took up the defense of the Free World against aggressive designs by the Union of Soviet Socialist Republics (USSR). In that role, America introduced security and financial institutions to prop up European and non-Western allies the world over against the USSR's expansionism. Washington's collective defense alliances, military assistance, and monetary aid proved durable and successful over the long haul in countering the Kremlin's advances.

Still, there were times of American retrenchment during the Cold War. The most notable disengagement came after the traumatic Vietnam War, when "there was great public doubt and confusion about the future direction of American foreign policy."[24] The fall of South Vietnam to the Communist North's invasion two years after the US military withdrew "had severely shaken American self-confidence."[25] To limit US international commitments and interventions, President Richard M. Nixon fell back on a strategy known as the Nixon Doctrine, which embraced "a devolution of American responsibilities in the Third World upon regional powers like Brazil, Iran, Indonesia, and Zaire" (now known as the Democratic Republic of the Congo).[26]

This mood of introversion lasted until the Soviet invasion of Afghanistan in 1979, which nearly coincided with the end of President Jimmy Carter's cautious retrenchment.[27] President Ronald Reagan introduced steps toward greater engagement in the lingering, post-Vietnam insular mood. His international involvement overtures carried forward into the post-Berlin Wall years and the presidency of George H.W. Bush. Even though, the post-Cold War era recorded cycler movements in US foreign policy, the Vietnam War still cast a shadow over war-making policies.

The chief two proponents of perceiving cycles in US foreign policy, as noted above, wrote books on the subject in the 1980s. In *The Cycles of American History*, Arthur Schlesinger described mainly domestic cyclical swings "between conservatism and liberalism, between periods of concern for the rights of the few and periods of concern for the wrongs of many."[28] The Harvard historian readily acknowledged the role of "sacrifices" during World War I "to make the great world outside safe for democracy," as a factor in the nation's fatigue during the 1930s. But he also called attention to domestic exertions to explain the change in American sentiments. After the activism of the Progressive Era as well as the Great War, Schlesinger wrote, the American people "had had their fill of crusades" by the interwar years. This disenchantment with "discipline, sacrifice, and intangible goals" played out, as we shall, see in post-Cold War presidencies too.[29] The eminent professor expressed in the mid-1980s an observation, which still holds abundant resonance for this current volume; he persuasively wrote: "Each swing of the cycle produced Presidents responsive to the national mood, sometimes against their own inclinations."[30] Using the presidential "bully pulpit," White House occupants could hope to change the public mood.[31] But presidents mostly reflected the prevailing feelings of the electorate as reflected in their reading of national polls and election returns.

The second authority, Frank Klingberg, also analyzed cyclical trends in American foreign policy as well as in domestic and cultural affairs. A political scientist at Southern Illinois University, Klingberg studied this pendulum phenomenon for over three decades after his start in the early 1950s. In 1983, he published a book, *Cyclical Trends in American Foreign Policy Moods*, on the subject. For an explanation of this cycler pattern, he pointed to what he termed "the historical alternation of moods in American foreign policy." To him, these "cyclical tendencies seemed to be based on the succession of causal factors in human nature and by much historical evidence since 1776." Professor Klingberg stressed that these trends present "an additional important element in the interpretation of past events and the prediction of likely directions for the future."[32] He identified oscillations between "extroversion" (a readiness to employ forward-leaning diplomacy, economic pressure, or military action to serve US purposes) and "introversion" (a desire to concentrate on domestic concerns with just routine economic and political intercourse with foreign powers).

Professor Klingberg identified several alternations in mood between 1776 and 1983. These phases, as cited above, averaged 21 years for the 4 introvert periods and 27 years for what became the 4 extrovert eras.[33] Accounting for these "mood cycles" in American history, Klingberg acknowledged that it was an imprecise science, requiring the weighing of multiple causes. To buttress his case, the university teacher pointed to similar phenomena in the "business cycles" and internal factors within human systems when confronted by imbalances and the need for changes. External factors, such as foreign wars and economic depressions, exerted powerful impersonal forces on American society.[34] There are other factors also at work on the direction of policy swivels.

US political party ideology and presidential instincts, this author saw in the post-Cold War presidencies, accounted for a degree of influence over America's pendulum-like swings in the exercise of its foreign relations. Presidents have drawn on their respective parties' past stances on issues and on the thinking of other politicians, government officials, and non-government experts as well as campaign pledges. Naturally, the sentiments of the body politic often influence presidential decisions. Presidents have singular power to shape the direction of foreign policy. Whereas domestic legislation on matters such as taxes and spending on government programs depend on extensive interaction and negotiations with Congress, the conduct of the nation's international affairs can be implemented by the commander-in-chief, White House aides, and executive departments such as state, defense, and commerce. Presidents, therefore, enjoy much greater latitude in the exercise of foreign policy than over internal issues that require Congressional approval.

When all is said and done, the general public does not pay much attention to world affairs, unless an event intrudes on their everyday life, as did the Pearl Harbor attack or the 9/11 terrorism. Presidents can act contra-mood, because they believe their decisions are the best for the country. When they set an independent course, the American public tends to fall in behind them.[35] For example, President George W. Bush resolved to take the United States into war against Iraq, and the American public followed him until US casualties mounted and no weapons of mass destruction (WMD) were found. Then deep disenchantment set in with the war and the president.

The Constitution grants the president broad latitude to handle the nation's overseas business, especially when security and defense are concerned. Since the Vietnam War, presidents have pushed for greater leeway in deploying the military forces. Even the 1973 War Powers Act, designed to rein in the president's ability to send US troops to foreign wars for more than 60 days without congressional consent, has often been circumvented by White House occupants.[36] They have jealously guarded their prerogatives over deciding on international intervention. Thus, presidential administrations have remained the prime mover in charting the nation's course overseas.

Another factor at work in America's foreign policy oscillations derives from the debate on how best to attain the benefits from spreading the country's values of liberty, democracy, and political tolerance. According to Christopher Hemmer, policy makers have agreed on the benefits but disagreed on the means to attaining them. Should the United States engage in crusades to impose its values on other lands? In this view, the country has to expand American principles "as a missionary, either converting or defeating those who reject core U.S. values like democracy." Or, should The United States "serve as model for others, letting the intrinsic attraction of its values do most of the work?"[37]

The United States achieved astounding success in the wake of World War II with its crusading impulse in Germany, Italy, and Japan. Immediately after the war, it also actively interfered to shore up Western democracies under threat from communist subversion. Other crusading enterprises have come to grief in Vietnam and Iraq (and quite possibly in Afghanistan too.) The costs in lives, money, and perhaps prestige are high for crusades. Crusading may also alienate allies when carried out contrary to their interests. Opposite of crusading image on the debate spectrum, according to Christopher Hemmer, is the notion that the United States can serve as a Promised Land, a term popularized by Professor Walter McDougall who also posed the Crusader State notion.[38] Professor Hemmer contends proponents of Promised Land proposition hold that America must "focus on perfecting democracy at home, thus making it a model that others want to emulate."[39]

Two distinct presidencies exemplify how the twin propositions of either crusading or symbolizing figured in the playout of intervention or retrenchment cycles. President George W. Bush used lofty language in his second inaugural address which matched his interventionist actions. He resolutely declared that those who "live in tyranny and hopelessness can know: the United States will not ignore your oppression." He added in his expansive manifesto that "when you stand for your liberty, we will stand with you." He dedicated his efforts to advancing democracy "with the ultimate goal of ending tyranny in our world."[40] With a pendulum change in public opinion, his successor gravitated from the hawkish crusader to the iconography of a shining beacon to the world. President Barack Obama frequently alluded to the necessity of refurbishing the Promised Land mantle when he spoke about the need to "reclaim the American dream" and "to focus on nation-building here at home."[41] His fixation was on mending America's promise as well as its dilapidated infrastructure.

This recurring debate by exponents of either one of the two poles on how best to advance American political values introduces an important variable in the nation's international role. The debate centers on the part American values play in foreign policy decisions. As such, it forms only one dimension of the battle between engagement and disengagement. In brief, statements and actions favoring the Crusader State approach lend substance to international engagement. The reverse posture highlights declarations and policies endorsing the Promised Land stance that emphasizes dissociation from militarily interfering or diplomatic muscle-flexing to proselytize for democracy.

The worldwide turbulence since the Berlin Wall collapsed also contributed to US foreign policy cycles. Without the lodestone of the Soviet Union to orient US strategy, Washington's foreign policy cycled—and could afford to cycle—between the poles of international activism and inaction. The post-Iron Curtain world held a host of lesser dangers from rogue powers, terrorist networks, criminal syndicates, and more recently from resurgent Russia and rising China. America's superpower status almost guaranteed that Washington had to pay attention to almost every trouble spot anywhere on the planet, like it or not. Its global dominance has vastly expanded since the end of the Soviet Union, while that of Britain, France, and Germany—key players during the Cold War—has greatly diminished. So Washington's decisions, even small ones, stand in sharp relief, because the world watches to see how it will respond to a crisis. Preeminence in military power enables a state to act or to refrain from action as its interests, values, and prospects dictate. As Thucydides notably phrased it: "The strong do what they can and the weak suffer what they must."[42] As such, vast power often confers the flexibility to choose policies. American leaders, therefore, exercised some power over the choice of their priorities, allowing for cycles.

Post-Cold War Foreign Policy Cycles in Brief

To test the hypothesis of engagement–disengagement alternation, it is necessary to re-study closely US foreign policy since the Berlin Wall came down in November 1989. The brief re-examination in this introductory chapter concludes that the four post-Cold War American presidencies perpetuated the cycles of engagement and disengagement established by their Cold War predecessors. Each of these four presidents initially undertook international policies that differed from the previous administration. The cycles were not precisely metronomic but they did yield recognizable rotations in policies and actions from administration to administration. Washington's international interactions are briefly sketched in the remaining pages of this introduction.

George H.W. Bush arrived in the White House on the tails of Ronald Reagan's generally successful presidency. Although Bush served for eight years as Reagan's vice president, he differed from his predecessor once in the Oval Office. Reagan's Pentagon re-built America's military forces as a direct challenge to the Soviet Union. The former California governor squared off against Moscow in other ways and contributed greatly to the downfall of America's chief nemesis. By escalating the Cold War confrontation in several geographic fronts as well as missile defense competition, the former California governor, pushed the Kremlin beyond the financial breaking point.

Despite Reagan's renewal of US internationalism, however, the 40th president spared the United States from any long-term, large-scale military invasions. He resorted unilaterally to military action only three times. Washington mounted an in-and-out armed intercession into the Caribbean island of Grenada to bring down a Marxist government. It sailed US naval forces into the Persian Gulf to protect Kuwaiti oil transports from being harassed by Iran's navy. And it committed US. warplanes to strafe Libya in retaliation for Muammar al-Qaddafi's terrorist bombing of a Berlin disco where two American servicemen died. President Reagan also deployed US forces multilaterally as part of an international peacekeeping force during Lebanon's civil war. Even though 241 American servicemen died in their Beirut barracks during a single truck bombing in 1983, the terrorist attack did not move Reagan to widen his intervention. The president's retaliation was confined to offshore barrages from US warships. He also withdrew US military units shortly after the truck-bombing attack without mounting potent retaliatory strikes on the terrorist perpetrators.

In spite of his sometimes tough rhetoric, Reagan was reserved in the exercise of US armed forces. Professor Colin Dueck observed that Reagan "had the ability to convince supporters of his core convictions while simultaneously pursuing policies that were actually more circumspect and less interventionist."[43]

The Reagan presidency, nevertheless, began the international re-engagement that had been lacking after the Vietnam War and Jimmy Carter's White House years. The shadow that Southeast Asian conflict cast over Washington foreign policy lessened when Ronald Reagan re-centered the United States on the world stage. The Reagan Doctrine, for example, overtly "pledged aid to insurgents battling against recently established pro-Soviet states in Afghanistan, Nicaragua, Angola, and Cambodia."[44] The Reagan White House also ended the détente policy with Moscow in the pursuit of either rolling back Soviet advances or bringing the USSR to its knees. Its forceful policies contributed to the USSR's fragmentation during George H.W. Bush's administration. Yet, Reagan was circumspect in the actual commitment of US military forces directly against the Soviet Union or its allies.

In contrast with his predecessor, President George H. W. Bush dispatched over half-a-million US troops to repulse Saddam Hussein's invasion of Kuwait in 1990. The Persian Gulf War was quickly won against Iraq's devastated Republican Guard. American and coalition air and ground power dazzled observers with its high-tech features and lightning lethality. The Bush administration decided against capturing Baghdad, deposing Hussein, or occupying Iraqi territory. Instead, it enlarged its basing and prepositioning of arms in the Gulf area. It stayed heavily involved in the Persian Gulf by setting up "no-fly zones" over large swaths of territory in Iraq's north and south. These air exclusionary zones lasted until the outbreak of the Iraq War in 2003. Over the years, the two zones recorded 350,000 air sorties and cost $30 billion. More forcefully, the jet patrols frequently fired missiles at ground targets, resulting in unremitting military operations in a time of peace. The Bush White House also began the active protection of the Kurds, who lived in the northern reaches of Iraq. As a result, the George Bush presidency marked a decidedly activist international phase in the cycle of American engagement and disengagement.

Before the Persian Gulf War, America's 41st chief executive played an outsized role in overseeing the Soviet Union's peaceful collapse, in removing the Red Army from Eastern Europe, and uniting East and West Germany back into a unified state after four decades of Cold War division. The Bush administration took a leading role negotiating among its European allies and with Soviet Russia over the terms for Moscow's withdrawal from its East European occupation. Such a role required Washington to arm-twist its allies to sign on to the American designed plan to let Europe be "whole and free" as President Bush phrased it in Mainz, West Germany in late May 1989.

The rapidity of the Soviet Union's disintegration nearly overwhelmed Washington officialdom. Meanwhile a flaying Moscow desperately struggled against the White House to retain its influence particularly over the form of German reunification and its opposition to a united Germany's membership in the North Atlantic Treaty Organization (NATO). The Kremlin failed all around. The vanishing of the USSR—something that almost no one predicted—occurred in a historical blink of an eye to astonishment in every world capital. Nor was the Soviet Union's descent into the historical dustbin the only blip on the Bush administration's radar.

Even as Soviet power began to unravel, Washington had to turn to other pressing problems. The Bush White House militarily deposed the narcotics-peddling dictator in Panama. It invaded the Central American country, ousted Manual Noriega, installed a legitimately elected president in the Panama Canal country, and departed without becoming bogged down in a hostile or prolonged occupation. It was a regime-change operation with few glitches that fell short of serving as a model when Bush's son intervened into Iraq. Largely forgotten today, the Panama episode momentarily distracted the White House from pressing issues in Europe, despite its smooth execution.

All this international activity took place in just one presidential term. George H.W. Bush lost his reelection bid to the Arkansas governor, William Jefferson Clinton, who had an entirely different approach to foreign affairs. But even before Bush left the White House, his administration's overseas actions anticipated those of his successor. President Bush started the pull back from an exuberant internationalism. Thus, he initially charted a policy that President Clinton embraced. George Bush did send US troops into Somalia for a humanitarian mission to feed millions of people in the destitute land during the last months of his presidency. But Bush hesitated to intervene militarily both in turbulent Haiti and in the fragmenting Yugoslavia. The incoming Clinton administration took up the same posture of disassociation toward the twin convulsions.

The early Clinton years were marked by an inattention to foreign policy concerns. The new president won the office by pledging to "focus like a laser beam" on the troubled domestic economy. His most senior aides saw it as their duty to keep international issues off Clinton's desk. His predisposition to work almost exclusively on domestic issues momentarily came to grief in the Black Hawk Down incident in Somalia just eight months into his first term. A fierce firefight between US Special Operations Forces (SOF) and residents of Mogadishu dashed Clinton officials' ill-conceived plans to inaugurate a nation-building program in a strife-torn country on the Horn of Africa. Pitching health care reform in California, President Clinton appeared shocked and out of touch about the Somali upheaval. So chastened by the international brouhaha surrounding the melee in Mogadishu's sweltering streets, the Clinton White House became even more skittish about entering into Haiti's political disorder and Yugoslavia's bloody civil war.

The president dragged his feet until pushed by members of the Congressional Black Caucus and concerns about adverse political repercussions from Haitian refugees washing up on Florida beaches. Finally, Clinton ordered the Pentagon to intervene and oust the ruling junta for the duly elected Haitian president. The same political inertia existed elsewhere. Neither the worsening carnage nor the humanitarian pleas moved

Clinton to enter militarily the Bosnian conflict within the fragmenting Yugoslavia until 1995, with the national elections around the corner. When the Republican challenger Robert Dole took up the Bosnian cause as a political cudgel, Bill Clinton relented and acted to ensure his reelection. By that time, the plight of the Bosnian Muslims had become a cause célèbre within Western humanitarian circles.

Although the Clinton administration adroitly, if reluctantly, managed the Haitian and Bosnian humanitarian interventions, it callously ignored Rwanda's frenzied mass murder (which recorded 800,000 deaths). It even blocked the Security Council from designating the unfolding massacre as an instance of genocide to escape responsibility for standing aside. Later, the Clinton White House quickly handed off the leadership of a proposed military intercession into East Timor to Australia and in Sierra Leone to Nigeria to deal with internal violence in both countries. The White House directed limited financial, training, and logistical support to the Nigerian peacekeepers in the West African country. It did next to nothing to arrest the political collapse in neighboring Liberia despite a historical connection with the United States. Washington committed to just an air campaign against Serbia to stem the sectarian violence in Kosovo, which ultimately prevailed after a much longer-than-anticipated bombing campaign.

In his last months in office, President Clinton reversed himself on a tough policy for the United Nations (UN) weapons inspections in Iraq, backed away from enforcing air traffic restrictions into Baghdad, anemically responded to the twin 1998 terrorist attacks on the American embassies in Tanzania and Kenya, and shrugged at a counterstrike for the skiff-bombing of the *USS Cole* in Aden, Yemen. The *Cole* attack killed 17 US sailors. By the time Clinton left the Oval Office, the United States looked to be in a full-bore retrenchment mode. His administration's international attention drifted from combating terrorism threats to a futile effort to resolve the Israeli-Palestinian conflict through White House-brokered negotiations.

George W. Bush initially treaded a similar pacific path as America's outgoing chief executive. Just two months into his tenure, Bush faced a diplomatic and military standoff with the People's Republic of China (PRC) over a downed US reconnaissance plane in the South China Sea. A reckless Chinese pilot crashed his jet into the American EP-3 forcing it to make an emergency landing on Hainan Island. The Bush foreign policy team defused the explosive showdown by measured diplomacy. Washington issued a letter expressing regret and sorrow (but not an apology). China released 24 Navy crew members and returned the aircraft two months later. The incident soon passed from recollection by all but a few commentators.

The same fate greeted a host of tiny incidents in the Middle East, which witnessed the United States de-escalate by retreating. FBI officials investigating the ring responsible for the *Cole* bombing fled Yemen when they received terrorist threats. US warships in their Fifth Fleet headquarters on the Persian Gulf island of Bahrain put to sea amid warnings of impending terrorism. Even US Marines, participating in a training exercise with Jordan's troops in the Gulf of Aqaba, abandoned the mission and left the field. Mostly forgotten now, these precipitous extrications during summer 2001 hardly signaled resolve on the part of the Bush administration toward political violence emanating from jihadi cells. Yet, by instinct, temperament, and political party ideology, George Bush junior turned out to be a war president twice.

The September 11 terrorist attacks transformed the American people and the Bush presidency. The unprecedentedness and ferocity of what the jihadi network al Qaeda termed the "planes operation" shocked and shook the American psyche. Americans rightly perceived the Twin Towers and the Pentagon as defining financial and military icons. The highly destructive assaults on both tilted the country and its political leadership into a warlike mood, which precipitated a lurch toward large-scale military intervention not only into Afghanistan (al Qaeda's haven) but also against Iraq (long suspected of possessing WMD).

The White House adamantly resolved to preempt the sinister risk of further terrorism from Afghan territory and the likelihood of a nuclear or chemical attack from the Saddam Hussein regime. The 9/11 terrorism revolutionized Bush's thinking toward America's enemies in a way that is hard to imagine in either Bill Clinton or Barack Obama in similar circumstances. All lay plain and clear before George Bush who elevated the doctrine of preemption to actual state policy and then acted upon the strike-first strategy against Iraq.

The two wars started off as astounding military victories. The US military's presence also entailed nation-building exertions and democracy-promoting activities. In time, however, the twin theaters sank into quagmires of protracted insurgency evocative of the agonizing Vietnam War, America's most frustrating conflict. Casualties and financial costs mounted, which tested the White House's resolve and strategy. Steep outlays in blood and treasure also cost the Republican president his party's control in the House of Representatives and Senate in the 2006 election. Dissatisfaction with the conduct of the war in Iraq, plus the White House's handling of Hurricane Katrina and corruption scandals, was so great that the opposition party for the first time in US history did not lose a single incumbent seat in Congress. The sweeping Democratic electoral victory chastened and chastised George W. Bush so much that it contributed to the administration's pull back from exercising US military power abroad.

Before that reckoning took place, the White Ho use expanded US counterterrorism operations into the Philippines, Somalia, Pakistan, and the Horn of Africa. Washington also backed and protected with vigorous diplomacy budding democracy campaigns in the "color revolutions" of Ukraine, Georgia, and Kyrgyzstan. In early 2005, the White House joined with Saudi Arabia and Europe (mostly France) in diplomatically forcing Syrian military forces out of their three-decade occupation of Lebanon in a revolt named the Cedar Revolution.

To his credit, President Bush retrieved America's failing military fortunes in the Iraq War by adopting a different strategy and by dispatching 28,500 additional combat troops to the war-torn country in 2007 in the face of unremitting media, pundit, and opposition party objections. But elsewhere, the White House rotated from international engagement to retrenchment. Similar to the other presidencies under review here, the foreign policy of the Bush White House altered course from its original trajectory in the last stretch in office. The Bush policy pendulum cycled from forceful intervention to policies of restraint. Bush's rescue of Iraq from sectarian warfare and unrelenting terrorism went unmatched in Afghanistan, where the insurgency tipped against US forces prior to his return to Texas.

Other White House decisions moved the foreign policy pendulum away from potential conflicts, fraught entanglements, or even troubled states, which had enjoyed previous Bush administration backing. In short, it embraced a risk-averse, non-military stance. For example, whereas it had once taken a firm line with the nuclear-arming North Korea, it caved into that rogue state's long-practiced routine of threats and promises. After the Democratic People's Republic of Korea tested its first nuclear weapon in 2006, the United States entered into arms-control talks with Pyongyang. The North Koreans agreed to shut down their plutonium-enrichment facility at Yongbyon, which it did temporarily. In return for the shutdown and a verbal pledge to submit to comprehensive international inspections of the nuclear plant, a divided Bush government agreed to strike the DPRK from the State Department's listing of terrorist states. Vice President Richard Cheney and others perceived the agreement as a capitulation to Pyongyang.

Toward Iran, another nuclear-arming state, President Bush resisted lobbying to bomb Iranian nuclear installations also in the last years of his term. A possible war next door in Iran raised concerns in George Bush's thinking about the high costs of another intervention. Instead, he opted for tougher economic sanctions against Iran. He also dropped his previous unilateralism and embraced West European assistance to halt Iranian nuclear-arming. Elsewhere, the Bush administration also ducked military involvement.

Whereas the Bush administration resented the painstaking deliberations of the Security Council in the run-up to its waging war against Iraq, it later looked to the UN to spare the United States from a humanitarian intervention into the Darfur region in western Sudan. The atrocities committed against the Darfurian peoples begged for an international rescue. But the escalating insurgency in Iraq deterred the Bush administration from sending US troops into another Muslim civil war. Over the course of several years, the Bush foreign policy team finally got the UN to dispatch peacekeepers to maintain a semblance of order, sparing America from interceding. Yet, during the lengthy Security Council talks, hundreds of thousands of people lost their lives and over 3 million their homes to the marauding Janjaweed ("devils on horseback") that the Sudanese government relied on to crush the rebellion in Darfur.

President Bush's more cautious international course was no more on display than in the Republic of Georgia, when Russian aggression flared in the Caucasus. The administration's reluctance to come to the aid of an attacked Georgia in mid-2008 was all the more striking since the White House backed the Transcaucasian state five years earlier. In that earlier political conflict, America went to the defense of the Rose Revolution, which secured Georgia's genuine independence from Russia's quasi-colonial rule. The Russians resented Georgia's movement westward toward Europe, NATO, and the United States. Deeply aggrieved by NATO's eastward encroachments into its traditional sphere, Moscow struck back after the Washington and other Western capitals recognized the independence of Kosovo, a former province of Serbia that Russia regarded as an ally. The Russian military took the side of two breakaway Georgian pocket-sized provinces in their conflict with Georgia's army. When the Georgian forces fired at the Russian troops, Moscow stepped up its war on the tiny state's army. Georgia's pleas for assistance fell on deaf ears in the West. Washington sidestepped a direct role in the confrontation with Russia. President Bush looked to Paris, which held the rotating presidency of the European Union (EU) at the time. Moscow suspended its invasion and bided its time until reinitiating interventions into Crimea and Ukraine half a decade afterward.

Before returning to Texas, George Bush set in motion a reversal of his earlier interventionist strategy that led to the protracted wars in Iraq and Afghanistan. His hawkish policies that typified his first years in office now belonged to history. Almost two years before the end of his eight-year term, he set in motion a disengagement cycle. His new restraint anticipated the retrenchment route so celebrated by his successor. President Barack Obama took up Bush's newfound disassociation and carried it to the next level. Thus, Bush's actions foreshadowed the next commander-in-chief's pendulum swing. His decisions conformed to the cycler pattern of post-Cold War presidents, who came into office with one trajectory in the engagement–disengagement cyclicity but were forced by circumstances to adopt the reverse phase of the cycle.

When Barack Hussein Obama strode into the Oval Office, he ushered in his campaign promises to end the war in Iraq and to "finish the fight" against al Qaeda in Afghanistan. President Obama moved promptly on both pledges in a manner that cycled American foreign policy away from its heavy militarization and democracy promotion of Bush's muscular international engagement. The new White House resident kicked the legs from beneath these two pillars of the George Bush era in his handling of terrorism and insurgency. In Iraq, where internal terrorism had fallen dramatically, Obama announced the departure of two-thirds of ground forces by August 2010 and the remaining units by the end of 2011. In Afghanistan, he nearly tripled the US ground forces in early 2010 but limited their stay by setting the start of their departure for July 2011. Obama's twin withdrawal from Iraq and Afghanistan, while generally popular at home, signaled a sweeping overhaul of America's international commitments elsewhere.

Although Obama reached out rhetorically to the Islamic world, Russia, and Iran, he embraced the use of drones against terrorists to a degree far greater than George W. Bush. He announced a strategic pivot to Asia, while scaling back on major US interventions in the broader Middle East. Like Bush, he relied on SOF to combat terrorist cells in difficult terrain. But Obama stepped up deployments of small teams of these elite troops to Iraq, Syria, Yemen, North Africa, and the Horn of Africa. But when it came to dispatching large contingents of US ground forces, he stayed clear of his immediate predecessor's major land invasions.

The Obama administration was surprised and overtaken by the political upheaval in the Middle East against longtime dictators in Libya, Egypt, Yemen, and Syria in early 2011. With the exception of the anti-regime uprising in Libya, the Obama White House largely sat on the sidelines, neither actively promoting democracy nor firmly backing its allied dictatorships. Notwithstanding the advance of democracy in Tunisia, the Arab Spring ended up reinforcing local strongmen against their rebellious citizens. The political upsurge, thus, did little to bring about consensual governments from Casablanca to Cairo. The resulting instability actually opened the gates to political Islam and terrorism as well as the return of dictatorial rule.

President Obama's handling of the Libyan crisis accentuated America's growing dissociation from its former leadership role among its allies. The White House's participation in the Western and Arabian Peninsula coalition to topple Muammar al-Qaddafi was so tenuous that critics' branded it as "leading from behind" after a staffer uttered the phrase. Yet, US warplanes, intelligence, and logistical support figured prominently in ousting Colonel Gaddafi from power. The removal of rogue regime brought no major American assistance to build a functioning state or install a democratic government. The Obama administration felt justified to wash its hands of the policies pursued by the George W. Bush's presidency, because Americans had turned away from them. Instead, Washington looked to European and others to pick up the burden.

As the Libyan air campaign raged, a high-profile counterterrorism operation contributed to President Obama's narrative that the United States could well afford to pull back from the smoldering conflicts east of the Suez Canal. American SOF entered Pakistan and killed Osama bin Laden in early May 2011. Washington interpreted and sold the arch-terrorist's death as mortal blow to his extremist cause. The US president propounded the assessment that his policies had hastened the end of al Qaeda. These sentiments served Obama's reelection hopes but the government's standoffishness figured in the sinister rise of another terrorist network.

The United States greeted the unfolding civil war in Syria with a similar hands-off posture as other conflicts in Yemen, Libya, and Egypt's Sinai Peninsula. The consequences of this inaction, however, backfired. Growing out of the fight against Bashar al-Assad, the Syrian dictator, there emerged a vicious terrorist band, the Islamic State of Iraq and Syria (ISIS) that sprang up originally in the Iraq War against US and Coalition armies. Anchored in the Sunni majority, ISIS either swept aside or co-opted other insurgent movements in the fight against the Damascus regime, whose ruthless despot gained vital support from Iran and Russia. Starting from a mild civil disobedience campaign in early 2011, the Syrian war rapidly descended into a horror show of beheadings, summary executions, and the mass flight of millions of refugees into neighboring lands and Europe. The Assad regime's resort to chemical weapons provoked President Obama to issue a "red line" against gas attacks on civilians. When Assad crossed the red line without consequences, he called into question the American leader's resolve.

Other events defied Washington's policies. In 2014, the Islamic State drove deep into Iraq where it proclaimed an Islamic caliphate, which was accompanied with countless barbarities against various sects and dissenters in the northern quarter of the country. The White House reacted by gradually deploying about 3700 troops (expanded unofficially to about 5000) and relying on airstrikes. President Obama, true to his campaign promises, wanted to steer clear of another American-led, large-scale land war and nation-building occupation in Iraq or Syria. Incrementally, Obama sent small numbers of special operations units into the Iraq and Syria theaters but he never came close to the preceding White House occupant's resource-heavy counterinsurgencies in Afghanistan or Iraq. His policies there and elsewhere, nonetheless, looked tentative and ineffective to his critics.

China and Russia also defied Barack Obama's resolve in two vital American arenas. The Chinese reinforced their naval presence in the South China Sea by extravagant coastline claims and by building artificial islands on top of reefs and shoals, which they militarized with landing strips and harbors for warships. Beijing's projection of its military power directly tested Obama's "pivot" to East Asia. Even more blatantly, Russia seized Crimea from Ukraine and then launched a hybrid war to hive off eastern Ukraine so as to weaken it and to impede Western encroachments on the Kremlin's historic sphere of influence. The US president reacted hesitantly to both, just as he did to offset the Islamic State's deep thrust into Iraq and its coordination of terrorist attack in France, Belgium, Denmark, and other countries.

During the last year or so of his presidency, Barack Obama incrementally and softly nudged the engagement–disengagement pendulum toward the military involvement rotation. By deploying teams of special forces, advisers, and aircrews to fight the Islamic state, he rolled back some of the Islamic States gains, enough to keep the lid on its advances in Iraq and Syria but far short of defeating the Islamists. He also deployed elite military forces to several countries in Africa to fight Islamist terrorists. Similarly, the president returned a US Army armored brigade to Western Europe; fielded military instructors; and rotated warplanes in and out of Eastern Europe and the Baltic states to put the Russians slightly on notice. In East Asia, he sailed US naval vessels near the disputed island chains without genuinely confronting China's widening claims to sovereignty over the open seas.

This barebones introduction to four presidencies sets the stage for and foreshadows more extensive treatment of American foreign policy after the Iron Curtain fell as well as its cyclicity. The pendular swings between engagement and disengaged stemmed from a host of factors, which will also be spelled out in much greater detail. Suffice it to write here that presidents and their aides took office with a formed predisposition toward international affairs. Each came into the White House bent on installing policies different from the preceding resident. They did not come into office with a tabula rasa. Indeed, their slates were well marked with historical information and analogies, together with campaign promises.

Membership in their respective political parties—whether Republican or Democrat—also played a part in shaping their outlook as well. Generally, the Republican Party focused on national security issues, advocated higher defense spending, and resorted to a hawkish orientation after the Vietnam War. Before that watershed, Republicans had been known to favor a more isolationist posture, or at least non-involvement in other nations' wars, since the 1930s. The Democratic Party, by contrast, had been known as the more internationalist one of the country's two main parties from the presidencies of Franklin Roosevelt, Harry Truman, and John Kennedy to Lyndon Johnson. The Democrats swung to the retrenchment side of the engagement–disengagement spectrum after leading the United States into the Vietnam War. In brief, the Southeast Asian war switched the international orientation of America's two major political parties. That divide held through the post-Vietnam period of the Cold War right through the post-Berlin Wall timeframe until the present.

Popular sentiments, party positions, electoral pledges, and personal traits all counted for a lot in influencing foreign policy. An early and prescient observer of post-Cold War pendulum swings in U.S. foreign policy,

Professor Henry Nau called attention to Washington's promoting "realist goals of stability at one time, liberal international goals of spreading democracy at another."[45] These alternating objectives often formed a part of the larger engagement or disengagement swings delinated in this book. Each presidential administration also strove to be unlike its predecessor, which played a major part in the cycler engagement–disengagement pendulum oscillations. Circumstances also played a role, as will be related in subsequent pages. Presidents are politicians foremost. As such, they adapted, hedged on campaign promises, and shaped their policies for polls, reelection, or historical legacies. They also altered their coming-into-office approaches near the end of their terms. When their new posture contradicted, modified, or even broke with their initial policies upon stepping into the Oval Office, they not only justified the change but also anticipated their successor's international stance. What is most relevant is that the four post-Cold War presidencies did precipitate the pendulum swings of intervention and retrenchment established during the Cold War period, albeit in briefer timeframes.

Notes

1. Theodore Roosevelt, *American Problems* (New York: The Outlook Company, 1910), p. 82.
2. Arthur M. Schlesinger, Jr., *The Cycles of American Politics* (Boston: Houghton Mifflin, 1986), pp. 23–48.
3. Frank L. Klingberg, *Cyclical Trends in American Foreign Policy Moods* (Lanham, MD: University Press of America, 1983), pp. 1–3.
4. G.W. Trompf, *The Idea of Historical Recurrence in Western Thought: From Antiquity to the Reformation* (Berkeley, CA: University of California Press, 1979), pp. ix–x and 2–3.
5. Schlesinger, *The Cycles of American Politics*, pp. 31 and 34.
6. Ibid., p. 28.
7. Klinberg, *Cyclical Trends in American Foreign Policy Moods*, p. 1.
8. Frank L. Kingberg, "The Historical Alternation of Moods in American Foreign Policy," *World Politics*, IV, no. 2 (January 1952), 239–273.
9. Samuel Merrill, Bernard Grofman, and Thomas L. Brunell, "Cycles in American National Electoral Politics, 1854–2006: Statistical Evidence and an Explanatory Model," *American Political Science Review*, 102, no. 1 (February 2008), 15.

10. James A. Stimson, *Tides of Consent: How Public Opinion Shapes American Politics* (Cambridge: Cambridge University Press, 2004), p. 165.
11. Schlesinger, *Cycles of American Politics*, p. 28.
12. Schlesinger, *The Cycles of American History*, p. xiii.
13. Klingberg, *Cyclical Trends in American Foreign Policy Moods*, p. xiii.
14. Brian McGing, *Polybius' Histories* (New York: Oxford University Press, 2010), p. 171.
15. Giambattista Vico, *The New Science*, trans. Thomas Goddard Bergin and Max Harold Fisch (Ithaca, NY: Cornell University Press, 1961), pp. 419–426.
16. Herbert Butterfield, *The Origins of History* (London: Eyre Methuen, 1981), pp. 121–125.
17. Paul Johnson, "Where Hubris Came From," *New York Times Book Review* (October 23, 2005), p. 15.
18. Niccolò Machiavelli, *Discourses on Livy*, trans. Harvey C. Mansfield and Nathan Tarcov (Chicago: University of Chicago Press, 1996), pp. 83–84.
19. George Santayana, *The Life of Reason: Reason in Common Sense* (New York: Scribner, 1958), p. 284.
20. Johnson, "Where Hubris Came From," p. 15.
21. Richard Snow, *I Invented the Modern Age: The Rise of Henry Ford* (New York: Scribner, 2013), p. 4.
22. George F. Will, "Colombia Illusions," *Washington Post*, September 10, 2000, p. B 7.
23. Klingberg, *Cyclical Trends in American Policy Moods*, pp. 9 and 71–72.
24. Cecil V. Crabb, Jr., *The Doctrines of American Foreign Policy: There Meaning, Role, and Future* (Baton Rouge, LA: Louisiana State University Press, 1982), p. 279.
25. John Lewis Gaddis, *The United States and the End of the Cold War: Implications, Reconsiderations, Provocations* (New York: Oxford University Press, 1992), p. 120.
26. Warren I. Cohen, *The Cambridge History of American Foreign Relations, Volume IV, America in the Age of Soviet Power, 1945–1991* (New York: Cambridge, 1993), p. 184.
27. Klingberg, *Cyclical Trends in American Foreign Policy Moods*, p. 135.

28. Schlesinger, *The Cycles of American History*, p. 24.
29. Ibid., p. 31.
30. Ibid., p. 32.
31. For an inside peek at how the Obama administration retailed the nuclear arms deal with Iran to Congress and the American people, see David Samuels, "The Aspiring Novelist Who Became Obama's Foreign-Policy Guru," *New York Times Magazine*, May 5, 2016, p. 27.
32. Klingberg, *Cyclical Trends in American Foreign Policy Moods*, p. xiii.
33. Ibid., pp. 169–174 and 131–136.
34. Ibid., pp. 8–18.
35. Colin Dueck, *The Obama Doctrine: American Grand Strategy Today* (New York: Oxford University Press, 2015), p. 11.
36. Arthur M. Schlesinger, Jr., *War and the American Presidency* (New York: W.W. Norton, 2004), pp. 20–25.
37. Christopher Hemmer, *American Pendulum: Recurring Debates in U.S. Grand Strategy* (Ithaca, NY: Cornell University Press, 2015), pp. 10–11 and 176.
38. Walter A. McDougall, *Promised Land, Crusader State* (New York: Houghton Mifflin Company, 1997), pp. 5–12.
39. Hemmer, *American Pendulum: Recurring Debates in U.S. Grand Strategy*, p. 11.
40. Peter Baker and Michael A. Fletcher, "Bush Pledges to Spread Freedom," *Washington Post*, January 21, 2005, p. A 1.
41. Scott Wilson, "Obama Hugs the Center in Pulling Troops from Afghanistan," *Washington Post*, June 23, 2011, p. A 1.
42. Thucydides, *History of the Peloponnesian War*, trans. Richard Crawley (London: J.M. Dent & Sons, 1910), p. 384.
43. Colin Dueck, *Hard Line: The Republican Party and U.S. Foreign Policy since World War II* (Princeton, NJ: Princeton University Press, 2010), p. 229.
44. Mark P. Lagon, *The Reagan Doctrine: Sources of American Conduct in the Cold War's Last Chapter* (Westport, CT: Praeger, 1994), p. xii.
45. Henry R. Nau, *Conservative Internationalism: Armed Diplomacy Under Jefferson, Polk, Truman, and Reagan* (Princeton, New Jersey: Princeton University Press, 2013, page 61.

Part I

CHAPTER 2

George Herbert Walker Bush: A Disorderly World

"There is nothing more difficult to take in hand, more perilous to conduct, or more uncertain in its success, than to take the lead in the introduction of a new order of things." —Niccolò Machiavelli

The raucous crowds that gathered at the Bornholmer Street border crossing in divided Berlin never imagined that they were to be present at the start of a new world order on the evening of November 9, 1989 when the Berlin Wall came down. Erected in 1961, the Wall halted most defections from East to West. Guarded by German troops, the gray stone slabs divided the city and symbolically the world. Political freedom prevailed in the West, and communism gripped the East. The Wall "will still be standing in fifty or a hundred years," boasted long-serving Erich Honecker, the German Communist Party chief.[1] That prediction proved dead wrong.

During that cool autumn twilight, protestors walked to both sides of the concrete Wall upon hearing implausible Western media reports that the German Democratic Republic (GDR, East German) officials had announced the opening of the Wall. East Berliners eagerly streamed through the checkpoint to enter into West Germany. The GDR leadership, caught off guard by the news, froze when senior *Stasi* officers (East German secret police) stopped preventing East Berliners from converging on the Bornholmer Strasse checkpoint to enter the city's Western sector. When a German news organization aired sensational assertions that the

T.H. Henriksen, *Cycles in US Foreign Policy since the Cold War*,
DOI 10.1007/978-3-319-48640-6_2

barrier stood open, throngs of people stormed through checkpoints. East and West Berliners flowed together, dancing in the streets, drinking toasts, and crying in joy. Others turned their anger on the Wall with anything handy to batter the hated 12-foot-tall, reinforced cement blocks. Within hours of the breach, the status quo ante was no longer retrievable. This accidental and peaceful revolution resulted from an "entirely unplanned sequence" of events, but the Wall could not be re-sealed.[2] Reunification of the two German states hurtled forward to a united county as before 1945. A year later, it was politically consummated as the Federal Republic of Germany.

When Berliners tore down the Wall dividing their city, they began the final unraveling of the mighty Soviet Union. Its disintegration, in turn, led to the end of the Cold War, which dated to the closing days of World War II. Without the Union of Soviet Socialist Republics (USSR) nemesis, the United States lost its strategic focal point, which for decades had orientated its worldview. The USSR's collapse, however, ushered in a much less orderly international landscape. Out of their mutual fear over lighting a nuclear fuse, Washington and Moscow kept the Cold War cold. They restrained their respective allies, checked the escalation of crises between them (after the 1962 Cuban missile standoff), and generally worked to avoid a mutually destructive thermonuclear war. The East-West standoff, therefore, possessed an orderly and even predictable quality. The Soviet Union's implosion meant America's overriding nemesis no longer threatened its well-being or security.

With the USSR's fragmentation in 1991, the United States enjoyed a "unipolar moment."[3] America was not all-powerful in world affairs but it surpassed others in its military, economic, and diplomatic capabilities. It lacked any peer rivals or overriding foreign threats to its security. What it did inherit was a disorderly and violent world. Contrary to expectations, post-Cold War America collected no sustained "peace dividend" due to slashed defense spending and reaped no respite from international emergencies. Because of its unsurpassed military dominance, powerhouse economy, and sense of diplomatic indispensableness, however, the United States possessed some luxury in deciding if, when, and how to intervene in foreign problems.

America remained a house divided about the wisdom of going to war beyond its shores before and after the Cold War. Whether to wade into foreign conflicts or even to embrace risky commitments were questions that tapped into deeply held sentiments in the American mind. Interventionists and non-interventionists offered conflicting visions of the country's interest. Except for the alliance signed with France during the American Revolutionary War, the United States went 165 years without entering into permanent alliances, until after World War II when it subsequently signed defense pacts with over 60 countries.[4] Instead, it followed for nearly two centuries the advice of George Washington and Thomas Jefferson; the latter's inaugural pledge—"entangling alliances with none"—encapsulated the isolationist proposition. During the World War I era, President Woodrow Wilson spoke of American international engagement to make the world safe for freedom. He, thereby, re-kindled the debate about America's international role.

The two schools of thought held contrary opinions about the nation's proper course in the post-1919 world. By the next decade, isolationism prevailed over involvement abroad. And the two worldviews, in update guises, exerted strong influences on the direction of American foreign policy ever since. In fact, they lay at the heart of the cyclical swings between American interventionism and retrenchment after the fall of the Iron Curtain according to one scholar. Christopher Hemmer detected pendulum swings in the debates about how to promote American values to other shores. To Professor Hemmer, policy-makers have agreed on the benefits but disagreed on the means to attaining them. Should the United States engage in crusades to impose its values on other lands? In this view, the country has to expand American principles "as a missionary, either converting or defeating those who reject core U.S. values like democracy." Or, should the United States "serve as model for others, letting the intrinsic attraction of its values do most of the work?"[5]

Decisions about entering into foreign conflicts or international commitments encountered isolationist impulses to stay free of foreign entanglements. Not only were these non-interventionist sentiments echoes from the 1930s, when millions of Americans longed to remain neutral as Europe and Asia lunged toward war. The heavy casualties suffered during World War I convinced them that the United States must abstain from another war. During the Franklin Roosevelt presidency, Congress passed "five formal neutrality laws that aimed to insulate the United States from the war-storms then brewing across the globe."[6]

Other non-interventionists excoriated American foreign policy for its imperial urge and reliance on excessive military force. Rather than dwelling on the loss of American blood and treasure spent in misbegotten ventures, they challenged what they believed were Washington's unrealistic assumptions about its benevolence abroad. In short, they took serious exception to the argument of American exceptionalism, when that notion justified unilateralism and militarism in the cause of US interests.[7] The high costs and frustrating end to the Vietnam War solidified their abhorrence of American militarism. These two insular strands—right and left—in American thought converged into the belief of America minding its own business, not acting as a global policeman.

The interventionists possessed counterarguments to the isolationists. They contended that by burying its head in the sand during the interwar period, America left the early aggression from Nazi Germany and imperial Japan go unchecked until it was too late to avoid a world war. For them, the 1938 Munich settlement that paved the way for Germany to take over Czechoslovakia's Sudetenland was an indefensible selling out of a small East European state for a short-lived and dubious peace. After Nazi forces overran the rest of Czechoslovakia the next year, the Munich appeasement came to symbolize shame and failure when confronting a threat. Britain's wartime Prime Minister, Winston Churchill, rebuked the "tragedy" of the Munich settlement as dishonorable and ultimately futile to satiate the Third Reich's thirst for conquests.[8] Foreign threats, in the engagers' opinion, must be addressed with diplomatic firmness or even military measures. Churchill became the engagers' standard bearer during nearly every international crisis ever since.

These intellectual and popular undercurrents offer context for the framers and implementers of the country's foreign policies. But these political winds never predetermined courses of action for or against overseas commitments. The post-Cold War presidencies felt the brush of history but they usually acted according to their own predilections and the political coalitions they built to capture the White House.

At most, the two schools of thought provided arguments, analysis, and analogies for and against overseas ventures. Pro and con arguments were often shaped by sketchy knowledge of American's past, however. The words "Munich" and "Vietnam" often served as shibboleths for each side against opponents. Even without direct reference to either event, the habits of the mind drew from their respective memories to influence outlooks and political discourse in the country.

Foreign Policy Cycles after 1989

The Cold War's termination resulted in neither enduring peace nor prevailing goodwill across the globe. Indeed, the collapse of the Soviet Union ironically entailed more, not less, upheaval and conflict for the United States to handle. Before the USSR's balkanization into several successor nations in 1991, it reached a quasi-accommodation with the United States to never again risk nuclear annihilation as during the 1962 Cuban missile crisis.[9] As a consequence, the bipolar standoff achieved more than a measure of restraint from both superpowers, keeping their relations close to an even keel.

The sudden breakdown of Moscow's hegemony, which both safeguarded and restrained its communist and non-communist allies, ensured a chaotic settling out for the new political order. No peer competitor rose suddenly to challenge American preeminence. But a cauldron of rogue nations, failed states, and Islamist terrorism boiled over onto the world scene. This disorderly world presented many threats and problems for American hopes of an immediate respite from international burdens, which had so taxed the country in lives, defense expenditures, and far-flung commitments across the planet.

This unstable atmosphere was not historically unprecedented after an arduous international struggle. The aftermath of World War I and II both witnessed much instability and bloodshed. The sheer magnitude of the 1914–1918 war—with 10 million military deaths and the horrors of trench warfare—made certain that the status quo ante could not be restored. Four monarchies fell. The Russian czar gave way first to a military coup and then the Bolshevik Revolution. The Kaiser, having helped catapult Germany into a bloody European war, abdicated and fled to The Netherlands. The long-crumbling rule of the Turkish sultan was replaced by a modernizing, secular regime bent on bringing Turkey into the modern era. Finally, the Austro-Hungarian Empire dissolved into several successor states with differing ethnicity and religions, promising trouble for decades. Eastern Europe suffered Bolshevik convulsions in Germany and Hungary. China entered a long period of turmoil that did not subside until the Communist victory in 1949.[10]

The post-1945 world also recorded its own set of tumultuous developments which played out over the next decades. The Soviets's Red Army followed up the defeat of the Nazi armies east of the Elbe River by consolidating a political grip on Eastern Europe and cutting off the "captive nations" from the West with an Iron Curtain, as Winston Churchill memorably phrased it. Germany was divided into two countries; East Germany fell to the Soviets and West Germany aligned with the United States and Western Europe. Moscow installed compliant communist governments in its new satellite states in Eastern Europe. It roped together these communist regimes into the Warsaw Pact, a military alliance arrayed against America and its West European allies in the North Atlantic Treaty Organization (NATO).

The defeat of Nazi Germany sparked a desperate flight of some 10 million refugees who fled Germany, Poland, and other nearby states in search of safety from the retreating Wehrmacht and the advancing Red Army. Shattered European states greeted the postwar era with little hope of peace, prosperity, or normalcy. It took the extraordinary Marshall Plan starting in 1947 to rescue the European economies and thereby their democratic governments. Administered by the exemplary George C. Marshall, Secretary of State, the Plan pumped some $13 billion (in 1952 dollars) into West Europe's recovery, saving the Continent from chaos and communism. Along with NATO, the aid program built a bulwark against the threat of Soviet conquest or subversion in the iciest days of the early Cold War.

Across the globe, Mao Zedong's peasant armies swept away first the Japanese invaders and then the Nationalist forces of Chiang Kai-shek. The Communist victory brought together the United States and Japan as allies against Mao's China. The international system separated into two large camps—one free and prospering and the other totalitarian and stagnate. Later, a non-aligned bloc formed to chart a neutral way, although in reality its members often tilted toward Moscow rather than Washington. With some notable changes, this Soviet-American rivalry remained largely frozen in place for the near half a century.

George Herbert Walker Bush and the Soviet Disintegration

When the East-West rivalry dissolved with the USSR's demise, the international environment birthed a still-unfolding global re-alignment with the rise of China, the resurgence of Russia, and the surfacing of medium-weight powers like India, Brazil, Iran, Japan, Indonesia, and Turkey. America's unipolar moment immediately after the USSR's fragmentation proved transient, although Washington remains an indispensable capital for international affairs and dominant military power. After four decades of nearly immobilized global politics between the two super blocs, the sudden breakdown nearly overwhelmed the newly installed George Herbert Walker Bush administration.

President Bush saw himself as distinctly different from his predecessor Ronald Reagan. In his inaugural address on January 20, 1989, George Bush held that America's purpose "is to make kinder the face of the Nation and gentler the face of the world." Critics, some from his own political party, interpreted the phrase as conveying timidity about his government's policies at home and abroad. He never completely shook his detractors' characterization that he was to the manor born and therefore too genteel to secure exclusive American interests. Two years later, after the Persian Gulf War, Bush spoke about a "new world order" linked to the United Nations (UN), which "is poised to fulfil the historic vision of its founders" embracing "freedom and respect for human rights."[11] These statements and other similar declarations gave rise to view that America's 41st president favored the UN agenda over that of the United States. To hard-liners, he was bent on soft-headed internationalism out of step with America's realist foreign interests.

Nothing could be further from the truth. Bush, in fact, was steelier than his disparagers acknowledged. He was prudent and cautious but not timid. After all, he had been a decorated World War II hero as a naval aviator who flew 58 combat missions. He was the lone survivor when his three-man plane was shot down in the Philippine Sea. At the war's conclusion, Bush attended Yale and then entered the world of business and politics. This latter profession he picked up from his father, who had been a US Senator from Connecticut. Like presidents before and after him, Bush strove to enlist the UN or other international organizations, such as the Organization of the Americas, in pursuit of US objectives. When resorting to military force, Bush (as other White House occupants) desired the political cover afforded by the UN Security Council's blessing. His tenure coincided with dominant US military power and diplomatic influence.

So, his detractors expected near-instantaneous reactions to any perceived threats or impediments to US priorities. When Bush permitted five Iraqi oil tankers to sail to Yemen and gave the Soviets three days to persuade Saddam Hussein to leave Kuwait, the British prime minister took him to task. When informed by the president, Margaret Thatcher quotably replied: "Well, all right, George, but this is no time to go wobbly."[12]

President Bush, in fact, did not "go wobbly," although his hawkish critics widely circulated the Thatcher quote.

When George Bush settled into the White House in January 1989, he came to the presidency after eight years as Ronald Reagan's vice president. That tour of duty stood him in good stead for his own residency at 1600 Pennsylvania Avenue. Having also served as a Texas Congressmen, US envoy to China, and Director of the Central Intelligence Agency (CIA), he had seasoned credentials in international affairs. He had met with scores of world leaders prior to taking the reins as America's commander-in-chief. This familiarity with world politics bred a cautious but firm approach in America's 41st president. His knowledge and confidence in US power were soon tested as the United States entered a hyperactive period overseas. America's international engagement crested during the Bush presidency and then waned in his successor's term. Bush's overseas endeavors built on and resulted from the active international course of his predecessor.

President Ronald Reagan confronted and tested the Soviet Union by backing, equipping, and training anti-communist guerrillas in Afghanistan, Angola, and Nicaragua in what became known as the Reagan Doctrine.[13] He also stressed the USSR with a massive arms buildup and a sketchy missile defense system. Already taxed by a failing military intervention into Afghanistan and a collapsing state-managed economy, Soviet Russia was fearful of further exertions. Reagan's forward policies contributed to the Soviets's debilitating woes. As Reagan prepared to depart for retirement in California, his personal friend and close ally Margaret Thatcher stated what was becoming obvious to all: "We are no longer in the Cold War now."[14] But the breakup of the sprawling Soviet Empire took place during the Bush presidency.

As the USSR visibly faltered under Mikhail Gorbachev, the White House scrambled to fashion a policy to take advantage of its foe's spiraling misfortune. Kremlin watchers struggled to comprehend the unfolding developments inside their beleaguered adversary. Gorbachev became General Secretary of the Communist Party in 1985, in part, to reform the stagnant Soviet economy. The former agricultural economist implemented *glasnost* (openness) and *perestroika* (restructuring) policies to breathe new life into the decaying economic and political apparatus. He also looked to the West for financial bailouts. In demographic terms, the Soviet Union also showed its systemic dysfunction with "very high rates of alcoholism, drug addiction, and crime."[15] Life expectancy, infant mortality, and governmental corruption reflected a society in disarray. Instead of resuscitating the dying Soviet system, Gorbachev jolted the sclerotic mechanism to its overdue death. Bankruptcy, political breakdown, and malaise became the new face of the USSR, dashing all the early Bolshevik promises of a worker's paradise.

Gorbachev's decentralizing moves loosened Moscow's controlling grip on the country's 15 Soviet Republics. The Russians held the top Communist Party positions in my republics despite their minority status among non-Russian populations. These resistive ethnic nationalities yearned for their freedom from Russian rule. Outside the USSR, the so-called Captive Nations of Eastern Europe and the Baltic countries asserted their sovereignty from the Kremlin's rule. Protests and turmoil broke out across many of the Soviet imperial holdings.

Among the Moscow's satellites, Poland led the growing resistance against the imposition of the Soviet-backed communist regime after World War II. In the early 1980s, the Polish workers' movement, Solidarity, protested for not only higher wages but also independence from party control. Solidarity, in addition, called for a free press, release of political dissidents, and a greater role for the Roman Catholic Church, which criticized the ruling party's crackdown. Moscow tentatively pushed back. But unlike its heavy-handed military suppressions in Hungary (1956) and Czechoslovakia (1968), Red Square did not dispatch tanks and troops to crush the protestors. The significance of Poland's opposition and the Soviet's indecisiveness must not be lost on a historical observer. One chronicler of the Soviet Union's rise and fall wrote: "in the imperial collapse, the Polish turning point would be only marginally less import than the foredoomed invasion of Afghanistan."[16] The political ferment pushed the Polish communist regime to concede partially free elections in June 1989. Of the 100 open seats, Solidarity captured all but one and then formed a coalition government. This independent leadership constituted the first democratic rule in Eastern Europe since the Iron Curtain descended.

The Polish bid for freedom pulled the proverbial finger from the dike. Neighboring countries under Soviet thrall soon followed suit. Hungary's break for freedom was of particular significance on two fronts. First, like Poland, it held elections in which the non-communist movements vanquished the regime's reinvented Socialist Party, thereby forming a representative government. Second, and equally consequential, the Hungarians broke open the Iron Curtain separating the communist nations from the democracies to the West. They took down the barbed-wire fence along their border with Austria, flinging open a route for thousands of fleeing East Europeans to seek freedom. Next, Germany, Czechoslovakia, Bulgaria, Yugoslavia, and the three Baltic states swept their communist rulers from power almost without bloodshed. Only in Romania did Nicolae and Elena Ceausescu cling tenaciously to power, ordering the Securitate (secret police) to fire on protestors in the streets. Seeing which way the wind was blowing, the Securitate, however, switched sides sealing the fate of their former masters. The Ceausescus were put up against a wall and shot to death by anti-regime opponents in December 1989. Thereafter, Romania joined the expanding democratic ranks.

Washington scrambled to keep up with the political tumult. After a brief hesitation, the Bush White House grasped that Moscow was geopolitically adrift without the ability or willingness to restore the old order. No Red Army soldiers marched from the barracks to clampdown on protests. American policy boiled down standing by and allowing change to proceed. Not for the first time in history, the best policy centered on steadying a wobbly foreign leader. The United States had two broad goals to gain from a weakened Gorbachev. It sought nuclear arms accords to lower the number of warheads aimed at the American homeland. And it wanted to sustain the freeing of Soviet satellites from Communist thralldom. George Bush and his closest aides reasoned that both objectives could best be obtained from Gorbachev. So, the Americans worried about the general secretary's political survival. Should he be replaced by either a military or party hard-liner, then America's priorities might be in jeopardy.

Nuclear weapons cast a dark shadow over American-Soviet relations since the early Cold War. These fearsome bombs could annihilate both powers, while destroying half the planet though the atomic blast or nuclear winter of smoke and soot blocking out sunlight. Both powers amassed huge armories of nuclear warheads that could be delivered against adversaries' cities by bombers, intercontinental ballistic missiles (ICBMs). Sensing an opportunity with a withering Soviet Union, the Bush White House resurfaced the Strategic Arms Reduction Treaty (START) talks, which the Reagan administration had proposed to Moscow. The abundance of weaponry and high financial costs of servicing nuclear arms made both superpowers amenable to reductions.

Two years of talks led to the signing of START I, a treaty that slashed about half of each side's nuclear weapons to some 6000—still many more than needed to destroy the planet. The agreement also cut back the number of delivery systems to 1600 each, whether they were long-range bombers, submarine-launched ballistic missiles or ground-based ICBMs. President Bush traveled to Moscow for the signing in July 1991. Years later, Moscow and Washington ratified the agreement, which rendered the world slightly safer from atomic annihilation. Secretary of State James A. Baker pressed ahead by persuading the newly independent successor states from the fragmenting USSR—Belarus, Kazakhstan, and the Ukraine—to sign onto the Lisbon Protocol in 1992. By agreeing to the protocol's terms, the former Soviet republics abandoned their nuclear arsenals which they obtained from Moscow.

The internationally activist government sitting in Washington followed up the START I signing with more arms-control accords. It embraced the senatorial initiative known as the Cooperative Threat Reduction program, which advanced in bipartisan fashion by US Senators Sam Nunn (Democrat, Georgia) and Richard Lugar (Republican, Indiana). The program received funding from the US Department of Defense in order to dismantle Soviet nuclear and chemical arms, lest these deadly instruments fall into rogue or terrorist hands.[17] Prior to leaving office after losing his reelection bid in November 1992, George Bush entered into the START II treaty, which shaved activated nuclear arms by more—3000 Russian warheads and 3500 American ones. The US Senate ratified the treaty four years afterward, and the Russian Duma took another four to do the same.

Engagement with the Gorbachev government was not confined to an arms-control treaty. The Bush foreign policy team swung into action to secure a range of American interests. Weeks after the Berlin Wall crumbled in November 1989, US and Soviet officials sat down to discuss the dramatic, unfolding events in Eastern Europe as the Kremlin's satellites strove to break from its tyranny. The face-to-face talks took place off the island of Malta on board American and Russian naval craft. Consciously selected to be reminiscent of the famous World War II shipboard meeting between Franklin Roosevelt and Winston Churchill off the coast of Newfoundland in 1941, the Mediterranean negotiations produced no stirring Atlantic Charter, which proclaimed the goals for the war against fascism. But they were historic nonetheless.

The Soviet-American rendezvous afforded the opportunity for the leaders to develop a personal bond. More concretely, President Bush put incentives on the table for his Soviet counterpart. He offered inducements to the economically strapped Moscow, including financial credits, most favored trade status, and promises to work for Russia to obtain observer status to the General Agreements on Tariffs and Trade, which would lead to more international commerce. Gorbachev happily accepted these benefits as they would bolster his perestroika reforms of the Soviet's centrally controlled economy. In reciprocation, the Soviet chief declared his intentions to halt supplying arms to the El Salvadoran rebels and to refrain from meddling in Nicaragua's free elections. The Central American country's polling unexpectedly posted a win for Violeta Chamorro, the non-revolutionary candidate, over the Marxist-influenced Sandinista incumbent Daniel Ortega. The White House interpreted the outcome as a victory. It secured peace in Nicaragua and then in the rest of Central America.

Not insignificantly, the vital question of German reunification evaded the Americans at the shipboard talks in Maltese waters. The East-West German divide lay at the heart of Cold War in Europe. For Washington, reuniting the split country rose to be the sine qua non-factor in making the Continent "whole and free" as President Bush phrased his goal. The Soviet position reflected the sober remembrance of two German invasions accompanied by immense destruction and loss of life during the first half of the twentieth century. Merely contemplating a strong, reunited Germany astride the Continent caused deep unease within the Kremlin and even the chanceries in London and Paris. France, for instance, recalled three German historic cross-border invasions deep into French lands within a 70-year period. And Britain suffered huge losses in blood and treasure during both twentieth-century conflicts, leading to its imperial decline. The Bush White House had its work cut out for it in convincing all parties to bury history.

American objectives were strategically clear but diplomatically problematic. The United States desired the Red Army out of Europe and the three Baltic nations, the East and West German states reunited, and the reunified Germany a member of NATO. While US statesmen eventually attained these lofty goals, they faced a strenuously uphill effort which seemed unattainable from the start. They concentrated on effectuating their objectives while soft-peddling calls for democratic and market reforms in the tottering Soviet Union. In fact, keeping Gorbachev in power served US interests more than liberalizing its old foe's economy or political system. In some respects, Gorbachev nearly became a quasi-ally of the Bush government. Elements within the floundering Soviet structure regarded Gorbachev as a traitor. Military officers staged coup against him in August 1991, months before the USSR dissolved. Held by his captors for days, the General Secretary reemerged physically unscathed but politically neutralized for his final months in office.

Moscow had deep reservations about a powerful, prosperous, and reconsolidated Germany within NATO, the West's premiere anti-Soviet alliance since 1949. Events, however, conspired to leave Moscow behind in the rapidly unfolding developments in Central Europe. The Germans themselves waited for neither time nor tide. The Federal German Republic, led by Chancellor Helmut Kohl, offered funds to sustain its smaller, bankrupt cousins in the East. There, the GDR felt the pressure of its own citizens for a brighter future with the Western state. For their part, communist functionaries dragged their feet, fearing a loss of political power in a new reality.

By early 1990, the political tide rose against the status quo. Beyond Germany's borders, its neighbors leapt ahead in casting off the Red Army-buttressed regimes in Poland, Hungary, Czechoslovakia, and Bulgaria. The GDR stood at a standstill, however. The East Germans stopped paying their taxes. Many citizens no long worked. They flocked to urban squares where they protested for elections and reunification with West Germany. In Berlin, the communist party reluctantly moved up elections to March to satisfy popular demand for a change in regime. The electoral results stunned the party, which believed that 40 years of communism would predispose the voters to its brand of socialism. The former Communist Party received just 16 percent of the ballots, whereas Chancellor Kohl's Christian Democratic Union's Alliance won 48 percent. The Social Democratic Party took 22 percent, and smaller parties got the balance. The fact that the two top vote getters were offshoots of West German political movements was not lost on any observer.

The results rattled not only Moscow but also European capitals. Paris and London drew the conclusion that it was futile to resist the inevitable prospect of one German nation. The Soviet Union, nevertheless, dug in its heels against a reunified German powerhouse in *Mitteleuropa*. After the German elections and the Bonn government's initiatives for economic and monetary union with East Germany, the Kremlin saw unification as inescapable. Moscow shifted to a fallback strategy of opposing a reconstituted Germany within NATO. At first, Moscow wanted Germany also in its Warsaw Pact of Soviet-controlled East European states and the USSR. This diversion evaporated when the Warsaw Pact went to pieces as the communist regimes fell apart in Poland, Hungary, and the Czechoslovakia. Next, the Kremlin flirted with notion of German neutrality from NATO. It looked with fear and loathing on German membership in the Western alliance, as simply an advancement of NATO toward the Russian border.

American officials beat back the Soviet feelers on a non-aligned Germany. They argued that an unaligned Germany could swing back and forth between East and West. It might also attract smaller states in Central Europe to its orbit, contributing to factionalism and instability on the Continent, especially if it adopted an anti-Moscow orientation. Washington, furthermore, argued that it was better for Soviet interests to have an economically ascendant Germany anchored within a democratic and peaceful NATO. As for American interest, German participation strengthened NATO, allowing for future US troop reductions in Europe. The US arguments were also intended to assuage apprehensions in Britain and France. None of its partners were eager for an American military withdrawal from Europe. The British, French, and Germans worried about a re-ascendant Russia, once it cast off its communist economic straitjacket. Even Mikhail Gorbachev wrote in his memoir that he favored the retention of US military forces in Europe as a stabilizing element and a defense against a German resurgence of militarism.[18] Jumping ahead, the resolution of the German question did, indeed, open the way for the United States to drawdown substantial numbers of troops over the years from its 300,000 peak at the end of the Cold War. By 2016, American forces had shrunk to about 30,000 troops, with only two US Army combat brigades in place.

In the final analysis, Gorbachev could not block German reconciliation and its NATO membership. America twisted his arm, and the Federal Republic of Germany offered desperately needed funds to the Soviet leader. Gorbachev let it be known to Secretary of State Baker that Moscow required some $20 billion in money and credits. The Soviet economy was bankrupt. Moscow wanted a bailout for debt repayments, consumer goods for its restive population, and industrial conversion from military output to civil products. The Bush administration provided modest aid, believing that most of the financial assistance would just "go down the rat hole" in the Soviet-managed economy.[19] The Helmut Kohl government reasoned that any money, if even misspent by the Russians, constituted an investment in attaining West German goals of reunifying with East Germany and ridding that state of the Red Army's occupation. Thus, Chancellor Kohl extended DM 12 billion and a further DM 3 billion in interest-free credits (approximately $7 billion and $1.7 billion, respectively).[20]

As for the United States, it redoubled its campaign for one, reunited Germany and for its membership within the Atlantic alliance. Washington took up a negotiating format dubbed "Two Plus Four," in which the "two" Germanys would meet with the "four" World War II victorious powers—the United States, Britain, France, and the Soviet Union to deliberate on combing the Germanic halves. Four months later, the negotiating parties signed the Treaty on the Final Settlement With Respect to Germany in September 1990. The signing in a Moscow hotel, not in one of the Kremlin's chandeliered rooms, took place without the high drama and orchestrated state pageantry of major treaty signings. Make no mistake: the treaty marked a singular American achievement, whose terms and strictures remain in force today.

Often referred to as the "two-plus-four" treaty, the agreement's articles set forth specific stipulations. Among the weighty provisions, it specified that East and West Germany constituted the new united Germany with the borders of the two pre-existing states. The treaty permitted the reunited country to join any alliances of its choosing, meaning NATO participation. The newly created state renounced any preparations "for aggressive war," and the manufacture or possession of nuclear, biological, and chemical weapons. The united Germany pledged adherence to the terms of the Treaty on Non-Proliferation on Nuclear Weapons. The new sovereignty also committed itself to a Bundeswehr of no more than 350,000 troops. The Bundeswehr forces were permitted to move into the former Eastern zone but without nuclear arms. Moscow also agreed to withdraw the Red Army forces from this zone by 1995 but did so two years earlier. Lastly, the treaty dissolved the Four Power framework that presided over a vanquished Germany since 1945.

Before assessing the legacy of the Bush government, a short account of the dismal fate of its Soviet partner must be briefly drawn. By the time Mikhail Gorbachev assumed the position of General Secretary of the Communist Party of the Soviet Union (CPSU) in 1985, the USSR's decrepitude was in its terminal stage. Perhaps, had he mimicked Deng Xiaoping's model of freeing the economy in China during the late 1970s while holding tight the CPSU's political power, then Russia's fate might have been different. But Gorbachev's pronouncements and reforms let loose mighty centrifugal forces that tore at the republic-structured political entity that spanned eleven (now nine) times zones and encompassed an array of ethnic groups. Moscow's plight was widely recognized before Ronald Reagan left the presidency in early 1989. As George Bush settled into the White House, the political crosscurrents assailing Gorbachev's hold on power accelerated. He lost the backing of the military and the KGB secret police which looked with dismay at his retreats. They interpreted as muddled thinking his reluctance to clamp down on East European dissent the way his Kremlin predecessors had in Hungary and Czechoslovakia.

Gorbachev worsened his standing and the cohesiveness of the dissolving USSR by endorsing the misnamed Union Treaty, which devolved Moscow's political and economic power to the constituent republics that made up the Soviet Union. The treaty soon cleared the way the USSR's breakup when republics asserted their sovereignty from the Kremlin. By August 1991, the hard-liners were fed up when they learned that Gorbachev intended to sign the Union Treaty with Kazakhstan. Elements of military leadership and KGB staged a coup, whereby they sequestered Gorbachev, who had been vacationing at his dacha in the Crimea. Almost in *opera buffa*-style, the ring leaders hurriedly released their charge when flummoxed by their own soldiers' refusal to fire on anti-coup protestors in Moscow and other cities. The coup flopped but not its consequences.

Although Gorbachev soon returned to power, his days were numbered as chief of the unraveling Soviet enterprise. A raft of republics declared their independence from the failing USSR. Foremost among them was the Russian Republic, the largest of the sub-states. Led by Boris Yeltsin, chairman of the Supreme Soviet in the Russian Republic, this polity became the Russian Federation. Yeltsin's star rose and Gorbachev's crashed. With the USSR's breakup, the Secretary General had no political platform. In fact, Gorbachev was left standing on a deck that had no ship beneath it. The Soviet Union dissolved and sank with just scattered debris left floating on the surface.

The Bush administration simply shifted horses from Gorbachev to Yeltsin, who stood as the best guarantor of the arms-control agreements and the German reunification treaty. The latter two-state settlements came off as low-profile denouement when compared to the toppling Berlin Wall drama. Yet, the two-plus-four accord diplomatically bound and codified the inter-state relationships of post-Cold War Europe. It stacked up as a far-reaching achievement, transforming Europe and America's relations with that continent and post-Soviet Russia. It capped the economic and political growth of what evolved into the EU during the 1990s from the far looser framework of the European Community. Securing the EU's ascent, the United States midwifed a prosperous bloc of democratic nations that, in effect, constituted another geopolitical pole in the multipolar world that followed the Soviet Union's vanishing.

President Bush and Secretary of State Baker strong-armed their reluctant, worried, and resistant counterparts to accept the American agenda. Behind the scenes, they drove a unilateral bargain that ruffled allied feathers. The White House firmly held that only a reunited Germany in NATO and a total Soviet withdrawal from Eastern Europe would guarantee peace on the war-wracked Continent. They dragged along the French, British, and Russians. On occasion, George Bush ignored London and Paris because US policy was "too important ... to review with allies in the usual way."[21] High-handed and cavalier, the Bush administration propelled the negotiations that led to a reunited Europe and saner nuclear arms levels with Moscow. This achievement endures to this day, even if it is underlauded by contemporary commentators. It stands in stark contrast to so many American train wrecks in the years afterward.

Bush: The Military Interventionist

If the George H. W. Bush legacy rested only on shepherding the peaceful reunification of the East and West Germany into one nation and its integration into NATO, it would still be a high-marked achievement. But his Soviet negotiations, including arms-control treaties, represented one intricate item on an otherwise full plate of international problems during his one-term presidency. Bush's tenure was nearly bookended by one militarized intervention at the beginning of his term and by another ground war at the end. Both the Panama incursion and the Persian Gulf War went according to plan. Neither bogged the United States down in lengthy occupations cum nation-building operations as subsequent conflicts. The military operations were parsimonious in American casualties and financial costs when compared with the wars of his son, George Walker Bush, a decade later. Both military ventures accomplished US objectives, although they did incur criticism from political opponents. Neither venture, despite their success, enabled George Bush to win a second term at the ballot box. A sagging domestic economy and lackluster reelection campaign tripped him up.

Operation Just Cause in Panama

The significance of the US military intervention into Panama is underrecognized. Obscured by the restoration of sovereignty in Eastern Europe, the disintegration of the Soviet Union, and the Persian Gulf War, the storm unleashed against Panama was of a lesser geopolitical magnitude. Plus, the Panama operations effectively attained its objectives with minimum casualties on either side. Smoothly executed with few unpolished surfaces inviting controversy to cling, the news media and the public quickly lost interest in what was regarded as a *fait accompli* from which the United States extracted itself in a matter of months. Yet, the brief, sharp incursion set the paradigm for subsequent US military actions in Somalia, Iraq, Bosnia, Kosovo, Afghanistan, and Iraq for the second time.

Panama included the concepts of regime change, unilateral American leadership with limited allied participation, and humanitarian justification as a political cover for practical US interests. These elements showed up in subsequent interventions. The Panama operation, as the first, post-Berlin Wall, armed intercession, set the stage and threshold for others. It also strengthened the engagement cycle inherited from the Reagan administration. In fact, the Panama invasion even swung the foreign policy pendulum higher than the previous Washington government.

Historically, Washington had a political stake in Panama at least from the earliest years of the twentieth century, when it was governed by Colombia. Panama occupied valuable real estate between the Pacific and Atlantic oceans. Its value boomed with California's exploding population, as settlers flocked to the new El Dorado at the start of the Gold Rush in 1849. Ships bound to and from California had to sail far south along the South American coast, round the Cape Horn, and then tack up the other sides of South America. In 1855, the Panamanian Railway spanned the isthmus and facilitated passenger travel between the two vast oceans. But direct East-West shipping awaited an isthmian waterway. French investors first attempted digging a canal under the direction of Ferdinand de Lesseps, who developed the Suez Canal in Egypt. The venture failed due to bankruptcy and the deaths of thousands of workers from malaria and yellow fever. This failure opened the way for the United States.

President Theodore Roosevelt hatched a plan of guile rather than gunfire to wrest the Panamanian territory from Colombian rule. When Colombia's parliament turned down requests for ratification of a treaty for a strip of land to build a trans-ocean seaway, Roosevelt outmaneuvered the Colombians. He made it known to the anti-Colombian rebels within Panama that the United States stood ready to back their independence from Bogotá's domination. Washington granted diplomatic recognition to Panama's sovereignty three days after its rebellion erupted. To safeguard the fledgling country, Roosevelt steamed warships to the Panamanian coast to stop Colombian vessels from landing troops to crush the revolt. His agents even bribed a Colombian admiral to leave the coast. To salve hurt feelings, Washington later transferred a payment to the Bogotá government. Soon afterward, it leased the Canal Zone, a ten-mile buffer on each side of the intended waterway, and restarted construction of a sea passage. The Panama Canal opened for trans-ocean traffic in 1914.

The United States kept a wary eye on Central American states after inaugurating the Panama Canal. As America's global role grew, the importance of the water transit loomed larger for transoceanic trade and warship navigation between the Atlantic and Pacific. During the Cold War, the Pentagon regarded the oceanic passageway as a strategic "choke point." Panamanians resented Washington's control over the Canal Zone but the political elite benefited from US financial transfers. The US exclusivity in the Canal Zone terminated when in 1977 President Jimmy Carter rammed through Congress a treaty returning the canal to Panamanian sovereignty, with both countries guaranteeing the waterway's neutrality. Shortly after, Carter signed two treaties with Panamanian General Omar Torrijos, who had seized power in 1968. The Torrijos-Carter treaties abrogated the 1903 US-Panamanian treaty and gave operational control to Panama for the Canal after 1999. The United States retained the right to defend the waterway from threats to its service for ships of all countries.

This status change did not end Washington's interest in Panama, particularly when it perceived instability developing in the small country. When longtime strongman Omar Torrijos died in 1981, his civilian successors were increasingly beholden to the military officers for their rule. Army General Manuel Antonio Noriega became the de facto ruler. He ran the country from behind the scenes through manipulation, intimidation, and strong-arm tactics. Behind his back, people called him Pineapple Face, a reference to his acne and resulting scars. But they bowed to his harsh rule.

Alarmed by increasing corrupt authoritarian rule within Panama, George Bush embarked on a forward policy to set things right in the isthmian dictatorship soon after moving into the White House. Trouble had been brewing in the country throughout the 1980s and was attributable in no small measure to Noriega. A onetime CIA asset, Noriega proved useful to the Reagan administration in funneling money and perhaps weapons to the Nicaraguan *contras* fighting the Sandinistas, until Congress legislated against *contra* support. General Noriega was also in the pay of the Medellín, the Colombian drug cartel, for letting narcotic shipments transit Panamanian territory for the US market and for money-laundering services. With the decline of the Soviet threat and winding down of the Central American guerrilla wars, Washington no longer needed to turn a blind eye toward Noriega's role in supplying cocaine to North American customers. In 1988, a US federal court in Florida issued an indictment against the despot for his role in drug trafficking. These changed circumstances failed to register with Noriega, who took delight in flaunting Washington's growing concerns.

In the waning days of the Reagan presidency, Washington's mandarins were tired of Noriega's antics. But it fell to the incoming George Bush administration to confront the wayward dictator. In May 1989, Panama held an election, in which Guillermo Endara was regarded as the winner by independent observers, who reported that the election had been stolen. Noriega voided the election returns, claiming "foreign" interference tainted the count. The United States recognized Endara as the new president. Even so, Noriega put up a crony as president. Washington countered by imposing economic sanctions on Panama. Afterward, tensions spiked between the United States and Panama. In the Panama Canal Zone, which US military forces garrisoned, a fraught standoff simmered with the Panamanian Defense Force (PDF).

The Bush White House had geopolitical worries about a Noriega-dominated Panama beyond what could have been seen as simply a personalized *mano-a-mano* struggle between the Panamanian dictator and an American president. Under the terms of the Panama Canal Treaty, passed during the Carter presidency, the United States agreed to turn over the chairmanship on the Canal Commission to a Panamanian official, selected by the government in 1990. American strategists still regarded the passageway as a critical artery. Bush was not keen on having a Noriega hack head up the commission. Ousting Noriega offered the best course for stability in Panama and the appointment of a reasonable commission chairman. The American government placed its hopes in the 1989 election. When Noriega stole the presidency from Endara, who won it with an estimated 62 percent of the vote, the United States resolved to lay down a tougher line toward the dictatorial regime.

The day after the election, President Bush declared: "the days of the dictator are over."[22] Next, the White House recalled the US ambassador to the Panama, reduced the embassy staff by two-thirds, and deployed an infantry brigade to strengthen the 12,000 troops already garrisoned in the Panama Canal Zone. The American forces, soon after, held more military exercises as means to step up the psychological warfare directed against the tyrannical ruler. Washington also took its case for regime change in Panama to the Organization of the American States (OAS). The OAS turned down the United States, because it long feared and resented what many Latin Americans viewed as the overweening behavior of the Colossus of the North in their hemisphere. US interference for over a century accounted for the OAS's demand for punctilious adherence to its principle of non-interference in the affairs of neighboring states. Secretary of State Baker concluded that "it was important to give the OAS a chance—if for no other reason than…the United States had exhausted every peaceful, diplomatic alternative."[23]

Manuel Noriega struck back against the US pressure tactics, which ended up aggravating the Bush administration. He took money from Libyan dictator Muammar al-Qaddafi and arms from Fidel Castro's Cuba for his paramilitary Dignity Battalions, which were a Praetorian militia owing allegiance alone to Noriega. The military strongman escalated his anti-US rhetoric. The tense tit-for-tat exchange between the two states generated internal critics in both countries. President Bush, for example, encountered criticism from his domestic political opponents who saw this policy as either ineffectual or war-mongering toward a small, isolated non-Western country. Inside Panama, the diplomatic spat with the Colossus of the North presented opportunities to men with a "lean and hungry look" eager to depose Noriega, if the United States could be persuaded to assist their putsch.

Behind closed doors, the top Bush officials hoped for a coup and a more reasonable Panamanian caudillo. The White House fine-tuned its anti-Noriega jibes to make it plain that they were directed toward the venal general and not the Panamanian people. A Panamanian army major, Moises Giroldi Vega, did, in fact, seize and hold the strongman in fall 1989. But, alas, the plotters failed and came to grief for a variety of reasons. Although US military intelligence officers were tipped off by the major's wife, their report was disbelieved by most White House officials. Only Bush believed the information and wanted to act on it. The debate and skepticism delayed any practical US response. Major Giroldi expressed the perfunctory rhetoric about his desire to restore democracy to Panama—a necessary justification for US backing of the usurpation. Many of his grievances, nonetheless, were about withheld military pay and service conditions. Thus, he lacked standing in the broader society. Most grievously, he bungled by allowing the captured Noriega to call his rescuers and, thus, to escape. Once free, he had his captors placed in custody, tortured, and executed. Next, the military dictatorship purged the ranks of the Panamanian Defenses Forces to root out Giroldi sympathizers. While a comic opera incident, the badly staged coup served as a wake-up call to the beleaguered Noriega.

The upshot was that the Bush administration could not count on another coup remove its Panamanian irritant. Yet, it persisted in attempting to foment an internal revolt by authorizing the CIA to offer a mere $3 million to would-be conspirators. Even these minimalist machinations blew up in the president's face when his intentions were revealed in the US media in November 1989.[24] Thereafter, Washington ruled out plots to overthrow the thorn in its side. Instead, it turned to a large-scale US military invasion to topple the despot.

Late in 1989, the Pentagon reinforced the garrisoned in the Canal Zone with an additional 10,000 soldiers. These reinforcements simultaneously acted as provocation and deterrent. Had Noriega placed discretion over foolhardiness, he might have remained in power. A misplaced sense of invulnerability and a clutch of toadies egged on the Panamanian Bonaparte, who persisted in taunting and threatening his powerful neighbor to the north. The spark that lit the fuse came when members of the Dignity Battalions shot and killed a US Marine officer riding in a jeep. In reaction, the President Bush summoned his top advisers to the White House. They held that only a stiff military response would end the string of provocations from Noriega and his henchmen. The presidential aides fretted about further threats and deaths of Americans, while the erratic martinet lorded over an increasingly impoverished thugocracy. A martial intervention risked casualties—American and Panamanian—but at the end of the day the United States and Panama would be rid of General Noriega.

White House officials wrestled with the legal justification for an armed incursion into a country, which after all had not attacked the United States. Intervention violated international law. For the United States, which set itself up as a guarantor of the global order, being compliant with international law carried an especial burden. Thus the Bush administration took pains to rollout an unassailable charge sheet against its target. It cataloged Noriega's stealing the May election, his narcotics dealing and the US federal indictment for these criminal offenses, his ultimate responsibility for the dead Marine officer, and his potential imperiling of the transfer of the Panama Canal authority to a responsible Panamanian official. The autocrat's illegitimate regime undercut his anti-US supporters in Latin America, because it placed them in the ranks of defending dictatorships.

The Bush government rested its case on the provisions of the Canal treaties. The agreements authorized the United States to address internal perils as well as external ones. In this instance, the dangers emanated from the Noriega and his thugs. Washington considered the hostile actions against the United States by the growing number of PDF's assaults against US military forces, their dependents, and even Panamanian civilians within the Canal Zone. Noriega inflamed the edgy atmosphere, when he announced that he would "sit along the banks of the Canal to watch the dead bodies of our enemies pass by."[25] As rumors circulated about an impending US attack, the Noriega-choreographed parliament declared: "the Republic of Panama is in a state of war for the duration of the aggression unleashed against the Panamanian people by the U.S. Government" on December 15, 1989.[26]

Washington took up this Panamanian declaration of hostilities. On December 20, 1989, the Bush administration launched a military invasion into Panama. Operation Just Cause aimed at regime change through the deployment of US armed forces, who marched out of their Canal Zone barracks, dropped from the sky in parachutes, or landed in the belly of Air Force transports. Planes and troops left from southern bases within the United States, achieving tactical surprise despite all the media speculation for weeks about the likelihood of an attack. The Pentagon's operations initially unfolded in a clockwork fashion with few notable glitches. The synchronized ground and paratrooper assaults succeeded in routing Panamanian forces. By the first days of 1990, US military units had crushed organized resistance in spite of unexpected doggedness by the 4000 PDF troops and the Dignity Battalions. Yet, the Panamanian defenders stood no chance to turn back 27,000 US troops who descended on their land in the biggest military deployment since the Vietnam War and the largest paratrooper drop since World War II.[27]

Two hitches in the execution of the armed intercession into Panama foreshadowed much larger difficulties for the United States during the Iraq War, nearly a decade and half later. One was the temporary disappearance of Noriega, who like Iraq's Saddam Hussein went into hiding. To root Noriega out of his hideaway, US authorities offered a $1 million reward for his whereabouts. Noriega eluded custody at first by hiding out and then taking sanctuary with the Roman Catholic's papal nuncio in Panama City. Following lengthy, convoluted talks among local US military commanders, Panamanian officials, the Vatican, and the nunciature itself, the ousted dictator walked out of his religious sanctuary and to the safety of American military authorities. Part of his motivation was to escape capture by a hostile crowd, which circled the Vatican embassy, demanding his death. Arrested by Drug Enforcement Agency officials, Noriega was whisked away to a Florida court, which indicted him. There, he stood trial for drug trafficking and racketeering, all the while protesting his innocence as a political prisoner. He was sentenced to a US penitentiary. After release in 2010, the onetime dictator was extradited to France where he served another prison term for money laundering. Next, he was handed over to Panamanian hands for a 20-year incarceration as punishment for several deaths.[28]

The second post-invasion glitch stemmed from the unanticipated chaotic landscape after the Panamanian military ceased resistance to US forces. Rioting, looting, and unruly crowds plagued Panama City and other urban centers. The Pentagon planned for short, minor disturbances but the scale and length of the street turmoil took it by surprise. As a result, the Department of Defense deployed an additional 2000 infantrymen to curb vandalism and restore calm. Although Panama's civilian unrest finally dissipated, it presaged far worse unrest in Iraq that contributed to an insurgency against the invading armies. As such, the Panama case should have alerted Washington policy-makers about a very likely turn of events in post-invasion Iraq, when residents took to the streets to pillage, destroy, and confront American-led Coalition soldiers.

Military operations were only a part of the US intervention into a Latin American country. Diplomacy figured largely in Bush calculations. With its long history of meddling in the Southern Hemisphere, the United States sought acquiescence, if not approval, from the Organization of American States prior to its military operations. After the fraudulent May 1989 elections, the OAS issued a condemnation of the electoral fraud but stipulated that "no state… has the right to intervene…in the internal or external affairs of another."[29] Subsequent Washington negotiations with the OAS failed to budge the Latin American countries to endorse US policy. South America remained aggrieved at its northern neighbor.

Overall, the Panama intervention accomplished its goals. It rid Panama of a corrupt desperado. The regime-change operation did move the country toward self-sustaining democracy. The Bush White House had a plan in place to install the rightful victor of the previous May presidential election, Guillermo Endara. From neighboring Costa Rica, Endara broadcast a message of hope to his fellow countrymen, as US paratroopers parachuted to earth. Thus, the United States was spared the post-invasion problems of Iraq, when it lacked a leader-in-waiting to pick up the reins of power, allowing American forces to withdraw speedily from the battlefield.

Despite the paucity of US financial assistance to the desperate country, Panama fared better than many of its neighbors. Since the intrusion, it has held several presidential elections declared free and fair by international observers. Its military stayed in the barracks and out of politics. An economic boom transformed the skyline of its major urban centers. The trauma of Noriega's venal and wicked dictatorship has receded. Whereas many subsequent US politico-military actions failed or left behind disfigured societies, Panama was clearly better off for Washington's interference. Once the attack unrolled, the White House moved quickly to take steps aimed at political cover for the invasion. It transported president-elect Endara and his two vice presidents to the Canal Zone; they were sworn into office by the head of Panamanian Commission on Human Rights. Thus, American might was seen as restoring democracy and not installing a foreign occupation. Washington also lifted economic sanctions and unfroze some Panamanian financial assets held in US banks to fund the new Endara government.

The OAS objected vociferously to America's invasion and the US military presence on South American soil in spite of Washington's charm offensive. Twenty OAS member states passed a resolution in Spanish "deeply deploring" the US invasion; six states abstained from the vote. Only the United States backed its own action. Its southern neighbors interpreted the attack as just another episode of "gunboat diplomacy" for Washington's exclusive interests. But their united and overwhelming opposition reached an unprecedented level in OAS history. The negative vote represented a singular defeat for the United States. Even though Endara, the new Panamanian president, spoke out in defense of the United States and its restoration of democracy in the tiny country, his voice counted for naught. If anything, the negative reaction to yet another case of Yankee trespassing below the Rio Grande presaged the international hostility that later greeted American armed interventions into the Persian Gulf and Southeastern Europe.

There is no gainsaying the fact that this international hostility to American interventionism played a part in the US cycler swings from overseas engagements toward retrenchment. Within both major political parties, there are found isolationist wings, which favor little or no foreign engagement beyond trade and routine diplomacy. Politicians and pundits of this school quickly echo foreign opposition to American overseas' actions. Author and politician, Patrick Buchanan, for example, concluded his book *A Republic, Not An Empire* with a warning: "entangling alliances, history shows, are transmission belts of war."[30] Public opinion itself has traditionally been wary of prolonged military interventions. Americans have never accepted long wars with expensive outlays in lives and funds. The US regime change in Panama set a post-Cold War precedent for American governments toward unruly dictators, which saw repetition in President Bill Clinton's assisted removal of Serbia's Slobodan Milošević and George W. Bush's toppling of Iraq's Saddam Hussein.

Several factors contributed to the Bush senior administration's escape from a domestic backlash for the Panama incursion. It was of short duration. Violent clashes tapered off after a week to just sporadic shots for a slightly longer period. The complete withdrawal of all American ground troops took place less than three months after the invasion. Casualties were light with 23 US troop deaths. The United States officially held that 324 Panamanian soldiers and 220 civilians died; the locals, however, claimed thousands more were killed.[31] Thus, the relative inexpensiveness of the Panama conflict generated no real groundswell against Bush's internationalism. The pendulum of strategic engagement still arched high at this phase of the Bush presidency. Before he left the White House, Bush policies had nudged the cycler swing toward disengagement, as will be described in the next chapter.

Notes

1. Frederick Taylor, *The Berlin Wall: 13 August 1961–9 November 1989* (London: Bloomsbury, 2004), p. 400.
2. Mary Elise Sarotte, *The Collapse: The Accidental Opening of the Berlin Wall* (New York: Basic Books, 2014), p. 177.
3. Charles Krauthammer, "The Unipolar Moment," *Foreign Affairs*, 70, no. 1 (1990–1991), 23–33.
4. For more on the debate about the dangers of overseas commitments dragging the United States into unwanted wars, see Michael Beckley, "The Myth of Entangling Alliances," *International Security*, 39, no. 4 (Spring 2015), 7–48.
5. Christopher Hemmer, *American Pendulum: Recurring Debates in U.S. Grand Strategy* (Ithaca, NY: Cornell University Press, 2015), pp. 10–11 and 176.

6. David M. Kennedy, *Freedom Fear: The American People in Depression and War, 1929–1945* (New York: Oxford University Press, 1999), p. 393.
7. Andrew Bacevich, *The Limits of Power: The End of American Exceptionalism* (New York: Metropolitan Books, 2008), pp. 121–122, 114–117, and 160; William Appleman Williams, *The Tragedy of American Diplomacy* (New York: W. W. Norton and Company, 1972), pp. 307–312 and Chalmers Johnson, *Blowback: The Costs and Consequences of American Empire* (New York: Henry Holt & Company, 2000), pp. 223–224.
8. Winston Churchill, *The Gathering Storm* (New York: Houghton Mifflin Company, 1948), pp. 292–295.
9. Graham Allison and Philip Zelikow, *Essence of Decision: Explaining the Cuban Missile Crisis* (New York: Addison Wesley Longman, 1999), pp. 94–105.
10. S. C. M. Paine, *The Wars for Asia, 1911–1949* (New York: Cambridge University Press, 2012), pp. 3–11.
11. George H. W. Bush, "Address Before a Joint Session of the Congress on the Cessation of the Persian Gulf War," March 6, 1991, p. 3.
12. Margaret Thatcher, *The Downing Street Years* (New York: HarperCollins, 1993), p. 824.
13. Mark P. Lagon, *The Reagan Doctrine: Sources of American Conduct in the Cold War's Last Chapter* (Westport, CT: Praeger, 1994), pp. 2–3.
14. Don Oberdofer, "Thatcher Says Cold War Has Come to an End," *Washington Post*, November 18, 1988, p. A 1.
15. Brian Crozier, *The Rise and Fall of the Soviet Empire* (Rocklin, CA: Prima Publishing, 1999), p. 403.
16. Crozier, *The Rise and Fall of the Soviet Empire*, p. 360.
17. Mitchell Reiss, *Bridled Ambition: Why Countries Constrain Their Nuclear Capabilities* (Washington, DC: Woodrow Wilson Center Press, 1995), p. 98.
18. Mikhail Gorbachev, *Memoirs* (New York: Doubleday, 1995), p. 533.
19. James A. Baker III, *The Politics of Diplomacy: Revolution, War, and Peace, 1989–1992* (New York: G. P. Putnam's Sons, 1995), p. 249.

20. Philip Zelikow and Condoleezza Rice, *Germany United and Europe Transformed: A Study in Statecraft* (Cambridge, MA: Harvard University Press, 1995), p. 352.
21. Stephen Sestanovich, "Not Much Kinder and Gentler," *New York Times*, February 3, 2006, p. A 27.
22. Michael Halloran, "U.S. Troops Go Slowly Into Panama," *New York Times*, May 12, 1989, p. A 6.
23. Baker, *The Politics of Diplomacy: Revolution, War, and Peace*, p. 183.
24. Tom Kenworthy and Joe Pichirallo, "Bush Clears Plan to Topple Noriega," *Washington Post*, November 17, 1989, p. A 1.
25. R. M. Koster and Guillermo Sanchez Borbon, *In The Time of Tyrants* (London: Secker & Warburg, 1990), p. 330.
26. Abraham D. Sofaer, "The Legality of the United States Action in Panama," *Columbia Journal of Transnational Law*, 29 (1991), 284–285.
27. For an account of the military operations, see Thomas Donnelly, Margaret Roth, and Caleb Baker, *Operation Just Cause: The Storming of Panama* (New York: Lexington Books, 1991), pp. 236–322.
28. Randal C. Archibold, "Noriega Is Sent to Prison Back in Panama, Where the Terror Has Turned to Shrugs," *New York Times*, December 11, 2011, p. A 1.
29. Cited in Robert C. Harding, *The History of Panama* (Westport, CT: Greenwood Press, 2006), pp. 112–113.
30. Patrick J. Buchanan, *A Republic, Not an Empire* (Washington, DC: Regnery Publishing, 2001), p. 387.
31. Lorenzo Crowell, "The Anatomy of Just Cause: The Forces Involved, the Adequacy of Intelligence, and Its Success as a Joint Operation," in *Operation Just Cause: The U.S. Intervention in Panama*, ed. Bruce W. Watson and Peter G. Tsouras (Boulder, CO: Westview Press, 1991), p. 95.

CHAPTER 3

George H.W. Bush: Interventionism Unbound

"Whereof what's past is prologue; what to come,
In yours and my discharge." —*William Shakespeare's* The Tempest

No political event defined George Herbert Walker Bush's presidency as sharply as the Persian Gulf War. His tenure was marked by several impressive achievements, as noted, with the peaceful management of the Soviet disintegration, German reunification, and Eastern Europe's restoration to the comity of democratic nations. These tested American diplomatic resolve and talent but demanded no projection of military power to the European Continent. The Persian Gulf conflict obliged the United States to exercise prodigious diplomatic finesse and to deploy large-scale air, land, and sea armaments to distant shores. The Bush administration unprecedentedly projected American military power into the heart of the Middle East. The Persian Gulf showdown blew up suddenly like a summer squall amid other international crises. As such, it reordered the Bush White House's priorities. The Oval office, by necessity, sidelined other issues so as to focus on countering Iraq's swift occupation of neighboring Kuwait. The US and allied military deployments and the war itself witnessed the largest ever US armed intrusion into the Middle East (up to that time). Armed might, nevertheless, formed just part of the effort. The conflict in the heart of the Arab Muslim world called for abundant and skilled diplomacy to reassure allies, build and maintain a transnational

T.H. Henriksen, *Cycles in US Foreign Policy since the Cold War*,
DOI 10.1007/978-3-319-48640-6_3

coalition, and even gain funding from non-participating powers such as Japan and Germany to pay for the war.

Finally, this crisis marked an apogee of American military and political interventionism as the pendulum arced high in the engagement cycle. Afterward, the dial oscillated back toward the non-engagement direction in the remainder of Bush's presidential term. This slide away from overseas commitments, in part, reflected the natural rhythm of relaxation following exertions of the Cold War. As such it conformed to the pattern evident since World War I through the Vietnam War of Americans looking inward after international conflicts. But before that disengagement, the United States was called upon to confront aggression that placed its interests in jeopardy by Iraq, a country not well known to most Americans. That first conflict with Iraq thrust America into Middle East in a greater way than any event since the establishment and US recognition of Israel in 1948.

Bush and the Hatching a Troublemaker

The conflict begun by Iraqi tank columns crossing Kuwait's border on August 2, 1990, was years in the making. While Iraqi grievances formed its justification for the attack, the country's dictatorship itself lay at the root of its aggression. Like many Middle Eastern nations, Iraq's modern state structure rested on an ancient culture and on a relatively recent delineation of boundaries. And like other dictatorial regimes of that region, its history missed the democratic evolution and modernization of Western states over the past two centuries.

Modern-day Iraq is superimposed over the three-millennial old lands of Mesopotamia (Greek for the land "between two rivers"), where the Tigris and Euphrates Rivers flowed from the country's highlands down to the Persian Gulf. Rich in both water and oil, Iraq is thus doubly blessed in contrast to much of the Middle East. Its vast oil reserves gave Iraq strategic importance since the mid-twentieth century. Its water, climate, and fertile soil geographically predisposed it to be the birthplace of such great, ancient civilizations as Sumer, Assyria, and Babylon, which contributed so much to the world's development in architecture, agriculture, law, urbanization, and literacy. The premodern Iraqi lands suffered the rise and fall of empires, the march and countermarch of armies, and the cruel vicissitudes of brutal governance.

Three hundred years ago, the Ottoman Turks imposed their rule over what would become Iraq. Recognizing the distinct ethnic features of the territory, the Ottomans divided its administration into three regions—Mosul, Baghdad, and Basra. In the north, Mosul was home to the Kurds, a distinct ethnic community, who yearned for its own sovereign nation for hundreds of years. In the country's mid-section, the Sunni people predominated. They constituted the backbone of the army and civil bureaucracy. In the south, close to the Iranian border, lived the Shia, who made up 60 percent of the population. They practiced a different version of Islam from the Sunnis and most Kurds. The Sunni-Shiite branches of Islam were at daggers drawn. A portion of the Arab Shiite population looked to Shiite Iran for physical safety and material help when ruled harshly by the Sunni minority, who made up about 25 percent of the population.

Ottoman power was crushed during World War I. Afterward, Iraq fell to Britain's governance under the League of Nations mandate system. London installed a monarchy derived from the House of Saud in next-door Saudi Arabia. Unlike British efforts to implant democracy in other colonial possessions, they ushered Amir Faisal onto the throne, who became Faisal I in 1920.[1] Then, in 1932, Britain granted Iraq independence. In the post-World War II period, Iraq as well as Egypt, Libya, Syria, and other Mid-East states succumbed to military coups. Moving from colonialism, monarchism, and finally to military dictatorships yielded arid soil for democracy to sprout. The divisions of the Cold War meant that often non-democratic states aligned with the Soviet Union and against the United States and the Free World. The West regarded most of the Middle East as a backwater, except for its increasingly vital petroleum reserves, which attracted Soviet meddling as well.

America's problems with Iraq really predate Saddam Hussein's rise to power, although in the end he set a collision course with the United States, but not before destabilizing his neighborhood. Iraq, in fact, made an abrupt about-face from Western alignment to Soviet ally after the 1958 military coup. Perpetrated by Brigadier Abd al Karim Qasim, the army killed off King Faisal II, other members of the royal family, and Iraq's nascent democracy. Once in power, Qasim yanked Iraq from the anti-Moscow Baghdad Pact (with Britain, Iran, Pakistan, and Turkey) and began to realign its relations toward the USSR in return for Soviet tanks, aircraft, and military training. Qasim's interlude was marked by political instability. Not until Saddam Hussein took power in 1979 as head of the Baath Party did Iraq experience the certainty of one ruthless tyranny that tamed the recurrent political unsettledness in the wake of Qasim's overthrow in 1963. Rising from poverty through guile, assassination, Egyptian exile, and conspiracy marked Hussein with a Stalin-like lust for power, revenge, and survival instincts. His accession to the Iraqi presidency coincided with the Iranian Islamic revolution and the Soviet military intervention into Afghanistan. Altogether they changed the face of the Persian Gulf arena in ways that drew the United States deeper into the turbulent region.

The Soviet military invasion into Afghanistan to prop up a Marxist ruler held consequences for the United States. President Jimmy Carter was persuaded by his hard-line National Security Advisor, Zbigniew Brzezkinski, to back the mujahideen by shipping out-of-date Lee Enfield rifles to the embattled fighters. Carter also responded by standing up a rapid deployment military force in the Middle East, which in time led to the formation of the US Central Command. Later, Ronald Reagan's White House substantially supplied money and arms, including the Stinger, a shoulder-fired anti-aircraft missile effective against Soviet helicopter gunships. The Kremlin's aggression threatened to destabilize the Persian Gulf, if Soviet forces marched southward for a warm water port, a desideratum since Catherine the Great ruled late eighteenth-century Russia.

America's troubles in the Persian Gulf, nevertheless, really took off when the shah of Iran fell. Shah Mohammed Reza Pahlavi advanced American interests and served as Washington's "policeman" when it scaled back its overseas commitments in the Vietnam War's aftermath. Coming to power in 1941 as a reformer in the footsteps of his father, he tried to modernize and westernize Iran in the White Revolution. The monarchy's liberalizing policies, plus corruption and cronyism alienated broad sectors of Iranian society but none more so than the country's Shiite clergy, who resented their loss of prestige, property, and political standing. Ayatollah Ruhollah Khomeini and his followers channeled societal discontent into a revolutionary wave that toppled the shah in 1979. They replaced him with militant theocracy. Not content with an internal transformation, the Islamic Republic of Iran extended its tentacles to Shiite communities living in Iraq and Lebanon so as to build militant movements.[2] Additionally, the Islamic Republic sponsored terrorist attacks in Western Europe, Argentina, and against American and Israeli targets in the Middle East. For the United States, Iran changed almost overnight from close ally to implacable foe. It labeled America the Great Satan and called Israel the Little Satan.

As for Saddam Hussein's Iraq, it watched with apprehension and calculation the Iranian revolution take root. Next door, Tehran looked on in horror at Hussein's persecution of Iraq's Shiite population. As Iraqi-Iranian relations soured, Hussein abrogated the 1975 treaty defining their joint border down the Shatt al-Arab waterway, Iraq's only access to the Persian Gulf. Then, the Iraqi dictator preemptively bombed Iranian military installations before launching a ground incursion into Iran in 1981. Hussein interpreted Iran's ongoing revolutionary convulsions as an opportunity to seize territory along the disputed river. Such a bold strike, he imagined, stood every prospect of symbolically enhancing his status within the Arab Middle East as the preeminent ruler since Egyptian strongman Gramal Abdul Nasser electrified the regions with his pan-Arabism oratory.[3]

The eight-year Iraq-Iran war turned out to be an unmitigated disaster for both nations. Neither could achieve a military breakthrough from the World War I-like trench warfare that consumed hundreds of thousands of young lives. Iran resorted to mass human wave assaults, and Iraq countered with poison gas shells. Stalemated, exhausted, and nearly bled white, Iraq and Iran entered into UN-negotiated cease-fire, when Tehran feared a wider application of Iraqi chemical weapons against it.[4]

For the United States, the Iraq-Iran war held several significant political and military ramifications, some of which did not emerge for years. Among the consequences was the fact that the Islamic Republic of Iran entrenched itself within society and intensified its anti-American sentiments. Iraq's indebtedness to its neighbors, chiefly Kuwait, eventually formed the backdrop for Saddam Hussein's war against the tiny Gulf kingdom. Another consequence of the intra-Persian Gulf conflict was America's fleeting modus vivendi with Saddam Hussein before it went to war against the Iraqi dictator. Washington viewed Hussein as a secular and modernizing strongman who was worthy of limited assistance in his fight against Iran.[5]

A Rogue Strikes

The incoming George H.W. Bush administration built on the Reagan White House's contacts with Baghdad as a logical counterweight to the vehemently anti-American ayatollah regime in Tehran. The Islamic Republic's implacable hostility dated from the clerics' ascension to power. Soon afterward, Iranian "students" took over the US Embassy in Tehran in November 1979, holding 52 diplomatic personnel for 444 days before freeing them. The Bush policy team addressed its relations with Iraq from a "realist" perspective. Unlike the US Congress, they were initially willing to look past Iraq's deplorable human rights practices so long as it helped check Iranian machinations. Thus, the White House extended financial guarantees to American farmers to sell grain to Baghdad. At first, Iraq reciprocated. It offered compensation funds to the families of the sailors killed on board the *USS Stark*, when an Iraqi missile hit the warship during the Iranian conflict.

As the 1990s opened, the United States backed away from its warming ties to Iraq, as the Hussein regime appeared increasingly belligerent. To elevate his pan-Arab standing, Hussein ardently embraced the Palestinian cause against Israel. He announced the building of chemical weapons so as "to make the fire eat up half of Israel with chemical agents" if it attacked Iraq.[6] The US Department of State reprimanded Hussein, stating that his remarks were "inflammatory, outrageous, and irresponsible."[7] Hussein paid no heed to the censure. He called for the US Navy to vacate the Persian Gulf. He advocated a return to the 1970s oil boycott by Middle Eastern petroleum exporters to boost revenues and to again damage Western economies.

Even a Washington distracted by momentous events in Europe and Asia took note of the changed tone in the speeches of its man in Baghdad. The Bush administration revoked $500 million in credits from the Commodity Credit Corporation for Iraqi purchase of US grain, a decision that angered American farm-state politicians and agricultural businesses. It also foiled Baghdad's illegal plot to buy nuclear triggering devices, halted the transfer of a huge artillery piece known as the "super gun," and thwarted the purchase of tungsten furnaces often used for nuclear weapons construction. Hussein's attempted acquisitions offered proof that Iraq hankered after nuclear arms.

By spring 1990, the Bush foreign policy team was absorbed by the historic breakup of the Soviet satellite empire in Eastern Europe. It was still dealing with the aftermath of the Panama intervention as well. In any event, Washington's fixation elsewhere contributed to its inattention to Iraq's building, warlike intentions. Secretary of State James Baker later wrote in his memoir that before Iraq threatened Kuwait, "it was simply not prominent on my radar screen, or the President's."[8] Top-level officials paid too little attention to a drumbeat of Iraq's statements and actions pointing toward a military invasion of Kuwait in mid-1990.

Like many of his countrymen, Saddam Hussein regarded Kuwait as little more than Iraq's 19th province, stolen from Baghdad by British mapmakers who placed it outside the country's boundaries. The Iraqi tyrant held other grievances against his neighbor to boot. He accused the small

Gulf kingdom and its neighbors of ingratitude for not canceling Iraq's wartime debts of some $30 billion incurred in the fight against Shiite Iran. Indeed, Hussein deeply resented his fellow Sunni Arab leaders' ungratefulness over the sacrifices made by Iraq against their mutual Shiite foe. He also contented that Kuwait siphoned off more than its share of oil from their jointly held Rumalia petroleum field. Moreover, he argued that all the Arabian sheikdoms pumped too much oil so as to fill their coffers. The oversupply on the world market exerted a downward pressure on prices. Hussein demanded that nearby states decrease their oil production to drive up the price. They refused. He became infuriated. In retrospect, the Iraqi autocrat was laying down a pretext for attacking Kuwait.[9]

To a surprised Washington, Iraq's Republican Guards rolled their T-72 battle tanks right up to Kuwait's border on July 24, 1990. The next day Hussein called in the US Ambassador, April Glaspie, for what became an infamous meeting. What took place between the Baghdad-based American envoy and the Iraqi dictator is still in dispute. To the Arabic-speaking ambassador's critics, she was too accommodating to Iraqi demands. Reportedly, she said: "As you know, we [the United States] don't take a stand on territorial disputes." This would have seemed to flash a green light to Hussein's aggression. However, she also added: "we can never excuse the settlement of disputes by other than peaceful means."[10] In subsequent testimony, the embattled diplomat defended her record in Baghdad but her State Department career was finished.[11]

The Bush administration also came in for condemnation for not laying down a clear marker to deter Iraqi aggression. In light of subsequent events and greater knowledge of Saddam Hussein, it seems unlikely that any red line would have halted his conquest. Strategically, the time was right to strike before the Americans filled the political void left by the rapidly declining Soviet Union. He acknowledged only his cause and his own maniacal powers to gobble up Kuwait and annex without incurring a counterattack. Like many dictators, he misjudged the West's resolve. Even two-thirds of the 21 member states of the Arab League condemned Iraq's conquest and annexation of the tiny kingdom.

What served to ignite international outrage against Baghdad's thrust into Kuwait was its ruthless occupation. The invaders did not stop at the seizure of Kuwait's oilfields, which rested on 20 percent of the world's proven reserves. Iraq's army behaved like a medieval horde. It swept through the capital Kuwait City plundering, pillaging, and raping. Iraqi soldiers looted shops, snatched paintings off the walls, confiscated 29,000 cars and drove them back to Iraq. They indiscriminately shot civilians and then stripped the bodies of valuables. Next, they torched palaces, office buildings, art museums, and even oil facilities. To gain an accounting of the losses, Kuwait's government set up a commission, the Public Authority for the Assessment of Damages Resulting from Iraqi Aggression in May 1991. This commission calculated the damages at $173 billion in 1990 dollars and reckoned over 600 Kuwaitis disappeared without a trace.[12]

Caught off guard by the ferocity and swiftness of Iraq's bloody infestation of Kuwait City, Washington scrambled to come up with a countering strategy. Within George Bush's circle of top advisers, discussions turned to either imposing stringent sanctions or conducing a military counteroffensive. Less risky than war, economic embargoes, nevertheless, take years to bite down on the targeted country's economy. Moreover, a sanctioned regime remains largely unaffected because shortages of vital goods fall on the ordinary populations who experience the privations in food and medicines.

What moved the Bush White House toward military action was the legitimate fear that Saddam Hussein might next invade Saudi Arabia. Internally, the West Wing staff was at first divided. Vice President Richard Cheney and National Security Adviser Brent Scowcroft favored the use of the American military. The Cheney-Scowcroft argument prevailed because it advocated the defense of Saudi Arabia, which clinched the debate. Should President Hussein overrun neighboring Saudi Arabia, he stood to preside over about 40 percent of the planet's known oil reserves. His bluster and unpredictability indicated the distinct likelihood that Republic Guard's tanks might move into the desert kingdom if it remained unprotected by the United States.

What benefited the United States in forging an international front against Iraq arose from Baghdad's regional isolation. Saudi Arabia and the Kuwaiti government-in-exile sided with the United States and its allies. Egypt and Turkey, two of the principal nations in the Middle East, backed a hawkish stance toward Iraq's aggression. Turgut Ozal, the Turkish president, argued that the Iraqi tyrant "must go" because "Saddam is more dangerous than Qaddafi," the belligerent leader of Libya who threatened stability in the Mediterranean basin with local conflicts and terrorism.[13] Other states indicated a willingness to back a tough Washington response. At the end of the day, only Jordan, Yemen, and Yasir Arafat's Palestinian Liberation Organization sided with the Republic of Iraq.

The United States also pressed its case through the Security Council as it pursued individual governments to line up against Iraq. Iraq's truculence, the warming Russian-American relations, and the pro-US posture of several Middle Eastern governments helped Washington's cause at the United Nations. On November 29, the Bush administration won a diplomatic coup by securing passage of Resolution 678, which called for the utilization of "all necessary means" (UN-speak for the military force) to effectuate the ten prior resolutions as well as military action if Iraq failed to march out of Kuwait by January 15, 1991. The vote constituted a rare event, since the last time the Security Council consented to war took place in 1950 when North Korea invaded South Korea.

What made it possible domestically for the Bush administration to flex its muscles abroad was that America's international engagement cycle was in the ascendency. Americans confidently looked outward beginning with the Reagan administration, which dispelled the "malaise" of Jimmy Carter's post-Vietnam presidency.[14] The national mood no longered favored withdrawal from overseas problems. Even with America's pronounced engagement mood, the White House needed to rally the country behind a war. Skeptics labeled the oncoming conflict as blood for oil, after Secretary of State Baker argued that the United States could not "permit a dictator...to sit astride that economic lifeline" referring to the Gulf's oil reserves. He tied the average American's employment to an economy dependent on the flow of petroleum. Bluntly, Baker added: "If you want to sum it up in one word, it's jobs."[15]

Right from the start, the White House ran into political headwinds from its political opponents. The Oval Office tackled the legislature's opposition head on by delivering a speech to a joint session of Congress on September 11, 1990. The president noted steady progress with Gorbachev on unshackling Soviet rule from Central Europe, which allowed for dealing with Persian Gulf crisis. The speech became memorable for Bush's floating the concept of a "new world order" by which he defined as "a world in which nations recognize the shared responsibility for freedom and justice."[16]

This new world order vision immediately triggered a critical firestorm from detractors, many from the right flank of Bush's own party. They denounced it as mushy internationalism that would subordinate American interests to a fuzzy brotherhood administered by the UN. Endless wars, according to the skeptics, would come from this new world order prescription.[17] The critics sprang too soon and too thoughtlessly, for Bush sought to enlist foreign nations in America's pursuit of its geopolitical order. Multilateralism had long been a plank in American internationalist platform. Bush just tried to put a fresh coat of paint on it, while reducing the US burden "in the world in which nations recognize *the shared responsibility* [author's emphasis] for freedom and justice."[18] Inside America, the president's opponents largely focused on what they saw as a march to war for oil.

The Republican White House faced an uphill partisan struggle with Democrats in the US Senate in spite of its considerable international backing gained for the dual-track approach of active diplomacy paired with military preparation. Still in the shadow of the Vietnam War, the Democratic Party leadership evinced a conflict-averse stance. They argued that the various UN economic sanctions must be given more time to pressure Saddam Hussein to pick up and leave Kuwait. They decried the notion that the "land of the free" would fight to restore a medieval monarchy to its throne. Even Congress's adjournment on October 28, 1990, to campaign for mid-term elections brought little respite for the embattled Oval Office. Congressional Democrats feared being bypassed by the White House before reconvening in January in a rush to war without a vote. So, they placed a provision in the adjournment resolution that permitted their leadership to reconvene hastily to hold a vote on any war-making authorization.[19]

As the UN's January 15, 1991, deadline neared for Iraq to vacate Kuwait, President Bush pushed the US Congress to authorize the use of force to execute the UN resolutions. On January 9, the House of Representatives passed the authorization easily. In the Senate, on the other hand, the motion barely scraped by with a 52 to 47 yes vote—the slenderest war vote in US history. If four more senators had cast ballots against going to war, Bush would have been at pains to take the country into a conflict anyway. Such an action promised a constitutional and political crisis. Washington's reliance on economic sanctions was unlikely to have curbed Hussein's grandiose ambitions. His possible attack on Saudi Arabia could well have added its oil revenues to his coffers. This new Babylonian Empire would have become even more formidable and aggressive.

Flush-with-oil-revenues Iraq would have continued its nuclear arms program already humming along at laboratories in Tuwaitha, Al Athir, and other facilities. After the Persian Gulf War, the world discovered the extent of Iraq's nuclear progress. During the conflict, the nuclear sites were bombed. Afterward, the International Atomic Energy Agency (IAEA), the UN's nuclear watchdog, dismantled the nuclear plants. The inadvertent discovery of Iraq's advanced nuclear program constituted a serious lapse and embarrassment for the IAEA. Had there been no war and no American victory, then Iraq would have almost certainly joined the exclusive atomic club at great peril to the world. Jaffar al-Jaffar, a prominent Iraqi scientist, estimated that Baghdad was "three years away, give or take a year" from manufacturing nuclear weaponry under the noses of the IAEA.[20]

The United States might have been able to deter Iraq from using atomic weapons; but a nuclear-armed Iraq would also have possessed a deterrence capability against the United States enabling Baghdad to meddle in its neighbors' affairs. Over the years, Washington governments have demonstrated a reluctance to challenge nuclear weapons states. Thus, the Persian Gulf War preserved America's nuclear monopoly regionwide, until Iran threatened it two decades later. Because of the IAEA's failure, the United States was loath to place its trust solely in the Vienna-based atomic-arms inspectors. So, Bush diplomats at the UN insisted on the establishment of a separate arms investigation entity. Passed in April 1991, the Security Council's Resolution 687 embodied provisions for setting up the UN Special Commission (UNSCOM). The resolution mandated UNSCOM to enforce Iraq's adherence to internationally imposed requirements to destroy biological, chemical, and missile facilities, plus assist the IAEA in its nuclear searches.

A Shield in the Desert

As it embarked on preparations for a military counteroffensive, the Bush administration mounted a full-court press to rally international support against Hussein's Kuwaiti annexation. The White House sought to pull together an international coalition. As Reagan's vice president, George Bush had met many world leaders before his presidency. His familiarity with the cast of players now facilitated coalition building. He met foreign representatives in the Oval Office or at his private summer home in Kennebunkport, Maine. As Bush himself noted, he "worked the phones," calling his counterparts to gain their participation in the anti-Hussein cause. What's more, America's 41st president hopscotched his Secretary of State around the globe to round up coalition partners and to seek out financial contributions for any ensuing conflict. James Baker's travels paid political and financial dividends. Germany and Japan—two pacifist nations after their devastating defeat in World War II—adjured war. Instead of fighting, Tokyo, Berlin, and other capitals handed over $54 billion in cash and in-kind contributions toward the $61 billion war.[21]

In the end, the Bush foreign policy team's diplomatic exertions forged a 30-nation coalition to oust the Republican Guard from Kuwait. One early product of the US efforts was the passage of economic sanction Resolution 661, which was the first of many economic embargoes aimed at the Republic of Iraq. The United States tried the sanction route in hopes of persuading Hussein to leave Kuwait and to release Western hostages seized when that country was overrun. Under no illusions, the Bush White House simultaneously readied for a Persian Gulf conflict.

Washington also understood that diplomatic steps were unlikely to deter Iraq from military actions against Saudi Arabia. But its proposals to dispatch reinforcements to the desert kingdom were initially met with skepticism from Riyadh. The Saudis held a dim view of American staying power if a conflict proved protracted and bloody. They recalled how the United States withdrew soon after its Marine Corps barracks in Lebanon were truck-bombed, killing 241 military personnel in 1983. Some Saudi officials fretted that Washington would scat once it took casualties. Other Saudis worried that the introduction of infidels, or "Crusaders," onto sacred Saudi soil would ricochet back on the House of Saud. Having Western armies march so near the holiest Islamic shrines amounted to blasphemy and sacrilege, inviting retribution. In this appraisal, the concerns proved to be accurate. Jumping ahead, the scion of a wealthy Saudi family, named Osama bin Laden, was deeply upset at Riyadh's permission for kaffirs (non-Muslims) to station forces near Mecca and Medina. This reputed defilement of Islamic sacred sites ignited bin Laden's fury against the Saudi monarchy as well as the United States and the West. He and his followers later mounted a series of terrorist attacks, including the catastrophic September 11, 2001, assault on the World Trade Center and Pentagon.

By gaining Saudi Arabia's participation in the anti-Iraq coalition, the United States was able to include other Arab governments in the group. Riyadh's involvement gave political cover from protests for Turkey, Egypt, and Syria to participate. All of Iraq's neighbors worried about the pugilistic and unpredictable strongman in Baghdad. But they also feared the tumultuous "Arab street" whose volatility threatened their regimes. Forging a regional partnership mattered both politically and diplomatically as well as militarily. Otherwise, the United States would have appeared self-serving in pursuing just its own strategic interests to protect the flow of oil to the West.

Washington excluded one regional nation—Israel—from its bloc despite its widely acknowledged military proficiency and its close diplomatic alignment to Washington. As the Arab world's sworn enemy at that time, Israel's participation, however welcome militarily and politically, was anathema to Mideast countries. George Bush recorded in his memoir: "The Israelis understood this point intellectually, although, it was emotionally difficult for them to stand aside."[22] The United States, nevertheless, still needed Israel's cooperation—or rather its forbearance. It implored Israel not to retaliate against Iraq, when Hussein rained down nearly 40 missiles on the Jewish state. It was touch-and-go for a time, but Israel held steadfast. As a defense, the United States struck Baghdad's launch sites with bombers, and SOF combed Iraq's western deserts for missiles.[23]

The Pentagon undertook Operation Desert Shield to defend House of Saud and its vast oil holdings from the rapacious grasp of its neighbor. It rushed paratroopers from the 82 Airborne Division and 2 US Air Force fighter squadrons as a spear point to a much larger deployment of tank divisions and bomber fleets. General Colin Powell, the Chairman of the Joint Chiefs of Staff, was initially a reluctant warrior. But Powell and Norman Schwarzkopf, the CENTCOM commander, agreed that America, if it went to war, should employ overwhelming force, not rely on an incremental bombing campaign that characterized early US actions during the Vietnam War. Their initial plan called for some 100,000 troops for military operations. As planning proceeded, the troop strength eventually leapt eightfold.

When the invasion buildup was completed, it encompassed 540,000 US troops and a further 250,000 allied soldiers. General Schwarzkopf commanded American, British, and other European military personnel. So as to present a united Arab-American front, the Pentagon enlisted a Saudi prince as an ostensible co-commander and intra-allied diplomat.[24] Saudi General Khaled bin Sultan was named Commander of Joint Forces to lead the Arab armies. Military hardware poured into Saudi Arabia, Qatar, and nearby countries. Ships, planes, and tanks accumulated just outside the borders of Iraq and its Kuwait acquisition in the weeks preceding January 15, 1991, the deadline for Saddam Hussein to withdraw his occupying army.

A Desert Storm Unleashed

The Persian Gulf War was a quick, sharp affair, which displayed spectacularly modern information warfare with laser-guided missiles, satellite-directed bombs, and stealth aircraft as never before seen in this 42-day conflict. The war opened with an aerial barrage two days past the announced deadline. First, US submarines fired salvos of Tomahawk missiles to suppress Iraqi air defense and communication nodes. Next came relentless shelling. From January 17 to February 24, the American-led air campaign rained down a modern-day version of fire and brimstone on the hapless Iraqi ground forces, pitilessly decimating troops and tanks alike. The dazzling high-tech features of the fighting were likened to Star Wars, a popular film, or to a Nintendo video game.

On February 24, Operation Desert Sabre rolled out with coalition ground forces attacking from the northeastern corner of Saudi Arabia toward Kuwait and southern Iraq. Three days later, they retook Kuwait and pushed 120 miles into Iraq assaulting Iraqi reserve units from their rear. By that time, the coalition's armored columns had smashed the elite Republican Guard divisions into near smithereens. Those Iraqi troops who did not perish in the allied onslaught deserted the battlefield or surrendered in droves. Their rout convinced President Bush to declare a unilateral cease-fire on February 28, 1991, just 100 hours after the ground campaign began. The exact number of Iraqis killed is unknown but estimates place it at between 10,000 and 100,000 deaths. Coalition deaths numbered almost 400 personnel.[25]

Despite its lopsided victory, the United States stopped well short of invading and toppling the tyrannical Iraqi leader. The Bush administration accomplished its UN-authorized mission to expel Iraq from the occupation of Kuwait. Halting the war while fleeing Iraqi soldiers streamed home was an act of mercy and political calculation. The Pentagon reasoned that slaughtering fleeing, unarmed men, who had dropped their weapons and ran along the Kuwait-Basra highway toward home, would sully the American-led victory and poison the postwar environment. General Powell put it clearly: "We don't want to be seen as killing for the sake of killing."[26]

An Armed Peace in the Gulf

By avoiding an invasion, occupation, and regime change, the United States escaped the passel of troubles that ultimately befell it after the 2003 Iraq War. The administration of Bush senior spoke with one voice on the wisdom of not pushing deeper into Iraq. George Bush the elder later wrote in his memoirs: "Had we gone the invasion route, the United States could conceivably still be an occupying power in a bitterly hostile land."[27] His Secretary of Defense, Richard Cheney, presciently forecast America's fate in a post-invasion Iraq: "Once you've got Baghdad, it's not clear what you do with it. It is not clear what kind of government you would put in place of the one that's currently there now.... How much creditability is that [non-Hussein] government going to have if it's set up by the United States military when it's there?"[28] Cheney raised the issues that, years after as vice president, he and other Bush junior officials dismissed during the Iraq War. A decade later, George W. Bush ordered a ground invasion to oust the Iraqi tyrant that bogged down America and its allies in a bloody insurgency at great cost in lives and dollars.

Despite the dodged bullet in Iraq, Bush detractors accused him of not finishing the job.[29] Indeed, the United States did leave a wounded tiger in the jungle. Hussein persisted in threatening regional stability. But US policy also left Iraq a regional counterweight to an increasingly belligerent Iran. Accordingly, Bush almost retraced Ronald Reagan's stratagem of seeing Iraq as a means to balance Iran's ascendancy in the Persian Gulf. The American president's approach held an element of realpolitik in its tactics. When the Bill Clinton moved into the White House, it cast aside the checkmate stratagem and treated both Baghdad and Tehran as hostile renegade powers.

Notwithstanding, the Bush administration's best laid plans to extricate the United States after the fighting stopped in the Gulf war, it was drawn back, in part, by its own shortcomings and by Hussein's misdeeds. Toward the end of the Persian Gulf conflict, George Bush prompted Iraqis to rise up against their despot. At a press conference on March 1, 1991, the president repeated his urgings: "In my own view, I've always said it would be—that the Iraqi people should put him [Hussein] aside and that would facilitate the resolution of these problems that exist, and certainly would facilitate the acceptance of Iraq back into the family of peace-loving nations."[30] On another occasion, the American leader called for the Iraqis to "get matters into their own hands."[31]

The president's exhortations did not fall on deaf ears. The disaffected Shiite and Kurdish populations rose up against their Sunni tormentors. Protests, civil disobedience, and violence erupted within the Republic of Iraq, momentarily shaking Hussein's hold on power. The regime's Republican Guards, many of whom had been deliberately spared by the US warplanes as they fled from Kuwait, took no similar pity on their fellow Shiite and Kurdish citizens. Hussein's Sunni security forces killed an estimated 300,000 people as they suppressed the revolt. An American blunder rendered the carnage even worse. During the post-conflict truce talks at Safwan, General Schwarzkopf wrongly conceded to the Iraqi generals' request to retain helicopter flights "to carry officials" because of the bombed out bridges and roads. Hussein used these helicopters later as gunships with devastating effect against the rebels.[32]

The Bush administration largely kept out of the internal fray, enabling the brutal Iraqi regime to survive. Although not intervening directly, its energetic internationalism all the same motivated the Oval Office to stretch a UN resolution to cover a forward policy on behalf of the Kurds that led America to perpetuate its involvement in Iraq's affairs for more than a decade. As the Kurds took flight to escape Hussein's wrath, they stirred Western humanitarian impulses and created dire problems for Turkey, a NATO partner. The fleeing Kurds crossed into Turkey, which already faced a Kurdish minority problem, particularly in the country's southeast corner. Kurds within Turkey as well as in neighboring Iraq, Syria, and Iran had narrowly missed statehood at the Versailles peace conference after World War I. Their surging nationalist aspirations collided with Ankara's efforts to control the Kurdish population. A desperate Turkey called on its allies.

Washington, working with London and Paris, relied on Security Council Resolution 688 for authority to act. The Anglo-American-French threesome set up an internal Kurdish sanctuary and a "no-fly zone" overhead. In the northern tier of Iraq, the "safe haven" afforded besieged Kurds a measure of safety from Baghdad. The United States deployed lightly armed American infantrymen and CIA agents under Operation Provide Comfort. The Kurdish enclave took advantage of its tenuous protection to gain autonomy from Baghdad and to develop the economy. From this unpropitious genesis, the Kurds gravitated toward consensual government. By nurturing democracy and economic growth, the United States contributed to one of the most unheralded achievements in the Middle East, as an afterthought. When pundits recount Washington's many missteps in the region, they often overlook the Kurdish success. Some 5 million Kurds forged a functioning and viable mini-state that withstood the vicissitudes of the Iraq War and the Arab Spring, which devastated one Mideast country after another.

To safeguard the emerging Kurdistan from Hussein's predatory air force, America, Britain, and France enforced an air exclusionary zone for Iraqi planes over the mountainous northern area. They feared that Hussein would return to bombing and gassing the Kurdish population. Their aviation patrols halted Baghdad's retaliation in the north. The three allies duplicated an aerial "no-go area" in the southernmost zone just below the 32nd parallel in mid-1992. It was extended to the 33rd parallel, nearly to Baghdad, four years later. The three allies, however, did not superimpose a protectorate over the southern belt as in the Kurdish north. Thus, Hussein's security forces operated ruthlessly. Iraqi planes found in either zone, however, wound up in the crosshairs of Western gunners. Removing Iraq's aircraft and firing on Iraqi air defense sites whose radar "locked on" Western aircraft, in fact, extended military operations from the official end of the Persian Gulf War in 1991 to the start of the Iraq War in 2003.

Before leaving office in January 1993, George Bush ordered a large-scale air campaign against Iraq. Hussein invited this attack when he thwarted the UNSCOM. UNSCOM was tasked with overseeing Iraq's compliance to destroy WMD and missile plants. The Iraqi despot disrupted the inspections, which he viewed as violation of his country's sovereignty. In reply, the Security Council found his actions in "material breach" of Resolution 687, the so-called cease-fire resolution. Still defiant, he dismissed the UN threat until over 100 American, British, and French warplanes struck Iraqi ground targets. After three days of bombing, Hussein called for a cease-fire. After the intense bombardment stopped, allied pilots continued over the years to strafe Hussein's radar and missile sites.

The engagement cycle still prevailed when President Bush inaugurated a muscular initiative to contain Iraq. The airstrikes and breaches of Iraqi airspace without a declaration of war blurred the line between peace and conflict not often witnessed contemporary times. Baghdad protested that the bombing runs destroyed mosques and private dwellings, not militarily sites. Both his successors to the Oval Office—Bill Clinton and George W. Bush—carried on the air strategy for containing Saddam Hussein. In fact, Bush's air warfare anticipated Barack Obama's widespread use of drone strikes, which also sparked intermittent criticism.

President Bush's brand of forceful international engagement resonated at the time with much of the American populace. Thousands lined Pennsylvania Avenue in Washington and millions watched on television the two-mile-long military parade on June 8, 1991. US troops marched down the broad thoroughfare accompanied by tanks, missiles, and helicopters, while F-117 stealth fighters streaked overhead. Everyone loves a parade, and many spectators celebrated a victorious, short, and happy war in the Persian Gulf. Even the flood tide of internationalism, as represented by the military commemoration on that sunny June day, could not forestall the cycle away from interest abroad that historically follows bursts of external endeavors.

Somalia: An International Curtain Call

Two months prior to leaving office, George Bush gave some thought to pivoting away from the indefatigable internationalism that marked his presidency. But rather his administration following months of discussion decided to embark on a large-scale humanitarian intervention into Somalia. Located in the Horn of Africa, Somalia abruptly became ungovernable after the ouster of its longtime strongman Mohamed Siad Barre in 1991. The country of 7 million people descended into anarchy as clans battled clans while the destitute population perished in droves from hunger and hardship. Some 300,000 deaths were reported by summer 1992. An additional 4 million souls were at risk of starvation. Relieving a humanitarian tragedy following a natural disaster presented mainly logistical problems about how best to deliver food, water, and medical relief. Somalia, on the other hand, was a society plagued by a war of one-against-all.

It seemed the height of folly to deploy the US Army and Marines into the vicious civil conflict where friend and foe, civilian and combatant, were indistinguishable from one another in densely packed urban environments. How could American troops protect themselves while handing out food? Initially, the White House and Pentagon dug in their heels against such a venture deemed irrelevant to America's geopolitical interests. As the crisis dragged on, George Bush and Colin Powell, as Chairman of the Joint Chiefs of Staff, relented in late November 1992. They faced a chorus of domestic humanitarian voices as well as international calls, orchestrated, in part, by the new UN Secretary General Boutros Boutros-Ghali. Particularly effective were accusations that the United States would not neglect a similar humanitarian tragedy if it unfolded in Europe. The so-called CNN factor, meaning television images of emaciated children, tugged at viewers' consciences.

A sympathetic American public formed a backdrop to the Bush administration's decision to intervene. Decades later, after repeated and costly US efforts to salvage and rebuild war-torn societies in Iraq and Afghanistan, popular sentiment turned against involvement in the broader Middle East. The American people became tired and fed up with the lack of progress or gratitude by those they had sacrificed money and lives to restore. The Somali intervention took place before that fatigue and cynicism set in, contributing to a turn inward away from international causes.[33]

Once again, the Bush administration went to the UN to get its blessing for a multinational intervention. The Security Council authorized a US-led operation to establish a secure environment for humanitarian relief. Operation Restore Hope eventually recorded the deployment of 30,000 American troops and 10,000 personnel from 24 other nations.

They streamed into Somalia in early December 1992, just after George Bush lost his reelection campaign. His opponent and future president William J. Clinton concurred in the assistance operation. In time, Clinton presided over a debacle in Somalia when the Pentagon's mission morphed from food distribution to hunting a clan chief. For George Bush, nevertheless, the Somali humanitarian expedition capped a vigorous internationalist cycle in American history.

The Cycle Begins to Reverse

The denouement of George Bush's four years in office came not in what he did but in what he did not do. Near the end of his presidency, George Herbert Walker Bush chose to intercede into Somalia. But the White House skipped another humanitarian tragedy flaring in the enclave of Bosnia and Herzegovina within southeastern Europe. The suffering in Bosnia differed from Somalia and Haiti, the autocratic island which stressed the Bill Clinton presidency soon after it took office. The tiny province of Bosnia and Herzegovina lay within the now-defunct country of Yugoslavia, which was violently fragmenting along ethnic and sectarian lines. And Yugoslavia—a federated state put together in the aftermath of World War I—lay in the heart of Europe, not a peripheral corner. What happened to Yugoslavia bore directly on its immediate neighbors (Italy, Austria, Hungary, Romania, Bulgaria, Albania, and Greece) and ultimately on East-West relations. Washington and Moscow nervously eyed developments inside the Balkans during the early 1990s. The disintegrating Yugoslavia abutted NATO, America's principle alliance. For hundreds of years, Russia looked upon the Balkans as its political sphere, where its interests demanded premier recognition. This is not the place to present Yugoslavia's history or dissect its descent into war—that will come in Chap. 5; suffice it to write just enough to provide context to the Bush administration's standoffish policy.

Along with European political exertions to avert the dismemberment of Yugoslavia, the United States sent its top diplomat to Belgrade in June, 1991. Secretary Baker urged each head of the six republics to forgo succession from the federation. He warned that Washington would withhold formal diplomatic relations with breakaway states. His brokering mission came up short.[34] Days after the Baker mediations, the parliaments in Croatia and Slovenia voted for independence from Belgrade unless all the republics reached a new compact enabling greater autonomy for the constituent states. Yugoslavia's central government met the autonomy bid with tanks and troops. Unexpectedly, the Slovene armed forces bested Serb-dominated Yugoslav National Army (JNA). Expediently, Belgrade accepted Slovenia's independence. Then, Serbia turned on Croatia with ferocity. Serb militias joined with regular JNA units. Together, they ethnically cleansed territory that they claimed as Serbian lands.

France and Britain introduced motions in the Security Council to condemn Serbia's murdering and deporting of Croatians. One dubious measure passed unanimously in late September 1991. It imposed an arms ban on all of Yugoslavia in order to suppress the spreading violence by clamping down on the influx of weapons to the combatants. Resolution 713, in fact, hurt the very people it intended to help, since the Bosnian Muslims and Croats lacked weaponry for self-defense. The federal JNA arsenals were already in Serbian hands, thereby minimizing their need for foreign arms. This mismatch whetted Serbian militaristic ambitions while leaving other populations vulnerable. Even more deleterious for the oppressed Balkan peoples was the lumping together of their fate with the UN.[35]

The licking flames arising from Yugoslavia evoked a human tendency among George H.W. Bush and his senior aides; they flinched from grasping the fire. His administration spoke nearly with one voice in opposing a military intervention. Neither the president nor his State and Defense departments wanted to be drawn into a wartime humanitarian tragedy. The Pentagon opposed entering into another conflict once it concluded the Persian Gulf War by spring 1991. Colin Powell grew testy when confronted by a newspaper's call for a "limited" role to save the Bosnians in ethnic battle. The Chairman of the Joint Chiefs of Staff argued against a "murky or non-existent" objective for the US military to perform. The Army general thought terms like "presence" and "surgical strikes" were vague to the point of meaninglessness. He reflected on his experiences with the blown up Marine Corps barracks in Lebanon and the war in Vietnam—internal conflicts in which the United States got caught up in a military escalation when limited means failed.[36] Going along with Powell's recommendation to stay out of Balkan horrors, James Baker expressed his reluctance about American military intervention in a memorable sentence: "We don't have a dog in this fight." As casual and callous as his characterization may have been, it did reflect the Bush White House's opposition to any military incursion. The Secretary of State added in another setting that the United States must not "fight its fourth war in Europe in this century," referring to the two earlier hot wars and the Cold War.[37]

Note for the record: at first, Europe swatted away any perceived American meddling in the brewing Balkan catastrophe. As the Soviet sword lifted from Western Europe, it no longer felt the need of American tutelage on how to resolve its own predicaments. "This is the hour of Europe, not the hour of the Americans" declared Jacque Poos, whose Luxembourg held the rotating presidency of the European Community (later the EU).[38] The Luxemburgish foreign minister spoke for many Europeans, who envisioned the Continent as an alternative geopolitical pole to the unipolar sway of the United States. Western European politicians felt no need for US protection against a faltering Soviet Union. Others, such as former President Reagan and former British Prime Minister Margaret Thatcher, castigated Bush for what they perceived as his coldhearted realism and indifference to Europe's well-known incapacity to handle its own problems without American leadership.

The United States, Britain, and France erred in looking to the Security Council in the early days to halt the Serbian attacks on the Bosnian Muslims, particularly against the city of Sarajevo. The Security Council became a cockpit of big power disputes. Russia, the Serb champions, blocked any action against Belgrade. Early in the crisis, Britain and France also displayed pro-Serb sympathies because of their wartime collaboration against the German invaders of the Balkans. In time, Serbian bloodletting and recalcitrance turned off London and Paris, which joined Washington in putting the screws to Belgrade. At the advent of the Balkan troubles, however, the United States stood as the foremost Bosnian Muslim patron.

While the outside powers relied on a divided United Nations, the Serbs seized the opportunity to strike out against their foes. They laid siege to the historic town of Dubrovnik on the Adriatic coast, overran Vukovar, where 5000 inhabitants of the city, lost their lives to Serbian militias, who even murdered hospital patients in their beds.

The Serb's military escalation spurred Washington into diplomatic action alone. To end Belgrade's frontal assault on Dubrovnik, the Bush administration convinced Serbs and Croatians to demilitarize Dubrovnik. Bush officials also succeeded getting both combatants to accept the placement of a UN Protection Force (UNPROFOR) to keep the peace between the two sides. Caught in the middle, UNPROFOR on occasion became Serb hostages or their human shields later during NATO airstrikes. Finally,

Bush diplomats gained Serb and Croatian acceptance of UN peace negotiators. The Secretary General Pérez de Cuéllar selected two envoys. Cyrus Vance had been President Jimmy Carter's secretary of state, and Britain's Lord Carrington had facilitated the transfer of white minority rule to the African majority in Rhodesia, now called Zimbabwe. Their efforts largely came to naught as the warring parties adopted intractable positions.

Serb aggression zeroed in on Bosnia and Herzegovina, whose 3 million population comprised under 20 percent Croatian, just over 30 percent Serb, and slightly over 40 percent Slavic Muslims, meaning European in custom and largely secular in religious orientation. On the surface, two beleaguered peoples—Croats and Muslims—had every reason to cooperate against their common enemy the Serbs. But the Bosnian Croats and Bosnian Muslims (known as Bosniaks) either fought each other or cooperated warily against their Serb oppressors. This one-against-all mentality perplexed the Bush foreign policy team as well as other outside diplomats in their search for an end to the carnage.

The conflict degenerated into a bitter triangular fight when Bosnia and Herzegovina held a referendum in March 1992 in which 99 percent of the Bosniaks and Croats voted for independence. The Bosnian Serbs boycotted the vote, pronouncing it illegal. In retaliation, they established their own state—the Republika Srpska with its capital in Pale. The independence referendum was the equivalent of a declaration of war against Serbia and their allied Bosnian Serbs. When Croatia, Slovenia, and Bosnia-Herzegovina joined the UN, Serbian took revenge mainly at tiny Bosnia-Herzegovina and the mostly Muslim-populated capital of Sarajevo. Encircled by Serb gunners, the city endured hunger and privation together with shells and bullets around the clock for three years.

The United States and Europe were at loggerheads over how to handle Yugoslavia's fragmentation. Both agreed on not invoking NATO to resolve the conflict and largely for the same reason. The Europeans thought that the Americans would dominate the effort because of their preponderant influence over the transatlantic alliance. And Washington feared that if NATO became involved, then the United States would have to shoulder the lion's share of the effort, as the leading power within the Atlantic pact. Also, both sides primarily saw NATO as an anti-Soviet alliance, not a regional peacekeeper. Later, NATO would take on a political-military role by bringing into its fold the newly freed post-Soviet states in Moscow's former Eastern bloc. It was not until the war on terror following the September 11 attacks that NATO truly embraced on out-of-theater military role. So, during the early stages of the Yugoslavia upheaval, NATO appeared irrelevant to the crisis.

America and Europe also subscribed to differing views of who was most at fault for the Balkan morass in its early stages. Reflecting their World War II perceptions, London and Paris were more partial to Serbs, who fought tenaciously as allies against the German armies of occupation. They pointed out that Croatian, Slovenes, and Bosnians also perpetrated atrocities, not just the Serbs. Washington, on the other hand, favored the underdog Bosnian Muslims, especially those in the cosmopolitan Sarajevo. Since it hosted the 1984 Winter Olympics, Sarajevo seemed more at one with the West than race-bound Serbia. Ethnically diverse Sarajevo resembled a microcosm of multicultural American society. Temporarily, Americans and Europeans agreed not to recognize the various secessionist states with diplomatic relations. This brief unity fell apart when the Germans broke ranks in December 1991 by succumbing to domestic pressure to extend diplomatic ties to Croatia and Slovenia. Since the European Community needed German assent to the Maastricht Treaty that created its follow-on structure, the EU, other European Council (EC) partners went along with Berlin in January 1992.

This outcome put off the Bush administration, which wanted to stay out of the Bosnian imbroglio but wanted the Europeans to embrace to its strategic guidance. In a form of retaliation, the US policy makers also granted diplomatic recognition to Bosnia-Herzegovina when it extended relations to Croatia and Slovenia in spring 1992. The Bosnian Serb's Republika Srpska greeted the news of Bosnia and Herzegovina's diplomatic breakthrough with an intensified siege against Sarajevo. All told, the bloody 44-month encirclement of the city cost the lives of some 11,000 residents, of whom 1500 were children. They died from sniper fire, mortar shells, or starvation. America and Europe stood aside from the barbarity except for limited UN declarations and modest humanitarian relief.

The Bush administration went to the Security Council, where it secured passage of UN Resolution 757, which imposed economic sanctions on Serbia. A month later, in June 1992, Washington won concessions at the G-7 summit (a forum for governments of the leading seven industrialized economies) from its fellow attendees. The G-7 governments agreed to deliver humanitarian supplies to the cut-off Bosnians to include "military means" to ensure it destination. Military means lay beyond serious consideration by the Bush White House. It concentrated on international bodies and political overtures. At the July meeting in Helsinki of the Conference on Security and Cooperation, President Bush spoke about doing "all we can to prevent this conflict from spreading."[39] Indeed, the Balkan conflagration did spread geographically, homicidally, and militarily. Russia, Greece, and Bulgaria watched warily as their Orthodox brothers in Serbia fought Muslims in Bosnia and Western-orientated forces in Croatia and Slovenia.

Washington was not unaware of the dangers posed by disintegrating Yugoslavia. Bush's National Security Adviser Brent Scowcroft and soon-to-be Secretary of State Lawrence Eagleburger (who took over for James Baker in mid-1992 when he left to run Bush's reelection campaign) had served in Belgrade earlier in their careers. They knew well the ethnonationalist passions lurking beneath the surface that if ever released meant murderous consequences for the region. Upon exiting from their official posts, Eagleburger and Scowcroft conceded in media interviews that Yugoslavia's bloodletting might have been minimized by US military intervention.[40] As loyal presidential aides, however, they held their peace.

By summer 1992, the United States was consumed by the national campaign for the presidency and congressional seats. American disengagement and indifference to the outside world rose to a new level. As the weeks passed George Bush's hold on the presidency loomed more and more uncertain, culminating in his November election defeat. In the course of the electoral contest, the White House looked away from any political risky ventures to retrieve the deteriorating state of affairs in southeastern Europe. Two months before the election, Secretary of State Eagleburger declared what many Americans believed: "Until the Bosnians, Serbs, and Croats decide to stop killing each other, there is nothing the outside world can do about it."[41] For the non-interventionist, Eagleburger's words provided comfort.

The departing Bush, however, retained still enough internationalist interest to rattle sabers at Serbia's atrocities against the Albanian population within the restive province of Kosovo. The White House wired a cable on December 24, 1992, to Milošević: "[I]n the event of a conflict in Kosovo caused by Serbian action, the United States will be prepared to employ military force against the Serbs in Kosovo and Serbia proper."[42] Known as the "Christmas Warning," the threat probably had less to do with the relative calm within Kosovo until the end of the decade than other factors. First, Belgrade's attention was focused on active and spreading conflict in Croatia and Bosnia-Herzegovina. Second, Kosovo's sectarian-nationalism burst forth later after the Dayton Accord.

The American president held firmly to his realpolitik stance against any intervention. But he ordered a massive airlift of food supplies to Sarajevo and its environs in December 1992. The United States additionally forced through Serb lines ground transports of food, shelters, and heating fuel. By this time, estimates pointed to over 100,000 deaths from starvation and exposure in the beleaguered Bosnia. No doubt the 11th-hour rescue effort saved thousands of lives. Humanitarian relief, nevertheless, did not even slow the Serb land grab. Unimpeded, the Serbian-dominated regular Yugoslav army and local militia ethnically cleansed more territory in the pursuit of an enlarged Greater Serbia. The Serbs rightfully drew the conclusion that the ineffectual UN Blue Helmets on the ground and occasional relief supplies amounted to little more salve for Western consciences.

Overall, Washington looked ineffectual in dealing with the Bosnian crisis, and this image passed to the incoming Clinton government before it finally led the effort to end the war in the benighted Balkans, as will be related in Chapter 5. The engagement cycle of George Bush's opening years in the White House no longer pervaded. Before George Bush lost his reelection bid, his administration backtracked from its overseas engagement. As such, it anticipated the inward swing of the Bill Clinton White House. This anticipatory phenomenon was not untypical of other US presidencies in the post-communist world, as will be shown. In the case at hand, George Bush's inward turn preceded his successor's presidency. An interventionist presidency after the tumbling of the Berlin Wall had grown reluctant to intervene abroad. Instead, Bush passed the poisoned Bosnian chalice to his successor.

Bush: In Retrospect

Because George Herbert Walker Bush was a one-term president, he was too-readily assessed as a failure. His election defeat stemmed largely from a troubled economy. Yet his domestic achievements ranked comparatively high. He signed into law the American Disabilities Act along with updating the Clean Air Act and reauthorized the Civil Rights Act. His broken pledge not to raise taxes hurt his standing within the right wing of his own party. His international attainments, by contrast, stood out over the decades as notable successes far exceeding any of his successors.

So much was admirably secured—the peaceable end of the Cold War, freedom of the Soviet bloc, reunification of Germany within NATO, the sensible conclusion of the Iraq War—that subsequent presidents never measured up in comparison. His popular opinion rating at over 90 percent approval just after the Persian Gulf War led to the forecast that he could cruise to a second presidential term. The American public, nonetheless, soon forgot the foreign victories and instead focused on their domestic concerns—nearly always a signal of a swing away from international issues and toward insular preoccupations, as seen in Winston Churchill's electoral defeat in Britain on the eve of the World War II victory.

Over two decades later, amid Barrack Obama's tenure which was not known for its activist international performance, overdue recognition gradually descended over America's 41st commander-in-chief for his overseas attainments. Historians and pundits revised their earlier judgments of Bush senior.[43] Admiration for George H.W. Bush's legacy initially fell short of the acclaim he deserved because the post-Cold War settlement, in part, seemed so inevitable and effortless. The stabile, peaceful world the Bush administration energetically ushered into being after the demise of the USSR lasted a quarter of century before a resurgent Russia and rising China shook its foundations. This geopolitical order, which appeared so rock solid and so inexpensively purchased with so little human and financial costs after the Berlin Wall, was now endangered by other great powers, terrorist networks, and sovereign debt. In retrospect, that Bush's construct now needed shoring up in the face of revisionist powers and violent forces made his accomplishments all the more praiseworthy.

Notes

1. For background on post-World War I Iraq and King Faisal, see Ali A. Allawi, *Faisal I of Iraq* (New Haven, CT: Yale University Press, 2014), pp. 361–381.
2. Vali Nasr, *The Shia Revival: How Conflicts within Islam Will Shape the Future* (New York: W.W. Norton, 2006), pp. 108–117.
3. Charles Tripp, *A History of Iraq* (New York: Cambridge University Press, 2nd ed., 2002), pp. 231–233.
4. Dilip Hiro, *Neighbors, Not Friends: Iraq and Iran After the Gulf Wars* (London: Routledge, 2001), p. 19.
5. William L. Cleveland, *A History of the Modern Middle East* (Boulder, CO: Westview Press, 2000), p. 405.
6. Joel Brinkley, "Israel Puts a Satellite in Orbit a Day after Threat by Iraqis," *New York Times*, April 4, 1990, p. A 3.

7. Micah I Sifry and Christopher Cerf, eds., *The Gulf War Reader: History, Documents, Opinion* (New York: Random House, 1991), p. 102.
8. James A. Baker III, *The Politics of Diplomacy: Revolution, War, and Peace* (New York: G.P. Putnam's Sons, 1995), p. 263.
9. Tripp, *A History of Iraq*, pp. 248–250.
10. George H.W. Bush and Brent Scowcroft, *A World Transformed* (New York: Vintage Books, 1999), p. 311.
11. Pamela Fessler, "Glaspie Defends Her Actions, U.S. Policy before Invasion," *Congressional Quarterly Weekly Report*, March 23, 1991, pp. 259–260.
12. John F. Burns, "A Cadillac and Other Plunder," *New York Times*, December 30, 2002, p. A 1; Dilip Hiro, *Desert Shield to Desert Storm: The Second Gulf War* (New York: Author's Choice Books, 2003), pp. 103–104; and Public Authority for the Assessment of Damages Resulting from Iraqi Aggression. Downloaded from http://www.paac.org. Accessed July 20, 2016.
13. Bush and Scowcroft, *World Transformed*, p. 332.
14. Kevin Mattson, *What the Heck Are You Up To, Mr. President?: Jimmy Carter, America's "Malaise," and the Speech that Should Have Changed the Country* (New York: Bloomsbury, 2010), pp. 21–31.
15. Thomas L. Friedman, "U.S. Jobs at Stake in Gulf, Baker Says," *New York Times*, November 14, 1990, p. A 14.
16. Bush and Scowcroft, *A World Transformed*, p. 370 and President Bush, "Toward a New World Order," *U.S. Department of State Dispatch*, September 17, 1990, p. 91.
17. Patrick J. Buchanan, *A Republic, Not an Empire* (Washington, DC: Regnery, 1999), pp. 5 and 359.
18. Ibid.
19. Michael R. Gordon, "In Case of War, Congress Wants Right to Meet," *New York Times*, October 25, 1990, p. A 12.
20. Anonymous, "Iraqi Scientist Discusses A-Bomb Effort," *New York Times*, January 28, 2005, p. A 8 and Dafna Linzer, "Arms Reports Name Western Suppliers to Nuke Program," *Washington Post*, December 18, 2002, p. 13.
21. Brian Callanan and David Weiler, "War Budgeting Strategies: Case Studies of The Gulf War and The Iraq War," Briefing Paper No. 39

(Harvard Law School), May 2008. Downloaded from http://www.law.harvard.edu/faculty/hjackson/WarBudgeting_39.pdf. Accessed July 20, 2016.
22. Bush and Scowcroft, *A World Transformed*, pp. 346–347.
23. Rick Atkinson, *Crusade: The Untold Story of the Persian Gulf War* (Boston: Houghton Mifflin, 1993), pp. 81–85 and 37–80.
24. HRH General Khaled bin Sultan, *Desert Warrior: A Personal View of the Gulf War by the Joint Forces Commander* (New York: HarperCollins, 1995), pp. 237–242 and 266–290.
25. Atkinson, *Crusade*, p. 477.
26. Colin Powell, *My American Journey* (New York: Random House, 1995), p. 521.
27. Bush and Scowcroft, *A World Transformed*, p. 489.
28. Cited by George F. Will, "What to Ask the Nominee?" *Washington Post*, November 17, 2004, p. A 27.
29. Angelo Codevilla, "Magnificent, But Was It War?" *Commentary*, 93, no. 4 (April, 1992), 15–20.
30. Michael R. Gordon and Bernard E. Trainor, *The Generals War: The Inside Story of the Conflict in the Gulf* (New York: Little, Brown and Company, 1995), p. 443.
31. "Remarks and an Exchange with Reporters Prior to Discussions with Prince Bandar sin Sultan of Saudi Arabia," February 28, 1991, George H.W. Bush Presidential Library. Downloaded from http://bushlibrary.tamu.edu/research/papers/1991/91022804.html. Accessed July 20, 2016.
32. Michael R. Gordon and General Bernard E. Trainor, *The Generals' War: The Inside Story of the Conflict in the Gulf* (Boston: Little, Brown and Co. 1995), pp. 443–448.
33. Jon Western, "Sources of Humanitarian Intervention: Beliefs, Information, and Advocacy in the U.S. Decisions in Somalia and Bosnia," *International Security*, 26, no. 4 (2002), 112–142. Downloaded from https://muse.jhu.edu/journals/international_security/v026/26.4western.html. Accessed July 20, 2016.
34. One author believed that Baker gave Serbia a green light to engage in military force to preserve the federation. Tim Judah, *Kosovo: War and Revenge* (New Haven, CT: Yale University, 2002), p. 138.
35. Laura Silber and Allan Little, *Yugoslavia: Death of a Nation* (New York: Penguin Books, 1995), pp. 197–198 and 350–358.

36. Colin Powell, *My American Journey* (New York: Random House, 1995), pp. 558–559.
37. Baker, *The Politics of Diplomacy*, p. 65.
38. David Gardner, "EC Dashes into Its Own Backyard," *Financial Times*, July 1, 1991, p. 2.
39. "U.S. Support for CSCE," *U. S. Department of State Dispatch*, 3, Issue 28 (July 13, 1992), p. 1.
40. Don Oberdorfer, "A Bloody Failure in the Balkans," *Washington Post*, February 8, 1993, p. A 1.
41. Richard Holbrooke, *To End a War* (New York: Random House, 1998), p. 23.
42. David Binder, "Bush Warns Serbs Not to Widen War," *New York Times*, December 28, 1992, p. A 6.
43. Peter Baker, "Hindsight Proves Kinder, and Gentler, to Bush 41," *New York Times*, April 4, 2014, p. A 14.

Part II

CHAPTER 4

William Jefferson Clinton: The Post-Cold War's Inward Look

"What you mustn't do is to identify diplomacy with escalating concessions."
—Henry Kissinger

"O brave new world, That has such people in't." —Shakespeare's The Tempest

When William Jefferson Clinton strode into the White House in January 1993, he also entered into another world from his immediate predecessors. The Cold War, which preoccupied American presidents since World War II, had ended. The sudden implosion of the USSR promised a hiatus in geopolitical threats to the United States. America stood momentarily without foreboding arch-adversaries. Not unlike the days after World War I, Clinton-led America beheld an international breathing space, letting the incoming administration look inward. After the conclusion of the four-decade-old Cold War, punctuated with hot and bloody conflicts in Korea and Vietnam, Americans welcomed a respite from international entanglements. Many citizens called for a "peace dividend" in which the federal government turned off the defense-spending spigot. Internal priorities—education, infrastructure, health care, and drug problems—beckoned for tax dollars. The 1992 national campaign took cognizance of these new realties. Domestic concerns assumed a commanding place in stump speeches and public debates as voters looked to internal woes.

In the months preceding the election, voters fretted about a sluggish economy, stuck at 7.5 percent unemployment. The ballooning national

T.H. Henriksen, *Cycles in US Foreign Policy since the Cold War*,
DOI 10.1007/978-3-319-48640-6_4

debt, made a singular political issue by the maverick presidential campaign of Ross Perot, worried Americans. Perot's hammering away at the elevated national indebtedness proved to be so powerful that he drew voters from incumbent Bush, enabling Clinton to capture the White House with just 43 percent of the popular vote. George Bush's sky-high approval ratings following the Gulf War counted for next to nothing with a largely domestic-focused electorate 18 months later. Indeed, Bill Clinton portrayed the incumbent as a "foreign policy president," who neglected his fellow citizen's bread-and-butter concerns. In some measure, Clinton's lack of experience and interest in foreign policy was almost a plus for the young governor. The presidential aspirant promised his audiences to "focus like a laser" on rehabilitating the ailing economy. His campaign uttered over and over the mantra that "it's the economy stupid."

The presidential race, nevertheless, did encompass a few foreign policy issues. Candidate Clinton, for example, embraced an assertive international stance to counter perceptions that he was merely a reincarnation of his fellow Democrat, Jimmy Carter. President Carter left office with an anemic legacy for his return of the Panama Canal to Panamanian authority, his tepid response to the Soviet invasion of Afghanistan, and his inadequate counter to the "student" hostage-taking at the US Embassy in Iran. Moreover, unlike George Bush's combat service in World War II, Bill Clinton sat out the Vietnam War which he protested as a student. Clinton was an adept political campaigner who turned the tables on the one-term president, however.

Candidate Clinton zeroed in on a chink in the Bush armor enough to raise doubts so as to blunt his perceived strength as a tested commander in chief and international statesman. He faulted Bush for leaving Saddam Hussein in power after the Persian Gulf War. The Arkansas politician also criticized the incumbent's handling of Chinese government's bloody crackdown of pro-democracy demonstrators in Tiananmen Square in the first days of June 1989. Later, Bush wrote in his memoir that the "stability of the US-Chinese relationship was too important to world peace to sever it completely."[1] Clinton made Bush appear a cold practitioner of realpolitik by abandoning American ideals for hardcore strategic interests with China. Rather than accolades for preserving the Sino-American relationship, Bush looked cynical as pictured by the Clinton campaign.

The presidential-aspiring Clinton seized upon Bush's lack of vigorous punishment for the perpetrators of Tiananmen Square bloodbath. He pilloried the sitting president for "coddling the old communist guard in

China."[2] Seeking votes, he pledged, if elected, to "link China's trading privileges [with the United States] to its human rights record."[3] Likewise, the Arkansas candidate charged the incumbent with failure to help Haiti and fleeing Haitians after the overthrow of the island's president in September 1991. Indeed, Clinton held the White House guilty of "racial politics" for turning back Haitian asylum-seekers looking to land on US shores.[4] The barbed attacks made Bush appear as an ice-hearted practitioner of American foreign policy.

When the election dust settled, the United States found itself with an inexperienced and sometimes uninterested commander-in-chief who lived and breathed domestic issues. William J. Clinton possessed no international expertise. Initially, he leaned on others to compensate. Forming his cabinet, he selected Warren Christopher, a lawyer and longtime veteran of the State Department. Christopher, in fact, handled relations with Iran during the hostage crisis during the Carter presidency. As to be expected, Clinton picked up other former Carter officials to serve in his administration, such as Anthony "Tony" Lake (National Security Advisor) and his deputy Samuel "Sandy" Berger before succeeding him in 1996. Long-term Democratic operative, Madeleine K. Albright became the US Representative to the UN. Because of his service in the House of Representative on defense issues, Clinton settled on Congressman Les Aspin for Secretary of Defense. Upon winning the Democratic Party's nomination, Clinton chose US Senator Albert A. Gore Jr. from Tennessee to be his vice presidential running mate because, in part, of his expertise in nuclear arms-control issues. As Vice President, Al Gore played an active role in working with Russia, which became a sensitive assignment when Moscow perceived its interest threatened in the tempestuous Balkans.

Clinton's New World Order

The incoming president's inaugural address struck an internationalist, even a Wilsonian, note so interesting in retrospect, given his campaign's heavy domestic orientation. Clinton uttered the usual warning of the United States employing military force when "our vital interests are challenged." But the 42nd president fused American purpose, Wilson-like, with world interests, when he added: "or the will and conscience of the international community is defied, we will act, with peaceful diplomacy whenever possible, with force when necessary."[5] With this pugnacious promise, the new leader evidently committed the United States to the role of world policeman, in a way for which George Bush came under fire. As it turned out, Clinton ended up reluctantly leading military interventions on behalf of humanity.

At first, however, President Clinton turned to internal matters, where his heart and expertise lay. Restoring economic growth ranked at the top of his to-do list. One means of rejuvenating the economy was through international trade. This course led to Clinton's espouse a globalization agenda—internationally integrated finance, stepped up international commerce, and easy foreign travel—as an engine for economic prosperity and peace among nations. His international legacy rests, in part, on expanded globalization during his presidency. So laser-like was Clinton's attention to the home front that he tried to cut himself off from problems abroad. Indeed, Christopher and Lake shared the portfolio to "keep foreign policy from distracting the President from his domestic agenda."[6] Keeping the presidential desk free of international issues proved as futile as it was unwise, as events would soon make clear.

One international issue did early on preoccupy the new occupant of the White House. And this item pertained to America's economy as well as its international orientation. Before leaving office, George Bush negotiated a free-trade pact with Canada and Mexico and passed it over to the US Congress. Now Clinton was at the helm to prod Capitol Hill to enact the North American Free Trade Agreement (NAFTA). Passage of this agreement required the president to cross swords with some of his key constituencies among labor unions and environmental activists. To assuage their concerns, Clinton added two side agreements to protect workers and the environment from the ill-effects of NAFTA.

Linking together over 450 million people, NAFTA led to soaring trade and financial investment across borders after coming into force January 1, 1994, although it failed to settle all disputes among the three signatories. This US, Mexico, and Canada pact paved the way for America's membership in the World Trade Organization (WTO). The WTO is a global entity dealing with trade rules between states to reduce trade barriers among producers, exporters, and importers. Clinton also took the United States into WTO membership one year after NAFTA came into force. The presidential team invested heavily in the belief that the WTO and NATFA were necessary not only for spurring American economic growth but also for contributing to worldwide development and, by extension, building peace and stability within and among nation-states. The easier flow of goods, peoples, and financing did create wealth and bettered lives.[7]

The Swing toward the Non-interventionist Pole

Clinton's accession to power furthered America's pendulum cycle toward the non-interventionist pole. Whether wearied of Cold War exertions or longing for home priorities, the electorate hungered for international restraint by its leader. Nor was the new White House resident interested in shaping public opinion through speeches and policy for any overseas actions. Bill Clinton was sensitive to the mood of the body politic. When he spoke to the UN on September 27, 1993, he cast his remarks for two different audiences at the same time. To his domestic audience, the commander-in-chief assured Americans that the country was not about to wade into the Bosnian imbroglio or other intractable hostilities in the tow of the UN. He warned "if the American people are to say 'yes' to UN peacekeeping, the United Nations must know when to say 'no' to too many commitments." For international listeners, the president reconfirmed America's overseas commitments. He stressed that the "United States plans to remain engaged and to lead."[8] A few days after his nuanced UN speech, Clinton faced an explosive foreign crisis that rocked his young presidency and entrenched more limits on American intervention for much of his first term.

Five thousand miles away and in a world apart from the plush UN General Assembly chamber in New York City, US military personnel fought back heroically and died in the hot, dusty streets of Mogadishu on October 3, 1993. In pursuit of clan warriors, US SOF swooped down in their MH-60 Black Hawk helicopters into the Somali capital. After the troops captured their prey, they came under fierce gunfire from every corner, window, or alley, as the small band of US Rangers and Delta Force operators fought their way to safety. Fifteen hours later, the Battle of Mogadishu subsided after claiming 18 American lives and possibly 500 Somali deaths. In raw numbers, the urban battle was a decisive US victory. The vastly outnumbered and surrounded SOF acquitted themselves with stoic bravery. They took back the two clan lords for which they had been sent, plus scores of followers. The relief column deployed to rescue the tiny contingent, in fact, succeeded. Together they made good their escape under blistering fire to the protection of the Mogadishu airport. A battlefield victory, nevertheless, is not always a political triumph. Mogadishu belonged in the category of an international debacle.

How did this blow befall the United States? The story began in the twilight of George H.W. Bush's presidency with his food-relief mission conducted under the legitimizing auspices of the UN, as noted in the preceding chapter. The Pentagon-run Operation Restore Hope set out to rescue the starving Somalian population beset by anarchy after the overthrow of the country's military dictator. This humanitarian goal was largely fulfilled within weeks of the first US troops setting foot in the country on the Horn of Africa in early December 1992. The American soldiers and Marines completed their mission without sparking fire-fights with rabble-rousing militias under various warlords and clan chiefs by eschewing confrontations with them. Instead, they concentrated on food distribution while not attempting to disarm or arrest the rifle-toting irregulars. On the eve of Bill Clinton's swearing-in ceremony, Bush's Department of Defense withdrew several hundred Marines as a start to the eventual turnover of food distribution to the UN forces. Other US military forces pulled out during the next months.

The formal transfer of duties from the United States to the UN took place in May 1993, under the Clinton administration's guidance. The new international force was named United Nations Operation Somalia. All but some 5000 American troops left the African country at that time; those remaining became part of the 30,000 member UNOSCOM contingent. Secretary of State Christopher cabled his satisfaction: "We have phased out the American-led mission in Somalia, and taken the lead in passing responsibility to the United Nations peacekeeping forces."[9]

Paradoxically, Washington's step back from the lead role coincided with a step up in UN operations, which directly involved the remaining US military forces in street battles. The Clinton administration deepened its intervention without due preparation, almost as if sleep-walking into the potential pitfalls that awaited it. Later, the Pentagon acknowledged its "mission creep" left it ill-prepared for the Somali backlash. In brief, the United States, along with the UN peacekeepers, moved from handing out food to imposing order on a chaotic land of feuding clans and militias. Stability was just the first step in what Washington officials saw as a project of "nation building" in Somalia. Rather than taking into account the scarcity of democratic traditions or even a homogenous population, they plunged ahead. In the course of Clinton's first summer in the White House, his administration changed course. Warren Christopher, the Secretary of State, cabled his enthusiasm about Somalia to his diplomatic corps: "[F]or the first time there will be a sturdy American role to help the United Nations rebuild a viable nation state."[10]

Priority one for UN and US force was the eradication of the warlords and their armed teenagers. Abundant small arms in the hands of young, unemployed Somali men confounded Western hopes for the clan-torn state. These "technicals" cruised the Mogadishu streets in pick-up trucks brimming with weaponry. In itself, the UN's anti-militia operations shattered two traditions. First, the blue-helmeted peacekeepers took up offensive operations rather than their routine passive peace-support patrols. Second, because the UN was in the lead, this configuration resulted in US fighting forces being, at least nominally, subordinate to UN commanders. What created the most unease back in the United States were reports of US troops engaged in hostile actions with Somali irregulars.

Congressional committees held hearings about the mounting US combat operations authorized by the UN. Reports caused unease about American Rangers and Delta Force commandos spearheading raids to capture or kill Mohamed Farrah Aidid, the chief of the Habr Gidr clan as a means to bring peace to Somalia. They signified the militarization of the UN operations. Madeleine Albright, America's ambassador to the UN, testified to Congress that US military participation in UN operations was necessary for "rebuilding Somali society and promoting democracy in that strife-torn nation." She went on to declare in a loaded phrase that "assertive multilateralism" served American international interest.[11] This two-word phrase became a target for critics of humanitarian deployments that did not contribute to tangible US policy goals. Amid this escalating political debate in Washington, the "black hawk down" incident took place in Somalia.

Tensions boiled over in Mogadishu after 24 Pakistani peacekeepers were killed in June and four US soldiers from a roadside bomb two months later. In retaliation, the US military hatched an operation to capture two Aidid confidantes meeting in the Olympic Hotel downtown in the seaside capital on the first Sunday of October.[12] The Task Force Ranger helicopters whooshed down on the hotel site, enabling the on-board elite forces to scoop up their two quarries. Soon, the commando raid ran into trouble when first one and then a second Black Hawk helicopter were shot down by militants in the streets. The embattled troops and their prisoners came under withering fire from hundreds of destitute Somalis, who shot, retrieved fallen arms, or scouted on the retreating column. After making good their escape, with the help of a relief column, the military and White House came in for a rude awakening.

The immediate repercussions hit squarely at all parties in the fight. For the Somalis, their killing American servicemen and dragging their bodies through humid streets led the US and UN personnel to withdraw from the country. Hunger and privation again wantonly stalked the Horn of Africa nation. The fighting also demoralized the decimated ranks of Aidid's followers. Many left the city fearing a searing US reprisal for the desecration of the dead, which violated Islamic beliefs.[13] The Clinton administration sustained a public relations blow from a stunned American public, who thought that the United States was only in Somali on a goodwill mission to feed and succor huddled masses. American television viewers recoiled at the graphic images of the bodies of their troops pulled behind exultant Somalis. Bill Clinton seemed over his head in international affairs and out of touch with the doings of his own administration in a far-off land. The Defense Department was blamed for "mission creep" by permitting the military operation to exceed its means.

The deepest impact occurred in how the United States conducted its future foreign policy. The Somali misadventure reverberated in the halls of power for some time. It profoundly influenced American policy toward other trouble spots such as Haiti, Rwanda, and Bosnia. It bred hesitancy in the president and his innermost circle. No-more-Somalias became a watchword deeply internalized if not openly uttered. It accentuated the international pendulum swing toward domestic affairs, away from foreign entanglements with potential military casualties and political defeats. Clinton was already homing in on the domestic economy and the midterm Congressional elections a year away. At the time of the Black Hawk Down action, Clinton was in California pitching his version of health care reform. When he learned of the calamity, he erupted in anger at his own officials for not informing him of the dangers in the Somali activities; to his staff he heatedly asked: "How could this happen?"[14] The president realized that adventuresome actions overseas had to be curtailed because they stood to jeopardize his domestic priorities.

The Somali lessons were further seared into the administration's thinking when Congress held hearings on the Mogadishu debacle. During the review, it came to light that General Thomas Montgomery, the highest-ranked officer on the spot, had requested AC-130 gunships and armored tanks in mid-September. Secretary of Defense Aspin greeted the appeal with inaction. Yet, experts cast doubt on whether the heavy arms could have arrived in time for the October 3 assault.[15] Two months after the snatch operation, Les Aspin resigned when a Congressional report held him and President Clinton responsible for the Somali blowup. By then, it was widely known that the White House wanted to rid itself of the ineffective former Congressman. The Oval Office replaced him with the Deputy

Secretary of Defense William Perry, who proved himself a much more able cabinet secretary.

The Clinton White House moved quickly to extricate the United States from Somalia. It canceled the armed pursuit of Aidid. Clinton pledged to help the Somalis "reach agreement among themselves so that they can solve their problems and survive when we leave."[16] Much to the chagrin of the comrades of the fallen SOF, the Washington administration required the US military to fly Aidid, the killer of American servicemen, to a peace meeting with other warlords and clan chiefs. A rickety peace deal was hammered out among participants, which did not hold after the American withdrawal. White House staffers disavowed the "mission creep" by Pentagon officials. In a formal statement four days after the Black Hawk Down incident, President Clinton pronounced about Somalia: "We have obligations elsewhere." He added that it was not America's job to "rebuild Somalia society."[17]

Next, Washington reinforced the US military presence in and nearby Somalia. It sailed the *USS Abraham Lincoln* aircraft carrier and its accompanying warships off the coast. It inserted an additional 1700 US Army soldiers into the East African country and held 3600 shipboard Marines in reserve. This sizeable show of force was designed to look muscular rather than betray a cut-and-run retreat. Finally, the Clinton officials publicly blamed the UN for the Ranger raid. Such recriminations fell on receptive ears since many Americans held the world organization in low regard. In reality, the commando operations never fell under UN control; they were run by the US military.

Operation Restore Hope actually notched laudable benchmarks. Estimates placed the number of Somalis saved from starvation from 100,000 to 250,000. The Secretary of State put a favorable gloss on the result when he declared: "We leave the country in a lot better shape than [when] we went in."[18] Soon after the departure of the foreign forces and aid workers, the country sank again into interclan warfare. Aidid died as he lived, in a hail of bullets in 1996. In its return to endemic violence, Somalia represented the first of many Middle East states in recent times to undergo widespread murder and mayhem when civil order broke down, as later in Iraq, Yemen, Syria, and Libya. The absence of foreign assistance in Somalia, it needs to be emphasized, led to a political vacuum. Into the bowels of this failed state walked al Qaeda, the fearsome terrorist network that instigated bombings of American embassies in Tanzania and Kenya in 1998 and afterward to foment other bloody attacks, including the September 11 terrorism.

The Somalia misstep strengthened anti-UN sentiments within the United States. It also temporarily damaged the credibility of the Clinton administration. In the short run, the Mogadishu street battle cast a dark shadow over the Clinton administration whenever crises abroad beckoned for US intervention. As such, it elevated the insular cyclical swing already rising in the American body politic after the Cold War.

Rwanda—A Tragic Non-intervention

The most horrendous victim of America's non-interventionist cycle occurred with the Republic of Rwanda soon after the missteps in Somalia. What gave the Rwanda crisis a particularly cruel salience arose from the fact that the genocidal-type massacre could have been mitigated, if not prevented by an American-led intervention. But the Clinton White House averted its eyes despite repeated appeals from many quarters to coordinate a relief operation to halt the ethnic slaughter in the Central African state. Fearing another Somali disaster, President Clinton and his top aides lost their moral and political nerve.

The same day—April 6, 1994—the United States completed its military withdrawal from Somalia, Rwanda descended into African killing fields. On that date, the Rwandan president Juvénal Habyarimana died when a missile struck his airplane, which crashed killing all on board. Among the casualties were government officials returning from peace negotiations in Tanzania. There, Rwanda's neighbors tried to broker a de-escalation of the hair-trigger tension between the Rwandan Hutu and Tutsi ethnic communities. Based on Rwandan history, the international negotiators feared that a spate of interethnic killings might ignite a firestorm of violence, which could engulf nearby countries as well. Tanzania successfully pressured Habyarimana to accept more Tutsi participation in his ethnically exclusivist government. The president's death took place under mysterious circumstances as the Kigali airport went dark just before the missile struck his aircraft. His murder, in fact, did open the floodgates to murder and mayhem in the country of then 7 million people, as observers feared.

The outside world knew about the tribal powder keg in the mountainous coffee-growing nation. Its history spoke volumes of Hutu-Tutsi retaliatory killings. Since Rwanda's independence from Belgium in 1962, the lush country had experienced repeated bouts of slaughter. To prevent a reoccurrence of violence, the Security Council passed Resolution 872, which established the UN Assistance Mission for Rwanda in October 1993.

Canadian Brigadier General Raméo A. Dallaire commanded UNAMIR, which incorporated a Belgian battalion along with 800 Ghanaian and 900 Bangladeshi troops. Beginning in early the next year, Dallaire sensed the impending catastrophe and called for additional forces, which the UN rejected.

The political atmosphere grew poisonous as the Hutu-dominated government mounted a hate-filled propaganda campaign against the Tutsi population. Radio Rwanda, the official broadcast station, and private stations, such as Radio Mille Collines, aired screeds against Tutsi and moderate Hutus. The Hutu extremists referred to Tutsi as "cockroaches" to be eliminated. They formed militias of young and uneducated Hutus, which were attached to the ruling party. The day after President Habyarimana's death these semi-militarized thugs wielding machetes and farm tools struck the Tutsi and pro-democracy Hutus in an orgy of killing. The lurid scenes invoked nightmarish landscapes similar to Hieronymus Bosch's paintings. The hapless Tutsi fled into neighboring countries, mostly Tanzania, where hundreds of thousands of refugees strained the food and sanitation facilities of their host.

The outside world watched in horror and passivity as the carnage mounted. General Dallaire pleaded for at least 5000 troops to stop or at a minimum slow the march of the barbarity. Not only was his request denied but also his tiny peacekeeping force was yanked out by a vote of the Security Council. France sent troops but only to secure the safe passage of French and other European nationals out of the country. The United States, so long the beacon of hope and last refuge, similarly washed its hands of the tragedy. The White House's calculated disengagement from intervening into the killing fields reflected the country's insularity impulse of the times.

By early May, the Clinton administration internally debated its options given calls for it to address the raging barbarity. UN Secretary General Boutrous-Ghali's appeals for international assistance resulted in the White House diving for political cover to avoid any intervention into Central Africa. The president's top aides, for example, discussed the means to pay for and organize relief efforts by Rwanda's neighbors rather than deploying US military personnel. The shadow of Somalia hung over the deliberations. Bill Clinton offered his perspective: "Lesson number one is, don't go into one of these things [Rwanda] and say, as the U.S. said when we started in Somalia, 'Maybe we'll be done in a month because it's a humanitarian crisis.'... Because there are almost always political problems and sometimes military conflicts, which bring about these crises."[19] So, America stood aside.

Deliverance for the Tutsi came when their Rwandan Patriotic Front (RPF) mobilized its forces and battled back the Hutu militias. The RPF units captured Kigali and then embarked on their own ethnic cleansing of the Hutu population, who fled into the Democratic Republic of the Congo (then called Zaire). Hastily established camps around the cities of Goma and Bukavu offered minimal services to the destitute Hutus, thousands of whom died from cholera or starvation. Those who survived lived in appalling conditions without access to proper sanitation.[20]

Because of the widening media coverage about the Rwandan genocide, the United States could no longer shrug off any responsibility to alleviate mass human suffering. On July 22, the president announced an increase in emergency assistance but proffered no means to halt the slaughter. The Clinton administration flew in clean water-producing equipment, food supplies, and other items, costing nearly $500 million, to a base in nearby Uganda. It also dispatched 4000 troops to distribute food and water and erect shelters.[21] Their mission was purely humanitarian; they scrupulously avoided any peacekeeping duties for protection of the refugees. With the Somali case in mind, the Pentagon leadership advised against any military activities that could drag it into combat operations. It even refused to electronically jam the Hutus' hate-laced radio transmissions that incited frenzied killings and directed the militias to locations where their prey was hiding. The administration interpreted any assistance as the first step on a slippery slope to intervention. The president and his top rung of officials at the Department of State, in the words of one scholar, handled the Rwandan genocide "as a peacekeeping headache to be avoided" not a "human rights disaster requiring urgent response."[22]

Fearful of "another Somalia," the Clinton government took advantage of the American public's cyclical disengagement mood to duck a humanitarian venture. Rather than shaping public discourse toward the use of a military rescue expedition, the White House impeded even the Security Council from advocating a relief operation. Clinton officials, moreover, strove to block the use of the word *genocide* to describe the Hutu-on-Tutsi savagery so as to head-off a call for robust US action.[23] Other Western states behaved as poorly as the United States. For example, France also neglected any responsibility despite its cultural and political ties to Rwanda. Within Africa, other countries lacked the capacity or will to intervene to end the grisly acts perpetrated first by the Hutu and then by the Tutsi.

In early 1998, Bill Clinton made a grand tour of the African continent. When the president stopped in Rwanda, he "acknowledged that the United States and the international community had not acted quickly enough to stop the genocide." He offered help to rebuild the country and "to support the war crimes tribunal that would hold accountable the perpetrators of the genocide."[24] Before that belated presidential mea culpa, Clinton had ridden waves of anti-intervention sentiments in the Balkans, Haiti, and even East Timor. After Somalia and Rwanda, the president persisted in his role of reluctant intervener, even when members of his own political party demanded action abroad.

Haiti and Presidential Hesitancy

The troubles engulfing the Republic of Haiti overlapped with those in Somalia and Rwanda. But Haiti differed from the latter two hotspots in geography and history. Haiti occupies the western third of Hispaniola Island, some 500 miles from the coast of Florida. Despite its proximity to the United States, Haiti has been the most impoverished country in the Western Hemisphere. The self-less nun Mother Theresa, who lived among the Calcutta slums, considered Haiti the Fifth World in terms of destitution. From its founding, the United States has always been sensitive to developments in its Caribbean backyard. Haiti's turmoil, bloodshed, and dictatorial rule periodically aroused Washington's attention for the last two centuries. Historically, only Cuba enjoyed a more arduous relationship with the United States. And even Cuba did not suffer from an extended US military occupation as Haiti did from 1915 to 1934 to restore order. Over the decades, Haiti faded in and out of American consciousness.

Beginning in early 1990, Haiti again blipped on Washington radars. The Haitian military junta found itself challenged by Jean-Bertrand Aristide, a young Catholic priest who in time was defrocked by the Vatican. A charismatic populist, Aristide led the Lavalas Movement (a name derived from the island's Creole which meant a flash flood capable of washing away everything) to electoral victory in December 1990 by championing the poor. The promise of political reform was soon dashed by Aristide's incendiary rhetoric laced with Marxist phrases and liberation theology themes. His attacks on the "bourgeoisie" and dismissiveness toward parliamentary practices catalyzed fear among army officers and wealthy citizens. This privileged strata engineered a military coup toppling Aristide just eight months after his taking office. Thanks to being the first democratically elected president in Haitian history, his overthrow by the army did not go unnoticed by the United States.

As Aristide's ouster nearly coincided with an abortive coup against Mikhail Gorbachev in the Soviet Union—a momentous event for American policy toward the disintegrating Soviet state—the George Bush administration treated the Haitian event circumspectly. It condemned Aristide's forcible removal from office. It offered him and his inner circle political asylum, which was accepted. It refused diplomatic recognition of the ruling junta and froze Haiti's assets in American financial institutions. From these funds in the US Federal Reserve Bank, the White House released a monthly $1 million to Aristide for expenses while in exile. But the Bush administration turned back Haitian asylum-seekers who fled on rickety watercraft to the United States.

As a presidential contender, Clinton faulted Bush for not doing enough to reverse Aristide's ouster. He brought up Bush's militarized-regime change in Panama against a drug dealer, without raising a finger to help a democratically elected president in Haiti. In a speech at the Los Angeles World Affairs Council three months before the election, Clinton charged Bush with "racial politics." Clinton said if he were president: "I wouldn't be shipping those poor people back" to Haiti as they sailed over the Caribbean toward US territory.[25] Clinton's passionate remarks rhetorically laid out a welcoming mat to the Caribbean poor. After his election, Clinton backtracked on his campaign promises. As one foreign policy commentator wrote after Somalia: "Haiti also marked a step in Clinton's disengagement from his Wilsonian rhetoric"[26] of internationalist engagement.

As president, Clinton ignored his campaign pledge. The trickle of Haitian migrants from dire conditions caused concern in the White House, for the president worried how the influx, especially into Florida, might impact his second-term political campaign. Clinton was particularly attuned to a possible political backlash due to Caribbean immigrants. When Arkansas' governor, he accommodated President Jimmy Carter's request during the Mariel boatlift from Cuba in 1980. Because Fidel Castro dispatched prisoners as well as genuine asylum-seekers to the United States, Clinton put many in Fort Chafee. When the refugees rioted against their incarceration, Arkansas' voters held it against their governor who lost his next gubernatorial election. Anxious about voter sentiment, President Clinton stationed US warships off the Haitian coast to turn back or sequestrate the would-be refugees until a solution could be found.

Members of his own party, nonetheless, pushed Clinton to search out an answer to Haiti's instability. He got the UN to summon the junta representatives to New York City's Governors Island for talks. The deliberations seemed to yield a positive settlement on October 3, 1993. Haiti's ruling junta agreed to democratic elections, modernization of the security forces to weed out the thugs, and the return of Aristide as the lawful president by October 30. Next, the UN established a mission to oversee the US-Haitian agreement. Clinton did not want American troops involved in a peacekeeping role on the island. The formation of the UN Mission to Haiti, or UNMIH, stalled because General Raoul Cédras, chief of the junta, reneged on his earlier commitment. Fifteen months later and after the United States had reluctantly militarily intervened into Haiti, UNMIH took up its duties. However prior to the US armed intrusion and the UN's peace-support mission, Clinton embarked on a tortuous path in dealing with the tiny, impoverished, and utterly defenseless republic. In all, its behavior betrayed how far the tide of American internationalism receded from its Bush-era exuberance.

Implementation of the Governors Island agreement called for the landing of small contingent of 1300 US troops and Canada's famed Mounties in Port-au-Prince to re-train the Haitian army for a non-political role in stabilizing the Caribbean country. Greeting the *USS Harlan County* at the docks was a mob of protestors orchestrated by the junta. To scare the US-Canadian security personnel when they stepped foot on Haitian docks, the crowd chanted "Somalia, Somalia" a week after the Mogadishu battle. Confronted with unruly demonstrators, the Clinton administration did the unthinkable; it ordered the amphibious warship to sail from capital's harbor. When a government turns tail and runs, its prestige falters. A fifth-rate power gave the world's sole standing superpower a political black eye. Years later, Secretary of State Madeleine Albright, who succeeded Warren Christopher, reflected in her memoir that the *Harlan County*'s humiliating military retreat amounted to "a low point in Clinton administration foreign policy."[27] It also marked a further notch in America's disengagement cycle.[28]

Clinton's political opponents were just as adamant about staying clear of Haiti as he was. At this juncture, both major US parties saw eye to eye about avoiding foreign entanglements, particularly in the Haitian case. The Senate minority leader Bob Dole threatened the Clinton administration with bringing up legislation, if it dispatched US troops abroad other than for genuine national security objectives. The Republican figure cast his opposition as one of the legislature reining in an overmighty executive branch. In reality, Dole played politics. Later, he favored intervening in Bosnia, when Clinton dragged his feet, as will be described. But even some of Clinton's fellow Democrats in congress proved less than eager to march into another Somali-type cauldron. Anti-interventionist impulses animated both political parties. Isolationist inclinations spanned the political spectrum after Somalia and the collapse of the Soviet Union.

The Clinton White House recognized that US-Haitian agreement was a dead letter. It fell back on sanctions—as better than doing nothing to offset its mortifying cave-in to the dockside rabble. The administration reinitiated its original anti-junta sanctions that it lifted when Port-au-Prince accepted the Governors Island agreement. Then, the administration returned to the Security Council to get additional economic restrictions on Haiti. It enforced the embargoes on oil and arms to the small Caribbean nation by ringing the island with US warships. Not feeling any personal pain, Cédras and company flouted their earlier agreement to make way for the return of Aristide. Meanwhile, the bulk of the population fell deeper into misery. Light industries crumbled. Workers lost their jobs and livelihood. Unemployment swelled to 70 percent. The poor went without food, electricity, and hope. One Harvard study pointed to 1000 deaths a month among children five years old and younger by November 1993 due to the punitive economic measures.[29]

America was not spared repercussions from its economic squeeze on the former French colony. The hard-pressed population voted with their feet—or rather with makeshift vessels—to flee the island for the North American continent. Those who survived the perils at sea mostly washed up on the Florida coast, presenting a problem for the Washington government on what to do with the refugees. The administration set out to rescue boatloads of the Haitian diaspora and domiciled them in the US naval base at Guantanamo Bay, Cuba, and a military base in Panama so as not to incur a backlash from US voters. Haiti's military troika and its cronies isolated themselves from material shortages by their horde of US dollars and by deal-making with high and low in next-door Dominican Republic.

Searching for other low-cost options—well short of intervention—the Clinton West Wing floated the idea of even stiffer economic penalties on the junta-ruled island. The president declared his intention to impose additional sanctions if the military rulers refused to vacate power by January 15, 1994. When the deadline came and went without a powerful riposte from the United States, Cédras was not alone in concluding that the American commander-in-chief possessed insufficient resoluteness to use military force for the restoration of Haitian democracy. Angered by the Oval Office's sanction bluff, Aristide denounced Washington's treatment of Haitian refugees as "racist" and compared the White House's asylum policy to the equivalent of a "floating Berlin Wall."[30]

Like the eighteenth-century Stuart pretenders to the English throne, the exiled Haitian president set up a court of followers across the sea where he presided over a legion of influence peddlers, pitchmen, and lobbyists. He had ample funding since the White House upped his monthly stipend to $2.5 million, paid from the proceeds of an international telephone carrier operating in Haiti. Aristide also cultivated the media and celebrities to expand his influence in Washington circles. Upper-echelon government officials tried to butter up the diminutive but fiery exiled president in hopes of taming his anti-Clinton broadsides. The Pentagon even conferred the status of a 21-gun salute on Aristide before according him an exclusive briefing by William Perry, the Secretary of Defense. Little mollified, the vituperative leader irritated the hand that fed him.

Within the president's own party, fellow Democrats from the liberal wing and the Congressional Black Caucus in the House of Representatives joined in criticizing Bill Clinton for what they all saw as irresolution on the Haiti issue. Eventually and glacially, the intra-party pressure would prove decisive in moving the White House, countercyclically, to intervene militarily into Haiti but not before exhausting sanctions and diplomatic approaches.

Spring 1994 saw the Clinton administration take another crack at UN-induced economic punishment. On May 6, the Security Council obliged the United States with a unanimous endorsement to emplace a harsher quarantine on the battered state. Backed by Aristide, who craved power, the White House imposed the new sanctions. It severed American commercial air links with the island nation and froze individual Haitian financial accounts in the United States. The junta hunkered down determined to hang on to their dictatorial regime. But the Haitian people resolved to seek a new and better life in the United States. By early summer, some 5000 Haitians weekly took to the open seas in open boats. By late summer, the number jumped to 30,000 a week. Large numbers reached American shores. Sanctions turned the lights out in Haiti but the consequences also beset the United States. Clearly, the status quo was unstainable. Intervention, nevertheless, went against the grain of the White House's hardwired insularity.

Grudgingly, the Clinton administration came around to the idea by mid-September 1994 that it must at least threaten military invasion of Haiti to budge the junta into leaving. It went back to the UN and obtained Security Council Resolution 940, which authorized the use of "all necessary means" to remove the military dictatorship. The resolution set no specific date for any intervention but it did call for "the restoration of democracy and prompt return of the legitimately elected President."[31] The resolution represented the first such military authority granted by the UN in the Western Hemisphere. It provided the White House a measure of political cover from Latin American critics as well as domestic voices raised against US military ventures.

Regardless of the UN's imprimatur and the Defense Department's preparations, the Clinton administration still with no appetite military intervention looked to an 11th-hour covert operation. Under presidential guidance, the CIA undertook a $12 million "secret enterprise" to bribe "friendly elements" within the Haitian armed forces with American dollars, weapons, and radios. The operation fell flat because no one took up the offer. The president searched for another non-military arrow in his quiver rather than wading into a militarized campaign. While the Pentagon readied its expeditionary forces, the commander-in-chief rolled the non-military dice yet another time to dodge a martial enterprise on Haitian soil.

President Clinton enlisted three top emissaries to offer a package to the junta to leave peacefully. Former president Jimmy Carter, former Chairman of the Joint Chiefs of Staff Colin Powell, and Democratic Senator Sam Nunn of George flew to Port-au-Prince to parlay with General Cédras and his two fellow junta members on September 17 with just 36 hours to reach a deal to permit a peaceful US military entry onto the island. The American delegation made it clear to the Haitian threesome that it would discuss only the "modalities" of their departure, not additional delays. As Haitian-destined US military aircraft cleared the runways, the junta relinquished power and decamped for Panama and a gold-plated exile with funds they looted from the Haitian masses.

Bill Clinton escaped a repetition of Somalia. The US paratroopers and soldiers conducted a "permissive invasion," meaning no combat resistance faced them. In reality, Haiti's enfeebled army and police numbered only about 7000 and lacked training and basic arms. They were lopsidedly dwarfed by America's two aircraft carriers—the *USS America* and the *USS Dwight D. Eisenhower*—and 20,000 troops alighting on Haitian soil.

The US force encountered no organized opposition from the islanders, who hoped for some modest improvement in their harsh lot. Washington returned Aristide to power a month after the intervention. Aristide's triumphal return was greeted by cheering throngs. His citizens' hopes for a better life were once more dashed by corruption, venality, and callous tyranny in the restored Aristide presidency.

The United States officially turned over its stabilizing mission to the UN in March 1995. By that time, Americans operations cost $1.2 billion. The Pentagon left 2500 US troops to serve in the UNMIH along with 5000 police and soldiers from 23 other countries. When the American participation ended with the exit of UNMIH in 1996, US expenditures for Haiti rose to $3.2 billion. Much good was done but most of it proved transitory like footprints in the sand.

For Clinton, all was well that ended well, despite the ever-present ghost of Mogadishu. He did bask in the Haitians' warm adulation during a brief visit seven months after the launch of Operation Uphold Democracy. In a made-for-photo-op moment, he stood amid admiring faces and declared triumphantly the "bringing back the promise of liberty to this long-troubled land."[32] The president hungered for a foreign success story to offset the Somali setback. Two years later, he was still beating a drum for his presidency's achievements on a small Caribbean island. In his 1996 State of the Union Address, the president trumpeted the restoration of Aristide to power. Clinton intoned "the dictators are gone, and democracy has a new day."[33] This pronouncement was far too sanguine. What the Clinton intervention wrought resembled a river artificially diverted to a new bed. Life followed in the new channel for a year or two, and then it wore back into its old course. Fortunately for the White House, the media moved onto other issues, leaving aside how little Haitian society changed after all the Oval Office's credit-claiming statements.

While the Haitian episode improved the president's image in handling international affairs, it fell short of moving the White House toward an assertive overseas role. Insular sentiments in the country and in its leadership still predominated. The historical cycle stayed lodged away from interventionism. Largely a domestic-issue president, Clinton concentrated on welfare reform, balancing the federal budget, and achieving a budget surplus. During his term, unemployment decreased, and the middle class prospered. Nor was his orientation out of sync with the insularity of average Americans. The arcane interethnic civil conflicts in far-off lands with unpronounceable names baffled the citizen in the street. They often saw little at stake for America to send its sons and daughters into harm's way. At peace and prosperous, America sent Bill Clinton into retirement with a high 66 percent Gallup poll approval rating.[34] But before that sendoff, Clinton faced other international troubles.

North Korea—Military Threats and Concessions

The Bill Clinton administration not only avoided a war with North Korea but its policies also wrote the playbook that every subsequent American president adopted in dealing with the rogue state. President Clinton deterred with military strength, negotiated arms-control agreements, and constrained with economic sanctions. Like his successors in the White House, Clinton rewarded bad behavior with aid or pledges of financial assistance for promises of peaceful behavior. Washington also failed to soften, let alone befriend the reclusive, warlike Stalinist regime. The North's implacable hostility persisted toward the United States no matter how many times Washington governments turned their cheek or opened their pockets.

The Democratic People's Republic of Korea (DPRK), as it is formally known, blinked on the warning radar of every White House since the Korean War until today. When the DPRK invaded South Korea in 1950, it ignited a savage war and divided the Korean Peninsula between a totalitarian state and one that eventually became a democratic nation after its authoritarian rulers passed from scene. The three-year war drew in China when the American-led UN forces threw the North Korean invaders back to near the Chinese border. As one of the hottest episodes during the Cold War, the Korean War cost the lives of 33,000 US servicemen, killed 3 million South Koreans, and annihilated several hundred thousand Chinese soldiers. The truce—not peace treaty—that ended the fighting froze the Korean peninsula into two warring states and never healed the divisions. The two remain at daggers drawn to this day. Separated by a four-kilometer-wide strip across the peninsula at the 38th parallel, the Demilitarized Zone (DMZ) is bordered on each side by the most militarized defense fortifications in the world. From time to time, the DPRK has fired across the DMZ or on South Korean islands off the coast. Propaganda blasts in clichéd Soviet-period phrases often lead up to attacks on the Republic of Korea (ROK), which Pyongyang considers a Washington puppet. American military forces, still garrisoned in the ROK, have also been the target of deadly attacks. In 1968, North Korean warships seized an American reconnaissance ship, the *USS Pueblo*, and held its crew for nearly a year. Over the years, it shot at US aircraft and hacked to death US soldiers near the DMZ.

Ominously, the Communist regime in Pyongyang chased after nuclear arms from the Korean War. It pressed the Soviet Union for material and technical assistance, which Moscow supplied. Over the years, the Kremlin trained North Korean engineers and it transferred a two-to-four-megawatt reactor for installation in Yongbyon, located 60 miles north of the capital. The Soviets also handed over short-range missiles and technical assistance so that the DPRK could manufacture its own versions. Subsequently, China sent scientists to assist the North Koreans in developing a nuclear capability and in manufacturing knockoffs of Soviet missiles. During the Reagan administration, the United States grew alarmed about the DPRK's nuclear progress as monitored from orbiting satellites. Ronald Reagan successfully pressured the Kremlin to get the North Koreans to sign the Nuclear Non-Proliferation Treaty (NPT) in 1985. The NPT required signatories to construct only civilian nuclear reactors for peaceful purposes of generating power. It also mandated that signers permit the IAEA, the UN's nuclear watchdog, to carry out inspections on their territory. In spite of the DPRK's signing and ratification of the NPT, it flagrantly ignored the treaty's provisions and boasted of its nuclear arms ambitions.

The USSR's disappearance from the world stage opened the way for North Korea to play its own leading role without Moscow's restraining hand. Along with other Soviet clients, such as Iraq, Syria, and Libya, the DPRK strode belligerently on the global scene. Soon these and other kin of Cain were dubbed rogue states for their dangerous behavior, terrorist sponsorship, and nuclear-arming. They confounded—and still confound—American governments long after the Soviet Union slipped into the historical dustbin. North Korea's nuclear avariciousness made it of particular concern to Washington and its allied governments in Tokyo and Seoul, which were even more proximate to atomic blast or radioactive fallout from a nuclear test north of the DMZ.

Late in the George H.W. Bush presidency, the North Koreans inadvertently revealed that they were cheating on the NPT by developing a capacity for nuclear weapons. In reaction, the Pentagon canceled the planned redeployment of 6000 US troops out of South Korea until the United States determined Pyongyang's nuclear intentions. More pointedly, Colin Powell, Chairman of the Joint Chiefs of Staff, uncharacteristically threatened the DPRK, when he stated: "if they [the North Koreans] missed Desert Storm, this is a chance to catch a re-run" of America's crushing defeat of Iraq in early 1991.[35] Powell's allusion to the lopsided victory made Pyongyang reconsider its opposition to the arms inspections as specified in the NPT.

Accordingly, the DPRK opened its Yongbyon nuclear facility to the IAEA inspection team headed by Hans Blix in May, 1992. Determined to restore his reputation after missing Iraq's nuclear progress before the Persian Gulf War revealed it, Blix bore down hard on the North Korean technicians. Under intense scrutiny, the Yongybon officials inadvertently handed over self-incriminating information, indicating that in 1990 they had reprocessed some 90 grams of plutonium suitable for nuclear arms. This violation of the NPT led the CIA to conclude that the DPRK had extracted between 8 and 16 pounds of plutonium from spent fuel in the Yongbyon reactor—a sufficient amount to produce one or possibly two nuclear bombs. This concern constituted the origin of the apprehensions that only have deepened since.[36] At that time, Pyongyang tried to hide its nuclear breakthroughs. Later, it boasted of its destructive capacity.

The Bush administration reacted mildly to Pyongyang's possible nuclear capacity at the urging of South Korea. Seoul reached out to the DPRK by asking the United States to remove any irritants in cross-DMZ relations. Washington obliged and transferred all of its nuclear bombs and artillery shells from its South Korean bases. The Pentagon also announced the suspension for one year of its annual joint combat training exercises with ROK forces in 1992. The de-escalation of tensions produced a short-lived détente between the two Koreas. North and South entered into the Joint Declaration on the Denuclearization of the Korean Peninsula at the end of 1991. This agreement pledged both sides to abstain from possessing nuclear arms, reprocessing plutonium, or enriching uranium for weapons. Americans, South Koreans, and East Asians hailed the treaty as a diplomatic masterstroke leading to a pacific peninsula. In retrospect, it was the first of many purported breakthroughs that led to a temporary lull in tensions that Pyongyang soon abruptly shattered by violating.

As George H.W. Bush prepared to leave office, Washington learned from overhead satellites that North Korea was secretly reprocessing plutonium in violation of its treaty promises. The outgoing administration passed the intelligence to the incoming William J. Clinton government. The new comers—the first administration to take office in the post-Soviet environment—took up the job of addressing the rogue-nation peril, of which the DPRK was a leading threat. North Korea had figured not at all in candidate Clinton's campaign for residency in 1600 Pennsylvania Avenue. Even in his Inaugural Address in early 1993, the new president skipped over the then 37,000 US troops stationed in South Korea when he paid tribute to "the brave Americans serving our nation today in the Persian Gulf and Somalia."[37] Those US forces at the DMZ stood "eyeball to eyeball" with the world's fifth largest army commanded by a fanatical anti-American regime.

Two months into his presidency, Clinton faced a brewing crisis on the Korean peninsula. Thanks to the alerts from US satellites about plutonium reprocessing for possible nuclear arms, the IAEA chief, Hans Blix, called for another inspection of the North Korea's nuclear facilities. His request coincided with Washington's reinstatement of the joint US-South Korean military maneuvers known as Team Spirit—the annual exercises suspended by President Bush for one year only. The combining of the two events—both perceived as threats by the edgy DPRK regime—generated an explosive atmosphere on the war-divided peninsula. Kim Il Sung, the North's all-powerful ruler, summarily rejected the Blix's inspection request and placed the army on a war footing, which sent shockwaves into the South. He also served notice that when the 90-day notification period lapsed, North Korea planned on exiting the NPT. Throughout the spring, war seemed imminent. The neophyte administration in Washington was knocked back on its heels by the sudden blowup in East Asia, which could conceivably lead to a second Korean War.

The Clinton White House looked to China—the DPRK's main patron since the disintegration of the Soviet Union—for assistance in reining in the warlike North Korean regime. Beijing implausibly replied that it was without influence in Pyongyang. Yet, the PRC and North Korea were ruled by fraternal Communist regimes, which shared an anti-American antagonism. As time passed, the DPRK increasingly depended on the PRC for transfers of fuel, food, and diplomatic protection from adverse votes in the Security Council. Clinton interlocutors were not taken in by Chinese protestations but they hesitated to take China to task. The White House changed track and turned to a diplomatic solution. Over several months, American officials met their North Korean counterparts in Geneva, Beijing, and at the UN in New York City.

Eager to keep North Korea in the NPT, the American negotiators entertained a DPRK proposal that the George Bush White House had earlier rejected because it had thought acceptance of the deal represented giving into blackmail and rewarding bad behavior. Nonetheless, the Clinton foreign policy team opted to consider the offer. The North cleverly exploited its leverage—the threat to go nuclear—to the hilt. Pyongyang proposed that in return for halting plutonium reprocessing and suspending the construction of out-of-date graphite reactors it was open to using modern nuclear technology on its territory. Specifically, the North insisted on the latest light-water reactor (LWR). This state-of-the art technology boasted several appealing features. It operated on ordinary water and not the heavy water (deuterium oxide) of the 1950-type graphite reactors in use in North Korea. The LWR generated more electrical power. The new reactors appealed to Clinton, because they came with "proliferation-resistant" locks to inhibit (but not totally block) the bleeding off of plutonium for atomic arms.

The Clinton administration accepted the proposal, much to the consternation of its critics. The actualization of the offer took over a year as the administration hesitated and re-examined it. The White House considered sanctions, too. But Pyongyang counter-threatened that economic sanctions were the equivalent of a declaration of war on the DPRK, something Washington desired to avoid. Besides, international sanctions were unattainable due to China's likely veto in the Security Council.

Framing any decision toward North Korea was the widely shared expectation that the Stalinist state stood at the brink of falling into the historical trash bin, as had all the East European communist regimes. The longer the DPRK limped along, the more anticipation grew that its demise was just around the corner. If it was only a matter of time, why should the United States, South Korea, and their allies ensnarl themselves in a costly war with North Korea? The extravagant expenses in money and lives would make for the ultimate Pyrrhic victory. The surrealistic regime in Pyongyang, so the thinking went, was destined to implode as did communist dictatorships in Eastern Europe. Better to indulge Pyongyang and await the inevitability of its collapse were the underlying assumptions of every US administration from Clinton's.[38]

Before moving to conclude an LWR agreement with Pyongyang, Washington did examine an airstrike operation to eliminate insular state's nuclear arms capacity. The Pentagon shelved the planning because it lacked the certainty that its bombers could eliminate the entire Hermit Kingdom's nuclear weapons program. Sites hidden inside the North's craggy mountains rendered any absolute destruction unlikely. Moreover, an air attack risked kicking up radioactive dust over South Korea, Japan, and much of East Asia. Nuclear particles raining down on hapless populations ensured a diplomatic nightmare for the Washington. An airstrike also guaranteed a Korean War redux, for Pyongyang was all but certain to lash back in spades at South Korea. The North Korean army was equipped with a vast array of long-range artillery and multiple rocket launchers designed to level Seoul less than 40 miles from the DMZ.

Bleak prospects led the already risk-averse Clinton White House to conclude the game was not worth the candle by incurring a war on the Korean Peninsula. So, it looked to negotiations and some sort of face-saving, war-avoiding deal with Pyongyang. By spring 1994, the bellicose North Korean regime edged toward conflict in its white-hot rhetoric. Outraged by what it saw as American perfidy for not moving forward on the LWR negotiations begun the previous year, Pyongyang ceased cooperation with the IAEA. It verbally exploded at the US deployment of additional troops and Patriot anti-missile batteries into South Korea, which Washington meant to reassure its ally of America's commitment to its defense. Kim Il Sung, the North Korean dictator, perceived Washington's reinforcements as preparations for a war of aggression. Inside the ROK, the population braced for war. Its stock market sank. Its panicked population horded food and expressed their fears to the media.

Bent on circumventing a war with the pugilistic North Koreans, the Clinton administration dispatched Jimmy Carter as a high-level envoy to Chairman Kim. The former US president unshelved the Light Water Reactor offer of the previous year. Carter's presence and LWR deal calmed Pyongyang's bellicosity. Carter and Kim brokered the outline of a deal, which awaited weeks of hard bargaining later. Acting beyond his instructions, Carter stole the public relations spotlight from Clinton thereby angering the West Wing staff.[39] The White House, nonetheless, pocketed the accolades from averting a North-South conflict and bringing the insular Kim regime to the bargaining table.

Soon after Carter's return, American and North Korean diplomats took up negotiations in Geneva, Switzerland. Both sides excluded South Korean participation, something that greatly rankled Seoul. Thrashing out an agreement with the irascible DPRK interlocutors was no picnic for their US counterparts. But the bargaining hit an unexpected hurdle when Kim Sung Il died on July 8, 1994, reportedly of a heart failure. As the much-mythologized father of the North Korean nation, Kim's sudden passing cast the talks into doubt. His son and crown prince, Kim Jong Il, took the reins of power. Despite his different temperament and background, the khaki-clad Kim junior let the negotiations go forward after a

30-day mourning period for his father. As for Washington officials, they held that the agreement must be viewed in its totality. The policy mandarin optimistically envisioned a reconciled North Korea ready to engage with the South and the international community. Historically, these hopes were not the first, or the last, time that the Western mindset misjudged the true nature of war-prone totalitarian regimes.

The United States and the DPRK signed the Agreed Framework in Geneva on October 21, 1994. This complex accord obliged Pyongyang to cease refueling the Yongbyon reactor. Compliance required closing down the out-of-date reactor, for it generated plutonium, which had nuclear weapons applications. Yongbyon's 8000 spent plutonium rods were to be placed in a cooling pond overseen by the IAEA. The North Koreans also agreed to suspend building two graphic reactors of older design. Significantly, they affirmed their return to the NPT. The NPT allowed for peaceful nuclear development but forbid its signatories from chasing after atomic arms. The DPRK soon enough broke this promise along with casting aside other provisions of the Agreed Framework.

As for America, the accord's terms were substantial. The United States agreed to head up an international consortium of donors to build first one and then a second proliferation-resistant LWR, each capable of producing 2000 megawatts of power. South Korea and Japan ponied up the bulk of the funds. The North Korean plant was modeled on the South's reactors, which each cost $4.6 billion to build in the 1990s. As a face-saving stratagem for the DPRK, which refused to work directly with South Korean scientists and technicians, the United States and Japan fashioned the artifice—the Korean Energy Development Organization (KEDO). In reality, South Korea ran KEDO. Thus, the North Koreans worked with KEDO, and not expressly with the ROK. The South swallowed its pride and anger for having been excluded from the Geneva negotiations. Seoul valued its relationship with Washington much more than giving into temporary pique. To tide over the energy-strapped North Korea until the first LWR reactor came on line in 2003, Washington agreed to annual oil shipments of 500,000 metric tons for the destitute country's power generators. The construction of the reactors never came to fruition, because the faltering agreement completely unraveled in the first year of the George W. Bush administration.

Despite the failings of the Agreed Framework, it de-escalated tensions on the peninsula for a time. The resulting calm permitted cross-border business talks. Pyongyang and Seoul reached terms for South Korean industries to open light manufacturing factories just north of the militarized border. Over the many ups and downs in the cross-DMZ relations, the prickly communist regime closed these commercial enterprises on occasion but then let them reopen to garner hard currency for its empty state coffers. Thus, the thaw enabled a détente to emerge between the two nations. The North periodically punctured the tranquility by provocatively shelling Southern territory or, more ominously, pursuing nuclear arms and long-range missiles. Every subsequent American president dealt with a belligerent and nuclear-arming North Korea through a similar pattern of deterrence and blandishments.[40]

The Geneva accord prompted a healthy partisan reaction by skeptics, who perceived it as a modern-day Munich settlement. Republican Robert Dole, the Senate majority leader, sniffed that the bargain "shows it is always possible to get an agreement when you give enough away."[41] Because the White House structured the Agreed Framework to escape a vote on Capitol Hill, it could implement the terms without passage through the US Senate as called for by the Constitution with a formal treaty. In order to head off Republican opposition beyond Congress, the Clinton administration sent briefers to present their case for the agreement to former President Bush and many of his onetime aides. This tactic largely worked.[42] The agreement dissipated prospects for war—a possibility that even Clinton detractors of the accord wanted to avoid. In short, there was no Congressional war party beating a drum to fight the DPRK.

Clinton's negotiations fell easily within the disengagement cycle of American foreign policy. The North Korean accord also accentuated the mood of disassociation from world affairs. The agreement permitted Washington to pass the North Korean threat to his successors. The president's own personal domestic orientation and the public's desire for a post-Cold War "peace dividend" either in lower taxes or in additional spending on education, health care, infrastructure, and welfare restrained Washington from international adventures.[43] Besides, the conclusion of the North Korean deal coincided with an unfolding political and human drama in southeastern Europe with Yugoslavia's disintegration, which captured the news media's attention. The North Korean deal fell from public awareness days after it was concluded. Domestic issues captured John Q. Public's attention. The stunning Republican victories in the House and Senate in the mid-term elections on November 4, 1994, turned on domestic concerns as reflected in Congressman Newt Gingrich's and Richard Armey's Contract with America. All but one of the contracts' proposed policies centered on domestic problems. The contract resonated with voters. The Republicans gained 54 seats in the House and took control of that chamber for the first time in 40 years. Neither the DPRK nuclear accord nor Yugoslavia's dismemberment captured the American public's interest.

Notes

1. George Bush and Brent Scowcroft, *A World Transformed* (New York: Alfred A. Knopf, 1998), p. 128.
2. Elizabeth Drew, *On the Edge: The Clinton Presidency* (New York: Simon and Schuster, 1994), p. 138.
3. Ibid.
4. David Lauter, "Clinton Blasts Bush's Foreign Policy Record," *Los Angeles Times*, August 14, 1992, p. A 1.
5. Transcript of President Bill Clinton's Inaugural Address appeared under the title "We Force the Spring," *New York Times*, January 21, 1993, p. A 11.
6. Drew, *On the Edge*, p. 28.
7. Michael Spence, *The Next Convergence: The Future of Economic Growth in a Multispeed World* (New York: Farrar, Straus, and Giroux, 2011), pp. 56–60, 92–97, and 222–230.
8. Thomas L. Friedman, "Theory vs. Practice" Clinton's Stated Foreign Policy Turns into More Modest 'Self-Containment,'" *New York Times*, October 1, 1993, p. A 2.
9. Michael R. Gordon, "Christopher, in Unusual Cable, Defends State Depart.," *New York Times*, June 16, 1993, p. A 13.
10. Ibid.
11. Madeleine K. Albright, "Myths of Peace-Keeping," Statement Before the Subcommittee on International Organizations, and Human Rights of the House Committee of the House Committee on Foreign Affairs, June 24, 1993, cited in *U.S. Department of State Dispatch*, 4, Issue 26 (June 24, 1993), p. 46.
12. Mark Bowden, *Black Hawk Down: A Story of Modern Warfare* (New York: New American Library, 1999), p. 43.
13. Mark Bowden, "The Lessons of Mogadishu," *Wall Street Journal*, April 5, 2004, p. A 18.
14. Drew, *On the Edge*, p. 317.

15. Mark Bowden, *Black Hawk Down: A Story of Modern Warfare* (New York: New American Library, 1999), pp. 417–425.
16. Douglas Jehl, "Clinton Doubling U.S. Forces in Somalia, Vowing Troops Will Come Home in 6 Months," *New York Times*, October 8, 1993, p. A 1.
17. William G. Hyland, *Clinton's World: Remaking American Foreign Policy* (Westport, CT: Praeger, 1999), p. 58.
18. Eric Schmitt, "Somalia's First Lesson for Military Is Caution," *New York Times*, March 5, 1995, p. B 15.
19. L.R. Melvern, *A People Betrayed: The Role of the West in Rwanda's Genocide* (London: Zed Books, 2000), p. 26.
20. Michael Barnett, *Eyewitness to a Genocide: The United Nations and Rwanda* (Ithaca, NY: Cornell University Press, 2002), pp. 149–151.
21. Bill Clinton, *My Life* (New York: Alfred A. Knopf, 2004), p. 609.
22. Holly J. Burkhalter, "The Question of Genocide. The Clinton Administration and Rwanda," *World Policy Journal*, 11, Issue 4 (Winter, 1994–1995), 53.
23. Samantha Power, *A Problem from Hell: America and the Age of Genocide* (New York: Basic Books, 2002), pp. 354–357, 505, and 520.
24. Clinton, *My Life*, p. 782.
25. David Lauer, "Clinton Blasts Bush's Foreign Policy Record," *Los Angeles Times*, August 14, 1992, p. A 1.
26. William G. Hyland, *Clinton's World: Remaking American Foreign Policy* (Westport, CT: Praeger, 1999), p. 65.
27. Madeleine Albright, *Madam Secretary* (New York: Miramax Books, 2003), p. 156.
28. Robert Fatton, Jr., *Haiti's Predatory Republic: The Unending Transition to Democracy* (Boulder, CO: Lynne Rienner, 2002), p. 93.
29. Raymond A. Joseph, "The Haitian Imbroglio," *Wall Street Journal*, April 6, 2004, p. A 16.
30. David Malone, *Decision-Making in the UN Security Council: The Case of Haiti* (New York: Oxford University Press, 1998), p. 101.
31. Richard D. Lyons, "U.N. Authorizes Invasion of Haiti to be Led by U.S.," *New York Times*, August 1, 1994, p. A 1.
32. Douglas Jehl, "From Haiti, Images of a Foreign Policy Success," *New York Times*, April 11, 1995, p. A 4.

33. William J. Clinton, State of the Union Address, January 23, 1996, U.S. Capitol. Downloaded from http://www.presidency.ucsb.edu/ws/?pid=53091. Accessed July 20, 2016.
34. Presidential Approval Rating—Bill Clinton, January 10, 2001. Downloaded from http://www.gallup.com/poll/116584/presidential-approval-ratings-bill-clinton.aspx. Accessed July 20, 2016.
35. David F. Sanger, "Cheney, in Korea Orders Halt to U.S. Pullout," *New York Times*, December 22, 1991, p. A 7.
36. Michael J. Mazarr, *North Korea and the Bomb: A Case Study in Nonproliferation* (New York: St. Martin's Press, 1995), pp. 82–88.
37. A transcript of President Bill Clinton's Inaugural Address, "We Force the Spring," *New York Times*, January 21, 1993, p. A 11.
38. Thomas H. Henriksen, *America and the Rogue States* (New York: Palgrave Macmillan, 2012), p. 143, and Paul French, *North Korea: State of Paranoia* (London: Zed Books, 2014), pp. 389–390.
39. Joel S. Wit, Daniel B. Poneman, and Robert L. Gallucci, *Going Critical: The First North Korean Crisis* (Washington, DC: Brookings Institution Press, 2004), pp. 221–238.
40. Victor Cha, *Impossible State: North Korea, Past and Future* (New York: HarperCollins, 2012), pp. 275–299.
41. Gerald F. Seib, "In North Korea: The Trouble Starts in Credibility Gap," *Wall Street Journal*, October 21, 1994, p. A 20.
42. Wit, Poneman, and Gallucci, *Going Critical*, pp. 337–339.
43. Bob Woodward, *The Agenda: Inside the Clinton White House* (New York: Simon & Schuster, 1994), pp. 126–133.

CHAPTER 5

Bill Clinton and Reluctant Interventions into the Balkans

"Our patience will achieve more than our force." —Edmund Burke

The Clinton administration tried to chart a course between Scylla and Charybdis in the Balkans, just as it had sailed through the Somali and Haiti crises. In those two latter humanitarian episodes, the White House sustained blows to its political rigging but escaped a shipwreck on deadly rocks. In his initial approach to the European tinderbox, Bill Clinton merely followed in the slipstream of his predecessor. George Bush Sr. avoided the breakup of Yugoslavia as if it were a medieval plague. The bloody turmoil, nevertheless, was not in a faraway place like Somalia, Haiti, or Rwanda. It could not be brushed aside, for it lay in the center of Eastern Europe and bumped up against member states within the NATO—America's premier alliance. Still, Americans and the White House both preferred to stand on the sidelines of history to escape a messy and violent ethnic war among the constituent parts of Yugoslavia. Humanitarian tragedy it was, but it held strategic consequences, which neither Somalia, nor Haiti, or Rwanda did. Despite its often Pilate-like stance, the Clinton White House still could not wash its hands of the problem.

T.H. Henriksen, *Cycles in US Foreign Policy since the Cold War*,
DOI 10.1007/978-3-319-48640-6_5

Background to the Balkan Morass

The roots of the Yugoslavian splintering lay not in the stars but in history. For centuries, the mini-nationalistic polities of southeastern Europe were seen as fractious, exclusionary, xenophobic, provincial, and self-contained. Their nature, in fact, gave rise to the term *balkanization* meaning a fragmented patchwork of smoldering ethnic and religious rivalries. The latter-day Austro-Hungarian Empire managed to rule over the region by practicing a nineteenth-century version of multiculturalism and semi-autonomy. Even its loose hold was repeatedly contested by nationalistic subjects. Serbia, one of its key territories, lit the fuse that exploded the powder keg when a Serbian student shot to death the Austrian Archduke Ferdinand in Sarajevo in July 1914. His assassination set in motion a chain of events culminating in World War I. Because the Balkans riveted the attention of Russia, Britain, Germany, and other European states for over a hundred years, the victorious powers after the 1914–1918 war resolved to put things right in the tumultuous arena.

Believing that a larger geographical state would be more economically and politically viable, the Great Powers recognized the self-creation of Yugoslavia after World War I as a constitutional monarchy. The mini-states came together on their own volition. The Versailles conference did not impose a political construct on the peoples in southeast Europe. It was made up from former principalities within the Austro-Hungarian and Ottoman empires. Initially, it was named the Kingdom of Serbs, Croats, and Slovenes. In 1929, the Balkan kingdom changed its name to Yugoslavia, reflecting its southern Slavic population. A decade later, Nazi Germany overran Yugoslavia to use as a gateway for invasion into the Soviet Union. Along with its Axis partners, Italy and Hungary, Berlin subdivided Yugoslavia into enclaves ruled over by Germans, Italians, or Hungarians. The occupation touched off a ferocious backlash. The bitter internecine struggle among anti-Axis resistance movements sowed toxic seeds for Yugoslavia's breakup half a century later.

After World War II, Yugoslavia joined the Soviet bloc. Ruled by Marshal Josip Broz Tito, an anti-Nazi guerrilla chieftain, the country broke with Moscow in 1948. Thereafter, it charted a semi-independent course from the Kremlin and toward its own version of socialism. Under Tito, Yugoslavia wrote a new constitution recognizing the realities of its political divisions. Its federalism provided for some autonomy to its six republics—Croatia, Bosnia and Herzegovina, Macedonia, Montenegro,

Serbia, and Slovenia. Two semi-autonomous territories—Vojvodina and Kosovo—were linked to Serbia. All the entities, therefore, were subsumed within the Federal Republic of Yugoslavia (FRY). What national cohesion existed began to dissolve after the 1980 death of Tito, who managed to hold the country together by force of personality and astute politics.

The five decades of communism failed to melt away Yugoslavia's ethnic differences and forge unity among the country's ethno-nationalities. Each clung to its respective tribal identity. The Soviet Union's collapse released pent-up ethnic nationalism within the fragmenting FRY. The divisions were made worse by Slobodan Milošević, a onetime communist functionary, who won the Serbian presidency on an election platform laced with pathological nationalism that he aimed against other ethnic communities, which looked to their own deliverances from Serbia. He tapped into animosities in a land where, to adapt William Faulkner's comment about the American South, where the past is not dead; it is not even past. Reawakening the Serb's sense of victimhood, Milošević enflamed passions across Yugoslavia's 24 million people. Croats, Slovenes, and Bosnians rebelled against Serbia's bid for dominance within Yugoslavia. Belgrade reacted by sending its military forces to crush the breakaway republics. The Serb militias engaged in extrajudicial killings, systematic rape, and intimidation. The aggrieved nationalities soon embraced similar "ethnic cleansing" atrocities against the Serbian peoples on their soil. In time, the macabre scenes erupting from Yugoslavia resembled the depiction in the *Book of Revelations* of the Four Horsemen of the Apocalypse—Pestilence, War, Famine, and Death.

Bill Clinton and the Slow Rescue

Uncorked by spiraling violence, the fermenting ethno-sectarianism of Yugoslavia's breakup poured onto the desks of the incoming Clinton administration. During his campaign for the presidency, candidate Clinton took issue with President Bush's inaction in the Balkan crisis. Once in the Oval Office, the new commander-in-chief soon walked in his predecessor's steps. Warren Christopher, the arriving secretary of state, signaled the new administration's non-involvement message during an appearance on CBS's Face the Nation program: "[T]he United States simply doesn't have the means to make people in that region of the world like each other."[1] Two weeks later, the president himself echoed similar disengagement sentiments when he intoned: "The United States should always seek an opportunity to stand up against—at least speak out against—inhumanity."[2] Speaking out, however, was as far as he was willing to go. Throughout Clinton's early handling of the Bosnian crisis, he faced criticism at home and internationally from human rights groups and media commentators. He dismissed and deflected the invective as best he could until he changed course near the 1996 presidential election. Overall, he did enough to appear half-responsive to the plight of the Bosnian victims in the meantime.

Like previous and future administrations in non-interventionist cycles, the Clinton White House looked to troop-less approaches by falling back on airstrikes alone. Because American airpower was often a ready weapon to avoid deploying ground forces, it became *the* instrument of choice, after economic sanctions. The internal discussion among Clinton policy makers revealed divisions. Colin Powell adamantly opposed sending American GIs in harm's way until the White House put forward clear political objectives for ground forces. The Chair of the Joint Chiefs of Staff despaired of the way America backed into the Vietnam War without a set of precise priorities. His hesitancy set off Madeleine Albright in what was a widely quoted outburst. The US representative to the UN (before being named secretary of state) declared: "What's the point of having this superb military that you're always talking about if we can't use it?" The four-star Army general shot back that US armed forces did not consist of "toy soldiers" to be "moved around on some sort of global game board." In his thinking, "tough political goals" must be defined first so that military forces "would accomplish their mission."[3]

The Clinton foreign policy team next searched for coalition partners for its "lift and strike" blueprint. This strategy proposed lifting the arms embargo, which hurt the outgunned Bosniaks more than the Serbs, who had access to the central Yugoslav armories. To compel the Serbs to allow the flow of humanitarian supplies, the United States also advocated striking them with air bombardments. The plan went nowhere with America's allies. The British and French, who supplied most of the soldiers in UNPROFOR, scuttled it out of fear that the Serbian military would lash back at their forces. London and Paris argued that Washington first commit soldiers to the UN peacekeeping mission before launching airstrikes. Even as Christopher traveled to Europe to sell the lift and strike option, his boss went "south on this policy." White House aides reported that Clinton's "heart isn't in it" because of doubts about settling the bitter ethnic feuds. But the US administration blamed the Europeans, since Washington had no policy except to state "all options are on the table."[4]

So, the policy makers returned to the lift-strike strategy. Four months later, in August 1993, Christopher finally won over the Europeans for NATO airstrikes, but only if both NATO and the UN agreed to targets. Because Russia held a veto on the Security Council and defended its ally Serbia, the so-called dual key arrangement never worked. Moscow always stood against aerial attacks against its Serbian dependency.[5]

The Clinton White House sought out other ways to keep the United States at arm's length from becoming embroiled in the Balkans. It latched onto a year-old prescription from the International Committee of the Red Cross (ICRC). The ICRC proposed "safe areas" to protect the endangered Bosniaks inside Bosnia-Herzegovina. Pushed by the Europeans, the Security Council passed Resolution 824 that embodied the "safe area" concept the next year on May 6, 1993. This resolution identified several Muslim-populated urban centers—Bihac, Gorazde, Sarajevo, Tuzla, and Srebrenica—to be safe areas. As such, the designated safe areas were to be "free from armed attacks and from any other hostile acts." The resolution, however, carefully skirted the term "safe havens," which connoted a legal definition in international law of immunity for refugees inhabiting them.

Until it designated geographical safe areas, the UN strove to stay neutral in the ethnic-sectarian conflict. Declaring an area safe signaled a departure in UN neutrality for the world body now saw the besieged Muslims as its wards.[6] The irony and tragedy of the so-called safe areas was that they became the most unsafe places. Srebrenica, in fact, was the scene of the most savage massacre of the entire war, where over 8000 Muslim boys and men were shot to death by Bosnian Serb Army in July 1995.

When the Clinton administration backed the Europeans' safe-area proposal, it masked its failure to win London and Paris over to its lift and strike alternative. More tellingly, it provided political cover for American disengagement from active leadership, while the Washington passed the blame and responsibility to the Europeans for the Yugoslav morass. In non-subtle language, Warren Christopher testified before the House Foreign Affairs Committee that Yugoslavia "at heart ... is a European problem."[7] Even with the Secretary of State's Pilate-esque testimony, the administration failed to scrub its hands of the worsening Balkans crisis. Within the United States, the plight of the besieged Muslims ignited a liberal internationalist movement to take up Bosnia's cause.[8] In time, liberal internationalism exerted political pressure through media commentary on the Clinton administration to go to the aid of Europe's latest victims of genocidal-type crimes.

Being Drawn into the Balkans

Try as it might to stay on the sidelines, the Clinton administration felt compelled again by the reportage of more atrocities to attempt collective action through NATO rather than unilaterally intervening. Joined by Paris, Washington won over NATO. The Atlantic alliance issued a ten-day ultimatum to the Bosnian Serbs to withdraw their heavy weapons from the highlands around Sarajevo. Washington also prevailed on Boris Yeltsin, the Russian president, to strong-arm the Serbs, who looked to Moscow for diplomatic bolstering. The Kremlin leaned hard on its client. As a result, the Serbs pulled out their guns and let 400 Russian troops serving in UNPROFOR file into their vacated trenches. Next, two American F-16 warplanes, operating within the NATO framework, blew four Serbian aircraft out of the sky for violating the "no-fly" zone imposed by the UN in October 1992. This aerial battling represented the first military action by NATO in its history to date.

Finally, Washington prodded NATO into "pinprick bombing" of Serb forces besetting Gorazde, one of the safe areas, ostensibly to protect the town's small peacekeeping contingent inside. Clinton praised the modest defensive bombardment: "This is a clear expression of the will of NATO and the will of the United Nations."[9] Incrementally, the United States edged away from its sedentary approach. Yet, the Clinton White House remained reluctant about entering foreign military ventures. Its tentative behavior during early 1994 took place at time of the horrendous atrocities in Rwanda noted in the previous chapter. The Clinton administration hesitated to become involved in either crisis, lest US forces suffer casualties as in the Black Hawk Down incident in Somalia a year earlier. One Clinton official explained the White House's inaction: "We were getting beaten up for Somalia, we were under siege for conducting 'foreign policy as social work' for being too concerned with humanitarian issues, the president's political capital was low and waning, we had become risk averse."[10]

Congressional opposition to what it interpreted as Clintonian dithering added a spur to administration policy makers. Pushed by Republican lawmakers, Capitol Hill even passed a bill to scrap the embargo on arms shipments to Bosnian Muslims so as to even the playing field with the Serbs. The president vetoed the legislation in August 1994, dismissing the law as tantamount "to the wrong step at the wrong time."[11] Yet, Congressional prodding and liberal internationalist advocacy had an effect on the White House's political calculations as the 1996 presidential campaign rose on the horizon. Even prior to announcing his presidential candidacy, Republican Senate leader Bob Dole joined a procession of critics, from the political left and right, to rail against Clinton's disengaged Balkan policy. Finally, the president reversed himself and gave a sop to his critics. Triangulating the restrictions, Clinton cleverly stated that the United States would no longer enforce the sanctions but left the armament quarantine in effect.[12]

Two Washington initiatives in 1994 eventually led to the peace settlement in Dayton, Ohio the following year. First, Clinton envoys patched up the former Muslim-Croat alliance that had broken down in early 1993, when the Bosnian Croats hived off their own statelet of Herceq-Bosna from the larger Bosnia-Herzegovina. American diplomats resorted to carrots and sticks to induce Croatia to corral its fellow countrymen in their mini-state in western Herzegovina to rejoin the front against the Bosnia Serbs. Washington's representative threatened sanctions against Croatia proper if it resisted. Clinton delegations also went to Germany, the main backer of Croatia, to exert leverage on the fledgling country. The stratagem succeeded. Croatia's President Franjo Tudjman pulled his protective 30,000 troops from the tiny Bosnian enclave until it agreed to re-enter the pact with the Bosnian Muslims. Tudman and his Bosnian Muslim counterpart Alija Izetbegović met in the White House to sign the Washington agreement, thereby escaping the international ostracism that befell Bosnian Serbs.

Signed under duress, the Croat-Muslim Federation fell well short of being a pact of fraternal brothers. Nevertheless, the arrangement functioned well enough to end the fighting between the two communities. Additionally, the armaments flowing through Croatian territory to the Bosniaks were no longer "taxed" by skimming off a percentage. Not all the arms flowed from above-board sources. It came to light after the Dayton settlement that the President Clinton approved a highly irregular source of transferred weaponry—Iran. The president authorized Iranian arms to help redress the Bosniaks' dearth of military hardware. Clinton's green light to the armament shipments contravened international agreements and betrayed Western allies. Members of Congress voiced disapproval but the incident soon passed from the nation's front pages.[13] For Clinton, the underhanded deal enabled him to get arms to the Bosniaks without Congressional or international approval. Opponents worried about arming a Muslim Trojan Horse that might threaten Western countries in time. Two decades later, some assault rifles did find their way into the hands of terrorists in France and Belgium. But hardly anyone remembered in 2016 the apprehensions voiced about the Iranian arms transfers, eventually contributing to terrorism.

America's second major initiative in 1994 drew Russia into the diplomatic inner circle to dampen the Yugoslav firestorm. As the principle backer of the Serbs, with whom it shared the Orthodox faith and a related culture, Russia's concurrence was the key to any settlement. If the Kremlin stood outside a peace framework, its stance presaged a return to Cold War divisions between East and West as well as guaranteed failure to bring peace to southeastern Europe. As a means to draw in Russia along with other powers, Washington joined in forming the Contact Group, which was made up of Britain, France, Germany, Russia, and the United States. Reminiscent of Great Power conferences of the nineteenth century, the Contact Group deliberated on terms and even maps to impose on the warring factions. When the Contact Group first put forward boundaries to the battling contestants in Geneva in July 1994, it got a unanimous reply—the breakaway mini-states all rejected the borders. The rejections entailed consequences that soon played out together with a dramatic turn of events that brought the conflict to a close.

The United States took advantage of the fissures that opened between Pale and Belgrade. The Bosnian Serbs' hard-line stance widened a rift with their key patron—Serbia. The Serbian president Slobodan Milošević desperately needed to have the international sanctions lifted on the squeezed economies in Serbia and Montenegro, which constituted the rump of the former Yugoslavia. Even before the Contact Group's extended an olive branch, Milošević had grown weary of his Bosnian Serb counterpart, Radovan Karadžić, whose stridency and histrionics repelled the Serb chieftain. Karadžić's refusal to compromise with the Contact Group widened intra-Serb divisions that the American delegation exploited before and during the Dayton negotiations.

A re-alignment of the political stars within Western Europe and the United States also played a part in eventual talks to broker a peace settlement. In France, the center-right politician Jacques Chirac won his third effort to capture the presidency in spring 1995. He turned French policy away from his predecessor's pro-Serbian orientation that harkened back to World War II. The Balkans' dangerous history, in fact, infused Chirac's thinking about the area. A palpable fear took shape in the minds of many about the recurrence of a World War I-type scenario, in which an incident could spark a wider war drawing in other powers. Chirac felt that the intensifying Balkan violence threatened to spill over into nearby countries, especially Bulgaria, Greece, Turkey, and even Russia unless extinguished.

In Britain, the Prime Minister John Major initially bucked Washington's lift and strike proposal as a threat to British troops serving as peacekeepers and as an invitation to a wider war. Criticized from within his Conservative Party by Margaret Thatcher, Major came around to the same disillusionment with the Serbs as the French and others expressed. Disenchantment peaked with the Serb cause, when a demonic atrocity occurred in mid-1995.

The United States and its quarrelsome Western European allies reached a watershed moment with the Republika Srpska and their prime backers in Serbia because of what occurred in a small town in easternmost Bosnia-Herzegovina. At Srebrenica (meaning the "place of silver" for its mining), one of the six UN-designated safe areas, the population had ballooned to over 40,000 destitute refugees from one of around 8000 villagers. When the Bosnian Serb militias and Serbia's regular army overran the safe area, they rounded up some 8000 boys and men, and in cold-blood mowed them down in the worst single atrocity since 1945. To their great shame, 400 Dutch UN peacekeeper idly stood by during the mass killings. When information transpired to the outside world, the news shook apart the diplomatic apparatus that contributed to the Srebrenica catastrophe.

But before a political re-alignment took place, there came the realization that the raging war must be stopped or it would endanger regionwide stability, dragging NATO into a possible conflict with Russia or Greece, as Serbia's allies. For their part, the Serb militaries heedlessly rolled on seizing Žepa, another safe area to the west of Srebrenica. The sad irony about the fall of the two Muslim enclaves lay in the fact that their elimination facilitated ethnically pure territories, largely in the control of one or the other ethnic-sectarian communities. Thus, the removal of Žepa and Srebrenica resulted in Serb-dominated lands, making the countryside ethnically purer than the previous configuration of "two spidery states, with thousands of kilometers of proposed borders."[14] Elsewhere a similar phenomenon was taking place, only it was the Serbs who were pushed off the land by an American-instigated attack against them.

Using an indirect approach to defeat the Bosnian Serbs, the Clinton policy makers turned to private military contractors to shape up the Croatian militia to fight the Serbian forces. Washington wanted to stay clear of direct US military intervention into an active war zone, just as it refrained from contributing soldiers to UNPROFOR. The State Department licensed and hired Military Professional Resources Incorporated (MPRI) to train the disorganized Croatian military in October 1994. Made up of former US military personnel, MPRI instructed what were little more than militias in modern tactics and operations.[15]

Early in August 1995, Croatia mounted a furious offensive against the Serb-controlled Krajina pocket. To the surprise of outsiders, including the CIA, the Croatians staged a blitzkrieg-like advance. In their Operation Storm, the Croatians swept aside the Serb defenders, seized territory, and shattered the Serbian myth of military invincibility. The Bosnian Muslims also went on the offensive against the hard-pressed Serb troops. The American plan succeeded in reversing the Serbian gains and counterbalancing Belgrade on the ground without employing US armed forces.

A hesitant-to-enter-the-conflict Clinton found his footing in the topsy-turvy Balkan politics. The White House kept the appropriate congressional committees informed of its plans, thereby lessening opposition from Capitol Hill. Its use of a private company to assist the Croatian martial recovery proved effective and creative, despite detractors of what they saw as mercenaries being sent to Croatia.[16] President Clinton's officials did much to re-orientate NATO during the event-filled summer, 1995. Working with allied defense ministers, Washington obtained an historic agreement that NATO, not the UN, would be the arbiter of airpower in the Balkans. This new arrangement canceled the unworkable dual-key formula that required clearance from the Security Council before bombing.

Rather than unilaterally entering the fray, the United States chose the political camouflage of a multilateral effort, which also spared it from deploying ground forces. NATO afforded the United States a semblance of international authority as well as the moral support of its allies. The new NATO air policy paved the way for the alliance to bomb Serb forces as the Croatian forces attacked them on ground. By this time, the Bosnian Serbs had alienated both Moscow and Belgrade, making them stand alone and vulnerable to NATO airstrikes. A sense of brutal realism engulfed the White House, when it turned a blind eye to Croatian ethnic cleansing perpetrated against Serbs living in Krajina.[17] The United States engineered a transformed political landscape by helping the Croatian martial recovery, getting NATO realigned from a fading anti-Soviet pact to a regional peacekeeper that prepared it for the Kosovo conflict four years later, and checking the Bosnian Serb aggression, while splitting Pale from Belgrade and even Moscow.

Washington worked to clinch a diplomatic breakthrough given the changed political environment. President Clinton stepped up his interest in reaching a settlement of the four-year conflict. He dispatched Richard Holbrooke, the newly confirmed Assistant Secretary of State for European Affairs, to take up a form of shuttle diplomacy among the Balkan players and European capitals. America's crisis diplomacy received a fresh spurt from another Bosnian Serb atrocity in Sarajevo, when Serb gunners again lobbed a mortar shell into the city's central marketplace, killing 38 people. In addition to being a reminder of Serb callousness, the bombshell was interpreted by Washington policy mandarins as a slap in the face to their renewed diplomatic effort. Thus, the crime demanded a disproportionate response to address the political as well as humanitarian sin.

The United States struck back furiously under the NATO aegis. The American-led NATO bombing firestorm struck Serb emplacements around Sarajevo in Operation Deliberate Force with 60 warplanes from US bases in Italy and the aircraft carrier *USS Theodore Roosevelt* sailing in the Adriatic Sea.[18] French and British artillery shells also fell on the Serb trenches. Hammed by airstrikes, the Bosnian Serbs consented to end the siege of Sarajevo. The local Bosnian Serbs thought they could hang tough but Milošević realized it was wiser to cut their losses and deal with the Americans. He forced them to accept his diplomatic mediation on their behalf and compelled them to sign the so-called Patriarch Paper (the head of the Serbian Orthodox Church witnessed the signing) granting Milošević "virtually total power over the fate of the Bosnian Serbs."[19]

Dayton and a Pax Americana

By mid-1995, the United States stayed disengaged from a ground war but Holbrooke led the peace talks to end the Yugoslav civil war. President Clinton wanted the political liability behind him before the 1996 presidential elections. For the most part, however, he took a backseat in the diplomatic activities that brought a resolution to the war in Europe's southeast corner.[20] He took a much higher-profile role in the Northern Ireland peace settlement than in the Balkan's reconciliation. In the last hours of his presidency, he recalled in the Oval Office "all the calls and meetings I'd had in that room on Northern Ireland, the Middle East, Russia, Korea, and domestic struggles."[21] He made no mention in his autobiography's concluding paragraph of the Yugoslav dilemma.

The hard-charging Richard Holbrooke took center stage in the Balkan drama's last act. The territorial and political resolution brokered at Dayton, Ohio, required braiding the local strands among the antagonistic Balkan participants and the self-interested neighboring powers, especially Russia, into a complex and comprehensive settlement. To do so involved hands-on diplomacy and deal-making par excellence. In a word, it was no mean feat. On the ground, Holbrooke and his associates got Croatia to halt its advance and return its army to the barracks. In return, the American diplomats promised Franjo Tudjman to seek the re-incorporation of eastern Slavonia within Croatian sovereignty. The United States equally pressed the Bosnian president, Alija Izetbegović, to break off the Muslim units from the joint counterattack against the Bosnian Serbs. Like the Croatian leader, he realized that American goodwill at the settlement talks was worth more than a few extra miles of real estate. Besides, the Americans might ground their warplanes, denying the anti-Serb forces close air support.

By the time the guns fell silent in late September 1995, the territorial geometry had been greatly reshaped. Prior to the Croatian-Muslim counterassault, Karadžić's militias held about 75 percent of the former Bosnia-Herzegovina mini-state. Now, the Republika Srpska holdings had been shrunk to about one half. Its geographical size almost matched the allocation meted out by the Contact Group meeting back in Geneva, although the configuration on the ground differed.

The years-long diplomatic logjam had been broken apart by local military advances on the ground, by changes in the relations among the players, and by alterations within the respective political entities themselves. When the Croatian and Muslim militaries marched toward Banja Luka, a major Bosnian Serb city, the United States halted the attack. Washington feared that the fleeing refugees might force Milošević to act on their behalf, although he was tired of propping up the Frankenstein monster that he helped create. Milošević looked to his own survival as the leader of Serbia. American negotiators sensed his desperation and irritation with Karadžić.[22] For their part, they needed Milošević as a dealmaker against the strident ultra-Serb chauvinists in Pale and in Serbia itself during the Dayton meetings later in the year.

As Washington saw the political tides break toward a negotiated settlement, it still needed to fit the Russian piece onto the chessboard. If the Kremlin went along with Washington, then the Serbs stood without a major patron. Additionally, the American diplomats shared the goal with London, Paris, and other NATO members of building a new post-Soviet relationship with a friendly and cooperative Moscow. Washington cultivated Boris Yeltsin, the Russian Federation president, to bring him into the diplomatic circle to resolve the Balkan war. President Clinton directly involved himself by meeting with Tudjman and Izetbegović in New York City. He asked the presidents of Croatia and Bosnia-Herzegovina to fly to Moscow and meet with Yeltsin "to do something for the peace process." Clinton wanted to "send a signal to the Serbs, and to allow the Russian people to see that he [Yeltsin] is part of the [peace] process."[23] Such a visit was to flatter the Russian leader and boost the prospects of his favored candidates in the upcoming Duma elections. Neither Balkan president was enthusiastic about their Moscow mission; but they accommodated the United States. And Washington secured its ulterior designs of a benign Russia, at least for a while.

The so-named Dayton Accords were a product of the 21-day negotiations convened at the Wright-Patterson Air Force Base in Dayton, Ohio starting on November 1, 1995. Washington summoned the parties to the relative obscurity and remoteness of an air base far from major urban centers to impede leaks about the progressing talks to the media. This tactic largely succeeded. The top American representatives were Secretary of State Warren Christopher and Richard Holbrooke, the architect of the talks. Croatia, Bosnia-Herzegovina, and Serbia (or FRY) each dispatched their respective presidents. Noticeably absent, if not missed, was Radovan Karadžić, the president of Republika Srpska. His role in atrocities sealed his exclusion from deliberations. He and General Ratko Mladić, who presided over the Srebrenica mass slaughter, were under indictment for war crimes and crimes against humanity by the International Criminal Tribunal for the former Yugoslavia. They risked arrest by traveling outside of the Republika Srspska. Serbia acted on behalf of the Bosnian Serb Republic as well as its own interests.

Marked by intense squabbles within a pressure cooker atmosphere inside the air force base's Hope Conference Center, the representatives collided over boundaries and the amount of square miles within each enclave. The Contract Group's percentage allocation among the contenders prevailed despite the fierce arguments over what specific lands fell within the borders. The Serbs within the Republika Srpska slugged it out to capture 49 percent of the fractured Bosnia-Herzegovina, while the three-president-structured Muslim-Croat Federation got the balance, including the long-besieged Sarajevo. To keep the talks on track, the Americans undertook an interior "shuttle diplomacy" of meeting with the protagonists separately and then conveying their demands to the others. Otherwise, direct contact among the sectarian-ethnic parties was almost certain to lead to a breakdown in the negotiations. Richard Holbrooke starred as the interlocutor-in-chief cycling back and forth among the delegations, arm twisting, cajoling, and deal-making to reach an agreement.[24]

Formally known as the General Framework Agreement for Peace in Bosnia and Herzegovina, the settlement called for the continuation of the October 5 cease-fire, respect for the sovereignty of the fractured Balkan states, resolution of issues peacefully, and respect for human rights as well as rights of refugees and displaced persons. Along with the Framework, there were 11 pertinent annexes and maps. It was initialed by the three regional presidents and by the representatives for the Contact Group. On December 14, 1995, the Dayton Accords were formally signed in the Élysée Palace. President Clinton witnessed the signing along with the other heads of state from the Contact Group.[25]

The Dayton Accords also laid out a military plan to execute its terms. The Implementation Force (IFOR), with a grant of UN authority, deployed days after the Paris signing ceremony. IFOR relieved UNPROFOR, the UN peacekeeping force, and took up peace-soldiering duties for what was advertised as a one-year commitment. The Oval Office committed just 20,000 troops toward the goal of 60,000 with the balance from 25 other NATO nations and non-NATO countries. The Russians participated with their own commanding general officer, although they had to accept subordination to the US command structure. It was the first time since 1945 that the United States and Russia cooperated militarily. The bulk of the soldiers were garrisoned in Bosnia and Herzegovina, where they separated and disarmed the former combatants. Surprisingly, IFOR encountered only sporadic demonstrations of hostility which petered out over the next months, allaying the worst fears of politicians and pundits.

At the time of entry, the American government had to "sell" involvement in the venture to its citizenry. President Clinton assured Americans in a television address that their participation in the peace force was in the country's national interest. Taking into account America's disengagement mood, the American leader announced a one-year timeframe. In reality, Washington knew that the IFOR mandate would have to be extended. As the December 20, 1996, endpoint neared, Clinton administration postponed it again and again prior to nixing the mission. In 2004, NATO transferred the mission to the EU, leaving only some 700 US troops in place.

Adding to the plausible danger that the swirling Bosnian vortex might draw Russia and Western Europe into a reprise of World War I, there was another cloud on the horizon. An obscure mujahedeen from the anti-Soviet resistance in wartime Afghanistan visited Sarajevo in 1994. Osama bin Laden offered his hosts the services of former guerrilla fighters and material support to his fellow Muslims. Before the Bosnian conflict subsided, mujahedeen journeyed to aid the Bosniaks from Saudi Arabia, Libya, and Kuwait. This trickle of fighters was an early version of the underground pipeline of youths streaming into Syria and Iraq in the chaotic aftermath of the Arab Spring. The Dayton Accords nipped this budding jihad before it took root.

The Dayton Accords' enactment brought to a conclusion the 4-year war, which killed 250,000 people and displaced or made refugees of another 2 million. Thus Yugoslavia's disintegration recorded the worst, war-related suffering and mass atrocities in Europe since the Holocaust and World War II itself. In a statement which he later abandoned for its implied criticism of the Clinton administration, Holbrooke wrote that the Yugoslav Wars "as the greatest collective security failure of the West since the 1930s."[26] Because of its disinclination to engage energetically, the United States shared responsibility for the collective failure and the costs it entailed.

Prior to resolution of the Bosnian crisis, US foreign policy officials were stung by criticism about mediocre American leadership early in the conflict. They pointed to achievements in securing NAFTA and General Agreement on Tariffs and Trade (GATT) trade agreements, developing relations with Baltic nations, and wooing former Soviet republics. So long as Yugoslavia bled, the perception persisted that America stood in the diplomatic shadows, while the carnage engulfed southeastern Europe. The Dayton Agreement and the IFOR went off cleanly, redeeming Clinton's foreign policy from charges of waffling and "ad hocism," if not murderous neglect and callous disregard for mass suffering. It did much to restore American leadership and prestige. The Euro-American cooperation after Dayton ended the worst chapter in transatlantic relations since Suez Canal in 1956, when Dwight Eisenhower clashed with the Anglo-French-Israeli intervention in Egypt. Without a Soviet threat to rally Western Europe to America's side, Europeans were prone to resent Washington "for *too much* leadership" in Holbrooke's words.[27] No resolution was final, however. The outbreak of violence in Kosovo was the other shoe dropping in the sectarian and ethnically charged Balkans.

Kosovo: The Balkans' Second Round

Just as World War I led to World War II, the Yugoslav Wars laid the groundwork for the Kosovo conflict. None of this was widely apparent in the afterglow of the Dayton peace. But it should have been because the Connecticut-sized enclave brimmed with same ethnic pathologies that had wracked the rest of Yugoslavia. Locking away the skeletons of war, ethno-sectarian hatred, and revenge in the Kosovo closet amounted to a temporary head-in-the-sand answer to its grievances. In this case, it was better, so argued Clinton foreign policy aides, that Washington's reach not exceed its grasp of what was possible at Dayton. Holbrooke considered "Kosovo as the most explosive tinderbox in the region." Rather than a comprehensive peace, the American diplomat left Kosovo out of the accord. He settled for the doable and for urgings to Milošević "to restore the rights of Kosovo's Albanian Muslims, which he revoked when he absorbed the formerly autonomous province into Serbia."[28] Not including it in the Dayton settlement reflected the Clinton administration's disinclination to wade too deeply into the Balkan morass.

Kosovo's absence from the Dayton Accords was not the same as it being forgotten. The Clinton government soon turned to additional economic measures to pressure the Milošević regime into ceasing its misrule in Kosovo. Not only did it leave in place the existing sanctions on the FRY (now made up only of Serbia, Kosovo, and Montenegro) but also blocked it from seeking funds from the World Bank and the International Monetary Fund to rebuild. Taking this tough line, it diverged from its West European allies, which contended that healthy economic growth held out the prospect for creating a lever for political change.

Kosovo appeared on the surface to be tranquil at the time of Dayton. Beneath the calm, however, stirred longings for an independent sovereignty that re-awakened after the Berlin Wall fell.[29] A manifestation of the re-kindled independence sentiments arose with the formation of a small movement, the Democratic League of Kosovo (recognized by its Albanian initials of LDK), in late December 1989. This largely academic grouping selected as its president Ibrahim Rugova, a professor of Albanian literature. Thanks to its pacifist approach and passive politicking, the Serbian authorities tolerated it.[30] They suppressed riots at Priština University when students went from parochial grievances to demands for Kosovo's independence.

But neither university students nor quasi-cultural parties like the LDK sufficed for a people yearning for statehood. Stronger nationalistic crosscurrents churned beneath the surface. The tipping point between a go-slow approach and a radicalized, violent campaign came with the Dayton Accords. Kosovars realized that the Dayton settlement left them out in the cold. Then the newly formed EU rubbed salt into that wound by granting diplomatic recognition to the FRY, which implied de jure sanctification of the status quo.

Resentful of their plight and the LDK's accommodations with Belgrade, more nationalistic Kosovars secretly formed groups to fight for independence from Serbia. These mini-parties sank their differences and merged into the Kosovo Liberation Army or KLA (the Ushtria Çlirimtate e Kovovës or the UÇK in Albanian) in mid-1993. Another source of unrest surfaced when the expelled Serbs from the Croatian-overrun Krajina pocket arrived in Kosovo seeking safety and new homes in mid-1995. The Kosovars hated this infusion of settlers on their land. They struck back with attacks on Serb farms and police stations as well as killing members of the Serb minority. Since Dayton changed nothing for the Kosovars, they took up the gun and bomb. Soon, an insurgency ripped through the tiny territory. Kosovars and Serbs fled the violence, clogging roads to neighboring countries in search of safety. Once again, world attention focused on the Balkans.

The United States worried about the likelihood that widespread killings would destabilize the entire Balkans, just as it had about the earlier Bosnian conflict. Contributing to Washington's apprehensions was the overall goal of the insurgents. The KLA issued statements about a war of liberation for Albanians residing in Montenegro and Macedonia in order to fashion a Greater Albania. For their part, the Serbs played up the KLA as a transborder terrorist front bent on "international aggression" for a "pan-Albanian ethnic movement."[31]

As a consequence, the Clinton Administration re-convened the former Contact Group (again it comprised Britain, France, Germany, Russia, and the United States) to consider, once more, sanctions against Serbia for its iron-fisted rule in Kosovo. The member states placed additional sanctions on the FRY, despite Russian opposition. Neither the Contact Group nor NATO wanted to intervene on the ground to end Serb attacks on the Albanian Muslim population. The United States favored only limited airstrikes to pressure Belgrade.

Washington, however, failed to persuade the Security Council to bless aerial attacks, because of opposition from Russia and China, which threatened vetoes. This led Milošević think that he had a free hand inside the province. As for the insurgents, they drew the conclusion that they were on their own. The result was more bloodshed as each side fought harder to gain the upper hand. The Serbs found themselves sinking into a quagmire. The Kosovo insurgency shaped up as a classic blind-man's-bluff conflict where the guerrillas are rarely seen, and the government forces overreact by striking back with blanket atrocities. The KLA insurgents also fought to marginalize Ibrahim Rugova and his moderate LDK. By early 1998, the KLA was on its way to sidelining the onetime professor and his small party. The Kosovo population came to see the KLA as the only force capable of ridding them of the hated Serb presence. This meant that in time the United States would be compelled to work with the KLA, an insurgent movement with lots of blood on its hands. Before that eventuality, Washington needed the Serbs to capitulate or to negotiate away their domination of Kosovo. Only stiff military action held out any prospect for wringing concessions from Milošević.

President Clinton, however, was uninterested in a solo military intervention. Nor was he interested in investing his political capital to shape public opinion toward a forward policy with presidential speeches to the American people. The UN or NATO auspices could provide some political cover from an electorate which remained loath to military ventures. His foreign policy, in the words of a former aide, "faced intense opposition from both right and left, from familiar enemies in the Republican Congress and a rising chorus of discontent about his strategy and motives."[32] Abroad, Russia's and China's veto-wielding power in the Security Council made the UN a fruitless venue for Washington. So, the White House turned to NATO, since the Euro-American alliance bordered on the Kosovo storm. In June 1998, at the NATO meeting of defense ministers in Brussels, the United States led its partners in drawing up a tough-sounding agenda intended to restrain Milošević's hand in Kosovo. The Serb strongman refused to blink. From his experience in the Bosnia fighting, he knew well NATO's reluctance to cross the line into a conflict. Indeed, NATO resisted moving toward another Balkan war. The EU did participate with the United States in enacting sanctions against financial investments in Serbia and Montenegro and in suspending commercial flights landing in either country.

Prodded by a hesitant Clinton administration hoping that half-measures might suffice, NATO fell back on a mere demonstration of military force to convince Milošević to pullout or negotiate a settlement. This diplomatic minuet vis-à-vis Serbia was a replay of the Bosnian showdown with the United

States choreographing deliberate steps to avoid an actual fight. Washington and its NATO allies lofted 80 warplanes in Operation Determined Falcon to strike fear in Serb hearts on the ground below on June 15, 1998. But the maneuver undercut its own threat by not buzzing Belgrade but instead flying outside Serbian borders in neighboring Macedonian and Albanian airspace. Unimpressed the Serbian security forces in Kosovo carried on their grisly campaign. Without a credible display of military power, the chances for a diplomatic breakthrough with Belgrade eluded the United States and its partners. Other hurdles popped up.

Russia opposed another American-led foray into the Balkans, a sphere Moscow claimed as its own backyard. In retrospect, the US-headed NATO intervention into the Kosovo trouble spot marked the start of the downward spiral in Russo-American relations that surfaced so dramatically in the Georgian War in 2008 and exploded during the Barack Obama presidency in 2014. In the course of the late 1990s, the Clinton government regarded Boris Yeltsin's Russia as pliant, impotent, and buyable. It also desired Moscow's acquiescence to America's intrusion in Kosovo. Bill Clinton worked to bring Yeltsin on board with Washington's plans. He telephoned the Russian leader and pushed for a $10 billion loan to Russia from the International Monetary Fund in 1996 right before the Russian presidential election which saw Yeltsin win a second term.

In the short run, Clinton's Russian policy reaped a rich harvest. The American president traveled to Moscow for a treaty-signing ceremony in the Kremlin's Catherine Hall on September 2, 1998. Together with Yeltsin, he put his signature on a security agreement to share information about ballistic missile tests and to clear out weapons-grade plutonium from their respective nuclear stockpiles as a concrete step toward a bigger de-nuclearization program. At the summit, Clinton declared that the two leaders "agreed that the Serbian government must stop all repressive actions...and pursue an interim settlement."[33] The Clinton-Yeltsin rendezvous marked a high point in Russo-American relations before they descended into acrimony and distrust.

During the last months in 1998, murder and mayhem intensified within Kosovo, and the West had to contemplate its options. The KLA assassinated and attacked Serb security officials. The Serbian army and police, in turn, struck back, often indiscriminately, killing scores by shelling farms and villages. The result was a tit-for-tat killing spree which produced lines of refugees along crowded roads. Despite information about KLA atrocities, the United States and its European partners lined up behind the

Kosovars against their brutal Serbian government, since it was seen as a cruel occupier of the Muslim mini-state.

Late in September, at the meeting of the North Atlantic Council (NATO's principle political decision-making body) in Portugal, the member-state representatives adopted a military plan known as Operation Allied Force. This military blueprint mapped out a phased air campaign that would escalate until it persuaded Milošević to relent. Next, the United States and its allies readied aircraft and crews for bombing operations. American diplomacy at the UN attained only partial success. The Security Council, where Russia held veto power, passed Resolution 1199. This resolution did call upon all parties to "immediately cease hostilities." But it also reaffirmed "the sovereignty and territorial integrity of the Federal Republic of Yugoslavia," in other words no separate sovereign state for the Kosovars.[34] The resolution reassured Moscow but it yielded little in the way to resolve the ongoing bloodshed or the fate of the majority in Kosovo.

Sobered by its UN approach, the Clinton White House turned to direct negotiations within the Contact Group to bring Moscow around to a UN-approved military intervention to stop Serbs killing Kosovars. Although the Kremlin grew weary of dealing with Milošević's difficult persona, it remained adamant against a US-led bombing campaign again in the Balkans. In the end, Yeltsin simply abstained from opposing Washington over military operations against the Serbian strongman but not until the next year.[35]

Late 1998 witnessed Milošević wheedling and wiggling to stave off a determined Madeleine Albright, who championed a hard-edged policy toward Serbia. In effort to get the Serbian dictator to buckle, the White House dispatched Richard Holbrooke to Belgrade. Faced with the reality of Operation Allied Force (the NATO air war plan), Milošević backed down slightly to the American diplomat. At their mid-October meeting, he accepted steps to reduce violence in Kosovo. Milošević agreed to NATO flights over Kosovo to monitor conditions on the ground and to the deployment of unarmed observers from the Organization for Security and Cooperation in Europe (OSCE). He agreed to the reduction of the Serb security footprint and two weeks later withdrew 4000 paramilitary police from Kosovo. He approved the return of some 100,000 internally displaced persons to their homes. Importantly, he resigned himself to begin a political process to chart the war-torn province's political future.[36]

On the surface, the US threat of bombing Serbia seemed to have achieved a diplomatic breakthrough with the Serbian autocrat. Milošević was far too wily to have not realized his gains from the Holbrooke-brokered agreement. He spared his country from air attack and ground invasion, which would have spelled the end of his rule. If he counted on Holbrooke, Albright, and NATO to restrain the KLA guerrillas, he got a rude awakening. The insurgents re-infiltrated the countryside they had fled during the summer Serb offensive. Shootings of Serbians ramped up again. The Kosovar's return angered the Serbs and confirmed their thinking that the West was duplicitous.

In retaliation against the guerrilla infestation, Belgrade launched Operation Horseshoe in late December 1998. A month later, its scorched-earth tactics of killing livestock as well as humans brought widespread suffering that plucked at the heart strings in Washington, Brussels, and London. Half-a-million Kosovo refugees spilled into Albania and Macedonia. In the hamlet of Račak, the Serb security forces shot to death 45 civilians that recalled the 1942 Nazi massacre of Lidice, a village in Czechoslovakia. As such, it outraged public opinion across Europe and enabled Secretary of State Albright to galvanize support for her bare-knuckled posture toward Milošević. She gained unexpected backing from the new government in London. Tony Blair, who became the prime minister after defeating John Major in May 1997, differed from his cautious predecessor. The New Labour Party leader exuded humanitarian feelings that recoiled at the barbarity practiced by the Milošević regime. When it came to a forceful policy toward Serbia, Blair put the "special" back in the Anglo-American special relationship.

Lifting a page from the Dayton playbook, the US secretary of state pressed for a summit among the Contact Group countries, Milošević's Serbia, and its Kosovar opponents. Madeleine Albright persuaded her counterparts on the Contact Group to summon the Belgrade government and the Kosovo combatants to the negotiating table. The warring sides were compelled to participate and to heed a cease-fire. If they resisted, they would incur punishment. The Serbs would be bombed and the Kosovars isolated internationally. Hence, both attended. She realized from the start that deliberations would fail to budge the Serb leader. The drill, she believed, had to be attempted in order to convince the Contact Group to back a military campaign against Milošević. The outcome went as Albright scripted it.

The peace talks convened in a fourteenth-century chateau in the town of Rambouillet, some 30 miles south of Paris, on February 6, 1999. Along with the American and Contact Group representatives came the Serb and

Kosovo delegates. Slobodan Milošević feared arrest as a war criminal and so sent his government's deputy prime minister, who acted on orders over the telephone from his boss in Belgrade. From the Kosovars came the LDK's Ibrahim Rugova, who was eclipsed by Hashim Thaçi a founder of the KLA. The Kosovo attendees selected Thaçi to head their delegation, despite the war criminal charge that hung over his head. Years later, Thaçi served as Kosovo's prime minister.

The British and French, reflecting European anxiety, favored preservation of the FRY's territorial integrity, lest a split-away ethnic Kosovo state set a precedent for other potential breakaway states, such as in Scotland, Belgium, and Spain's Catalonia. Thus, London and Paris wanted autonomy for Kosovo and good behavior toward it from Belgrade. This half-loaf strategy satisfied neither of the two contenders. The Kosovars wanted an immediate grant of independence, not a three-year waiting period before holding a referendum to determine sovereignty. They rejected disarmament of their insurgent fighters, even by outside NATO forces. For its part, Belgrade could stomach limited autonomy only for the rebellious province. It recoiled against a NATO presence, even if its troops disarmed the guerrillas. In the end, the Kosovars swallowed the autonomy feature and Thaçi signed the Rambouillet accord in Paris on March 18, as urged by Albright.

The Serb delegates stayed home. To Belgrade, Ramouillet constituted an ultimatum, not a fair-minded settlement. They especially reacted against the difficult-to-swallow Appendix B of the accord, which authorized NATO troops, "vehicles, vessels, aircraft free and unrestricted passage and unimpeded access through the Federal Republic of Yugoslavia," not just Kosovo.[37] This blatant infringement of sovereignty raised Serb hackles. In the eyes of the Belgrade regime, this intrusive, NATO footprint also represented a threat to the longevity of Milošević's rule. To no one's great surprise, least of all Albright, the Serbs rejected the accord. The secretary of state had become so hawkish toward Milošević that the impending air campaign acquired the appellation of "Madeleine's war."

The American administration as a whole, however, was much more hesitant about fighting Serbia, a country that never attacked the United States or a neighbor. On the eve of the NATO bombing of Serbia, Albright noted that President Clinton's "eyes were as grim as I felt."[38] Clinton came around to the military option only after Milošević's intransigence and atrocities persisted against the Kosovar Albanians. Standing aside in face of the ongoing bloodshed took more forbearance than asking Congress to vote for military action. Besides, it was not in American or European interests to have Belgrade destabilize Eastern Europe with ethnic cleansing, horrific carnage, and refugee columns crossing frontiers for safety.

The White House, nevertheless, knew well the non-interventionist mindset among the American people and their representatives on Capitol Hill. As a result, Clinton officials worked for weeks to persuade congress to vote for its military approach. They won over members of both major political parties with a 58–41 vote in the Senate at the 11th hour and earlier with a House vote of 219–191.[39] Winning legislative backing stood the president in good stead when the air campaign dragged on beyond what had been anticipated as a quick action. On the first night of the bombing campaign, Secretary of State Albright echoed the consensus when she said: "I don't see this as a long-term operation."[40]

The troops-will-be-home-for-Christmas forecast was no more accurate in the Kosovo aerial campaign than in predictions for World War I's quick end when gunfire first sounded. The air bombardment lasted 11 weeks from its inauguration on March 24, 1999. It was flawed at the outset according to airpower champions who advocated a full-throttled first punch rather than an incremental build-up in intensity. Unlike the Persian Gulf War, where 2700 warplanes struck Iraq in the first week, the Kosovo air offensive opened with 400 aircraft before ratcheting up to about 1000.[41] This incremental formula reflected the tentativeness of the American initiative. If less would suffice, then this was all for the better. The United States did take the lead by flying nearly 60 percent of the sorties, with France ranking next in contribution with almost 100 planes. The Pentagon also supplied the bulk of the refueling aircraft, intelligence capability, and the damage-assessment analysis after the bombing runs.

Despite American dominance, the NATO allies, chiefly France, engaged in target-selection disputes with the Pentagon. Washington suspected Paris's lingering pro-Serb sympathies as a factor in the wrangling. The two allies also shared differing opinions on strategy. France endorsed limited destruction of Serbian civilian infrastructure to ease the rebuilding and integration of the FRY into the West's institutions after the war. The Clinton administration, however, worried about a prolonged war given the American public's disengagement sentiments of the times, which coincided with antiwar protests in West European cities.

President Clinton's management of the Kosovo War mirrored his tentativeness in the use of military force. At the advent of the air operation,

Clinton emphasized: "I do not intend to put our troops in Kosovo to fight a war."[42] Ever sensitive to public opinion polls, the president spoke to ease Americans' anxieties about casualties and military missions. Throughout Washington power circles, it was well known that the Oval Office occupant harbored aversions to dead troops arriving in body bags at Dover Air Force Base, for the negative impact they had on his approval ratings. Clinton, in fact, felt compelled to restrain America's foremost ally when Tony Blair frequently urged the introduction of ground combat soldiers. Two days before the 50th anniversary NATO summit in Washington on April 23–24, 1999, Blair met Clinton in the White House where the US president asked him to soften his insistent calls for sending troops against the Milošević dictatorship because the air offensive went on longer than predicted. In return, the US president promised to re-examine his war plans.[43]

Air assaults alone produced controversy within and outside NATO circles. Germany, Italy, and Greece voiced their disenchantment with the slow progress of the bombing. As Her Majesty's government grew dissatisfied with just aerial attacks on Serb targets and the French insisted on reviewing proposed American targets, the Pentagon stuck to its story that the barrage from the sky would in time bring Belgrade to its knees. The Defense Department's line, however, wore thin as weeks passed. Finally, a foot-dragging White House slightly revised its adamant opposition to a land war. Responding to a question, the president announced: "[W]e have not and will not take any option off the table" on May 18.[44] But he resisted stating any specific change in the air strategy. Criticism from pundits and politicians mounted as the bombing persisted and Serbian civilian casualties rose. The mistaken bombing of the Chinese Embassy in Belgrade, which killed three staff members and inflamed Sino-American relations for months, also took a toll on the air-only option. Frustration with its one-and-done air effort finally trigged a re-assessment in Washington.

Behind the scenes, Clinton advisers urged the president to re-think his no-ground-troops stance in light of military factors and domestic political considerations. They were all aware of past failed Democratic presidencies—Harry Truman, Lyndon Johnson, and Jimmy Carter—due to bankrupt foreign ventures. Fearing a repeat of history for his presidency, Clinton moved off the dime.[45] His National Security Advisor, Sandy Berger, initiated a planning document termed "Plan B-minus" that called for 175,000 NATO troops, of which the United States would contribute 100,000 soldiers. The plan envisioned an intervention taking place in early September. On June 2, the media reported that Bill Clinton called for a meeting the next day of the Joint Chiefs of Staff at the White House "to discuss options for using ground troops if NATO decides to invade Kosovo."[46]

Planning for a land intervention ended before it really got underway because Milošević capitulated on June 3. The autocrat realized the threat posed by Western troops on Serbian soil. A ground intervention was *the* key factor in his capitulation.[47] He understood that a defeated and debilitated Serbian security force was no longer a secure prop for his regime. It is worth recalling that the presence of foreign soldiers in the Rambouillet accord caused Belgrade to walk away from the signing, for they also posed a danger to the regime. Additionally NATO armies operating in Russia's backyard constituted a grave loss of face for the Kremlin's long-standing policy against Western encroachments in its sphere. Consequently, Moscow pushed Milošević toward negotiations with Washington rather than risk NATO garrisons so close to its borders.

In the end, Slobodan Milošević loved power more than standing up to the United States. He accepted a cease-fire and the FRY's participation in overall political settlement for Kosovo. Belgrade pulled out its 50,000 military and police forces, allowed refugees and internally displaced people to return home, and, most crucially, permitted the basing of a NATO-organized peacekeeping force within Kosovo. Milošević kept NATO troops out of Serbia proper. As these issues were resolved, NATO continued the bombing until June 9. By this date, the Security Council passed Resolution 1244, which authorized NATO's troop deployment into Kosovo and put the province under UN supervision for humanitarian relief and refugee return. The Serb military and paramilitary police retreated from Kosovo without serious incident.

The conflict, thus, dissipated rapidly, except for a brief but ugly flare-up at the Priština airport, when a Russian army column from Bosnia attempted a seizure of territory, much as the Red Army had done when it raced for Berlin in the closing days of World War II. The standoff was resolved peacefully in Washington, London, and Moscow without Russia getting its own sector as happened in 1945 Berlin.[48] The Russian and Serbian animosity toward Kosovo revived when the rebellious province unilaterally declared independence from Belgrade in 2008. Neither Russia nor Serbia completely recognized its statehood. Nor did Milošević's surrender spare his regime. Washington plotted his political demise and backed the street protests to his reelection in 2000, which ousted him from office. Six years later, he died in a prison, on trial for war crimes at the International Criminal Tribunal for the former Yugoslavia.

Dodging International Involvement

Looking at the US interventions in Bosnia and Kosovo, an observer might conclude that the Clinton presidency more clearly represented an activist cycle than a disengagement phase in American foreign policy. The explanation set forth above, however, points to the reluctance, hesitations, and delays in implementation of the twin military engagements. They recall Winston Churchill's famed observation that the Americans always do the right thing after exhausting all other possibilities. Clinton never exulted in being a wartime president during the interventions. Unlike George W. Bush, he never relished the commander-in-chief role in conducting the air wars in the Balkans. Rather, his orientation was clearly toward the country's domestic issues. Moreover, the Clinton administration relied on air power to carry out its policies rather than large-scale ground invasions more typical of the interventionist actions of its predecessor and successor presidencies.

The final Clinton years, moreover, witnessed a pronounced retreat from international interventions. Never relishing overseas combat ventures, the Washington administration doubled down on ways to avoid anymore. After the Balkan airstrikes, the United States shouldered some postwar burdens of deploying ground forces as part of the international peacekeeping contingents needed to disarm locals, calm roiled populations, and preserve stability long enough for commerce and governance to take root. Clinton's foreign policy team took cognizance of the costs and challenges of peace-soldiering after the back-to-back interventions into the turbulent, former Yugoslavia. Their disinclination to lead other armed intercessions was matched in the Pentagon, congress, and the American public. Not a few commentators held that the repeated humanitarian deployments were wearing out the military forces, making them unfit for the defense of genuine US interests. In fact, President Clinton incurred charges by politicians and pundits for his "social work" abroad, global "care giving," and want of "strategic coherence" in sending armed forces hither and yon for dubious purposes.[49]

It was no surprise that the White House quickly looked to hand off to others two humanitarian crises in the post-Kosovo period. When violence flared in Sierra Leone, the United States chose to first broker a cease-fire and then the Lomé Agreement enabling it to stage manage the formation of the UN Assistance Mission for Sierra Leone (UNAMSIL). This UN effort spared direct American involvement in the West African state. But the UNAMSIL presence only delayed Forday Sankoh, a homicidal warlord, from his goal in taking over the coastal nation's lucrative diamond mines. When the agreement collapsed and UNAMSIL stumbled, Britain dispatched paratroopers into its onetime colony to restore order. They arrested Sankoh and put to flight his drugged teenaged militia. The violence moderated there only to burst forth in neighboring Liberia, a country with a special historical tie to the United States having been partially founded by former America slaves. Still, Clinton managed to stay clear of an activist role. Liberian troubles were not properly dealt with until George W. Bush came into office. Working with the UN and neighboring countries, Washington then effected a regime change and free elections that returned normalcy to Liberia in 2005.

Halfway around the world, another war-humanitarian crisis beckoned for the Clinton administration's attention in 1999. In the enclave of East Timor, the largely Catholic population (dating from Portuguese colonial rule) voted overwhelmingly in favor of a UN-sponsored referendum for independence from Muslim-dominated Indonesia. Reacting to the polling, anti-independence Muslim militias crossed into the eastern half of the island of Timor. Backed by the regular Indonesian military, the rampaging militias looted and burned shops and homes. They killed several hundred East Timorese and compelled some 300,000 to flee as refugees into West Timor. Seeking to escape another onerous peacekeeping mission, Clinton's foreign policy officials prodded Australia to lead the UN-initiated International Force East Timor to impose order and to protect the East Timorese from the marauding Muslim bands. The White House assisted INTERFET with logistical support in the form of air and sea lift capacity as well as intelligence and communications capabilities. Australia, Britain, Canada, New Zealand, Thailand, and the Philippines contributed soldiers and military personnel with medical and engineering expertise to restore services in the ruined territory, which became an independent state in 2002.[50]

The Clinton government touted the turnover of the peace and healing missions to Australian leadership as a case study in outsourcing regional responsibilities to other nations. In an era when the United States was repeatedly referred to as a global policeman, Clintonian Washington was relieved to dodge the expense and effort of managing another rescue mission in a faraway land. The last years of Bill Clinton's presidency recorded other efforts to shift gears from the Balkan exertions to an even more limited international exposure. It mostly stayed clear of dealing with threats emanating from the Middle East.

Iraq Finessed and Counterterrorism Shirked

Of all single-country threats during the 1990s, Iraq constituted the gravest danger, even more so than North Korea as discussed in the previous chapter. Iraq's propensity to offer rewards for terrorism against Israel worsened. Saddam Hussein, despite major wars against Iran and Kuwait, also lost none of his saber-rattling recklessness toward his neighbors or the United States. Internally, the Iraqi dictator ruled with an iron hand, murdering perceived rivals and wiping out substantial members of the Shiite and Kurdish communities to preserve his power and that of his co-religionist Sunnis. Madeleine Albright stated: "Of all the headaches inherited by the Clinton administration, Saddam Hussein was the most persistent."[51]

After the conclusion of the Persian Gulf War in 1991, George H.W. Bush instituted an armed containment policy toward the Republic of Iraq that was sketched in Chap. 3. The Bush White House established no-fly zones in Iraq's northern and southern quadrants. Together with the British and the French (until 1998), American aircraft patrolled the skies. In the country's northern zone, the military flights afforded limited protection to the Kurdish minority, who also hosted several thousand allied infantrymen for its security. Washington also obtained Security Council resolutions for sanctions on Iraq and, most importantly, for UN arms inspectors to search for WMD facilities.

All these measures passed to the incoming Bill Clinton government in 1993. The new president not only stuck to the active containment agenda but also stiffened his stance in the Gulf region, at least until the last years of his tenure. Clinton kept in place the no-fly areas, economic sanctions, and UNSCOM arms inspections because like his predecessor, he thought Hussein was beyond the pale for normal diplomacy. Clinton, too, conceived that it was possible that Hussein might meet an untimely end, in either a coup or assassination. Because Iraq, as an American adversary, could not play a counterbalancing role against Iran, Washington initiated a "dual containment" strategy to box in both Iraq and Iran. Treating both rogue nations as pariahs was a departure from the Reagan and early Bush administrations which sought to position Iraq as a counterweight to Iran.

Six months after settling into the White House, the former Arkansas governor faced an unexpected crisis from Iraq. It came to light that the Baath Party's General Intelligence Department, the dreaded Mukhabarat, hatched a plot to assassinate former President George Bush, while celebrating the second anniversary of the Kuwait's liberation by US armed forces. Both the CIA and Federal Bureau of Investigation concluded that the evidence against the Mukhabarat was airtight. After a Washington debate on the form of a response, the United States ordered its warships in the Gulf to fire 23 Tomahawk cruise missiles at the Muhabarat headquarters in Baghdad, reducing it to rubble. Wags quipped that since the retaliation took place in the dead of night, the only victims of the attack were the cleaning personnel in the building. More serious commentators thought the counterstrike was far too irresolute for the Iraqi offense.[52] It did nothing to chasten the impetuous belligerent in Baghdad.

Thereafter, the Clinton administration settled into its "containment-plus" doctrine. It recorded blips of occasional intense anti-Hussein air attacks on a trend line that pointed down before flat-lining at the end of Bill Clinton's time in office. Other crises also intruded to shift the White House's attention to Somalia, Haiti, North Korea, Rwanda, and the two Balkan conflicts. Sanctioned and ostracized, Hussein struggled at first to breakout of the US-orchestrated cordon sanitaire. Over time, Baghdad's Arab-street pleasing resistance against Washington garnered Hussein widening re-acceptance and even respectability among the Middle Eastern populations and their rulers, some of whom also bristled at America's Iraq policies and support of Israel. Resourceful Iraqis smuggled oil exports to Turkey and Iran for re-shipment to other petroleum consuming customers. Meanwhile, Hussein's regime found ways to siphon off UN funds intended to purchase food and medicine for ordinary Iraqis. It played on popular grievances to fuel anti-American and anti-UN sentiments.

Most frustratingly for the Clinton White House, Hussein stonewalled and thwarted UNSCOM weapons inspections. His antics heightened suspicions that Iraq had secretly embarked on fabricating chemical and biological weapons, if not pursuing nuclear-arming. The delays and roadblocks to UNSCOM investigations wore away at the agency's patience and effectiveness. The last straw came with Hussein expelled some UNSCOM team members as spies for cooperating with the CIA. Infuriated by the Hussein's cat-and-mouse countermoves, the UNSCOM chief, Richard Butler, removed his inspectors from Iraq in autumn 1998. The former

Australian diplomat later wrote a book about the UN's ineffectiveness and the dark consequences of a nuclear-armed Saddam Hussein.[53]

The United States and Britain (France refused to take part) retaliated for Baghdad's opposition to the arms inspection. They hoped to chasten the strutting Iraqi president into compliance with a punishing, four-day bombing campaign in December 1998. Operation Desert Fox logged 650 sorties by Anglo-American warplanes and counted 325 cruise missiles fired against not only suspected WMD sites but also airfields, communication nodes, and military facilities. Damage assessments indicated a high rate of target destruction. As Desert Fox got underway, President Clinton, in an Oval Office address, asserted a rationale for the bombardment that eerily foreshadowed George W. Bush's justification of the Iraq War. He declared that "someday, make no mistake, he will use it [WMD] again as he has in the past," referring to gassing of the Kurds in 1988. Clinton also noted the regime-change option that formed a key component of his successor's Iraq policy. He explained that the only means to do away with the recurring ominous dangers emanating from Baghdad "was with a new Iraqi government."[54]

The political circumstances at home muted Clinton's stern words. Republican critics accused the president of trying to impede his impeachment over the Monica Lewinsky scandal that enveloped much of his presidency during the previous year. The president's confidants refuted the accusation.[55] The issue about the timing of the airstrikes was little more than a tempest in a teapot in the longer scheme of domestic and international policies.

Both the sex scandal and the bombing's message soon subsided with Clinton's acquittal in the Senate and his wind down of the anti-Hussein attacks. The Desert Fox bombardment marked an inflection point in the administration's Iraq-containment policy. Afterward, the White House looked past its headache in the Persian Gulf. Madeleine Albright selected a special coordinator, Frank Ricciardone, to oversee a transition in Iraq. But the so-called czar for overthrowing Saddam quickly ran aground on the shoals of Mid-East politics, intrigues among exiled Iraqi politicians, and lethargy within his own government. Other issues also intruded, and Iraq lost its urgency for the Oval Office.

The Republicans, who held majorities in Congress, poured scorn on the West Wing's calculated avoidance from what became a near-fixation by some of their party members. The Iraq hawks, within and without Republican Party, laid the intellectual basis in the late 1990s for what developed into the George W. Bush administration's war doctrine against Iraq. Politicians and pundits took issue with what they interpreted as Bill Clinton's fickleness toward Iraq's perceived WMD build-up and his outsourcing of American security to UN arms inspectors. The president's opponents (including many Democrats) on the Iraq issue passed bipartisan legislation on Capitol Hill in the form of the Iraq Liberation Act of 1998. Iraq generated such cross-party concern that the bill received substantial votes in the House and unanimous approval in the Senate. When President Clinton signed the bill on October 31, it became the law of the land to remove Saddam Hussein and try him before an international tribunal. The American people's representatives were on board with regime change, although it would take place five years later. The legislation's other particulars included the establishment of Radio Free Iraq to beam anti-Hussein broadcasts, and the funds for arming and equipping of Iraqi opponents to overthrow the dictator. The legislative act authorized $97 million to implement its provisions.

Aside from the president's circumscribed Balkan interventions, Bill Clinton's dissociation from forward policies abroad was further confirmed by the paucity of dollars spent carrying out provisions of the Iraq Liberation Act. When the president left the White House, his administration had expended less than $3 million of the authorized funds, most of which went for administrative-startup costs. The president had taken the measure of the American people, concluding that they were uninterested in risky foreign adventures. Rallying them to international activism demanded the expenditure of considerable political capital and significant presidential effort. Clinton chose to follow the lines of least resistance instead of arousing his fellow citizens to an unpopular, uncertain, and perilous course against the Republic of Iraq during the last two years of his presidency.

The White House took careful note of what the Soviets had termed earlier as the correlation of forces now confronting the United States vis-à-vis Iraq. Clinton foreign policy officials considered how stubbornly Serbia resisted during the drawn-out 78-day Kosovo bombing operation. Air power against Iraq looked even less than a sure thing as Baghdad was expected to hold out much longer than Belgrade. Using ground forces against Hussein was left off the table by the Washington mandarins. Intra-allied squabbles were almost certain to worsen. During Kosovo campaign, US military planners ran into problems with NATO partners, particularly France, over target selection. As the bombardment lengthened, NATO countries increasingly became disenchanted with the rising toll the shelling inflicted on the Serbian civilian population and infrastructure. Iraq promised to be worse.

The overall Euro-American camaraderie, moreover, started to sour even before George W. Bush assumed the presidency, exacerbating transatlantic relations on many issues. No longer reliant on the United States as its protector against the Red Army, Western Europe's goodwill receded toward Washington as time passed.[56] One data point in this worsening of Euroatlantic ties can be seen in the fact that Bush Sr. mobilized a 34-nation coalition against Iraq in the Persian Gulf War. Yet, Clinton at the time of Operation Desert Fox counted only on British steadfastness. Saddam Hussein had managed to come off as the scrappy underdog versus an over mighty America, as he wove his way back into the good graces of many Middle East countries.

American domestic considerations dominated the White House's thinking. Aside from the electorate's risk-aversion to foreign military enterprises, Clinton ran up against pushback from members of his own party. Seventy-five Congressional Democrats wrote him in early 2000, imploring the White House to lift sanctions on Iraq, because of the hardships caused Iraqi citizens who lacked food and medicine. America's economy was also a factor in presidential thinking. Owing his victory over incumbent President Bush to the country's lackluster economy, Clinton naturally watched closely the state of the nation's economic well-being. The president worked to avoid anything that might interfere with its humming along as it did in the late 1990s.

Disruption of Iraq's oil flow of nearly 3 million barrels daily constituted a threat to America's and the West's economic health. Therefore, the Oval Office shied away from muscular military policies aimed at the Persian Gulf nation. It kept its containment policy in place but pared the frequency of the air-to-ground missile strikes out of anxiety that a US aircraft might be downed by one of Hussein air defense batteries as the presidential election season neared. The outgoing Clinton team backed Vice President Al Gore in his bid for the top office. A complication arising from an Iraq attack, so the thinking went, could endanger Gore's prospects.

In light of the coming national contest, the Clinton White House also squelched the chances of a new arms-inspection team in Iraq. In fact, it made a U-turn in its prior approach at the end of August 2000. Previously, the United States pushed for a replacement for UNSCOM after it withdrew out of frustration over Hussein's hide-and-seek maneuverings. In response to American urgings, the UN formed the UN Monitoring and Verification

Commission (UNMOVIC). It placed Hans Blix, a former Swedish official, at the head of UNMOVIC. At the stroke of midnight, nonetheless, the White House abandoned its effort and sided with its three main Security Council opponents to deployment of UNMOVIC. Stemming from their Iraqi commercial interests, China, France, and the Russian Federation objected to intrusive weapons searches within Iraq. Washington joined the three in announcing that UNMOVIC was unready to resume the former UNSCOM inspections. It was not dispatched until George W. Bush, who defeated Gore in the November election, pushed the Security Council to send the sidelined UNMOVIC into Iraq.

America's disengagement during Bill Clinton's waning days in the Oval Office was even more pronounced than its suspension of international arms inspections or its decrease in airstrikes. Its policy to contain and box in Iraq lay in shambles. By the time Clinton left office, Iraq was no longer an isolated pariah. The no-fly-zone stratagem fell apart after Venezuelan President Hugo Chávez first punctured the exclusionary perimeter in August 2000. As chairman of the Organization of Petroleum Exporting Countries, the Latin American populist and anti-US leader lost no opportunity to jab at the Colossus of the North. Chávez flew into Bagdad as a snub to the United States. On his heels, several other international officials jetted into Iraq, setting off what was dubbed as "air diplomacy." Washington simply stopped enforcing the no-flight restrictions on commercial planes in and out of the country. No effort was made to fill the breach with new policies.

By this date, Iraq was no longer ostracized for its cross-border invasion and punishing occupation of Kuwait. The bulk of the Middle East had moved on from its earlier censorious isolation of Saddam Hussein. His financial support of the Palestinian cause, including money to the families of the terrorists carrying out attacks against Israelis won him plaudits from the Arab street.[57] Additionally, the United States encountered renewed opposition for advocating the continuance of economic sanctions and limited airstrikes on Iraqi military targets. From West European capitals to Saudi Arabia and Turkey, governments questioned Washington's dissolving agenda. Some wanted to do business with Iraq; others saw a Sunni-run Iraq as a counterbalance to an expansive, Shiite Iran in the greater Gulf arena. The late-term Clinton presidency, desperately trying to broker an Israeli-Palestinian peace, accommodated its allied Arab rulers and went along with their wishes by scaling back its Iraq policeman duties as it headed toward the exits.

THE HOLIDAY FROM TERRORISM

Bill Clinton's "selective engagement" in the Bosnian and Kosovo conflicts, which reaped favorable reviews, broke down when it came to the intensifying menace of terrorism. One commentator maintained that Clinton's selective engagement contained the caveat that this policy lacked "criteria for defining the national interest" and degenerated into "tactical manipulation." As such, Clinton "stumbled from crisis to crisis, trying to figure out what was popular… and what choices would pose the lowest risk to his presidency."[58] Overplaying military restraint, Clinton's approach cost America much from Osama bin Laden and al Qaeda. It is not that the Clinton White House lacked for pertinent intelligence alerting it to the pernicious and perilous nature of the burgeoning terrorist risk. No, ample evidence and warnings presented themselves to officials and non-officials about the escalating dangers posed by Islamist terrorists in the years leading up to the September 11, 2001, mega-terrorist attack on American soil. A crescendo of terrorist violence from the Muslim world had been rising since the 1960s. By the Clinton era, there were frequent bombings and shootings inspired by Islamist cells. Al Qaeda's sinister hand was recognizable in many of the attacks by its three trademark elements—suicidal, spectacular, and symbolic.

Within Clinton's National Security Council, officials voiced anxiety and debated the proper response to the rising terrorist danger. They considered the merits of a passive defense and/or preemptive offense.[59] Bin Laden and his al Qaeda network owed their ascendancy up to the uppermost ranks of international terrorism by harnessing Islamic triumphalism after the Soviet Union's defeat in Afghanistan. In the wake of the Red Army's retreat from the mountainous land in 1989, the local mujahedeen and the foreign fighters rejoiced in their humbling of a superpower. A coterie of Arab fighters operating in Afghanistan believed they could duplicate their USSR-bleeding tactics against the sole remaining superpower, the United States. This cost-imposing strategy required tying down and draining American power in far-flung anti-terror wars.

Cobbling together al Qaeda (known in English as the base) from six movements and forging a headquarters capable of instigating, coordinating, and funding a series of terrorist assaults was due to the skill of bin Laden and his able lieutenant, Ayman al Zawahiri, an Egyptian medical doctor. Al Qaeda was behind the 1993 Black Hawk Down incident in Somalia, the 1998 bombings of the US embassies in Tanzania and Kenya, and the boat-bombing of the *USS Cole* in Yemen's Aden harbor in 2000, which nearly sank the guided-missile destroyer and killed 17 sailors. Al Qaeda was not just all bombs and no message. The terrorist front communicated its worldview through television appearances by al Qaeda leaders and by issuing anti-American *fatwas* (religious edicts).[60]

Given the multiple terrorist bombings, pointed taunts, and ominous warnings of the 1990s, it is difficult in retrospect to explain Washington's feckless response to the rising tide of jihadi murder and mayhem. Prior to the cataclysmic terrorist assaults on the symbols of American financial and military prowess at the World Trade Center and the Pentagon, the anti-terrorist strategy was one of muddle, complacency, and missed opportunities to eliminate Osama bin Laden before the 9/11 attack. Washington officials knew of bin Laden's use of terrorism to re-establish a transborder caliphate encompassing any territories where Islam once-historically prevailed. Al Qaeda matched its extravagant real estate claims with vicious and callous attacks aimed at soft, civilian targets. As it turned out, Washington's countermeasures paled in comparison to the terrorists' bold attacks.

When the United States fired salvos of cruise missiles in retaliation for al Qaeda's truck bombing of the two American embassies in East Africa, President Clinton addressed the nation from the Oval Office. He reviewed the casualties from the blasts, 257 killed of whom 12 were Americans and several thousand injured. Then, the commander-in-chief vowed: "We will meet it [terrorist threat], no matter, how long it may take." He further pledged that "there will be no sanctuary for terrorists."[61] For Bill Clinton, nonetheless, there was no follow-through to the tough talk. All in all, he elevated Richard Clarke, a Cassandra about the threats posed by al Qaeda, to be the first national coordinator for counterterrorism. Clarke drafted the "Political-Military Plan Delenda," which used the Latin word *delenda* to convey the meaning that al Qaeda must be expunged or annihilated. This chapter laid out military strikes as well as diplomatic options, all to no avail. The Clinton administration never again mounted a lethal operation against the shadowy terrorist network hosted by the radical Taliban regime. Nor was the Defense Department eager to deploy ground troops or even SOF to strike al Qaeda in Afghanistan.[62] A mood of disengagement and risk-avoidance hung over Washington departments.

In retrospect, the Clinton administration's counterterrorism response projected inadequacy to the grave threat presented by al Qaeda. Washington opted first for economic sanctions through the Security

Council, which authorized both resolutions. It hoped the ineffective sanctions might induce Kabul to surrender bin Laden and close his training camps which instructed an estimated 10,000–20,000 militants in the black arts of terrorism from 1996 to September 11. Mullah Mohammed Omar (the Taliban's spiritual leader and emir or commander of the faithful) refused to hand over or expel bin Laden. Economic sanctions hardly bit at Afghanistan's subsistence economy, already heavily reliant on illicit opium exports to the lucrative European market. Just before leaving office the Clinton administration pushed an arms embargo through the UN in December 2000. Given its weapons resupply links with Pakistan's Inter-Services Intelligence (ISI), however, the Taliban regime was not pinched hard by the UN moratorium on arms sales to Afghanistan.

By this time, the CIA had re-established connections with the Taliban's chief adversary, the North Alliance, in hopes of hatching a plot to neutralize bin Laden. Dominated by Tajik and Uzbek peoples, the Northern Alliance had been at war with the Taliban since 1996, when the rebel movement lost control of the capital to the Pashtun-controlled Taliban movement. When told by CIA agents that President Clinton preferred bin Laden's capture rather than assassination, the charismatic Tajik chieftain, Ahmed Shah Massoud, mockingly replied: "You guys are crazy—you haven't changed a bit."[63] The Lion of Panjshir's observation explains why the arch-terrorist lived to mastermind the most deadly foreign attack ever on American soil. At that time, the United States was still gripped by an inward-facing attitude.

The topic of terrorism received scant attention from the public as Bill Clinton prepared to depart from Washington. In the course of the presidential debates in October 2000, the skiff-bombing of the *USS Cole* by two suicide bombers in Yemen's port of Aden came up only once. Vice President Al Gore and Texas Governor George W. Bush squared off mostly on domestic issues. Neither the exiting Clinton nor the incoming Bush administrations retaliated for the terrorism attributed to al Qaeda, which almost scuttled the warship. Americans and their elected officials simply shuffled on after the ship attack. Inexplicable in retrospect, the country slept through the wake-up call before the 9/11 terrorism. After his presidency, Clinton mused in his autobiography that his "biggest disappointment was not getting bin Laden."[64]

Over a decade after the infamous September 11 attack, a taped recording came to light of a talk by Bill Clinton in which the former president claimed that he could have killed Osama bin Laden in 1998. Speaking to business officials in Australia, former President Clinton ironically divulged, hours before the al Qaeda hijacked planes crashed into the World Trade Center and Pentagon, that: "I could have killed him, but I would have to destroy a little town called Kandahar in Afghanistan and kill 300 innocent women and children."[65] Like many might-have-been turning points in history, this revelation comes more as a sad footnote than an historical irony. Bill Clinton's unwillingness to employ effective military operations against bin Laden comported with his overall reluctant foreign policy orientation during his years in office.

Notes

1. Thomas L. Friedman, "Bosnia Reconsidered," *New York Times*, April 8, 1993, p. A 5.
2. Elizabeth Drew, *On the Edge: The Clinton Presidency* (New York: Simon and Schuster, 1994), p. 153.
3. Colin Powel, *My American Journey* (New York: Random House, 1995), p. 576.
4. David Owen, *Balkan Odyssey* (New York: Harcourt Brace & Company, 1995), p. 172.
5. Clinton, *My Life*, p. 534.
6. Laura Silber and Allan Little, *Yugoslavia: Death of a Nation* (New York: Penguin Books, 1995), p. 274.
7. Elaine Sciolino, "U.S. Goal on Bosnia: Keeping War Within Borders," *New York Times*, May 19, 1993, p. A 1.
8. As a representative account of the lament for Bosnia and a stinging indictment of Western reaction, see David Rieff, *Slaughterhouse: Bosnia and the Failure of the West* (New York: Simon & Schuster, 1995), pp. 14–15, 227, and 256–257.
9. Michael E. Gordon, "Modest Air Operation in Bosnia Crosses a Major Political Frontier," *New York Times*, April 11, 1994, p. A 1.
10. Cited in David Rothkopf, *Running the World: The Inside Story of the National Security Council and the Architects of American Power* (New York: Public Affairs, 2005), p. 339.
11. Todd S. Purdum, "Clinton Vetoes Lifting Bosnia Arms Embargo," *New York Times*, August 12, 1994, p. A 1.
12. Clinton, *My Life*, p. 667.

13. Tim Weiner, "Clinton Withholds Bosnia Data from Congress," *New York Times*, April 17, 1996, p. A 1.
14. Silber and Little, *Yugoslavia: Death of a Nation*, p. 350.
15. P.W. Singer, *Corporate Warriors: The Rise of the Privatized Military Industry* (Ithaca, NY: Cornell University Press, 2003), pp. 127–129.
16. Roger Cohen, "After Aiding Croatian Army, U.S. Now Seeks to Contain It," *New York Times*, October 28, 1995, p. A 5 and Clinton, *My Life*, pp. 666–667.
17. Silber and Little, *Yugoslavia: Death of a Nation*, pp. 352–354.
18. Robert C. Owen, ed., *Deliberate Force: A Case Study in Effective Air Campaign* (Montgomery, AL: Air University Press, 2000), pp. 506–515.
19. Holbrooke, *To End a War*, p. 106.
20. Bill Clinton's 950-page political memoir, *My Life*, cites the Balkans five times.
21. Clinton, *My Life*, p. 950.
22. Richard Holbrooke, *To End a War* (New York: Random House, 1998), p. 293.
23. Holbrooke, *To End a War*, p. 214.
24. The single best account of the negotiations is by the already cited book by Richard Holbrooke in *To End a War*, chapters 16 through 20.
25. General Framework Agreement for Peace in Bosnia and Herzegovina, November, 21, 1995, U.S. Department of State. Downloaded from http://www.state.gov/p/eur/rls/or/dayton/52577.htm. Accessed July 20, 2016.
26. Richard Holbrooke, "America, a European Power," *Foreign Affairs*, 74, Issue 2 (March/April 1995), 40.
27. Holbrooke, *To End a War*, p. 359. The italics are Holbrooke's.
28. Ibid., p. 357.
29. Tim Judah, *Kosovo: War and Revenge* (New Haven, CT: Yale University Press, 2002), pp. 25–31 and 53–54.
30. Noel Malcolm, *Kosovo: A Short History* (New York: New York University Press, 1998), p. 348.
31. Tim Judah, *Kosovo: War and Revenge* (New Haven, CT: Yale Nota Bene, 2002), pp. 249–254.
32. Sidney Blumenthal, *The Clinton Wars* (New York: Farrar, Straus and Giroux, 2003), p. 629.

33. Strobe Talbott, *The Russia Hand: A Memoir of Presidential Diplomacy* (New York: Random House, 2002), p. 347.
34. United Nations Resolution, 1199, October 28, 1998. Downloaded from http://www.un.org/press/en/1998/19981024.sc6588.html. Accessed July 20, 2016.
35. Talbott, *The Russia Hand*, pp. 301–302.
36. Ibid., p. 302.
37. John Pilger, "What Really Happened at Rambouillet?" And What Else Is Being Kept under Wraps by Our Selective Media?" *New Statesman*, May 30, 1991, p. 1.
38. Albright, *Madam Secretary*, p. 406.
39. Clinton, *My Life*, p. 850.
40. Wesley Clark, *Waging Modern War* (New York: Public Affairs, 2001), p. 135.
41. Benjamin S. Lambeth, *Transformation of American Air Power* (Ithaca, NY: Cornell University Press, 2000), pp. 258 and 264.
42. "In the President's Words: 'We Act to Prevent a Wider War,'" excerpts in the *New York Times*, March 25, 1999, p. A 6.
43. Peter Riddell, *Hug Them Close: Blair, Clinton, Bush, and the 'Special Relationship'* (London: Politico's Publishing, 2003), pp. 106–116.
44. Katharine Q. Seelye, "Clinton Resists Renewed Calls for Ground Troops in Kosovo," *New York Times*, May 19, 1999, p. A 10.
45. Blumenthal, *The Clinton Wars*, p. 648.
46. Jane Perlez, "Clinton and Joint Chiefs of Staff to Discuss Ground Invasion," *New York Times*, June 2, 1999, p. A 14.
47. Many experts attribute Serbia's surrender to the threat of a ground invasion. See, for example, Clark, *Waging Modern War*, p. 425; Benjamin s. Lambeth, *NATO's Air War for Kosovo: A Strategic and Operational Assessment* (Santa Monica, CA: RAND, 2001), p. 76; and Ivo H. Daalder and Michael E. O'Hanlon, *Winning Ugly: NATO's War to Save Kosovo* (Washington, DC: Brookings Institution Press, 2000), pp. 158–160, 214.
48. Clark, *Waging Modern War*, p. 394.
49. Jim Hoagland, "The Trouble With Playing Global Cop," *Washington Post*, September 2, 1999, p. A 39; Kay Bailey Hutchinson, "The Case for Strategic Sense," *Washington Post*, September 13, 1999, p. A 27; and Michael Mandelbaum, "Foreign

Policy as Social Work," *Foreign Affairs*, 75, no. 1 (January/February, 1996), 16–32.

50. Jamsheed Marker, *East Timor: A Memoir of the Negotiations for Independence* (Jefferson, NC: McFarland & Company, 2003), pp. 202–210.
51. Madeleine Albright, *Madam Secretary* (New York: Miramax Books, 2003), p. 272.
52. David von Drehel and R. Jeffrey Smith, "U.S. Strikes Iraq for Plot to Kill Bush," *Washington Post*, June 27, 1993, p. A 1.
53. Richard Butler, *The Greatest Threat: Iraq, Weapons of Mass Destruction, and the Crisis of Global Security* (New York: Public Affairs, 2000), pp. 234–241.
54. No author, "Clinton's Statement: We are Delivering a Powerful Message to Saddam," *New York Times*, December 17, 1998, p. A 16.
55. Blumenthal, *The Clinton Wars*, pp. 545–546.
56. T.R. Reid, *The United States of Europe: The New Superpower and The End of American Supremacy* (New York: Penguin, 2005), pp. 10–11, 22–25, and 227.
57. Rachel Ehrenfeld, *Funding Evil: How Terrorism is Financed—and How to Stop It* (Chicago: Bonus Books, 2005), pp. 101 and 116.
58. Hyland, *Clinton's World*, p. 203.
59. Richard A. Clarke, *Against All Enemies* (New York: Free Press, 2004), pp. 214–226 and 227–229 and Daniel Benjamin and Steven Simon, *The Age of Sacred Terror* (New York: Random House, 2002), pp. 350–383.
60. Osama bin Laden 1996 fatwa, "Declarations of War against the Americans Occupying the Lands of the Two Holy Places." Downloaded from http://www.pbs.org/newshour/updates/military-july-dec96-fatwa_1996/. Accessed July 20, 2016.
61. "U.S. Missiles pound targets in Afghanistan, Sudan," CNN.com, August 20, 1998. Downloaded from http://www.cnn.com/US/9808/20/us.strikes.01/. Accessed July 20, 2016.
62. For an explanation of the U.S. military's reluctance to carry the fight to al Qaeda, see Richard H. Shultz Jr.'s "Showstoppers: Nine Reasons why we never sent our Special Operations Forces after al Qaeda before 9/11," *Weekly Standard*, 9, no. 19 (January 26, 2004), 26–29.

63. *The 9/11 Commission Report: Final Report of the National Commission on Terrorist Attack Upon The United States* (New York: W.W. Norton, 2004), p. 139.
64. Clinton, *My Life*, p. 935.
65. Michael Muskal, "Bill Clinton: 'i could have killed' Osama bin Laden in 1998," *Los Angeles Times*, August 1, 2014, p. A 3.

Part III

CHAPTER 6

George Walker Bush and the International Outreach

"So foul a sky clears not without a storm." —William Shakespeare's King John

"Trying to plan for the future without a sense of history is like trying to plant cut flowers." —Daniel Boorstin, Librarian of the US Congress

George Walker Bush's foreign policy veered sharply from the caution, disengagement, and hesitancy of his predecessor to a forceful interventionism that surpassed other post-Cold War presidencies. Large-scale military incursions into Afghanistan and Iraq were followed by ambitious nation-building and democracy-promotion exertions in both lands. Under American auspices, counterterrorism operations expanded into the Philippines, Somalia, Pakistan, and the Horn of Africa. President Bush's first term also witnessed the formation of a global anti-terrorism coalition, a close re-alignment with Pakistan, and diplomatic exertions to buttress democracy in the "color revolutions" of Ukraine, Georgia, and Kyrgyzstan. In early 2005, the White House joined with Saudi Arabia and Europe (mostly France) in pushing Syrian military forces out of their three-decade occupation of Lebanon in the Cedar Revolution. George W. Bush's policies, in turn, generated international opposition from friends and foes, strained America's resources, and bred its own backlash at home.

The former Texas governor's first nine months in White House recorded a moderate international policy. Ten weeks into his presidency, for example, Bush faced the so-called Hainan Incident. In that showdown with

T.H. Henriksen, *Cycles in US Foreign Policy since the Cold War*,
DOI 10.1007/978-3-319-48640-6_6

China, the incoming government defused it in the best crisis-management tradition without escalation or triumphalism. A US reconnaissance aircraft flying 70 miles from Hainan Island was set upon by two J-8 fighter planes from the People's Republic of China. One of the Chinese pilots collided into the US Navy EP-3 intelligence airplane on its routine signals-gathering mission. The PRC fighter jet broke in two, crashed into the sea below, killing the pilot. The damaged American propeller craft had to make a forced landing on Hainan Island. Chinese military officials placed the 24 Navy crew members under guard and interrogated them repeatedly and at all hours of the night. A brief diplomatic standoff ensued until Washington issued a letter of regret and sorrow (but not an apology) to the Beijing government. The White House made no concessions but finessed the diplomatic tempest. China released the crew on April 11, ten days after the mid-air crash. The disassembled EP-3 was returned on July 3. There was no cowboy internationalism on Bush's part.

Three brief terrorist incidents during President Bush's first June in office also indicated that the new commander-in-chief started walking in the same cautious footsteps of the previous White House occupant, despite his tough rhetoric on the campaign trail. As such, the trio of events elicited a Clintonesque reaction which struck observers as odd coming from the new president, who roundly derided the sitting government's irresolution during his election campaign.[1] These soon-forgotten episodes in mid-2001, additionally, drew a decidedly timorous response so out of step with that of the post-9/11 Bush administration. First, FBI agents investigating the skiff-bombing of the *USS Cole* fled Aden in haste when notified of intercepted cellphone threats. Second, on the other side of the Arabian Peninsula, US warships berthed in Bahrain, the US Fifth Fleet's headquarters, headed seaward after receiving terrorists' alerts. Finally, US Marines taking part in training exercises with Jordanian troops hastily redeployed back on their ships and steamed clear of any land danger once they received a terrorist warning. None of these events made much political impact once the September11 attack took place two months later. In retrospect, however, they hardly signaled resoluteness on the part of America's defense forces or the new commander-in-chief. The foreign policy pendulum seemed decidedly anchored in disengagement mode.

During his campaign, however, candidate Bush sounded strong internationalist policy themes. In this manner, he followed closely Republican Party pronouncements during the 1990s. The former Texas politician called for a return to basics in national security policy and for strengthening alliances with Western Europe and Japan, the latter of which he believed had been shunted aside for a China-first orientation by the Clinton White House. Likewise, he argued that Clinton had let the strong Persian Gulf coalition atrophy, despite ongoing saber-rattling from Saddam Hussein. At his party's convention, he returned to the need for more defense money: "America's armed forces need better equipment, better training, and better pay."[2] By personal temperament and political instincts, candidate Bush gave more than an inkling of his predisposition toward a terrifying menace.

September 11 and the Return of American Interventionism

The al Qaeda-orchestrated "planes operation" ended the decade-long interregnum from the fall of the Soviet Union. This "holiday from history" left America unprepared for the sudden terrorist attack on its own soil. Prior to the 9/11 terrorism, Americans had looked inward from global issues, except briefly during the short Persian Gulf War. Washington's internationalism addressed mostly humanitarian plights in Somalia, Haiti, Bosnia, and Kosovo. The pocket-sized military expeditions did not break the rhythm of American society or its citizenry. None overextended America's armed forces in the manner of the great wars of the twentieth century or even the conflicts in Korea and Vietnam. The 9/11 violence was profoundly different, for it marked the opening of several counterterrorist battles, which still persist today.

The demolished World Trade Center and damaged Pentagon snapped the disengagement cycle of American public opinion. The four commandeered and crashed commercial jets undeniably initiated much more than a change in the cycle of American foreign policy. The 9/11 terrorist highjackings set the stage for an expansive strategy of counterterrorism, military invasion, territorial occupation, democracy promotion, and nation-building, which initially enjoyed wide public support.

Stunned by the events of the day, President Bush took to the airwaves from the Oval Office to rally the nation for war. Then at a memorial service at the National Cathedral in the capital, Bush called the terrorist perpetrators the "evil ones," and pledged to pursue them to the ends of the earth. Next, he traveled to the lower Manhattan and the site of Ground Zero where the 110-storied Twin Towers once proudly stood and 50,000 people had worked. Still swirling with dust and noxious particles in this resting place for most of the 2996 dead, the president took up a bullhorn to address the crowd of hardhats, rescue workers, and gawkers. He spoke for Americans, when he pledged that "the people who knocked these buildings down will hear all of us soon."[3] The warlike statement heartened the crowd and resonated widely across the country. It was to be one of the high points of Bush's tenure, a presidency not marked by many rhetorical pinnacles.

Before the Senate and the House of Representatives sitting in joint session, Bush gave his third speech in the trilogy following the 9/11 catastrophe nine days earlier. He spoke like a wartime commander-in-chief laying out a martial campaign to carry the fight to the enemy. He delineated the case against Osama bin Laden, al Qaeda, and their Taliban hosts in Afghanistan. Wisely, he laid down the strategy that prevails today of separating "our many Muslim friends" from the Islamist terrorists, "who are traitors to their own [Islamic] faith." The president called attention to the fact that the terrorists "want to overthrow existing governments in many Muslim countries, such as Egypt, Saudi Arabia, and Jordan."[4] The conflict was to be a counterterrorism operation, not a religious crusade against the over 1 billion Islamic faithful.

Rather than moving ahead without Congressional authority, President Bush complied with the US Constitution and demonstrated respect for the separation of powers between executive and legislative branches by seeking approval from Congress for military action against the 9/11 jihadis. Out of these turbulent days came a significant legislative measure that contributed to the expansive use of America's military power and to its foreign policy reach. The US Congress passed the Authorization to Use Military Force (AUMF), which granted the president "authority under the Constitution to take action to deter and prevent acts of international terrorism."[5] At the time of passage, just a week after the horrific destruction of the Twin Towers in Lower Manhattan, the Joint Resolution seemed almost perfunctory given the scale of al Qaeda's terrorism. Soon afterward, the AUMF slipped from public attention for almost a decade. Then, its disinterment was marked by the resolution's application by President Barack Obama to a broad range of terrorist networks unconnected to al Qaeda, which will be related in a subsequent chapter. With the war-fighting authorization in hand, the Bush administration returned to its goal of building an international coalition. So began the most fervent international interventionism of any post-Cold War president, as the engagement phase of the foreign policy cycle marked.

Coalition Building

Prior to its counterattack on Afghanistan to root out al Qaeda's headquarters and to oust the Mullah Mohammed Omar regime for hosting Osama bin Laden, the Bush administration undertook a burst of international diplomacy. Washington lined up NATO partners, pursued Russia, and looked to friendly nations beyond Europe. Keen to make its case of turning over every stone before attacking Afghanistan, it appealed to the Taliban rulers to hand over the terrorist mastermind. The Taliban rejected American requests and even Saudi Arabian pleas, despite the desert kingdom being the chief backer of the Islamic Republic of Afghanistan. The two Muslim states shared their adherence to purist Salafist Islam. For his part, Mullah Omar took refuge in the *Pashtunwali* code that once hospitality is granted to a guest then the host must protect his visitor. The American and Taliban governments underestimated the costs of honoring this ancient custom.[6]

Thereupon, Washington strengthened its resolve to oust the Taliban from power. It strove to assemble a broad coalition to fight Islamic terrorism and to mount an Afghan invasion. Forging coalitions forms a part of the American way of war. Allies and international approval provides legitimacy and justification for interventions. The Bush administration laid the groundwork for an array of distinct coalitions ringing Afghanistan. At the outer edge, it moved to reduce tensions with such major players as China and Russia. The Bush White House dropped lingering resentments over the Hainan Incident with Beijing. It discarded its "strategic competitor" label used to define Sino-American relations. It nearly recognized China as a cobelligerent for Beijing's anti-terrorism policies in the Muslim-populated Xinjiang province in the westernmost reaches of the country despite State Department opposition. The Bush foreign policy team pursued warmer relations with Russia for a more direct quid pro quo from Moscow than just goodwill.

The Pentagon needed the Russian Federation's acquiescence for flyover rights and to establish airbases for its Afghan attack in the nearby countries that Moscow regarded as its "near abroad." Gaining entry into Russia's sphere of influence proved easier than anticipated given the recent downturn in Russo-American relations. The Kremlin had bitterly resented the American-led NATO bombings in 1999 of Serbia over Kosovo's rebellion against Serbian rule. Moscow saw in Muslim-dominated Kosovo a reflection of its battles against Muslim separatists in Chechnya. Washington's muscling into the Balkans, first with the Bosnian crisis and then Kosovo, infuriated the Russian leadership, who perceived the NATO advances as trespassing on their doorstep.

Washington encountered a changed Russian leadership. When the affable, often intoxicated, and politically out-of-step, Boris Yeltsin unexpectedly resigned his presidency, he cleared the way for his handpicked successor Vladimir Putin to move from prime minister to president in 2000. A steely personality, Putin drove Russo-American relations into the political freezer much as they had been during the Cold War. But before that downturn, the new Russian president mostly stood aside while the Bush team searched for rentable bases in Central Asia. After all, the Kremlin chief shared America's goal to defeat political Islam, lest its Afghan variant further inflame Islamist violence in the Russian-dominated Caucasus.

Three Central Asian nations directly shared borders with Afghanistan—Tajikistan, Turkmenistan, and Uzbekistan. Of these, Uzbekistan attracted the most Washington attention for a mix of reasons. Geographically, Uzbekistan was the most propitiously placed, for it shared the closest border with the Northern Alliance, the Taliban's foe. The Bush administration secured expanded use of the Uzbek's Karshi-Khanabad airport (known as K-2 by US airmen). In return, Uzbek president Islam Karimov raked in millions of US dollars and took delivery of military aid to combat the Islamic Movement of Uzbekistan, which endangered his government.

Similarly, the United States reached out to Turkmenistan, although it lacked the close proximity of Uzbekistan to the Northern Alliance. Only Tajikistan, which shared a frontier with Afghanistan, initially resisted Washington's courtship. Poorest and most fractured of the 15 former Soviet republics, Tajikistan was the most dependent on Moscow's goodwill. It took Putin's intercession to convince the government in Dushanbe to accede to American requests to fly over, refuel, and undertake other operations from its territory. Additionally, the Bush administrations pursued landing rights with other Central Asian nations that did not share a border with Afghanistan. It nailed down agreements with Kazakhstan and Kyrgyzstan.

President Bush's foreign policy team also went beyond the Soviet successor republics in their quest for allies to facilitate the Afghan attack. Among the most pivotal was Pakistan, with which the United States shared a tortuous history since their close Cold War cooperation. In the course of the East-West standoff, Washington looked upon Islamabad as a key ally against the Soviet Union. The two worked together in repelling the Red Army's invasion of Afghanistan by backing the mujahedeen resistance. After the Berlin Wall crumbled, the Clinton administration shunted Pakistan aside for closer ties with its archrival India. Pakistani leaders interpreted warmer Indo-American relations as a betrayal. The Pakistanis also pursued their own interests in Afghanistan, which included keeping the rugged country out of India's orbit. Pakistan's secretive ISI Directorate regarded the Taliban jihadis from their beginnings as ready allies against Hindu-ruled India. The ISI, therefore, helped the Taliban to seize power to exclude Indian influence in Kabul. Pakistani objectives conflicted with American interests.

The Bush White House tasked Secretary of State Colin Powell with the job of returning Pakistan to the American column. The former four-star Army general was able to speak soldier to soldier to Pervez Musharraf, a former general who came to the Pakistani presidency through a military coup. Powell persuaded Musharraf to sever ties with the Afghan Taliban regime, grant US landing rights on Pakistani airbases, share intelligence, and open the country's airspace to American warplanes. George Bush contended that the former career Army officer "single-handedly got Musharraf on board."[7] Powell's diplomatic coup notwithstanding, neither he nor his successors ever ended the underground support by elements within the ISI for the Taliban movement, even though it fomented violence in Pakistan's tribal belts.[8]

Money also played a major role in returning Pakistan to the American camp. Over the years, the United States poured in billions of dollars, making Pakistan the fourth largest beneficiary of its foreign aid after Afghanistan, Israel, and Iraq.[9] The Bush administration also looked past Musharraf's redrafting of the Pakistani constitution so as to extend his presidency for another term. Such pragmatism differed from President Bush's zealous democracy promotion in a host of countries after the Iraq invasion.

The Pentagon did gain access to two Pakistani bases—Pasni and Jacobabad—for its Afghan invasion. What's more, the Pakistanis allowed supply ships to dock at the port city of Karachi. Off-loaded materiel found its way onto trucks driven by local men, who drove convoys across the country into the elevated terrain of Afghanistan in what became a vital logistical link to the Western war against the Taliban. Overall, the Pak-American partnership functioned reasonably well, although it was subject to fraught moments as when the US breached its sovereignty with CIA drone strikes or military ground raids. Washington and Islamabad shared the same jihadi enemies, whose presence within Pakistan threatened citizens' lives and societal order. But overt collaboration with the hated Americans was not in the best interest of the South Asian country's rulers. So, its military and civilian officials winked and nodded their complicity in the drone killings. These CIA aerial strikes enhanced the survival of Pakistan's leadership but it was loath to acknowledge the fact.[10]

Washington's sudden intervention into Central Asia also necessitated a working relationship with America's bête noire in the region—the Islamic Republic of Iran. Washington and Tehran had been at sword's point since the overthrow of the pro-American shah and the ascendancy of a theocratic regime in 1979. Bitterness over the Iranian "student" seizure of the US Embassy and abduction of its staff began America's post-shah animosity. Other crises followed which had the effect of pouring kerosene on the blazing antagonism each time it seemed to subside. Iranian clerics often called America the Great Satan and whipped up chants of "death to America" from street demonstrators. Therefore, the US-led military intervention promised to trigger another set-to between the two powers.

Unexpectedly, their interaction went much better than the Bush administration anticipated. Part of the explanation for the Iran's mild reaction to the US military presence lay in the fact that Tehran looked upon the Taliban regime as a mortal enemy. Not only did the Taliban rulers practice the strict Salafi doctrine of Islam which considered the Iranian Shia branch of Islam as heretics, but also they persecuted, tortured, and murdered the Shiite population within Afghanistan. Another Iranian grievance against the Taliban regime stemmed from its negligent suppression of narcotics exports from Afghanistan's luxuriant poppy growing fields. Afghan drugs were the bane of Iranian youth, whose widespread addiction caused massive problems for the country. So, the clerical regime momentarily suspended its fierce hatred of the United States.

Elsewhere the Bush foreign policy team jumped into action to fight what it termed as the Global War on Terror, or GWOT. It perceived threats in the Middle East, Africa, and the Pacific. Failed states, such as Somalia, and fragile ones, such as the Philippines, possessed "ungoverned spaces" which afforded havens for terrorists' attacks on the West. As a consequence, Pentagon officials searched for bases from which to counter the spread of political Islam. On the northeastern corner of Africa, the United States set up an anti-terrorist headquarters in Djibouti's Camp Lemonier, a former French Foreign Legion outpost that opened on the Gulf of Aden. Eventually, some 4000 soldiers, sailors, airmen, and other personnel arrived and instituted a counterinsurgency strategy for the entire Horn of Africa region. They sought to prevent, or at least limit, terrorist factions from establishing sanctuaries to recruit, train, and export terrorists to other fronts. The Special Forces trained local troops, tried to ameliorate ruinous conditions that bred terrorism, and gathered intelligence. In short, they aimed for a "pre-emptive strike on the hearts and minds of those living in the Horn."[11]

Halfway around the globe, 600 US military personnel extended similar assistance to the Philippines as part of the GWOT. In the southern islands of the archipelago, SOF descended on the Zamboanga Peninsula of Mindanao, which was home to an aggrieved Muslim population who fought the larger Catholic population. A tiny bandit-terrorist group, Abu Sayyaf, sprang from the decades-long local resistance to the Manila government. With very tenuous links to al Qaeda, Abu Sayyaf undertook a range of criminal activities, including abduction, rape, murder, and extortion in the name of Islam. The Manila government limited the US special-forces soldiers to training and mentoring roles for the Filipino armed forces, who did the actual fighting against the Abu Sayyaf terrorists. This indirect approach, with US troops in support functions, evolved into a standard operating procedure in other parts of the world.[12]

Rallying America's Allies

The 9/11 terrorism mended US relations with its European allies, which had cooled after the USSR's breakdown. Without the Soviet threat, Western Europe became less likely to toe the American line on matters of security and foreign policy. But the 9/11 terrorism stimulated a wellspring of sympathy and goodwill toward the United States, which the Bush administration capitalized on for its plans. The day after the attacks, NATO hastily convened a meeting of transatlantic ambassadors to consider invoking Article 5, requiring a collective defense of a member state under attack by an outside power. The attendees issued a statement: "If it is determined that this attack was directed from abroad against the United States, it shall be regarded as an action covered by Article 5 of the Washington Treaty," which established NATO.[13]

After NATO examined the US intelligence findings, the alliance's General Secretary George Robertson concluded that "it is now clear all roads lead to al Qaeda."[14] Invoking Article 5 meant that NATO members were at war against al Qaeda. In a role reversal of sorts, NATO's

European members flew planes to patrol the East coast of their ally across the Atlantic. In retrospect, the giant West European reconnaissance planes flew unnecessary missions to defend their American ally from a shadowy terrorist cell. But the gesture heartened America for its display of solidarity. Not all Europeans joined in America's rush to war in Afghanistan. Anti-American protestors took to public squares to oppose the US counterattack against a terrorist-sheltering regime.

Washington gratefully accepted NATO's air protection. But the Bush government exhibited much less enthusiasm for NATO military participation in the Afghan military expedition for two reasons. First, the Pentagon recalled the complex and circuitous decision-making process during the 1999 Kosovo air campaign. Selecting targets and getting decisions from NATO allies proved arduous and time consuming. The Secretary of Defense Donald Rumsfeld preferred an unencumbered chain of command, where he and his civilian and military aides made decisions without NATO's bureaucratic bottlenecks. Second, NATO was notorious for its underspending on defense. What militaries it possessed were orientated toward Cold War's conventional warfare. The Afghan conflict promised to be one requiring small numbers of specially trained troops, conducting unconventional tactics behind enemy lines and in close coordination with bombing aircraft.

Instead, the Pentagon looked to Britain and Australia for special forces rather than NATO's armies. Meeting at NATO headquarters in Brussels, the members pressed the US Defense Department for combat assignments in the war. In reply, Paul Wolfowitz, deputy to Rumsfeld, bluntly replied to European appeals: "If we need collective action, we will ask for it."[15] America's standoffishness ruffled European feathers even after the start of the intervention. A French official characterized the secondary role allotted to most NATO countries as "washing up the dirty dishes" after the United States "did the cooking."[16] The metaphor was fleeting, as the United States soon needed its NATO partners in Afghanistan and later Iraq.

Still, by the commencement of the military campaign, President Bush could proclaim: "More than 40 countries in the Middle East, Africa, Europe, and across Asia have granted air transit and landing rights." Even without participation by Muslim governments in the military operation, Bush held that "we are supported by the collective will of the world."[17] Traditional American friends such as Australia, Britain, Canada, and France were joined by Poland, Denmark, Norway, and Germany, all of which inserted military units on the ground. Even Japan and the Netherlands patrolled warships in the Arabian Gulf.

Attacking Afghanistan

The September 11, 2001, attack swung America into a foreign policy engagement cycle. Americans backed their 43rd president in his march against the phantom-like terrorist circuit hosted by Afghanistan. President Bush set in motion several initiatives to target al Qaeda and its mastermind. He convened a War Cabinet of his top policy makers in the White House's Situation Room on September 13. The president wanted to eliminate the terrorist perpetrators in their Afghanistan liar. Unexpectedly, George Tenet, the Director of Central Intelligence (i.e. the head of CIA), outlined a plan for an immediate attack on al Qaeda and their Taliban protectors. A few days later at the presidential retreat Camp David, Tenet and Cofer Black, the head of the CIA's Counterterrorism Center, fleshed out the Agency's strategy using PowerPoint slides. It envisioned an innovative mix of CIA field officers on the ground, Special Operation Forces working with local militias, and heavy bombing from US Air Force and Navy planes.

The Pentagon was caught largely flatfooted with no prepared contingency plan for an intervention into Afghanistan. The Chairman of the Joint Chiefs of Staff, General Henry B. Shelton, offered a bombing and Tomahawk missile strategy to deal with the threat. But the Clinton appointee's recommendations were judged inadequate to eradicate the terrorist scourge from the remote country. Indeed, Shelton's plan smacked of the former administration's failed "cruise missile" response to the 1998 embassy bombings in East Africa, when mostly deserted Afghan camps were blown up.[18] So, the president and civilian officials at the Pentagon adopted the CIA playbook with some modifications.

The Agency augmented its contacts with intelligence services in such unsavory countries as Libya, Syria, and Uzbekistan—all with abysmal human rights records. The Bush administration felt justified supping with devils, even if long spoons were not used. The CIA also engaged in a range of anti-terrorist actions, some of which became controversial in time, such as "black sites" or secret prisons in foreign countries used to detain, interrogate, and water-board suspected terrorists. Additionally, Langley acquired covert bases from which to loft drones (remotely piloted aircraft) for surveillance and strike missions to rub out terrorists or insurgents in

Afghanistan and Pakistan, plus Yemen. At the request of George Tenet, President Bush signed a series of intelligence memoranda authorizing the CIA under Title 50 of the US Code to conduct covert and lethal operations against al Qaeda.[19] Thus, Bush's muscular course of action departed substantially from Clinton's law enforcement orientation, which relied on forensic evidence, arrest, legal procedures, and jury trials to deal with terrorism.

For the intervention into Afghanistan, George Bush's strategy called for CIA field officers to enter Afghanistan first and establish contact with the anti-Taliban movement. The Northern Alliance had been fighting the Pashtun-dominated Taliban since 1996 when the radical Islamist movement took over Kabul. The CIA operatives came armed with millions in $100 bills to hand out to the local militia chiefs. Some of the American intelligence personnel had long-standing relations with local chieftains, providing them familiarity with local forces and the country itself.[20] Once on the ground, the SOF called in airstrikes and worked with Northern Alliance militias against the Taliban fighters.

This triumvirate of airstrikes, Special Forces, and local, pro-American militias proved to be a winning and cost-effective combination. It routed the Taliban's disorganized and ill-trained rifle-toting irregulars. The small US military footprint heralded an innovative counterterrorism prescription that later served as a template for similar American operations in Yemen, Somalia, and Syria. Nevertheless, it failed to get Osama bin Laden and his top lieutenants, who escaped over the border into Pakistan, where they engineered a comeback in Afghanistan three years later.

The swiftness of the victory caught the United States unprepared for a governance role in Afghanistan. Nor had Washington officials given much thought about the political structure or the reconstruction of a post-Taliban state. Days before the commencement of bombing on October 7, President Bush asked his national security affairs advisor: "Who will run the country?" Condoleezza Rice admitted that no real thought had been given to the question.[21] In fact, the security adviser, like many of her fellow Vulcans—as the Bush foreign policy team termed themselves—opposed the use of US military forces for peacekeeping or society-building. Their preoccupation was regime change.[22] They held the previous Clinton administration in contempt for its stability-soldiering missions in Somalia, Haiti, Bosnia, and Kosovo. The planning void for the post-invasion period was an ominous omission first for Afghanistan and later Iraq, which placed both occupations in jeopardy from raging anti-American insurgencies.

The Plunge into Nation-Building

Invading a foreign country is one thing, but building it into a replica of America's democratic pluralism is quite another. Nation-building and democracy-promotion goals constituted a volte-face from George W. Bush's earlier utterances. "Sending our military on vague, aimless, and endless deployments is the swift solvent of morale," said candidate George Bush about Clinton's humanitarian deployments in Somalia and Yugoslavia.[23] His principle foreign policy advisor during the presidential campaign, Condoleezza Rice, put the argument even more precisely about the military's role: "It is not a civilian police force. It is not a political referee. And it is most certainly not designed to build a civilian society."[24]

First in Afghanistan and then in Iraq, the Bush administration came around, after initial hesitation, to the proposition that it must occupy, develop, and instill democracy in its newly acquired subjects.[25] This assessment constituted a huge commitment to societal transformation under the most unpropitious conditions. This projection of US power, ideology, and vast resources drew upon the post-World War II precedent of implanting democratic institutions and building prosperity within defeated Germany, Italy, and Japan. But those countries and other West European beneficiaries of the Marshall Plan all had more than a brush with industrial economic development and democratic traditions. Afghanistan, the world's second poorest nation after Somali, represented an extraordinarily backward economic and political state.

The rapidity of the US-led victory over the Taliban caught Washington unprepared and off balance much as a tug-of-war team stumbles when its opponents unexpectedly let go of the rope. On the eve of the American bombing campaign, the incoming chairman of the Joint Chiefs of Staff, Air Force General Richard B. Myers, speculated about the conflict lasting a year or more. The Taliban resistance folded after a few months. The US war machine hardly revved up before the need arose for occupation, administration, and government services.

A great impediment to democratic state-building rested not solely with the need for overnight implementation but with the President Bush's own initial predilections against it. During his run for the Oval Office, the Texas governor disparaged the Clinton administration's deployments of US troops for peacekeeping and rudimentary nation-building tasks in Somalia, Haiti, and the Balkans. He resolved to avoid a similar pattern. One week into the Afghan aerial bombardment, Bush firmly re-stated his position—"I don't want to nation-build with troops"—to his advisers in a strategy meeting.[26] Later, in his second-term inaugural address, he wholeheartedly embraced the global spread of freedom and liberty as America's mission. At the outset of the Afghan campaign, he recalled his electioneering rhetoric, however.

The president was not alone in his abhorrence to nation-building prospects. Colin Powell voiced a similar disdain for societal transformation in the forlorn land. As the Taliban fled Kabul, the secretary of state reiterated a common refrain: "We will turn it [Afghanistan] over to Brahimi and the U.N."[27] The UN Secretary General Kofi Annan had recently appointed Lakhdar Brahimi, an Algerian diplomat, to the post of UN special representative to Afghanistan. Brahimi and the UN did play a role in trying to stabilize the turbulent nation but its military and civilian capacities fell well short of what was needed to cure the deeply fractured country at war since 1979. The secretary of defense joined the chorus opposing a long-term US presence to remake the face of the country. Donald Rumsfeld thought it "highly unlikely" that American soldiers and Marines would assume "a part of a semipermanent peacekeeping activity in the country."[28] The Bush administration, while embarking on an interventionist cycle, still displayed a reluctance to go full bore into lengthy occupations cum civil society reconstruction akin to that America carried out in postwar Germany and Japan. In the meantime, Washington turned to the United Nations to handle governance.

The UN did summon a conference to form an Afghan government from the country's opposition figures. Meeting in Bonn, Germany, two weeks after Kabul fell to the United States and its local allies, Afghan political figures and tribal representatives bickered and jousted until they settled on a governmental framework. Signed on December 5, 2001, the Bonn Agreement set up an interim government, established basic administrative functions, and laid out a roadmap to democracy. The conferees picked Hamid Karzai, an English-speaking former deputy foreign minister, to be the interim president. Karzai hailed from an anti-Taliban Pashtun subclan in the country's south. In addition to support from Washington, Karzai gained the approval of Iran and Russia, two nations uneasy about instability on their doorstep. The Bonn attendees doled out other administrative posts in a rough attempt to balance ethnic representation at the national level. The agreement mandated elections for president in 2004 and for a parliament the next year. Even though the Bonn conference was not strictly a democratic answer, it resulted in a reasonable ethnic inclusion of the country's various peoples. In hopes of preempting subversion from a powerful and ruthless warlord, Karzai brought into his fledgling government the Uzbek commander Aburrashid Dostrum. Later, Karzai relied on other warlords to govern. These decisions telegraphed the new president's reliance on unsavory figures—a dangerous turn for the re-born country.

Next, Washington secured Security Council passage of resolution 1386 that defined an international framework for assistance. That UN action established the International Security Assistance Force (ISAF) for peacekeeping and security operations. Soon after, ISAF commanded 5000 troops in Kabul. Next, the Security Council passed resolution 1401 in late March 2002 that set up the UN Assistance Mission in Afghanistan (UNAMA). UNAMA sought to integrate the international reconstruction and administrative functions throughout the country. It parceled out government tasks among participating foreign nations. This crude division of labor put European powers in charge of standing up a Western-styled judiciary, modern health services, and a contemporary-trained police force. It fell to the United States to form a countrywide military, known as the Afghan National Army.[29]

Washington also pulled together former protagonists that flanked Afghanistan. Iran, long an adversary of Taliban-ruled Afghanistan, pledged $500 million for reconstruction projects. Tehran also prevailed on the warlord Ismail Khan, who it backed, to attend and to cooperate with the Bonn conference. India, which also despised the Taliban, bestowed billions of dollars for construction projects during the next decade to stabilize the new Kabul government. Pakistan officially joined the American camp on Afghanistan, although elements within its intelligence branch still assisted the Taliban to mount an insurgency against the Karzai administration. Russia, the most wary of the US intervention into its sphere, acquiesced to the Pentagon's enlarging footprint in Afghanistan and neighboring states, once part of Soviet Union. All these neighbors acted for self-interest but it was Bush's foreign policy aides who harnessed and channeled their political ambitions to American reconstruction plans.

For its part, the United States inched into the occupation business. By the end of the first quarter in 2002, the Pentagon had dispatched nearly 20,000 troops, who combed the borderlands for Osama bin Laden and his entourage. Some also tried to seal the transit points into Pakistan to prevent the master terrorist's escape. Closing the frontier by this late date amounted to shutting the barn door after the horse galloped free. On the heels of the burgeoning military "boot print" came a raft of American civilian agencies. The Agency for International Development and the Department of State sent staffs to assist in state-building and rural regeneration. Inasmuch as its ISAF partners proved initially reluctant to venture into the countryside, the United States dispatched Provincial Reconstruction Teams (PRTs) to aid and to protect the rural population. Made up of troops and civilian-aid experts, the 60- to 80-member PRTs varied in quality and performance. In the end, they proved only of marginal effectiveness when the Taliban insurgents returned to Afghanistan.

The Bush White House rhetorically broke further with its opposition to assisting governance and development projects in prostrated Afghanistan. President Bush flew to the Virginia Military Institute to deliver a speech invoking the name and career of that school of arms' most illustrious graduate—George C. Marshall. On a bright sunny day in mid-April 2002, the president recalled that the five-star general was "best remembered for the peace he secured" in the Marshall Plan. Bush declared that "we, too, must follow" a similar path in Afghanistan. He noted that the famous European Recovery Program was acclaimed for "rebuilding Europe and lifting up former enemies showed that America is not content with military victory alone."[30] Hours after the commander-in-chief spoke about reconstructing Afghanistan, his secretary of defense argued that the president did not envision deploying US troops in a peacekeeping role. Donald Rumsfeld noted that troop-contributing allies to the ISAF opposed expanding the ISAF mission beyond the capital.[31]

For its part, the Kabul government turned to warlords, who had gained power and influence since the anti-Soviet war. The Karzai government depended on these powerful local chieftains to ensure order in the domains beyond the capital. Relying on these warlords alienated the rural population from the central government. The warrior chieftains and their thuggish henchmen rode roughshod over the countryside, demanding bribes and inflicting harm on all who challenged them. Their depredations re-kindled favorable memories for some past Taliban practices. Before the Taliban seized Kabul in 1996, Afghanistan experienced a brutal period marked by corruption, human rights abuse, and warlordism. The Taliban ushered in stability and security, even if they sternly enforced a strict Islamic orthodoxy. They severed the arms of thieves and stoned adulterers. Now, Karzai's Kabul, in part, turned back the clock to the pre-Taliban period. Bad governance, corruption, and local grievances undermined the legitimacy of the new Kabul administration to such a degree that American and international programs to restore and reconstruct the country were nearly doomed to fail from the outset.[32] President Karzai won reelection against 17 other candidates in October 2004. A little more than a year later, the country's first democratically elected parliament in 30 years took office. Beneath the surface, however, the Taliban insinuated themselves back into the southern reaches of Afghanistan, while Kabul's corruption and its fractured civil institutions clouded long-term prospects for a peaceful and democratic nation.

After the start of the Iraq War in early 2003, Afghanistan suffered shortages in military and civilian assistance. Just months after the American-led invasion to topple Saddam Hussein, Iraq's new rulers faced a brewing insurgency that further diverted manpower and attention from Afghanistan, which seemed peaceful on the surface compared to the savage sectarian violence washing over Iraq. Beginning in 2005, the Taliban re-commenced isolated assassinations and bombings, which raised Afghan anxieties. By the end of the same year, Iraq was embroiled in a fierce insurgency that threatened an American defeat. To the Bush policy mandarins, Afghanistan became a neglected stepchild as Iraq exploded with scenes reminiscent of Rodin's *Gates of Hell.* Iraq's sharp spike in violence and Coalition troop casualties grabbed the political spotlight in Washington circles. It would not be until Barack Obama's presidency that Afghanistan again loomed large in Washington's power corridors.

A Global Approach to Counter Terrorism

Before either insurgency in Afghanistan or Iraq metastasized into looming quagmires, the Bush administration had swiveled toward a maximalist diplomatic initiative. The large-scale military invasions of Afghanistan and Iraq represented watershed events in the engagement cycle of US foreign policy. Less sweeping but another interventionist action came from the White House. In 2003, the president announced the Proliferation Security Initiative (PSI) to interdict the shipment of nuclear, chemical, and biological weapons to terrorists and rogue nations, such as Iran and North Korea. The PSI also sought to impede the trafficking in WMD delivery systems, that is, missiles and bombs. Ten other countries joined with United States at the time of the launch. Three months later, in early September, they released a set of principles.[33]

The PSI made it clear that only an endorsement of the Statement of Interdiction Principles was necessary to participate; it required no membership in an organization. The United States held that the PSI was a participatory activity, not an organization. Before Bush left office, nearly 70 countries signed the statement. Notably the PRC and its troublesome ally North Korea did not. The PSI formed the basis for several shipboarding searches that netted WMD materials. In one high-profile instance, German intelligence officials uncovered aluminum tubes often converted to nuclear centrifuges aboard the *BBC China*, an Antigua and Barbuda-flagged vessel, sailing in the Mediterranean bound for Libya in September 2003. Assisted by the US Navy, the German inspectors confiscated the nuclear-related items in the ship's hold.

The PSI project lived on into the Barack Obama administration, which backed and celebrated its ten-year anniversary in Warsaw, Poland. Yet, it lacked the prominence given to it by the Bush presidency. By 2013, over a hundred countries endorsed the PSI. Determined opposition to the anti-proliferation campaign still came from China, India, Indonesia, and, of course, North Korea. In some respects, the PSI functioned as a defensive measure like many arms-control agreements, such as nuclear treaties with the Soviet Union and Russia or even Barack Obama's nuclear agreement with Iran, which will be noted in Chap. 9. In other ways, however, the PSI embraced an offensive strategy to halt WMD proliferation and missile-delivery capabilities by taking steps to close off "the flow at sea, in the air, or on land," as outlined in the Statement of Interdiction Principles.[34] It mobilized nations to mount assertive operations rather than enforce compliance on weapons development through diplomacy, as in most arms-control agreements.

The Bush administration set an even more interventionist vector to combat international terrorism in the wake of the 9/11 attacks. Its Global War on Terrorism involved covert as well as overt military operations. The war on terror produced a new cabinet post for the new Department of Homeland Security, plus laws and regulations to dry up financing for terrorism. President Bush declared to other countries that "either you are with us, or you are with the terrorists."[35] This near-ultimatum whetted the perception of American unilateralism and hawkish internationalism. Yet, his words and deeds, despite their uncompromising tone, prodded many other nations to step up cooperation with Washington and crackdown on suspected terrorist cells within their own societies. During the Bush and then Obama era, the freshly minted regulations and data searches infringed on civil liberties, while setting out to safeguard Americans from terrorism within the country.

Abroad, Washington often waged counterterrorist missions with the SOF; they were expertly trained, nimble, and resourceful elite troops who were well suited for dispatching shadowy terrorist circuits in forbidding jungles or mountains. Donald Rumsfeld "authorized the Special Operations Command (SOCOM) as a lead command for the war on terror planning and missions."[36] The Secretary of Defense also presided over a substantial growth in SOF capacity. Its budget quadrupled from $2.3 billion in 2001 to over $10 billion in the 2013 fiscal year, which still represented just 4 percent of the base defense budget. Personnel figures underwent similar swelling and stand now at over 70,000, which comes to 5 percent of the Defense Department's total.

SOCOM expanded its reach by inserting elite special operators in scores of countries, training and mentoring local forces, and by winning over villages to fight insurgents and terrorists beyond their role in Afghanistan, Pakistan, and eventually Iraq. In the Philippines, for example, US military personnel instructed and mentored Filipino army units in the best practices to beat back Abu Sayyaf's banditry and terrorism. From 2002, the Pentagon spent roughly $1 billion over the years to supply Manila with fast patrol boats, arms, and equipment for anti-terrorist operations. On the other side of the globe, SOCOM set up shop in Camp Lemonier in Djibouti, from which they struck back at the terrorist menace in Yemen, Somalia, and elsewhere in the Horn of Africa. Special Forces conducted training and guided indigenous soldiers in counterinsurgency operations in Kenya, Mali, and Algeria. The Djibouti outpost along with a secret base in Saudi Arabia served as launching pads for CIA drone strikes against jihadis in Yemen and Somalia. One of the spy agency's most famous kills in the Horn of Africa region took out Anwar al-Awlaki, the American-born chief of al Qaeda's branch in Yemen.[37]

To sum up, the Bush government augmented the scale and scope of America's military and intelligence presence worldwide. It held to the belief that preemptive military engagement after 9/11 would disrupt or deter plans for terrorism inside the United States. There is more than a shred of legitimacy to this argument as no serious terrorist violence recurred on George W. Bush's watch. The US military frontier, nevertheless, advanced under the direction of Bush junior in ways not seen since World War II. Yet nothing the military special operators or Agency field officers undertook in a passel of failing African and Middle Eastern states came remotely close to matching the enormity of the ground invasion into Iraq with tens of thousands of troops.

Notes

1. Thomas L. Friedman, "A Memo From Osama," *New York Times*, June 26, 2001, p. A 17.
2. James Mann, *Rise of the Vulcans: The History of Bush's War Cabinet* (New York: Viking, 2004), pp. 255–256.
3. Bill Sammon, *Fighting Back: The War on Terrorism—Inside the Bush White House* (Washington, DC: Regnery Publishing, 2002), pp. 187–188.
4. George W. Bush, "Address to the Joint Session of Congress and the American People," September 20, 2001. Downloaded from http://georgewbush-whitehouse.archives.gov/news/releases/2001/09/20010920-8.html. Accessed July 20, 2016.
5. Public Law 107-40, 107th Congress, September 18, 2001. Downloaded from http://www.gpo.gov/fdsys/pkg/PLAW-107publ40/pdf/PLAW-107publ40.pdf. Accessed July 20, 2015.
6. Thomas Barfield, *Afghanistan: A Cultural and Political History* (Princeton, NJ: Princeton University Press, 2010), p. 268.
7. Mann, *Rise of the Vulcans*, p. 342.
8. Stephan Tanner, *Afghanistan: A Military History from Alexander the Great to the Fall of the Taliban* (New York: Da Capo Press, 2002), p. 292.
9. "Aid to Pakistan by the Numbers," Center for Global Development. Downloaded from http://www.cgdev.org/page/aid-pakistan-numbers. Accessed July 20, 2016.
10. Peter L. Bergen, *Man Hunt: The Ten-Year Search for Bin Laden from 9/11 to Abbottabad* (New York: Crown Publishers, 2012), pp. 72–73, 121, 142, 244, and 249.
11. Charlie Coon, "Troops in Horn of Africa Hope to Keep Terrorists at Bay by Helping People," *European Starts and Stripes*, November 21, 2004, p. 1.
12. Eric Schmitt and Thom Shanker, *Counterstrike: Untold Story of America's Secret Campaign Against Al Qaeda* (New York: Time Books, 2011), pp. 164–179 and 194–198.
13. Suzanne Daley, "For First Time, NATO Invokes Pact With U.S.," *New York Times*, September 13, 2001, p. A 1.
14. William Drorzdiak and Rajiv Chandrasekaran, "NATO: U.S. Evidence on Bin Laden 'Compelling,'" *Washington Post*, October 3, 2001, p. A 11.

15. Suzanne Daley, "Alliance Says It Will Fight, If It Asked," *New York Times*, October 3, 2001, p. A 1.
16. Joseph Fitchett, "U.S. Allies Chafe at 'Cleanup' Role," *International Herald Tribune*, November 26, 2001, p. 1.
17. Patrick E. Tyler, "U.S. and Britain Strike Afghanistan, Aiming at Bases And Terrorist Camps," *New York Times*, October 8, 2001, p. A 1.
18. George Tenent, *At the Center of the Storm: My Years at the CIA* (New York: HarperCollins, 2007), pp. 175–179.
19. Dana Priest and William M. Arkin, *Top Secret America: The Rise of the New American Security State* (New York: Little, Brown and Company, 2011), pp. 32–34 and 203–208.
20. Gary C. Schroen, *First In: An Insider's Account of How the CIA Spearheaded the War on Terror in Afghanistan* (New York: Ballantine Books, 2005), p. 38.
21. Bob Woodward, *Bush at War* (New York: Simon & Schuster, 2002), p. 195.
22. Mann, *Rise of the Vulcans*, p. 331.
23. Frank Bruni, "Bush Vows Money And Support For Military," *New York Times*, September 24, 1999, p. A 10.
24. Condoleezza Rice, "Promoting the National Interest," *Foreign Affairs*, 79, no. 1 (January/February, 2000), 53.
25. Woodward, *Bush At War*, p. 339 and Ali A. Allawi, *The Occupation of Iraq: Winning the War, Losing the Peace* (New Haven, CT: Yale University Press, 2007), p. 250.
26. Woodward, *Bush at War*, p. 241.
27. Ibid., p. 241.
28. Patrick E. Tyler, "U.S. Sees Limited Mission in Postwar Afghanistan," *New York Times*, November 28, 2001, p. A 1.
29. James Dobbins, John, et al., *America's Role in Nation-Building: From Germany to Iraq* (Santa Monica, CA: Rand, 2003), pp. 132–134.
30. James Dao, "Bush Sets Role for U.S. in Afghan Rebuilding," *New York Time*, April 18, 2002, p. A 1.
31. Ibid.
32. Sarah Chayes, *The Punishment of Virtue: Inside Afghanistan After the Taliban* (New York: Penguin Press, 2006), pp. 163, 168–170, 173, and 228–290.

33. Proliferation Security Initiative: Statement of Interdiction Principles, US Department of State, September 4, 2003. Downloaded from http://www.state.gov/t/isn/c27726.htm. Accessed July 20, 2016.
34. Ibid.
35. George W. Bush, "Transcript of President Bush's Address to a Joint Session of Congress," *Washington Post*, September 21, 2001, p. A 24.
36. Donald Rumsfeld, *Known and Unknown: A Memoir* (New York: Sentinel, 2011), p. 654.
37. Mark Mazzetti, *The Way of the Knife* (New York: Penguin Press, 2013), pp. 307–310.

CHAPTER 7

George W. Bush's Overstretch Abroad

"We cannot escape history." —Abraham Lincoln

"No one in his right mind would, or ought to, begin a war if he didn't know how to finish it." —Carl von Clausewitz

The preemptive Iraq War marked the apogee in America's cycle of internationalism since the Berlin Wall toppled. George W. Bush's pirouette toward military intervention and democracy promotion in Iraq and elsewhere saw no equivalent among his post-Wall predecessors or successor. None embraced Bush's Wilsonian faith in exporting democratic institutions to the degree the 43rd president expressed in early 2005 during his second inaugural address: "So it is the policy of the United States to seek and support the growth of democratic movements and institutions in every nation and culture, with the ultimate goal of ending tyranny in our world." He directly linked others' "imperative of self-government" with "the urgent requirement of our nation's security and the calling of our time."[1] Tersely stated, democracy delivered for security for the United States.

Bush's cri de coeur came as America recoiled from the mounting human casualties and financial costs from two large-scale conflicts far from its shores. His fellow countrymen soon lost faith in the presidential project amid the rising toll in blood and treasure expended in unforgiving lands for what seemed as ungrateful beneficiaries. Americans entered the two

T.H. Henriksen, *Cycles in US Foreign Policy since the Cold War*,
DOI 10.1007/978-3-319-48640-6_7

wars with confidence. But the intractable nature of insurgent warfare discouraged them as years past. Prior to that fateful reckoning, the United States waded into its most controversial conflict since the Vietnam War. Like Vietnam, the Iraq War would have a frustrating end after the United States withdrew its military forces. Despite many differences, the two conflicts shared similar outcomes. In both wars, Washington tired of its exertions and left the battle field enabling its enemies to attack again.

Iraq—The War of Choice?

The onetime Texas governor did not set foot in the White House as a prospective warrior president or uber-democracy champion.[2] He inherited a troublesomely aggressive Saddam Hussein from the Clinton administration, which presided over the breakdown of international sanctions and WMD inspections in Iraq, as noted in Chap. 5.[3] Throughout his 18-month presidential campaign, in fact, Bush never spoke of military intervention into Iraq. There were elements within Bush's Republican Party and without the party machinery who were stridently anti-Iraq, however. Some wanted Hussein forcefully ousted by the United States. They championed the concept of "preemption" to deal with the Iraqi dictator because, in their opinion, international containment of Iraq was steadily eroding. Specifically, these thinkers, who were later identified as "neoconservatives" (or neocons), had formerly urged President Clinton to use military action against Iraq to remove the autocratic regime.

Not a few of this hawkish persuasion were to hold influential positions on President Bush's foreign policy team. Donald Rumsfeld and Paul Wolfowitz, secretary and deputy secretary of the Defense Department, respectively, joined John Bolton (US Representative to the UN), Robert Zoellick (US Trade Representative and other positions), and Peter Rodman, who served as Assistant Secretary of Defense for International Security Affairs, in favoring a preemptive course of action against Saddam Hussein.[4] Vice President Richard ("Dick") Cheney also fell prominently into the war-minded camp. Years later and speaking though a biographer, the first President Bush made tough-minded comments about his son's vice president and Rumsfeld, secretary of defense until late 2006. The elder Bush held Cheney and Rumsfeld responsible for influencing the second President Bush toward war with Iraq. But in the end, Bush 41 acknowledged that Bush 43 held the reins of power when the nation entered into the Iraq War.[5]

This loose, neocon grouping originated from onetime Democrats who embraced Franklin Roosevelt's New Deal. But after the Vietnam War, the neocon contingent lost faith in the Democratic Party's hesitant foreign policy and disinclination to employ military power for American interests. The anti-Iraq neocons called attention to Hussein's sponsorship of terrorism when he offered $25,000 payments to the families of Palestinian suicide bombers, who killed Israelis. Hussein's past spoke for itself—wars against Iran and Kuwait, plus gassing his own Kurdish population and Iranian soldiers in the thousands. His record and persistent recklessness pointed to recurring threats. Thus, sooner rather than later, the United States had to push Saddam Hussein from power. Neocons differed on the means to bring down the Iraqi tyrant. Some espoused a direct military approach; others ascribed to US-backed subversion by the Iraqi military.[6]

The neocon faction favored implementation of the Iraq Liberation Act, passed in 1998, which was stillborn because the Clinton White House barely effectuated its provisions. The main thrust of that act aimed at the overthrow of Hussein by his own people and his trial before an international tribunal. This overwhelmingly bipartisan legislation set aside $97 million to establish a Radio Free Iraq to beam in anti-Hussein broadcasts and to arm and equip an internal opposition to oust the dictator from power. President Clinton signed the bill but he spent only $3 million, mainly for office expenditures, by the time he left office. The incoming Bush officials held that Clinton dragged his feet in executing the Iraq Liberation Act and then passed the buck to them to resolve the festering problem in Baghdad.

With Hussein, the sword was always half out of its scabbard, a fact recognized by even the departing Clinton administration. Days before exiting the Pentagon, William S. Cohen released an ominous intelligence report, warning that Hussein had reconstructed Iraq's WMD infrastructure. The secretary of defense's document listed suspected biological and chemical warfare plants. Cohen's January 10 report called attention to restarted activity at the factories since UNSCOM departed Iraq in 1998.[7] Given Saddam Hussein's provocative antics over the years, the review flashed alarming signals. In retrospect, Cohen's intelligence proved inaccurate. Its importance lies in establishing the fact that not only did the George W. Bush administration err but so did the Clinton government in its fears over non-existent Iraqi WMD stocks.

When George Walker Bush moved into the White House, his administration initially trod closely to the footsteps of his predecessor toward Iraq.

President Bush's secretary of state picked up the quest to get a "smart sanctions" proposal through the Security Council. Together with the British government, Colin Powell tried to win passage of targeted sanctions so as to alleviate the suffering of the ordinary people from the lack of adequate food and medical treatments. The former general faced an uphill struggle against the entrenched interests of China, Russia, and France, all of which wanted normal business transactions and oil exports to resume. In hindsight, Powell's UN failure paved the way for a much more aggressive approach to Iraq.[8]

President Bush's national security advisor (before going on to become secretary of state) Condoleezza Rice joined the White House staff with notions of deterring Iraq and other rogue nations. Before the election, the Stanford professor wrote in *Foreign Affairs* magazine that states like Iraq and North Korea lived on "borrowed time, so there need be no sense of panic about them." Instead of going to war with rogues, she advocated "classical" deterrence to keep them in check while the administration concentrated on big power relations.[9] Thus, Rice, Powell, and the president were set to manage, not attack, the Baghdadi troublemaker. Besides, the fledgling administration focused on issues other than Iraq until after the 9/11 terrorist attack.[10]

The Rush to War in Iraq

The 9/11 catastrophe drastically overturned George W. Bush's international priorities. In the days and months leading up to the plane hijackings, Washington's attention on Iraq had slipped to the backburner. Other headaches supplanted Saddam Hussein. Domestically, the White House vigorously pushed tax cuts in Congress and worried about the sharp jump in unemployment to 4.9 percent. Internationally, the White House had been absorbed in the $8 billion emergency bailout of Argentina's economy and the Hainan incident with China over the forced landing of the US reconnaissance aircraft, noted in the previous chapter. Terrorism was off its radar screen for all but a handful of officials.

In retrospect, the Bush administration had been far too complacent about the dire warnings over the menace posed by Osama bin Laden and in his al Qaeda network.[11] Once the plane jihadis struck, a psychological switch was thrown, and the Bush administration raced to war against not only al Qaeda in Afghanistan but also Saddam Hussein in Iraq. The bold execution of the plot to hijack four commercial jets and then to crash them into the World Trade Center, the Pentagon, and possibly the US Capitol Building, caught even the Cassandras by surprise for its audacity and devastation. The sheer destructiveness wrought by what al Qaeda termed "the planes operation" shook America and shattered its long-established feeling of invulnerability from foreign attack. The "pancaking" down of the 110-story Twin Towers of the World Trade Center into smoldering rubble, the death of nearly 3000 people, and the marred face of the Pentagon—all darkly clouded the American psyche, and none more so than that of President Bush.

The unprecedented attack revolutionized the US commander-in-chief's thinking about threats to America's citizens. Having failed to respond adequately to the intelligence about the threat posed by al Qaeda to the US mainland, the Bush administration convinced itself that Iraq's Saddam Hussein possessed WMDs which he would unleash against the homeland. Had it not been for that great calamity on a bright September morning, it seems almost inconceivable in retrospect that the Oval Office occupant would have rushed preemptively to invade Iraq. Just moments after learning that a "second plane hit the second tower," the president gazed at the innocent faces of the schoolchildren he was visiting in a Sarasota, Florida classroom. He thought to himself: "Millions like them would soon be counting on me to protect them. I was determined not to let them down."[12] Later, the president reflected that September 11 "redefined duty. And it redefined my job. The story...is the key to understanding my presidency."[13]

All lay plain and clear before George Bush even though the US invasion of Afghanistan began just weeks earlier. Near the Thanksgiving holiday 2001, the president asked his secretary of defense for an estimated war plan for Iraq. Donald Rumsfeld ordered General Tommy Franks, the commander of the Defense Department's Central Command (which held responsibility for the Greater Middle East), to revise and streamline the off-the-shelf Operation Plan 1003, which military planners drafted after the Persian Gulf War in 1991. Op Plan 1003 hewed closely to the strategy of the first Gulf war; it called for another 500,000 troop-intervention army and a six-month military buildup in nearby states. The Pentagon chief commanded the four-star general to update the battle plan and to cut the number of troops.[14] Rumsfeld became converted to the military proposition that explosive lethality and high-speed mobility could smash an adversary to smithereens before it knew what had hit it. Early in 2002, the civilian Pentagon chief uttered the notion of "shock and awe" which came to mean overwhelming the Iraqi forces with an updated form of blitzkrieg warfare, using fast-moving armored tanks, mechanized infantry, and heavy close-in air support preceded by a bombing and missile blizzard to suppress the Iraqi air defenses.

President Bush's request for military planning coincided with the White House's call for a return of weapons inspectors to the Persian Gulf country to search out Iraq's suspected WMDs. After the UNSCOM head, Richard Butler, yanked his inspecting team from Iraq out of frustration with Hussein's harassment and roadblocks in 1998, the Clinton administration and the UN formed a new investigative body known as the UNMOVIC. By mid-2000, the Clinton White House had developed cold feet. It applied the brakes on pushing UNMOVIC into Iraq, lest it stir up trouble for Vice President Gore's election run to replace the retiring Bill Clinton. In a startling turnabout, President Clinton joined with Iraq's trading partners France, Russia, and China to postpone the posting of UNMOVIC. On the heels of the Afghan intervention, George Bush picked up the UNMOVIC gauntlet and insisted that the UN send it into Iraq to ferret out illicit nuclear, chemical, or biological weapons in Hussein's domain. The timing of the two requests—a battle plan for Iraq and a resumption of arms inspections—was not a coincidence. Rather, they were steps toward a confrontation with the longtime Persian Gulf nemesis. In time, Iraq's purported WMD caches served as George Bush's casus belli against Saddam Hussein.

President Bush made his intentions publically known in his first State of the Union address. Speaking before both Houses of Congress on January 29, 2002, he lumped together the Republic of Iraq with two other troublemaking countries—Iran and North Korea—as "rogue states" joined in "an axis of evil, arming to threaten the peace of the world." Then the president rattled his own saber: "I will not wait on events, while dangers gather."[15] The "axis of evil" phrase stuck in the national discussion as a marker on the road to war, invasion, and regime change. Accounts of war preparations and military plans recurrently popped up in the news media by spring 2002.[16]

Even the Department of State got into the act of preparing for a post-Hussein Iraq. It held meetings with experts and exiles on its "Future of Iraq Project" in July and August, 2002. These sessions examined how government institutions might be remodeled or improved after Hussein lost power. The conferees set out recommendations for eliminating corruption, curbing police abuse, establishing an independent media, and restoring civil institutions. The State Department officials compiled 13 volumes of reports and findings that flagged a host of post-invasion woes.[17] But the study fell well short of a step-by-step blueprint for the country's rehabilitation and governance. Even so, the Pentagon ignored the document with its insights and predictions of likely problems.[18] Hence, the United States went to war with no carefully drawn up roadmap for the day after Saddam Hussein fell from power.

A year before the US-orchestrated air and land assault into Iraq, CENTCOM embarked on extensive readiness for high-intensity combat. It upgraded and enlarged its bases and facilities in the Persian Gulf by extending runways, constructing armories, storing ammunition and supplies. Kuwait, Oman, and the United Arab Emirates opened their ports and airfields for foreign military forces. Not all the sheikdoms on the Arabian Peninsula flung open the gates to their airports and depots, however.

Saudi Arabia conspicuously absented itself from a public role in another ground attack on Iraq. Its participation in the Persian Gulf War ricocheted back on the desert kingdom, when Osama bin Laden (the scion of a wealthy Saudi businessman) took up arms against his homeland for allowing "Crusader" troops near Medina and Mecca, the holiest shrines in the Islamic religion. During the course of the second Gulf war, Riyadh did secretly permit some US forces to operate from their long-established airbases. Prior to the conflict, Washington turned to the nearby sheikdom of Qatar to serve as another launching pad for the projected invasion. The government in Doha expended millions of dollars to modernize Al Udeid, an outpost on the Gulf coast, to replace the Prince Sultan Air base in Saudi Arabia.

Except for the tiny sheikdoms on the Arabian Peninsula, the United States received little encouragement from its traditional allies in the region. Egypt and Syria joined Saudi Arabia in publically opposing the second conflict against Iraq. All had backed Washington in the 1990–1991 war. Hostilities this time differed from the first Persian Gulf War when Saddam Hussein's brutal invasion of Kuwait demanded a unified response to expel Iraq's Republican Guards. The second conflict lacked a similar justifiable pretext. Besides, Cairo, Damascus, and Riyadh rightly feared the regional instability that would result from Hussein's ouster. They also looked askance at any large-scale US military presence for its likely deleterious political repercussions across the Middle East. Even Iran, which stood to gain from Hussein's dispatch, vigorously objected to the coming military intrusion. It feared the close proximity of US forces to its borders. Washington's intervention, therefore, was unpopular before it took place.

The Bush administration's quest for allies beyond the immediate Mid-Eastern ring of states also proved less than rewarding. America's closest ally, Britain, of course, teamed up with the country with which it had enjoyed a "special relationship" since World War I. The British government in the hands of Tony Blair, New Labour's prime minister, initially acted as a brake on President Bush's "impatience" to take the fight unilaterally to Iraq. Bush accepted Blair's counsel and allayed his fears: "I agree with you, Tony. Afghanistan is the priority. We will come back to Iraq in due course."[19] George Bush honored his promise to Blair, and a year later he staked his global campaign against Islamic terrorism on a war with Iraq.

Britain's loyalty aside, the United States encountered great skepticism from other nations about the wisdom of going to war against Iraq. Both French and German governments opposed military action, believing that UNMOVIC must be given time to carry out thorough inspections. President Bush met with government heads of both European countries to assure them of American restraint. Returning from Moscow after signing an arms-control treaty that limited the number of deployable nuclear warheads (to between 1700 and 2200—a two-thirds reduction by 2012) with Vladimir Putin, the Russian president, George Bush stopped first in Germany in late May 2002. Speaking in the newly reconstructed Reichstag building, the president answered a question regarding a possible American-engineered regime change in Baghdad by repeating what he earlier said privately to German Chancellor Gerhard Schroeder: "I have no war plans on my desk, which is the truth."[20] The next day while in Paris, the US president reiterated the mantra that he had no plans on his desk for an Iraq war.

Profound incredulity and unease greeted Bush's denials both in chancelleries and in public squares, where demonstrators gathered to protest what they saw as American bellicosity. Diplomatic and military exertions went head amid Bush's protestations. By mid-2002, the news media brimmed with accounts of the military buildup in the Persian Gulf and with possible scenarios for how the US might overthrow Saddam Hussein. Commenting on press stories about military preparations, the *Economist* editorialized with a Churchill paraphrase: "Never in the field of human conflict has so much war planning been revealed to so many by so few."[21]

The sense of impending conflict was heightened by the White House's espousal of its warlike theory of preemption in the conduct of international relations. The president took the lead in cultivating the political ground for a preventative attack on Iraq's supposed WMD stocks. In his commencement address to the June 2002 graduates of the US Military Academy, he unveiled his still-sketchy doctrine for a preventive war that departed from America's long-standard containment and deterrence formulas to grave danger. At West Point, Bush cautioned: "If we wait for threats to fully materialize, we will have waited too long." Devoid of any memorable phrase as in his State of the Union, his remarks on a sunny spring morning, however, carried more import, for they enunciated a "strike first" strategy. Ergo, America would take "preemptive action when necessary."[22]

The importance of the speech in laying out a military strategy against Iraq was obscured by the White House's announcement of a new federal department. The Washington press corps glommed onto the news about the proposed creation of the massive Department of Homeland Security to prevent terrorist attacks on US territory. This new Cabinet department was the first in the security field since Harry Truman's proposal for the Department of Defense in 1945, which combined the War and Navy departments.[23] The standing up of an additional security cum intelligence bureaucracy demonstrates in another way George W. Bush's commitment to his international war on terrorism, albeit a somewhat more defensive dimension of the struggle.

After Labor Day, 2002, the West Wing picked up the political pace in its campaign to persuade the American people and their Congressional representatives of the necessity of regime change in Iraq. It made top officials available for television interviews to voice anxieties about Iraq's mega-death arms. Condoleezza Rice appeared on CNN, where the national security advisor memorably declared: "We don't want the smoking gun to be a mushroom cloud."[24] A few days later, President Bush spoke to the General Assembly, importuning UN members to enforce the suite of resolutions against Baghdad and implying an American attack, if Iraq failed to mind international law. He forcefully affirmed to the audience that Security Council resolutions requiring Iraq's disarmament "will be enforced—or action will be unavoidable." Brandishing a battle-ax, George Bush painted a red line: "If the Iraqi regime wishes peace, it will immediately and unconditionally forswear, disclose, and remove weapons of mass destruction, long-range missiles, and all related materials."[25] Vice President Cheney went to work on fellow Republican Dick Armey in September 2002. The House majority leader initially balked at invading Iraq unprovoked. Cheney persuaded Armey by confiding that Saddam

Hussein was near to miniaturizing nuclear arms and was cooperating with al Qaeda—both falsehoods.[26]

Six thousand miles away, Saddam Hussein took heed of the warlike writing on the wall. He expressed his willingness to re-admit the international weapons inspectors to Iraq. His timing gave rise to charges of a firing-squad conversion. Whatever cynicism lay behind his change of heart, the Iraqi dictator's newfound openness to the long-stalled UNMOVIC searches enabled France, China, and Russia to try to slow down American assertiveness toward the Baghdad. Each voiced anxiety about instability in the Gulf due to US military action. Because each power stood to benefit from doing oil and other business with Baghdad, their warnings seemed self-serving and received short shrift in Washington. As events slid toward armed hostilities against Iraq, the troika, particularly France, threw up impediments as the United States readied for war.

In the meantime, the American case against Baghdad's presumed WMD manufacturing got a boost from the British Isles. Tony Blair's government released a white paper asserting that Iraq was circumventing international barriers to acquire chemical and biological weapons. The document, "Iraq's Weapons of Mass Destruction," contained photos and diagrams to lend it credibility. At the end of the dossier, Prime Minister Blair assessed that "the policy of containment is not working."[27] In reality, the British assessment relied on secondary sources and even a paper written by a graduate student in California. After the Anglo-American intervention into Iraq, it came to light that the intelligence estimate was bogus. Her Majesty's government stood accused of fabricating a sham justification for war. The subsequent revelations did much to undo Blair's reputation and political legacy.

In autumn 2002, though, the British report reinforced a similar conclusion in Washington's National Intelligence Estimate (NIE). The NIE represented a summation of the smorgasbord of entities within the American intelligence community. Near the same time as the British findings, the NIE's overall appraisal held that the Republic of Iraq possessed biological weapons and renewed its chemical arms production with an arsenal of some 500 metric tons. That alarmist picture fell apart two and half years later when the presidential Commission on Intelligence Capabilities of the United States Regarding Weapons of Mass Destruction threw cold water on it: "These assessments were all wrong."[28] In the critical short term, the faulty British and American reports about Saddam Hussein's WMD capacity added to the steady drumbeat for a military invasion.

A Striking First Doctrine

During that same autumn, the White House returned to the preventive warfare theme that George Bush lifted the curtain on in his West Point remarks in June. Those comments and similar snippets in other utterances led to a raft of rumors inside the Washington Beltway. When the White House issued its National Security Strategy in September 2002, the strategic blueprint rattled the Washingtonian establishment with its doctrinal rationale for an Iraq War. The landmark security manifesto laid down two hawkish courses of action. It outlined a formula for a preemptive attack rather than waiting for aggression from an adversary. Secondly, it set a threshold for American global military dominance. The National Security Strategy pulled no punches in its advocacy for hitting first:

> While the United States will constantly strive to enlist the support of the international community, we will not hesitate to act alone, if necessary, to exercise our right to self-defense by acting preemptively against such terrorists, to prevent them from doing harm against our people or our country. [We will deny] further sponsorship, support, and sanctuary to terrorists by convincing or compelling states to accept their sovereign responsibilities.

This dramatic assertion—that third-party states must accept their sovereign responsibility to deny terrorists shelter—drew less immediate push back from other powers. It did contribute to the growing belief by Russia, China, Iran, and other states that America was bent on forcibly imposing its will on them. Its prescription for global military dominance over any competitor was certain to touch a raw nerve in other capitals:

> The United States must and will maintain the capability to defeat any attempt by an enemy—whether a state or nonstate actor—to impose its will on the United States, our allies or friends....Our forces will be strong enough to dissuade potential adversaries from pursuing a military buildup in hopes of surpassing, or equaling, the power of the United States.[29]

George Bush's strategic architecture also articulated standard features from preceding national security statements. Like others, it endorsed traditional American purposes such as fostering democracy, strengthening alliances, and promoting economic growth, plus encouraging free markets and commercial trade. Its critics bypassed what they saw as routine boilerplate and zeroed in on America's military supremacism and preemptive attack. Pundits and professors tore into Bush's grand scheme. They characterized it as perilously provocative, dangerously hegemonic, heedlessly boastful, tactically unwise, foolishly setting an ominous precedent, and totally incompatible with past American diplomacy.[30]

For all its unilateral and martial tone, the security strategy fell within America's historical tradition before the Cold War. John Lewis Gaddis, known for his rigorous Cold War studies, pointed out that the White House harkened back to the early nineteenth-century prescriptions of John Quincy Adams. The Yale history professor bucked the academic and intellectual currents flowing against the Bush doctrine by exhuming the career and writings of America's sixth president. Coming into office after the burning of the White House by the British in 1814, Adams set down an azimuth which subsequent presidents reaffirmed. According to the Yale teacher, it was Adam's strategic vision that inspired several fateful events in the US history. In his book, *Surprise, Security and the American Experience*, Gaddis attributed to Adams's guidance the 1818 invasion of Florida by President Andrew Jackson, the annexation of Texas by President James Polk, and Admiral George Dewey's preemptive attack on the Spain's fleet in Manila Bay. He explained that Theodore Roosevelt's Caribbean gunboat diplomacy drew inspiration from John Quincy Adams. Professor Gaddis praised Adams as "the most influential American grand strategist of the nineteenth century." He points out that Washington's "preemptive interventions in Venezuela, the Dominican Republic, Haiti, Nicaragua, and ultimately Mexico derived justification on the grounds that instability" furnished European powers, such as Britain, France, and Germany, an excuse to interfere in the Western Hemisphere.[31]

President Bush's security framework did depart from the multilateral precedents instituted by the United States after World War II. In the early Cold War era, the United States latched onto non-military mechanisms, such as international law and international organizations, in order to entrench its new dominance. Participating within international organizations or regional blocs, however, necessitated some abandonment of unilateralism to foster compromise and to achieve unity. During the presidencies of Franklin Delano Roosevelt and Harry S. Truman, Washington tempered its unilateral impulses by establishing and participating in international institutions and security agreements that required it to work through consensus with other states for the purpose of containing and deterring Soviet expansionism. These cooperative arrangements included the UN, Marshall Plan, NATO, International Monetary Fund, and World

Bank. The institutions served US interests in varying degrees by consolidating American ascendancy and freezing out the Soviet Union from Western funds, finance, and commerce to build its economy.[32]

Did George W. Bush's foreign policy, therefore, revert to the pre-World War II period when the United States often acted unilaterally? In some ways, it did. Even this assessment needs refinement, because other recent presidents also acted overseas without international approval from the UN or regional alliances. Ronald Reagan, for example, intervened into the Caribbean island of Grenada to overthrow a Marxist regime despite disapproval from Britain, America's best ally and the island's patron. George Herbert Walker Bush, to take another example, sent 20,000 troops into Panama to oust Manuel Noriega, onetime CIA asset turned drug kingpin. Bill Clinton provides another instance when he regime-changed on the island of Haiti. President Clinton went further when he ordered a preemptive missile barrage of al-Shifa, a chemical plant in Sudan suspected of manufacturing nerve agents but in a country officially at peace with the United States.[33] But George Bush junior, nonetheless, pushed unilateralism and interventionism to unaccustomed levels since the Wall crumbled.

The Quest for Consent at Home and Abroad

Once the White House issued its National Security Strategy, the administration set out in earnest for a green—or at least amber—light to drive its war policy. In early October, President Bush stated without equivocation that the Iraq regime "has developed weapons of mass death" and "has scientists and facilities to build nuclear weapons and is seeking the materials required to do so."[34] The administration also released a declassified edition of the NIE, which was shorn of the caveats, dissent, and doubts about Iraq's WMD capabilities in the classified version. The declassified text came close to policy advocacy, for it endorsed the White House's version of the threat without any of the skepticism in the classified NIE. A week after its publication, Congress voted to grant Bush wide latitude to use force against Iraq. By then, the White House had reinforced the NIE release with other war-prompting efforts.[35]

Two hurdles, or rather two very different constituencies, had to be overcome—one domestic and the other international. The administration took on the challenges, first at home and then abroad. To win Congressional authorization for the use of force against Iraq, the West Wing mounted a briefing campaign for members of the House and Senate about the deadly menace presented by Saddam Hussein. To rally the American people to his side, George Bush pitched his anti-Baghdad themes in speeches. This campaign culminated on the eve of the Congressional vote to authorize the use of force. In a televised address in Cincinnati, the commander-in-chief reassured the public that "we will act with allies at our side" against the Republic of Iraq which "could have a nuclear weapon in less than a year." Bush also expressed hope that Iraq's disarmament "will not require military action."[36] The White House's drumbeat for war accomplished its goal. Opinion surveys noted a rise in pro-war sentiments, as Americans grew concerned about Iraq's WMD. At the start of the Iraq War, one poll noted that 71 percent of the sampled cross-section endorsed George Bush's forceful disarmament policy.[37]

Congress jumped on the war bandwagon when the White House sent over a joint resolution for authorizing force against the threat posed by the Hussein regime. With the West Wing's assent, the Republican-controlled House of Representatives modified it, passed it, and sent it along to the Democratically dominated Senate which also passed the bill. The House of Representatives voted 296 to 133 (with 126 Democrats, six Republicans, and one independent against) to authorize the president the use of military force "as he determines to be necessary and appropriate" against the Republic of Iraq. Then the Senate backed the resolution by 77 to 23 (29 Democrats went along with 48 Republicans).[38] The US Congress and nation, therefore, backed Bush's doctrine of preemptive war. George Bush signed the authorization to use force on October 16, 2002, five months before the Iraq intervention. When the war started to go badly, some Democratic lawmakers, particularly those running for president in 2008, argued that the White House had misled them about the presence of WMD in Iraq. Presidential officials countered that both branches were privy to the same intelligence, which turned out to be faulty in the extreme.

To its credit, the George W. Bush presidency adhered to the Constitution and the War Powers Act by going to Congress to gain authorization to use military force (AUMF) against both the al Qaeda terrorist network in 2001 and separately the Baghdad dictatorship in the next year. At the time of their passage, the two AUMF resolutions enjoyed much popular and legislative support, demonstrating public approval of America's active international engagement. Coming so soon after the 9/11 attacks, Bush's war thumbing resonated among the population. In retrospect, the moment proved to be an apex of the post-Cold War expansiveness. It was not to last, as the protracted wars in Afghanistan and Iraq, along with the ballooning price in lives and dollars took a heavy toll on the country's cycler internationalism, even before Bush left office.

A far less receptive international community greeted the Bush administration's war plans. Washington ran into a buzz saw of opposition in the Security Council from Saddam Hussein's three, long-standing, commercial partners—Russia, China, and France. Many other countries agreed with the United States that the Iraqi dictator possessed a reckless streak. Was he also pursuing biological, chemical, and even nuclear weapons? The United States and Britain answered affirmatively. Russia, China, and France demanded irrefutable proof of WMD in Iraqi arsenals. Still, other countries were on the fence.

This stiff opposition from three permanent Security Council members presented the White House with a dilemma. Either it had to prove the existence of Iraqi WMD to the skeptical trio or Washington had to go it alone without a UN blessing for its planned military action. Colin Powell championed the alternative of seeking UN approval. He persuaded George Bush to endorse a Security Council resolution to dispatch UNMOVIC to Iraq to search for WMD stockpiles or manufacturing sites. Others in the Cabinet meetings, chiefly Vice President Richard Cheney, opposed the UN route as futile and a waste of time. Powell won this first round. Security Council Resolution 1441 passed unanimously in early November 2002. It required that Baghdad allow arms inspectors to resume their search in line with Resolution 687 (passed in April 1991). The previous resolution mandated that Iraq destroy all its WMD and missiles capable of delivering the deadly arms. UNSCOM had been established to ensure Baghdad's compliance. But as narrated above, Hussein frustrated its searches through cat-and-mouse tactics until it pulled out in exasperation. This time, Hussein grasped at the unanticipated UN escape hatch from an all-but-certain US military incursion by opening his country to UNMOVIC two weeks after the UN vote.

The White House encountered another impasse within the Security Council. Resolution 1441 also included a controversial provision for the use of force against Iraq. Leading up to its Security Council passage, the United States wanted an automatic move to hostilities if Iraq were found in "material breach" of the previous resolutions calling for its WMD surrender. Led by France, several council members demanded a second vote before resorting to "all necessary means" (that is to say war) to enforce Iraq's compliance to international law. Bush's Cabinet was divided. Cheney, joined by the Pentagon chief, Donald Rumsfeld, perceived the second vote as a trap to block America's muscular pressure on Hussein to come clean on WMD stocks. Powell argued that the administration needed the UN imprimatur to carry out its policies or risk adverse world opinion for acting unilaterally against the Persian Gulf nation. The secretary of state carried the day with the president, who reluctantly agreed to the two-step process. The resolution won a 15-to-none vote in the Security Council. The UN Monitoring, Verification, and Inspection Commission resumed WMD inspections on November 18. The resolution required a report on UNMOVIC's findings by the end of January 2003 to coincide with the White House's own timetable to reach a decision on the Iraq invasion.

The interim between UNMOVIC's start and its report bristled with tension, uncertainty, and recriminations. A month after the inspectors entered Iraq, George Bush denounced the slow pace of UNMOVIC: "We're not interested in hide and seek in Iraq."[39] The president's outburst was at variance with the UN Secretary General's assessment of Baghdad's openness to the investigators. Sparring with the White House, Kofi Annan held that "cooperation seems to be good."[40] Early in 2003, Bush warned that "time is running out on Saddam Hussein" and fumed: "I am sick and tired of games and deception."[41]

The Bush administration perceived Hussein as trying to run out the clock on a US-orchestrated invasion during the first months of 2003. It was widely known that the Pentagon wanted the attack to take place in the spring to escape the scorching summer heat. But no amount of Iraq's procrastination slowed the massive military buildup in the Persian Gulf. Mountains of arms, ammunition, and war materiel piled up on bases bordering Iraq. By start of 2003, General Tommy Franks opened his new CENTCOM headquarters in Qatar, thereby relocating his command center from Tampa, Florida to the frontlines of the invasion force. At the same time, the Pentagon transported its first major troop presence to bases in the Arabian Peninsula.

UNMOVIC's chairman delivered the keenly anticipated report to the UN on January 28, 2003. Hans Blix, a veteran Swedish diplomat and arms-control expert, negatively described Iraq's uncooperativeness with UN arms inspectors.[42] His 15-page statement revealed Iraq's failures to prove conclusively that it had ended and uprooted its WMD capacity. Blix stated: "Iraq appears not to have come to genuine acceptance—not even today—of the disarmament which was demanded of it and which it needs to carry out to win the confidence of the world."[43]

But the centerpiece of UNMOVIC's findings was that the inspectors found no WMD. This conclusion refuted the Bush administration's assertions of what turned out to be a case of phantom WMD. Furthermore, the International Atomic Energy Agency's chief, Mohamed ElBaradei, reported that his team also uncovered no proof that Iraq had tried to restart its nuclear weapons sites since they were discovered in 1991. Blix and ElBaradei asked for more time to conduct more inspections. The Bush foreign policy team greeted the reports with disbelief and rejection. They refused the inspectors' requests for additional searches.

The day after the delivery of the twin inspection reports to the Security Council, the American president contradicted them. In his State of the Union address, George Bush announced that US intelligence found that the Baghdad regime neglected to disclose "30,000 munitions capable of delivering chemical agents" along with substantial amounts of botulinum toxin and anthrax. Next, Bush uttered a sentence that haunted his presidency for years when he spoke: "The British government has learned that Saddam Hussein recently sought significant quantities of uranium from Africa."[44] Bush's assertion stood uncontested for several months beyond the opening US attack on Iraq.

President Bush's justification for war rested on Saddam Hussein being in "material breach" of his obligations to turn over all WMD. Clearly, the Iraqi autocrat did not comply with his obligation. The invading soldiers found about 5000 two-decade-old chemical warheads for artillery shells or aviation bombs.[45] But these antiquated munitions containing nerve or mustard agents were dismissed by experts as not the types of WMD that formed the real justification for the invasion. Instead, Bush critics held that only active programs, not the inert rusting shells uncovered in dilapidated bunkers by US troops, justified intervention. It came to light ten years later that some of the soldiers suffered health problems from the leaky munitions.[46] The administration did not stick with a narrow, technical, legal pretext for war—that Hussein failed to meet his international legal obligations. Rather, the Bush officials spoke of Iraq's large offensive nuclear and biological capabilities, plus active chemical weapons as the rationale for invasion.

The White House's war rationale dissolved over time. First and foremost, the US military forces found no functioning nuclear or biological sites even though they scoured every suspected corner of the country. The chemical shells, they unearthed, were in a state of decay. As time dragged on, the absence of WMD took on the aspects of the Chinese water torture, drip by drip, no evidence of WMD came to light. To the American people, the Bush administration's case for war twisted slowly in the wind, damaging its credibility at home and abroad. In time, bumper stickers appeared: "Bush lied, people died." This damning shadow never left Bush's legacy, although the president was not found to have lied by the committees charged to investigate why no WMD turned up in Iraq.[47]

In 2008, the Senate's Select Committee on Intelligence, Chaired by John D. Rockefeller IV (Democratic from West Virginia), published its findings. The report found that George W. Bush's statements on Iran's nuclear weapons program "were generally substantiated by intelligence community information." The report concluded the same about the president's statements concerning chemical and biological weapons.[48] The report neither put to rest the conviction that the White House intentionally misled the American people nor restored faith in intelligence community, some members of which felt pressured to back the White House's line.[49] They sensed pressure from the Bush administration, especially Vice President Cheney, to confirm the existence of WMD. The misuse or distortion of intelligence became a watchword for decision-making in the future.[50]

The Commission on the Intelligence Capabilities of the United States Regarding Weapons of Mass Destruction—a bipartisan body—found no evidence of the White House lying about WMD or pressuring the intelligence community to verify the presence of mega-death arms within Iraqi facilities. Rather the commission uncovered a steady stream of alarmist CIA intelligence briefings to both the Clinton and Bush administrations about Iraq's WMD. The commission reported that the intelligence community was "dead wrong" about Hussein's WMD stockpiles. George W. Bush and his national security team acted on the grossly inaccurate intelligence findings but apparently did not shape the CIA conclusions.[51] The charge that "Bush lied" still reverberated in public discourse more than a decade after the invasion and the commission's report.[52] Such an ill-advised and ill-conducted war seemed to demand a schemer, not just a wrongheaded culprit.

Another revelation further undercut the government's credibility. Under CIA auspices, a former US ambassador, Joseph C. Wilson traveled to the African nation at the center of British allegations that Iraq sought yellowcake to manufacture bomb-grade uranium for its nuclear program. Once in Niger, Wilson investigated the claim. Three months into the Iraq invasion, Wilson very publically stated that no evidence existed for Bush's assertion of an Iraqi pursuit of African uranium.[53] Next, Wilson took a cudgel to Bush's 16-word statement in a high-profile campaign, including an influential book on the misstatement.[54] These factors, plus later revelations about the US intelligence community's failures, leached away the president's political standing.

After the State of the Union address in early 2003, Bush's adjutants knew they were in for a fight in the Security Council to avoid a veto of their Iraq invasion plans. UN Resolution 1441 just papered over the deep divisions in the council. Without proof positive of the WMD from UNMOVIC inspectors, it seemed improbable to secure passage of a military-action resolution to enforce Iraq's compliance with a host of UN's anti-WMD demands. Only WMD evidence and an impeccable spokesman might persuade the French, Russians, and Chinese not to block the US request. The Oval Office thought it could square the circle. It commissioned its secretary of state to deliver the administration's intelligence brief against Baghdad.

Colin Powell's appearance before a specially convened Security Council meeting on February 5 riveted attention on him and the American case. Former general Powell's appearance invoked the hallowed recollection of Adlai Stevenson, the UN ambassador during John Kennedy's presidency. Stevenson's magnetic presentation to the Security Council during the Cuban Missile Crisis that brought American and Russia to the brink of nuclear war four decades earlier lingered in America's collective memory. Stevenson showed photographs taken by U-2 reconnaissance aircraft of Soviet nuclear-tipped missiles in a secret base on the Caribbean island. Stevenson's high-profile moment in the public eye etched itself into history so it became a marker for Powell's delivery.

Secretary Powell's presentation was commensurate with that of Stevenson. The former Army general delivered a crisp indictment of the Hussein regime lasting an hour. He called out Iraq's alleged cheating with satellite photos, radio intercepts, and audiotapes, which corroborated human sources. Voiced with confidence and conviction, Powell's remarks seemed to leave little doubt about the Iraqi tyrant's duplicity and WMD stockpiles. The onetime four-star officer also endeavored to link the Iraqi despot with the al-Qaeda terrorist network. Soon, his assessment, and that of the United States, turned out to be a sandcastle washed away in a rising tide of refutation, which left Powell's sterling reputation in tatters before he resigned at the end of Bush's first term. He was replaced by Condoleezza Rice. Well before those developments, the White House faced immediate troubles within the Security Council.

The United States and Secretary Powell fell substantially short of convincing the stonewalling trinity on the Security Council about Iraq's purported arms of mass destruction. France, Russia, and China resisted American prodding for a resolution calling for military operations. The French were the most skeptical about the accusations of secret WMD caches. They instead insisted that the weapons inspectors be allotted more time to conclude their work. Although devoid of a veto seat on the council, Germany, normally a staunch US ally and a major NATO power, dug in its heels against a war too. Only Britain hung in with the United States. Paris, Berlin, and Moscow jointly issued a statement urging "a substantial strengthening" of the "human and technical capabilities" of the arms investigators within Iraq.[55] In the short term, the face off spawned a verbal war between Washington and European capitals. One commentator framed the showdown in a memorial phrase that heightened animosity. He wrote: "Americans are from Mars and Europeans are from Venus."[56] Europeans understandably resented the characterization. The standoff soured Euro-American relations for years, although it did not stop Germany and France from continuing to deploy military units to Afghanistan.

Sensing defeat in the Security Council for a war resolution, President Bush switched tactics. He abandoned the plan for a war-authorizing vote. Instead, he argued that Resolution 1441 alone sufficed; it justified coercive disarmament because Iraq failed to fulfill its legal obligations to provide "accurate, full, final and complete disclosure" of it WMD.[57] No further UN consultation was needed. The administration adopted a "coalition of the willing" strategy to bring into its pro-war camp as many partners as possible no matter how minimal their military contribution. Several NATO countries did participate in the ad hoc coalition. But Washington's unilateralism aroused anti-American demonstrations in many European cities, particularly in France and Germany.[58] President Bush's go-it-alone course incurred harsh international rebukes. They prompted Condoleezza Rice, the national security adviser, to react with a steely barb: "Punish the French, ignore the Germans, and forgive the Russians."[59] Her rejoinder hardly contributed to improved transatlantic relations.

Washington's travails with allies were not behind it, for next Turkey stiffed the US request for ground transit. Bush officials asked their fellow NATO member and longtime American friend for permission to land an Army division of tanks, armored vehicles, and thousands of troops on Turkey's Mediterranean coast and travel over land so as to invade Iraq from the north as well as from the south thereby confronting the Republican

Guard with a two-front war. The new government in Ankara dominated by the Justice and Development Party—an Islamic movement—voted against the appeal even when Washington sweetened it with a $26 billion aid package. America went to war with the handful of close allies. It was another sign of America's unilateralism and interventionism under the Bush presidency.

Invasion, Regime Change, and Occupation

After a year of preparation, the assault into the Republic of Iraq went off without a major glitch on March 19, 2003. At 5:30 in the morning local time, US warplanes struck with decapitation airstrikes intended to remove Saddam Hussein from power. Radar-evading F-117A jets dropped satellite-guided bombs on Doha Farms—a suspected Hussein hideout south of Baghdad. Flawless execution went unmatched with flawless intelligence. The Iraqi dictator escaped because he was hiding elsewhere. Bad intelligence turned out to be almost a byword of the whole intervention from no WMD facilities to little understanding of Iraq's historical cross-currents of fratricidal, clan-based sectarianism which erupted into an anti-American insurgency overlaid with sect-on-sect fighting.

Hours after the bombing runs, the land war commenced with Abrams tanks, armored Bradley Fighting Vehicles, and thousands of US Army soldiers and Marines speeding toward Baghdad. On another front, British military forces converged on the southern city of Basra. Overhead, Coalition airpower delivered the "shock and awe" of bombardment on the hapless Republican Guards in a devastating re-run of the previous Persian Gulf War in the course of the war, the US-organized Coalition lofted into the air some 1800 allied warplanes, which blew to pieces the Republican Guard's T-72 Soviet tanks and troop fortifications. The brief conventional phase of the war lived up to its billing, as a "cakewalk war" by one of the neocons pushing for the Iraq War.[60] Before long, the cakewalk turned into a protracted insurgency, where America's technological superiority was of less use.

The US invasion army was small at some 137,000 soldiers and Marines, along with 40,000 British Tommies and other Coalition personnel. Iraq's armed forces numbered over 400,000 troops; they possessed little of the technical and tactical skills required for modern warfare. The Coalition side experienced imperfections, too. America's pell-mell advance suffered from deficiencies in resupply of food and fuel, battlefield intelligence, and preparedness for sandstorms. Since much more went right than wrong, nevertheless, the United States easily defeated and deposed Saddam Hussein, who morphed from president to fugitive. Major combat operations almost completely ceased on April 14. Back at the Pentagon, the spokeswoman, Victoria Clarke, delivered a postmortem: "The regime is at its end, and its leaders are either dead, surrendered, or on the run."[61]

The final curtain did not come down on this manageable phase of the war until the US commander-in-chief appeared in a tightly scripted photo-op event on the flight deck of the aircraft carrier *USS Abraham Lincoln* on May 1. George W. Bush announced the end of major combat operations in triumphal tones in front of a large banner which read Mission Accomplished. He never uttered the two-word phrase. In fact, he cautioned that the "war on terror is not over."[62] Still, the symbolism of president's jaunty arrival in a plane on the ship, dressed in a flight suit, and his boastful banner, nonetheless, came back to haunt him for the rest of his years in office. His detractors mocked him with references to "mission accomplished," as the Iraqi insurgency drained away American lives and resource. For the purposes of this book, the near-theatrical scene pointed to another signpost of the engaged, interventionist cycle of US international policy.

Not long after American forces raced toward Baghdad, they were hit from the rear by irregular combatants known as Fedayeen. While the lightly armed Fedayeen caused minimal damage to US armored vehicles, they constituted a harbinger of the coming resistance to the occupation. Before the emergence of an insurgency, however, the American and British troops found themselves overwhelmed by protestors, looters, and vandals. Simply stated, there were too few "boots on the ground" to properly handle the demonstrations that exploded with the collapse of the country's central authority.[63] The Humpty-Dumpty of civil life lay shattered and all the Coalition forces could not put it together again for half a decade—and not until entirely new strategies and more troops arrived. The rioters coupled with the Coalition's inability to rein them in formed the roots of the budding insurgency. By the time Tommy Franks, CENTCOM commander, retired in late June, an incipient hit-and-run warfare was taking hold in Baghdad and the western stretch of the country. Introducing a counterinsurgency campaign fell to Franks's former deputy John Abizaid who took over the CENTCOM command. General Abizaid, an Arabic-speaking officer, oversaw Phase VI operations, the occupation stage of the overall Cobra II war plan.

Iraq nearly tumbled into the abyss with a sectarian conflict wrapped within an anti-occupation insurgency. Saddam Hussein's former officers and Baath Party members were just one opponent faced by the US-organized Coalition. Radicalized Islamists within the Sunni sect engaged in a Hobbesian conflict to touch off a sectarian war with the Shiite population. Overseen by a psychopath named Abu Musab al-Zarqawi, the Sunni-dominated al-Qaeda in Iraq network murdered with abandon by snipers, suicide bombers, throat-slitters, or Improvised Explosive Devices (IEDs) along roadways or in crowded markets. This Iraq branch of al Qaeda central was the forerunner to the Islamic State of Iraq and Syria, which shot to infamy during Barack Obama's second term. For its part, the Shiite-run government resorted to semi-official death squads who fiendishly drilled holes in their Sunni prisoners' heads with power tools, if they did not first shoot them.

The reason to dwell on the Iraq insurgency stems from the fact that this conflict altered America's cyclical swing toward international engagement. Long story short, the bitter Iraq fighting first checked and then reversed America's international engagement mood. The Iraq insurgency was characterized by the use of IEDs which resulted in more than 60 percent of the nearly 4500 American deaths in the war. Bomb-sniffing dogs saved countless troops from death, wheelchairs, or disfiguring burns. More were spared when the United States belatedly built and shipped to Iraq about 27,000 heavily armored "V"-bottomed Mine Resistant Ambush Protected (MRAP) vehicles which deflected explosive blasts outward. Robert Gates, who replaced the forced-out Rumsfeld in 2006 as Pentagon chief, labored intensely for an accelerated production of MRAPs. Not until mid-2008, though, did adequate MRAPs arrive in Iraq so that the Pentagon could divert some to Afghanistan.[64] The tardy deployment of protective vehicles was just one of many Washington stumbles in prosecution of the Iraq War. Billions of dollars in aid was misspent or wasted, sometimes on ridiculous programs or uncompleted, worthwhile projects.[65] Other failures included the scandal at Abu Ghraib where Iraqi prisoners were abused and humiliated, but not tortured, by US military personnel. Waste, fraud, and nontrivial errors disillusioned Americans at home. The faltering Iraq War redirected American sentiments toward "inwardism" and rechanneled US foreign policy away from military intervention.

The civil side of the intervention gravely faltered as well. To administer the country, Washington established the Coalition Provisional Authority under the direction of L. Paul Bremer, who equated his powers with those of a Roman proconsul. Ruling from the US-protected Green Zone in Baghdad, Bremer mistakenly disbanded the Iraqi army rather than remobilizing it as a civilian force to police the streets, clear rubble, pick up garbage, and perform other civic duties. Just keeping soldiers paid and complaisant was a wiser course until a new force could be constituted. Instead, the disgruntled men, with military training and arms, went over to insurgent ranks. The de-Baathification policy was another ill-advised order. The Baath Party had ruled Iraq for decades. Top Baath Party members deserved trial, prosecution, and severe penalties, if found guilty of crimes. But many lower-ranking members simply joined the party for a card to get a job. Bremer's purge did not distinguish among the committed and the careerists or cowards in the party. Without a bureaucracy staffed by Baathists, the country ground to a halt.[66] Simple civic functions collapsed, rending the country ungovernable and discontented.

As it became clear that Iraq possessed no real WMD threat, Washington turned with vigor to its second reason to remove Saddam Hussein from power. It proceeded to promote democracy by forming political parties, holding elections, and establishing parliamentary governments. Noble in purpose, this democracy implantation occurred on arid soil. Making up about 60 percent of the population, the Shia captured the majority of parliamentary seats in elections and formed a government determined to marginalize the Sunni and Kurds. American official prodded Prime Minister Nouri Kamil al-Maliki, who came to office in 2006, to be inclusive of minority politicians. Al Maliki, who had been an exiled dissident during the Hussein era, never overcame his animus for the other ethnic communities. He treated his position as a personal fief, appointing Shiite military officers and political hacks to positions. In time, al Maliki's misrule undermined the unitary Iraqi state.

Meanwhile, the insurgency went from bad to worse for the Coalition. By 2006, Iraq sank into paroxysms of violence and bloodshed. Despite the killing of Abu Musab al-Zarqawi by US forces, his network, al Qaeda in Iraq, went on a killing spree. Although its attacks murdered thousands of Shia, the Sunni terrorist movement also murdered thousands from its own ethnic community. Al Qaeda in Iraq also strictly enforced Sharia religious tenets, such as mandating men grow beards, demanding that women wear Islamic dress, and prohibiting smoking or alcohol, all of which irked the local populations. The insurgents also elbowed aside Sunni sheiks' smuggling and black market businesses.[67]

The United States appeared on the brink of suffering a military defeat in Iraq by mid-2006, as Iraq cartwheeled toward a Dantesque hell with pervasive blood-chilling butchery. American casualties shot up from 486 deaths in 2003, the year of the invasion, to 904 fatalities in 2007. Wounded rates soared as well. Iraqi citizens perished in the thousands.[68] The uppermost ranks of US military and civilian brass advised George Bush to pull out American forces from Iraq. General George Casey, the US commander of multinational forces in Iraq, adopted a strategy of withdrawing Coalitions troops, thereby, handing the fighting over to the hard-pressed Iraqi units, which the United States had hastily established.

The savagery struck many Americans as a hopeless struggle to bring peace, reconciliation, and true democracy to such a benighted land. The war, moreover, was nearing a cost of a trillion dollars in military and non-military expenditures. For good reasons, Americans turned against the war and the president. Congress formed a ten-person panel in the Iraq Study Group to assess the Iraq War and make recommendations. Nine months later in late 2006, the group issued its report with 79 recommendations. Among them, it called for turning over the conflict to Iraq and for withdrawing American military forces to nearby countries, where US forces could still strike at regional terrorist organizations. The group's recommendations were recognition of the bleak prospects in Iraq.[69]

Two factors—one major and one less so—retrieved the war from failure. The chief source of change lay with Sunni populations to the west and north of Baghdad. Violent attacks and rigorously enforced Islamic strictures generated a backlash among the Sunni tribes. Aggrieved Sunni sheiks, particularly Abdul Sattar Abu Risha, banded together against the al Qaeda in Iraq terrorists. US Army officers cultivated strong ties with the Sunni sheiks, who threw their lot in with the Americans in what became known as the Sahwat al Anbar (the Anbar Awakening). The American military furnished arms, money, and firepower in the larger battles. The Sunni tribes provided manpower and intelligence, allowing the Coalition forces to locate and eliminate their common enemy. Without the Awakening movement, it is difficult to imagine a victorious wind down in the insurgency.

Another driver in transforming the battlefield emanated from a crucial decision by the White House. Battered by collapsing polls and many lost Congressional seats in the 2006 mid-term election, the Oval Office felt the weight of history as America faced either defeat or a hasty retreat from Iraq. Whatever George W. Bush's failings in regard to the entry into Iraq or misunderstandings the nature of democracy's prospects in its barren landscape, he made a courageous decision. He decided to double down by backing a plan to secure the Baghdad population from sectarian violence with 28,500 additional US troops in early 2007. As one scholar put it, in the "boldest stroke of his presidency," Bush dismissed contrary voices from the Joint Chiefs of Staff and chose a population-centric counterinsurgency formula.[70] By the time George W. Bush left office in early 2009, Iraq was well beyond the civil war that nearly destroyed the country. And every year afterward, it marked a greater degree of peace and stability until the total evacuation of all US ground combat forces and their Coalition allies under President Obama in late 2011.[71]

Bush's Other International Interventions

On the heels of the Iraq invasion, the United States got behind several initiatives to advance Bush's democracy agenda. Washington employed diplomatic pressure, made use of tough rhetoric, dispersed financial aid, and even deployed military forces to back democratic movements. Among the first beneficiaries of America's invigorated democracy campaign arose in the troubled West African country of Liberia. Once an American colony, Liberia descended into civil war under its corrupt and brutal warlord-president Charles Taylor. As violence in countryside swept toward the capital city of Monrovia in mid-2003, Washington felt compelled to act. It sailed a flotilla of US Navy warships to the Liberian coast. Absorbed by the budding Iraqi insurgency and wary of another Mogadishu urban firefight, however, it was loath to enter the fray. US officials demanded that the warring parties work out a cease-fire and that the embattled president leave office. Seeing that the jig was up, Taylor fled to exile in Nigeria for safety. Two hundred US Marines went ashore to provide logistical support for Nigerian peacekeepers, who restored order. Two years later, Liberia's democratic election notched a victory for Ellen Johnson-Sirleaf, a former UN official, who became the first woman president in postcolonial Africa.

Hardly had the Marines waded onto the Liberian shore when Washington noticed trouble again in the Republic of Haiti. Like Liberia, Haiti shared an unhappy history with the United States, including a 19-year American military occupation of the Caribbean island state in the early twentieth century. The Dickensian conditions within Haitian society often caused hordes of asylum-seekers to flock to Florida and other southern states. The Bill Clinton administration carried out a military incursion to oust an army junta and to install a defrocked priest, Jean-Bertrand Aristide, into the presidency, as previously related. When Aristide reverted to the corrupt practices of his dictatorial predecessors, he incurred the wrath of peasants, urban poor, and former soldiers. Unrest migrated from the countryside to the capital of Port-au-Prince. Across the Caribbean, the United States shrank from putting another military operation on a crowded policy plate in early 2004. The Iraqi insurgency was crackling across the country like a prairie wildfire, giving unease to Bush's foreign policy advisers. Yet, Washington shifted gears to apply pressure on Aristide to resign, which he did in February before leaving the country for exile in Africa. Washington dispatched 200 Marines to participate in a stabilizing operation with hundreds of peacekeepers from Canada, Chile, and France before the UN took up the peace-soldiering duties. In 2006, Condoleezza Rice worked with a contact group of nations (Brazil, Canada, and France) to oversee elections and a return to democracy for the troubled and impoverished republic.[72]

Thousands of miles away on the Eurasian landmass, three democratic "color revolutions" also captured Washington's attention and assistance. The Republic of Georgia, Ukraine, and Kyrgyzstan underwent political changes that mattered much to America's newfound democracy emphasis. In Georgia, the country's November 2003 election produced discord because the challenger, Mikheil Saakashvili, disputed the outcome as fraudulent. The Columbia University-trained lawyer's followers poured into the boulevards in the Rose Revolution. The Bush government switched its backing from Eduard Shevardnadze, the president, to his challenger, because the incumbent government reeked of corruption, cronyism, and incompetence. Washington wanted to preempt a Russian intervention on the side of Shevardnadze, a Kremlin ally and the last foreign minister of the Soviet Union before its dissolution. The White House dispatched Donald Rumsfeld to Tbilisi to meet with the disputing parties. The secretary of defense hinted at the deployment of US military forces to the region and demanded the Russian troops leave their Georgian bases. The crisis dissipated when Shevardnadze resigned the presidency. Russia was a sore loser and persisted in drawing Georgia into its orbit, as described subsequently.

Several hundred miles north of Georgia, another democratic transition unfolded in a manner that once more commanded the Bush administration's interest. The issue involved a disputed election in Ukraine. Yet again, thousands of demonstrators thronged the squares and streets in the capital and many other cities to protest the outcome. The world considered Ukraine's November 2004 election tainted by irregularities. The

United States scorned the voting returns as did many European capitals. Colin Powell asserted: "We cannot accept this result as legitimate because it [the election] does not meet international standards."[73]

After 17 days of non-stop civil unrest in Kiev's Independence Square, the Orange Revolution, as it became known, prevailed, ushering into the presidency the Western-leaning Viktor Yushchenko. The democracy movement owed a portion of its success to the United States. Two years before the popular upsurge hit Ukrainian streets, the United States funneled $58 million to strengthen democracy in the closed society by training activists, sustaining a pro-democracy website, and broadcasting independent news coverage of political events. Thanks to the Ukrainian military's participation in NATO's Partnership for Peace exercises, its army stayed in its barracks rather than suppress the pro-democracy marches.[74] But America's coup in Ukraine's democracy birth, as will be described, stoked Russia's countermoves to assert Moscow's influence in its bordering states.[75]

The third democratic eruption in the so-called color revolutions took place in Kyrgyzstan. To foster political pluralism, the United States and a bloc of European governments funded and tutored fledgling democratic groups in the Central Asian country, along with similar programs in other former Soviet republics. Under the Freedom Support Act, Washington provided $12 million to finance civil society centers to nurture a free society in Kyrgyzstan a year before its parliamentary elections in March 2005. From these sparse seeds bloomed the "Tulip Revolution" which saw anti-regime rallies, calling for the ouster of the fraudulently reelected President Askar Akayev. The repressive dictator, despite being propped up by the Kremlin, fled to Moscow. Russia was furious at the West because Kyrgyzstan belonged to its Collective Security Agreement.[76] That a Muslim country rose up in a democratic rebellion to unseat its tyrant heartened President Bush with possibilities for duplication in the Middle East.

In fact, it was in Lebanon where the Bush administration boasted of its first "demonstration effect" of American policy in the Middle East after liberating Iraq and Afghanistan from dictatorial rule. According to Washington, Iraq's election in January 2005 ignited a "Baghdad Spring," which spilled across to the eastern Mediterranean states. Whereas Afghanistan and Iraq had been dominated by homegrown tyrants, the Lebanese protesters, in fact, objected to foreign rule. Syria had occupied Lebanon since 1976. At the time of its intervention, Damascus claimed that it marched into the Levantine country because the civil war there threatened to wash into Syria. Everyone knew that Damascus longed to restore Lebanon to Greater Syria, as it was in the times of the Ottoman Empire.

The Lebanese chafed at occupation by the Syrian military and intelligence services until early 2005. Their opposition to the Syrian presence was catalyzed into an open revolt by the bomb-blast death of Rafik Hariri, a former prime minister and stalwart opponent of the Syrian hold on his country. Demonstrations broke out in Beirut with demands for the return of sovereignty, political freedom, and democracy. The Western media tagged the protests as the "Cedar Revolution." The revolt made headway as outside powers rallied to its cause. The United States found close company with France (the former colonial ruler in the Levant) and Saudi Arabia to press the isolated regime of Bashar al-Assad into withdrawing his army.

Lebanon marked the high tide of the Bush presidency's democracy boosting. Exalting the US democracy campaign, Condoleezza Rice went on to appeal to Egypt, Saudi Arabia, and other regional nations to embrace liberty by holding fair and free elections, indulging free speech, and granting women equal rights. America's top diplomat proclaimed: "Freedom and democracy are the only ideas powerful enough to overcome hatred and division and violence."[77] As it turned out, subsequent events soon proved how unpropitious conditions were for consensus governments in the Middle East.

The Pendulum Reverse with Iran, North Korea, and Darfur

The vigorous cycle of US military and diplomatic involvement abroad began its swing back toward disengagement after half a decade of US exertions. By George Bush's last years in office, the American public had taken stock of its copious expenditures in blood, treasure, and tears in the two raging conflicts. Their most critical eye focused on Iraq; its sheer intractableness dampened American spirits. Feelings of regret and outrage over the Iraq War were compounded by the absence of any meaningful arsenals of WMD. Disillusionment permeated the nation's psyche that America had waged the Iraq War for false reasons. This fact darkened the public's attitude toward George Bush. Emotions stayed more muted about the conflict in Afghanistan. Besides the fighting being at a lower tempo, Afghanistan was actually home to the terrorism movement that struck the United States on September 11. So to many Americans and politicians,

Iraq became the "bad war" and Afghanistan the "good war." Simplistic to be sure, this characterization overshadowed and dominated complex public feelings about the wars. Pride and admiration in the US armed forces mingled with anguish and remorse for the few who paid a terrible price.

These sentiments converged in a growing unpopularity for overseas involvement and for the presidency of George Bush, who appeared to be leading the country into endless wars. American voters registered their disapproval of President Bush's international priorities and his handling of Hurricane Katrina during the 2006 mid-term elections. The Democrats took control of both the House and Senate from the president's Republican Party for the first time in a dozen years. Bush took cognizance of this electoral defeat by announcing that Donald Rumsfeld was stepping down. The defense secretary had been associated with the hawkish interventionist wing of the Bush administration. He had also become the target for the failing counterinsurgency and for insufficient protective vehicles against roadside bombs. Together with Vice President Cheney and top civilian appointees at the Pentagon, Rumsfeld beat the war drum for Iraq. Bush's decision, therefore, reflected more than a mere personnel change. Instead, it represented "a shift in the center of gravity and worldview of Bush's foreign policy team" in the words of one presidential historian.[78]

There were substantial ramifications from Americans' mood swing away from international commitments. The idealism associated with the Bush democracy agenda receded, and the administration took on the trappings of realism. Robert Gates, who replaced Rumsfeld, had been allied with realists in George H.W. Bush's presidency, such as National Security Adviser Brent Scowcroft, who wrote a prominent newspaper article in 2002 opposing the coming Iraq War.[79] The redirected Bush presidency now kept its sword in the scabbard when facing foreign crises.

After revelations came to light in 2002 that Iran had two secret nuclear facilities, the United States accused the Islamic Republic of pursuing WMD. What followed was a convoluted history of Iranian denials, Western-imposed economic sanctions, and enumerable diplomatic meetings to get Tehran to come clean on its bomb-making progress, to negotiate away its atomic advances, and to open its suspected nuclear plants to international inspection. These efforts came to naught during George Bush's tenure. Meanwhile, the Bush administration felt the sting of focused lobbying from neoconservatives and others to bomb the Iranian nuclear sites. By 2006, the intensifying bomb-Iran campaign was in full cry.[80] Once again, Dick Cheney and the vice president's fellow travelers took a hard line. Bush demurred. He spoke with Rice, who sided with those preferring sanctions.[81] The president also consulted the Defense Department, whose military brass unanimously opposed an air bombardment of Iranian nuclear capacities. They cautioned that US intelligence was sketchy on the location of all the nuclear arsenals. Some nuclear capacity might survive airstrikes and be used against American targets. Further, Iran might hit back with devastating attacks of its own, leading to a wider war, which could dwarf the already ongoing bitter fighting in Iraq.

In the end, President Bush stood firm against the pro-war proponents. With American allies, he pursued economic sanctions on Iran. The release of the 2007 NIE further undercut the neocons' war pitch, as it judged with a high degree of confidence that Iran suspended its nuclear arms program in 2003. Its missile program proceeded apace. By this point, Bush had firmly opted for sanctions, not bombs, to halt Iran's nuclear arms aspirations.[82] The neocons' thundering was not silenced when George Bush turned away from a military course. But, as one critic observed they "created an Iraq syndrome that tarnishes the idea of intervention for several decades."[83] That retrenchment sentiment took early root in Bush's second term and entrenched itself deeply in Barack Obama's presidency.

Two other major cases stand out as examples of Bush's new newfound war-averse posture. Both North Korea and Russia engaged in gauntlet-throwing provocations. And the United States left the challenges unaddressed by any forceful rejoinder. Rather, the Bush White House chose to finesse the threats, not tackle them. North Korea had long bedeviled US foreign policy in East Asia. It bristled with warlike hostility toward the United States, South Korea, and Japan since the Korea War, as outlined in Chap. 4. Its desperate pursuit of nuclear arms and long-range missiles transformed the DPRK from just a Stalinist state frozen in a time-wrap to a regional menace.

President Bush's handling of the DPRK threat ran the gamut from forceful to conciliatory during his tenure. Early in his term, Bush identified North Korea as one of the three (along with Iran and Iraq) members of the "axis of evil" in his 2002 State of the Union address. Unlike Iraq, he did not militarily attack North Korea, although the secretive regime was further along the road to a nuclear threshold than Saddam Hussein. Even with mounting woes in Iraq and Afghanistan, Bush could not completely take his eye off North Korea once information surfaced about the reclusive state's enrichment of uranium in 2002, which violated the Nuclear Nonproliferation Treaty and Agreed Framework with Washington. At an

October 4 meeting in Pyongyang between DPRK and American diplomats, North Korea's Deputy Foreign Minister, Kang Seok-Ju, acknowledged American allegations about his country's uranium enrichment. Later, the North Koreans retracted the admission and dismissed it as a mistake in translation.[84]

Another confirmation of Washington's suspicions about the North's quest for enriched uranium came from revelations surrounding the black market network of Abdul Qadeer Khan, the Pakistani scientist who resolved to make money on his country's nuclear breakout. He journeyed to North Korea over a dozen times and sold it centrifuges needed for the enrichment process.[85] As an upshot, the Bush administration withheld further oil transfers to North Korea as stipulated in the Agreed Framework. The American suspension of oil, and the North's relentless nuclear-arming led to the breakdown of the 1994 accord.

During President Bush's second term, the White House opted for diplomacy to rein in Pyongyang's atomic bomb pursuits, as it did with Iran. In the North Korean case, Bush foreign policy officials participated in the Six-Party talks (along with China, Japan, South Korea, and Russia) with the DPRK to freeze Pyongyang's publicly announced goal of an atomic arsenal. Drawn out and tedious negotiations netted agreements, which then lagged for implementation due to the North's much publicized illicit activities in narcotics, money laundering, counterfeiting $100 bills, and conventional arms sales. In response, the United States put in place economic sanctions, not military plans. And in counterresponse, North Korea tested its first nuclear device in an underground explosion in October, 2006. Washington replied with tough talk but nothing else. The great fear overhanging the production of nuclear material centered on its falling into jihadi hands. With nuclear terrorism in mind, Bush warned Pyongyang about "a grave threat to the United States" by transferring nuclear material to "any state or non-state actor."[86]

At this juncture, the United States was bogged down in bloody and financially draining insurgencies in Iraq and Afghanistan. Little wonder, the Bush administration opted for a "discretion as the better part of valor" approach. The earlier Bush doctrine of preemptive attacks on gathering dangers fell by the wayside in this new reality. Washington turned to the UN, where it got a Security Council resolution demanding that "the DPRK not conduct any further nuclear tests or missile firings."[87] Laborious and mostly futile negotiations followed to convince China, the DPRK's main ally, to rein in its wanton ward. In short, nothing happened.

Near the end of the Bush presidency, the United States entered into a controversial agreement with North Korea, which amounted to an even sharper departure from tough policies and actions of earlier years. Led by career Foreign Service officer Christopher Hill and backed by Condoleezza Rice, the administration negotiated with Pyongyang to shut down its plutonium-enrichment facility at Yongbyon and to render a full accounting of its nuclear program to the participants in Six-Party talks.[88] To gain inspection access to the DPRK's nuclear plant, a divided Bush government agreed to strike the xenophobic and opaque country from the State Department's terror listing.

Secretary of State Rice pressed for approval of the decision because the North verbally promised a "comprehensive and vigorous" verification protocol without a written agreement. When the president asked for clarification on the absence of a signed accord, the secretary of state replied: "Mr. President, this is just the way diplomacy works sometimes. You don't always get a written agreement."[89] But Vice President Cheney vigorously opposed the secretary of state and the delisting scheme. George Bush sided with Rice. Attorneys quip that a verbal agreement is not worth the paper it is printed on. This ironic observation sums up the worthlessness of the bargain struck with Pyongyang by a much-less-assertive Bush administration in its final days.

The Bush deal was at best a speed bump to North Korea. Washington struck North Korea from the official Department of State listing of state sponsors of terrorism in October 2008. This enabled the DPRK to receive less scrutiny on trade and aid deals. Months earlier, Pyongyang blew up the nuclear reactor's cooling tower in Yongbyon as international television crews filmed its destruction. True to form, the North Koreans then returned to their threat mode by announcing steps to re-activate their nuclear program. They barred IAEA inspectors from the Yongbyong site, and test-fired missiles into the Sea of Japan. Before the end of the year, the DPRK scuttled their bargain with the United States. Subsequently, Pyongyang tested nuclear devices in 2009, 2013, and early 2016 as well as tested missiles that one day might carry a nuclear warhead to the US homeland. In response to these three post-Bush atomic detonations (during the Barack Obama administration), North Korea paid no penalty, as will be discussed below.

Another case of American unwillingness to intervene militarily arose with the humanitarian crisis in Darfur. This westernmost corner of Sudan had been seething with racial discontent for years. Although almost completely Muslim, Darfur held deep divisions between the Arab and African populations. Its predominately black non-Arab peoples suffered under the arbitrary rule of the Arab government in Khartoum. A civil war erupted in 2001 in which the Darfurians scored early successes against the Sudanese army. Alarmed by the regular army's defeats and humiliations, the Khartoum government of President Omar al-Bashir resorted to a vicious paramilitary force, the Janjaweed, to crush the widening revolt. The mounted Janjaweed ("devils on horseback") marauded through villages killing, raping, and ethnically cleansing the African farmers. Hundreds of thousands died and nearly 3 million were displaced. The "Save Darfur" cry became popular on many American university campuses. By early 2003, many observers called the Darfur massacres a case of genocide.[90]

American experts appointed by Colin Powell assessed the systemic violence as genocide in Darfur. Condoleezza Rice met with Bashir in Khartoum, where the new secretary of state delivered Washington's message to the Sudanese government to halt its barbaric retributions against civilians. Words alone failed and Bush foreign policy advisers found themselves blocked at the UN in their efforts to send peacekeepers to protect innocent lives in Darfur. Working through the Security Council proved fruitless at first, because China opposed any penalties on the oil-rich Sudanese government, which exported its crude to thirsty Chinese customers. Bush's own Pentagon also opposed unilaterally dispatching US armed forces to yet another Muslim country, which after all was not of vital national interest to America. Thus, the White House responded with presidential speeches, diplomacy, and reliance on the UN, not with military action as had Clinton in the Balkans during the 1990s. Even Congress grew frustrated with the inaction. In July 2004, the US House of Representatives unanimously passed a resolution that called on the White House to "seriously consider multilateral or even unilateral intervention to stop genocide in Darfur."[91]

Three years after the Congressional resolution and many thousands of deaths later, Bush's aides secured passage of UN Resolution 1769, which authorized the "Deployment of United Nations-African Union's 'Hybrid' Peace Operation in a Bid to Resolve Darfur Conflict." United Nations and African Union Mission in Darfur (UNAMID) provided for a force of 36,000 military and police personnel.[92] The presence of UN peace soldiers curtailed some of the worst excesses of the government militias, if not all of them. Writing in her memoir years afterward, Rice vented her exasperation: "But until I left the State Department there was no greater source of frustration than Sudan."[93] Clearly, the Bush presidency had ironically gone from searing impatience with the UN in the lead-up to the Iraq War to patient acceptance of its deliberations to rescue US policy in Darfur. The UN route spared Bush from another intervention.

America Punts Again: The Republic of Georgia and Russia

The Bush White House executed another break with its former muscular posture during the Georgian crisis in mid-2008. The United States, as noted above, had championed the 2003 Rose revolution to secure the Republic of Georgia's genuine independence from Moscow's quasi-colonial embrace of the former Soviet republic. America's diplomatic backing ensured that Mikheil Saakashvili, a Western-orientated reformer, assumed the presidency after a disputed election. The Bush administration made the youthful politician a poster image for its "freedom-agenda." Thus, when the Oval Office did not come to Georgia's aid in its war with Russia, its abandonment was all the more pronounced.

Once in office, Saahaskhvili drew Moscow's ire. The nationalistic president tilted his tiny nation toward the West against Russian wishes. The Kremlin already nursed a deep humiliation over the West's interference in Kosovo by bombing Russian-aligned Serbia and ousting Slobodan Milošević from power. The Russians resolved to push back against any further American influence in their near-abroad. They figured that Georgia was ripe for subversion. The Republic of Georgia's Achilles's heel developed from "frozen conflicts" in its rebellious enclaves of Abkhazia and South Ossetia, populated with non-Georgian peoples. During the 1990s, both these pocket-sized provinces rebelled against Tbilisi's rule. They obtained a measure of autonomy from Georgia and protection from Moscow.

Events beyond its control sealed Georgia's fate with Russia. When the United States and European states at long last diplomatically recognized Kosovo's independence from Serbia in 2008, their actions precipitated Russian hostility toward Georgia as a protégé of the West.[94] Hardly had the ink dried on Kosovo's independence declaration than Moscow set the stage for a conflict with the Republic of Georgia. The Russian Duma passed a resolution calling on the Tbilisi to recognize Abkhazia and South Ossetia as sovereign states. The Duma also urged the Kremlin to protect the citizens of each. Russian authorities openly armed separatists in the two breakaway provinces. Russia's new president, Vladimir Putin sent a letter to the separatist leaders, pledging his practical support.

Fighting broke out in South Ossetia between Ossetian separatists and Georgian regular troops in the first week of August 2008. The conflict quickly escalated as Russian forces engaged the Georgian army. Harassed and cornered, Saakashvili unwisely went to war against Russia over its "creeping invasion" of Abkhazia and South Ossetia. Some Georgians held out hope that the Bush administration might send the US Calvary. After all, the same American government stood up for Georgia against Russian muscle-flexing five years earlier during the Rose Revolution. Even though the heirs to the Red Army underperformed against Georgian forces, the Russian military overmatched by several fold Tbilisi's defenses. David failed to slay Goliath in this contest.

As Ronald Asmus wrote in *A Little War That Shook the World*, the August conflict had everything to do with Georgia seeking to break free from its semi-colonial relationship with an overweening and interfering Kremlin. The war also represented a signpost to the future. It demonstrated that Russia no longer felt obliged to work with the West. Thus, it marked one of the clearest instances of Moscow's emerging anti-American game plan. The war was payback for all of Moscow's perceived humiliations and slights over NATO's eastward expansion toward its borders, the EU's enlargement, and the West's intervention in Kosovo against Moscow's interests.[95] Turning the tables on Washington and European capitals, the Kremlin adopted a faux analogy by equating Georgia with Serbia and Saakashvili with a new Milošević to justify the Russian invasion of Georgian territory for "peacekeeping." The Kremlin's military offensive constituted an early rollout of its subversive operations in the annexation of the Crimea and the hybrid war in eastern Ukraine in 2014, as will be subsequently analyzed.[96]

The Bush administration found an exit door to escape from rescuing Georgia. It retreated from America's long-standing assumption that only the United States was strong enough to stand up to Russia. Dating from the Cold War years, Washington thought that Europe lacked the strength and coherence to face down Moscow. Searching for a way to avoid going to the assistance of a besieged Georgia, now George Bush turned over the lead for ending the Russo-Georgian war to the Europeans. The American foreign policy mandarins knew full well that Europe was less keen on Georgia's independence streak than even the United States. In some respects, Bush's abdication was a "prototype" for his successor's policy of "leading from behind" in the 2011 Libyan bombing campaign or of staying clear of the Syrian imbroglio. In any event, the American leader looked to Paris, which held the rotating presidency of the EU in mid-2008. No surprise, Georgia stood virtually alone against its powerful neighbor, which reversed the small Caucasus nation's drift toward the West and its hoped-for membership in NATO and the EU.

The Bush administration's predicament stemmed from its earlier overextension. The country wearied of wars and expenditures in foreign lands. Moreover, the president was a lame duck with just a few months left in office. In late summer, the American economy faltered as it plunged into a deep financial crisis, which led to the multiyear Great Recession. Even before that severe economic downturn, George Bush's poll numbers plunged. One CNN poll recorded that "71 percent of the American public disapproves of how Bush is handling his job as president." Poll analysts contented that no prior president had ever crossed the 70 percent disapproval threshold. And even though the violence in Iraq had dissipated markedly by mid-2008, only 38 percent of Americans believed things were going well for the United States in the Persian Gulf nation.[97] Widespread dissatisfaction with President Bush's policies made it easy for Barack Obama to promise the polar opposite of the incumbent's international interventionism.

Bush's end-of-term pullbacks from his earlier interventionist strategy anticipated what was to be an extraordinary disengagement by his successor in the White House.[98] Even before Bush returned to Texas, his administration had set in motion a shift away from the robust engagement that so characterized his first years in office. The cycles of US foreign policy have not been rigidly confined to the exact start and end of presidential terms. Overlaps in policies typified other presidencies. Americans sensed that their country overreached itself in Iraq and Afghanistan, and these sentiments seeped into White House thinking.

Notes

1. President Bush's Second Inaugural Address, January 20, 2005. Downloaded from http://www.npr.org/templates/story/story.php?storyId=4460172. Accessed July 20, 2016.
2. James Mann, *Rise of the Vulcans: The History of Bush's War Cabinet* (New York: Viking, 2004), pp. 258–259.

3. Charles Tripp, *A History of Iraq* (New York: Cambridge University Press, 2nd ed., 2002), pp. 278–279.
4. Stefan Halper and Jonathan Clarke, *America Alone: The Neo-Conservatives and the Global Order* (New York: Cambridge University Press, 2004), pp. 146–147.
5. Jon Meacham, *Destiny and Power: The American Odyssey of George Herbert Walker Bush* (New York: Random House, 2015), pp. 625 and 740.
6. David Wurmser, *Tyranny's Ally: America's Failure to Defeat Saddam Hussein* (Washington, DC: American Enterprise Institute, 1999), p. 137.
7. Steven Lee Myers and Eric Schmitt, "Iraq Rebuilt Bombed Arms Plant, Officials Say," *New York Times*, January 22, 2001, p. A 1.
8. March Lynch, "Smart Sanctions: Rebuilding Consensus or Maintaining Conflict?" *Global Policy*, June 28, 2001. Downloaded from https://www.globalpolicy.org/component/content/article/170-sanctions/42169.html. Accessed July 20, 2016.
9. Condoleezza Rice, "Promoting the National Interest," *Foreign Affairs*, 79, no. 1 (January/February, 2000), 61.
10. Robert S. Litwak, *Regime Change: U.S. Strategy through the Prism of 9/11*(Washington, DC: Woodrow Wilson Center Press, 2007), p. 125.
11. Richard A. Clarke, *Against All Enemies: Inside America's War on Terror* (New York: Free Press, 2004), pp. 229–240.
12. George W. Bush, *Decision Points* (New York: Crown Publishers, 2010), p. 127.
13. Ibid., p. 151.
14. Bob Woodward, *Plan of Attack* (New York: Simon and Schuster, 2004), pp. 30, 81–82, and 98.
15. George W. Bush, State of the Union Address, January 29, 2002, in National Archives and Records Administration. Downloaded from http://georgewbush-whitehouse.archives.gov/news/releases/2002/01/20020129-11.html. Accessed July 20, 2016.
16. Thom Shanker and David E. Sanger, "U.S. Envisions Blueprint On Iraq Including Big Invasion Next Year," *New York Times*, April 28, 2002, p. A1; Eric Scmitt, "U.S. Plans For Iraq Is Said To Include Attack On 3 Sides," *New York Times*, July 5, 2002, p. A1 and Thomas E. Ricks, "Timing, Tactics On Iraq War Disputed," *Washington Post*, August 1, 2002, p. A1.

17. John Barry and Roy Gutman, "Rumors of War," *Newsweek*, August 12, 2002, p. 36.
18. Eric Schmitt and Joel Brinkley, "State Dept. Study Foresaw Troubles Now Plaguing Iraq," *New York*, October 19, 2003, p. 1.
19. Philip Stephens, *Tony Blair: The Making of a World Leader* (New York: Viking, 2004), pp. 198 and 200.
20. David E. Sanger, "In Reichstag, Bush Condemns Terror as New Despotism," *New York Times*, May 2004, p. A 1.
21. Editorial, "The Need for One Voice on Iraq," *Economist*, July 30, 2002, p. 14.
22. White House, President Bush Delivers Graduation Speech at West Point, June 1, 2002. Downloaded from http://georgewbush-whitehouse.archives.gov/news/releases/2002/06/20020601-3.html. Accessed July 20, 2016.
23. Among media coverage, *The Washington Post*, almost alone, understood the significance of the president's attack doctrine. See its editorial, "Taking the Offensive," *Washington Post*, June 4, 2002, p. A 16.
24. Julia Preston, "U.N. Spy Photo Shows New Building at Iraq Nuclear Sites," *New York Times*, September 6, 2002, p. A 1.
25. President's Speech to the United Nations General Assembly, September 12, 2002. Downloaded from http://georgewbush-whitehouse.archives.gov/news/releases/2002/09/20020912-1.html. Accessed October 1, 2015.
26. Barton Gellman, *Angler: The Cheney Vice Presidency* (New York: Penguin, 2008), pp. 215–222 and 227.
27. Patrick E. Tyler, "Britain's Case: Iraqi Program to Amass Arms Is 'Up and Running,'" *New York Times*, September 25, 2002, p. A 1.
28. Commission on Intelligence Capabilities of the United States Regarding Weapons of Mass Destruction, March 2005. Downloaded from http://govinfo.library.unt.edu/wmd/about.html. Accessed July 10, 2016.
29. National Security Strategy, The White House, September 17, 2001. Downloaded from http://georgewbush-whitehouse.archives.gov/nsc/nss/2002/. Accessed July 20, 2016.
30. Peter Slevin, "Analysts: New Strategy Courts Unseen Dangers," *Washington Post*, September 22, 2002, p. A 1 and Judith Miller, "Keeping U.S. No. 1: Is It Wise? Is It New?" *New York Times*, October 26, 2002, p. A 19.

31. John Lewis Gaddis, *Surprise, Security and the American Experience* (Cambridge, MA: Harvard University Press, 2004), pp. 15–20.
32. Norman Graebner, *Foundations of American Foreign Policy: A Realist Appraisal from Franklin to McKinley* (Wilmington, DE: Scholarly Resources, 1985), p. 354.
33. Daniel Benjamin and Steven Simon, *The Age of Sacred Terror* (New York: Random House, 2002), pp. 353–365.
34. Cited in Bob Graham, *Intelligence Matters* (New York: Radom House, 2004), p. 181.
35. Ibid., pp. 181–184.
36. Karen De Young, "Bush Cites Urgent Iraqi Threat," *Washington Post*, October 8, 2002, p. A 1.
37. Richard Morin and Claudia Deane, "71 % Of Americans Support War, Poll Shows," *Washington Post*, March 19, 2003, p. A 14.
38. Jim VandeHei and Juliet Eilperin, "Congress Passes Iraq Resolution," *Washington Post*, October 11, 2002, p. A 14.
39. Walter Pincus and Karen DeYoung, "U.S. Sets Late January Decision on Iraq War," *Washington Post*, December 19, 2002, p. A 1.
40. Betsy Pisik, "U.S., U.N. Spar over Iraq Report," *Washington Times*, December 13, 2002, p. 1.
41. Serge Schmemann, "Bush Warns Hussein again but Sidesteps any 'Deadline,'" *New York Times*, January 15, 2003, p. A 1.
42. Hans Blix, *Disarming Iraq* (New York: Pantheon Books, 2004), pp. 135–143.
43. Julia Preston, "U.N. Inspectors Says Iraq Fall Short on Cooperation," *New York Times*, January 28, 2003, p. A 1.
44. George W. Bush "State of the Union Address," *Washington Post*, January 28, 2003. Downloaded from http://www.washingtonpost.com/wp-srv/onpolitics/transcripts/bushtext_012803.html. Accessed July 20, 2016.
45. This valid legal argument was made by Kim Holmes, "Uncomfortable Truths: Explaining away Iraq's Real WMD," *Washington Times*, October 72, 2014, p. A 14.
46. The full extent of the harm caused to US soldiers by the chemical shells was commented on by a journalist in 2014. See C.J. Chivers, "The Secret Casualties of Iraq's Abandoned Chemical Weapons," *New York Times*, October 14, 2014, p. A 1.
47. Judith Miller, *The Story: A Reporter's Journey* (New York: Simon & Schuster, 2015), pp. 145–149 and 216–219.

48. For a summary of the report, see Fred Hiatt, "'Bush Lied'?: If Only It Were That Simple," *Washington Post*, June 9, 2008, p. A 20.
49. Scott Shane, "Ex-C.I.A. Official Says Iraq Data Was Distorted," *New York Times*, February 11, 2006, p. A 6.
50. Paul Pillar, *Intelligence and U.S. Foreign Policy: Iraq, 9/11, and Misguided Reform* (New York: Columbia University Press, 2011), pp. 142–143 and 145–157.
51. Commission on the Intelligence Capabilities of the United States Regarding Weapons of Mass Destruction, March 31, 2005. Downloaded from http://govinfo.library.unt.edu/wmd/about.html. Accessed July 20, 2016.
52. Laurence H. Silberman, "The Dangerous Lie That 'Bush Lied,'" *Wall Street Journal*, February 9, 2015, p. A 13.
53. Joseph C. Wilson, "What I Didn't Find in Africa," *New York Times*, July 6, 2003, p. A 16.
54. Joseph C. Wilson, *The Politics of Truth* (New York: Carroll & Graf Publishers, 2004), pp. 325–341.
55. Craig S. Smith and Richard Bernstein, "3 NATO Members and Russia Resist U.S. On Iraq Plans," *New York Times*, February 11, 2003, p. A 1.
56. Robert Kagan, *Of Paradise and Power. America and Europe in the New World Order* (New York: Alfred A. Knopf, 2003), p. 3.
57. John Diamond, "White House Getting under Europe's Skin," *USA Today*, February 21, 2003, p. A 9.
58. For more information on the Security Council wrangling, see Woodward, *Plan of Attack*, pp. 167, 174–184, and 221–226.
59. Elisabeth Bumiller, "Bush's Tutor and Disciple: Condoleezza Rice," *New York Times*, November 17, 2005, p. A 1.
60. Kenneth Adelman, "Cakewalk in Iraq," *Washington Post*, February 13, 2002, p. A 27 and gloatingly again in "'Cakewalk' Revisited," *Washington Post*, April 10, 2003, p. A 29.
61. Cited in Anthony H. Cordesman, *The Iraq War: Strategy, Tactics, and Military Lessons* (Washington, DC: CSIS Press, 2004), p. 123.
62. Reginald Dale, "Bush Never Said 'Mission Accomplished,'" Center for Strategic and International Studies. Downloaded from http://csis.org/blog/bush-never-said-%E2%80%9Cmission-accomplished%E2%80%9D. Accessed July 20, 2016.
63. Thomas E. Ricks, *Fiasco: The American Military Adventure in Iraq* (New York: Penguin Press, 2006), pp. 147–161.

64. Robert M. Gates, *Duty: Memoirs of a Secretary of State* (New York: Alfred A. Knopf, 2014), pp. 120–125.
65. Peter van Buren, *We Meant Well: How I Helped Lose the Battle for the Hearts and Minds of the Iraqi People* (New York: Metropolitan, 2011), pp. 117–121.
66. L. Paul Bremer III, *My Year In Iraq: The Struggle To Build A Future of Hope* (New York: Simon & Schuster, 2006), pp. 39–42, 44–45, and 260–261.
67. Jim Michaels, *A Chance in Hell: The Men Who Triumphed over Iraq's Deadliest City and Turned the Tide of War* (New York: St. Martin's Press, 2010), pp. 91–94.
68. For casualties in Iraq and Afghanistan, see icasualties.org. Downloaded from http://www.icasualties.org/iraq/. Accessed July 20, 2016.
69. *The Iraq Study Group Report: The Way Forward—A New Approach* (New York: Filibust Imprint, 2006), pp. 82–88.
70. Kimberly Kagan, *The Surge: A Military History* (New York: Encounter Books, 2009), p. 28.
71. Michael R. Gordon and Bernard E. Trainor, *The Endgame: The Inside Story of the Struggle for Iraq, From George W. Bush to Barack Obama* (New York: Pantheon Books, 2013), pp. 675–680 and Peter R. Mansoor, *Surge: My Journey with General David Petraeus and the Remaking of the Iraq War* (New Haven, CT: Yale University Press, 2013), pp. 260–270.
72. Rice, *No Higher Honor*, pp. 401–403.
73. Steven R. Weisman, "Powell Says Ukraine Vote Was Full of Fraud," *New York Times*, November 25, 2004, p. A 10.
74. Oleksandr Sushko and Olena Prystayko, "Western Influence," in *Revolution in Orange: The Origins of Ukraine's Democratic Breakthrough*, ed. Anders Aslund and Michael McFaul (Washington, DC: Carnegie Endowment for Peace, 2006), pp. 140–141.
75. Edward Lucas, *The New Cold War* (New York: Palgrave Macmillan, 2014), pp. 70–71.
76. Ibid., p. 173.
77. Condoleezza Rice, "Remarks at the American University in Cairo," June 20, 2005. Department of State Archives. Downloaded from http://2001-2009.state.gov/secretary/rm/2005/48328.htm. Accessed July 16, 2016.

78. James Mann, *George W. Bush* (New York: Times Books, 2015), p. 107.
79. Brent Scowcroft, "Don't Attack Saddam," *Wall Street Journal*, August 15, 2002, p. A 17.
80. Norman Podhoretz, "The Case for Bombing Iran," *Commentary*, June 1, 2007, p. 23 and Norman Podhoretz, *World War IV: The Long Struggle against Islamofascism* (New York: Doubleday, 2007), pp. 182 and 185.
81. Rice, *No Higher Honor*, pp. 420–424.
82. Bush, *Decision Points*, pp. 415–420.
83. Jacob Heilbrunn, *They Knew They Were Right: The Rise of the Neocons* (New York: Doubleday, 2008), p. 274.
84. Victor Cha and David C. Kang, *Nuclear North Korea: A Debate on Engagement Strategies* (New York: Columbia University Press, 2003), pp. 130–148.
85. Gordon Corera, *Shopping for Bombs: Nuclear Proliferation, Global Insecurity, and the Rise and Fall of the A.Q. Khan Network* (New York: Oxford University Press, 2006), pp. 92–93, 99, 101–102.
86. David E. Sanger, "Bush Urges Quick Action on North Korea," *New York Times*, October 10, 2006, p. A 1.
87. United Nations Security Council Resolution 1718, October 14, 2006. Downloaded from http://www.un.org/sc/committees/1718. Accessed December 15, 2014.
88. Christopher R. Hill, *Outpost: Life on the Frontlines of American Diplomacy* (New York: Simon and Schuster, 2014), pp. 252–268, 279–285, and 309–310.
89. Dick Cheney, *In My Time: A Personal and Political Memoir* (New York: Threshold Editions, 2011), p. 487.
90. Julie Flint and Alex de Waal, *Darfur: A New History of a Long War* (London: Zed Books, 2008), pp. 123, 179–183.
91. House of Commons Resolution, 467 in the 108th Congress, July 22, 2004. Downloaded from https://www.congress.gov/bill/108th-congress/house-concurrent-resolution/467. Accessed September 15, 2015.
92. UN Resolution 1769, dated July 31, 2007. Downloaded from http://www.un.org/press/en/2007/sc9089.doc.htm. Accessed September 15, 2015.
93. Rice, *No Higher Honor*, p. 585.

94. Ronald D. Asmus, *A Little War That Shook the World* (New York: Palgrave Macmillan, 2010), pp. 87, 146–149.
95. Asmus, *The Little War That Shook the World*, pp. 90–91.
96. President Clinton's point man on Russia in the 1990s dissected the twisted logic and self-serving Russian statements. Strobe Talbott, "Russia's Ominous New Doctrine?" *Washington Post*, August 15, 2008, p. 26.
97. "Poll: More disapprove of Bush than any other president," CNN Poll, May 1, 2008. Downloaded from http://www.cnn.com/2008/POLITICS/05/01/bush.poll. Accessed September 29, 2015.
98. Dan Eggen, "Bush's Overseas Policies Begin Resembling Obama's," *Washington Post*, September 15, 2008, p. A 2.

Part IV

CHAPTER 8

Barack Hussein Obama and the New Retrenchment

"History doesn't repeat itself, but it does rhyme." —*Mark Twain, reputedly*

"History is a cyclic poem written by time upon the memories of man." —*Percy Bysshe Shelley*

Barack Obama's presidency marked a decided backward step from the muscular internationalism of his immediate predecessor. On its face, the US Senator from Illinois won the White House largely to reverse George W. Bush's assertive international engagement and to refute his military interventionism. President Obama's foreign policy, in fact, recorded the sharpest turn inward among any of the post-Cold War presidents. In some respects, Barack Hussein Obama's international stance appeared such an acute departure from previous overseas ventures because junior Bush's interventionism also represented a break from the overall circumspect engagement of his father and the generally conflict-avoidance Clinton presidency. During his presidential campaign, Obama's advisers emphasized the use of "soft power diplomacy" rather than the hard power of the Bush junior era.[1]

Obama's international stance, however, never matched the isolationism of the interwar period when White House occupants sidelined America's engagement during the rise of German and Japanese radical doctrines and exuberant militarism of the 1930s. Rather, America's 44th president scaled back American leadership in large-scale ground invasions while not

T.H. Henriksen, *Cycles in US Foreign Policy since the Cold War*,
DOI 10.1007/978-3-319-48640-6_8

completely abandoning all of America's participation in international ventures. Hence, his restraint greatly contrasted with the younger Bush's diplomatic and military muscularity.

Barack Obama's retrenchment prescription for American foreign policy became known during his pursuit of the White House. He stumped for the presidency with a selective message condemning the Iraq War while endorsing the fight against al Qaeda terrorists and the Taliban in Afghanistan. His outlook resonated with the widespread war-weariness in the American body politic. He tapped into wide sectors in American society that felt a deep disenchantment with the human and monetary costs of both wars, but held a particular dislike for the conflict in Iraq. Because no nuclear production plants or chemical weapons facilities were uncovered in the Persian Gulf country, many Americans saw little rationale for the invasion or the occupation's mounting costs in lives and resources. Candidate Obama frequently called attention to the fact that he even opposed the Iraq War before it began. In October 2002, five months prior to the US invasion, Obama, as an Illinois state senator, delivered a speech in Chicago against going to war. His opening comments defined his position: "I don't oppose all wars. What I am opposed to is a dumb war."[2]

As a presidential candidate, Obama frequently voiced opposition to Iraq as "a misguided war." In a carefully crafted newspaper essay, the presumptive Democratic presidential nominee wrote in July 2008 that he even opposed the military surge in Iraq, which is still widely credited as a key factor in decreasing anti-American violence and bringing to heel the al Qaeda insurgents. In that same opinion article, he stated that his first day in the White House a new order would go out to the US military in Iraq to "safely redeploy our combat brigades at a pace that would remove them in 16 months," which would be by summer 2010.[3]

At the Democratic Convention, in his acceptance speech, the presidential nominee made plain his intentions when he declared: "I will end this war in Iraq responsibly and finish the fight against al Qaeda and the Taliban in Afghanistan." He returned to this oft-spoken theme about the Iraq War being a "war of choice," unnecessary to combat terrorism. "You don't defeat a terrorist network that operates in 80 countries by occupying Iraq."[4] Earlier, the presidential candidate spelled out his views in a magazine article entitled "Renewing American Leadership." That pre-White House perspective offered no isolationist message. Indeed, it advocated a re-seizing of the "American moment," which he judged needed to be reclaimed by "rebuilding alliances, partnerships, and institutions necessary to confront common threats." Although the candidate wrote that "Iraq was a diversion from the fight against terrorists" who struck American on September 11, 2001, he also dwelt on classic internationalist themes, such as calling for "global engagement," "strengthening the pillars of a just society," and "vibrant free societies" for citizens everywhere.[5]

The nation's first African-American president rode into power on a crest of optimism with one poll showing 79 percent of his fellow citizens feeling that he could restore the economy and end the war in Iraq after two years. This initial optimism surpassed the forecasts of the five preceding incoming White House occupants, with the nearest being Ronald Reagan in 1981 at 69 percent. Outgoing President Bush in the same poll left office with just 22 percent of Americans having a favorable view of his handling of the nation's overseas activities and troubled domestic economy, which was mired in what became known as the Great Recession. The severe economic downturn figured high in Americans' polling decisions, too.[6]

One of Barack Obama's first acts in the White House was to sign an executive order banning torture and degrading treatment of prisoners to seize the higher moral ground. Before long, he let Eric Holder, his attorney general, go after CIA interrogators of terrorist suspects on torture charges. His pledge to close down the maligned Guantánamo Bay detention center within a year ran into adverse political realities and court rulings. Removing and transferring the nearly 700 terrorism suspects raised fears that the former inmates would return to the battlefield. Politicians and ordinary citizens also feared that the freed detainees would live in their neighborhoods. Thus, Congress refused to fund a transfer of detainees to US prisons. The new White House resident gradually went about transferring prisoners to other countries. In the span of seven years, he reduced the total to slightly less than 100 by mid-2016.

Barack Obama moved quickly to set the stage for his brand of foreign policy. Here the president's caution and hesitancy, which became hallmarks of his years in the White House, revealed themselves early on in his first months in office. His persistent questioning and requests for additional options slowed the decision-making process.[7] He strove to evade committing American forces to action in the way that brought so much ruin to his predecessor's presidency and to the image of the United States as an overly assertive military power.

President Obama's selections for the top security spots, nonetheless, reflected a steady course. He retained Robert Gates as the secretary of defense, who George Bush selected for the position when Donald

Rumsfeld left the post after the big Republican loss of Congressional seats in the 2006 mid-term elections. He picked his campaign rival Hillary Clinton to be Secretary of State. For the directorship of national intelligence, he settled on Dennis Blair, a retired admiral. When the new president chose Leon Panetta as head of the CIA, the surprising choice caused a stir because the former California congressman and chief of staff in the Clinton administration lacked recent intelligence experience, since his Army service decades earlier. Panetta, an accomplished political operator, was not perceived as a reformer of the battered Agency. Rather, he was seen as a caretaker.[8] The conformist cast of the new appointees belied President Obama's plans for an emphatic break from his predecessor's policies and his calculations to manage international affairs from within the West Wing.

The applause for his Inaugural Address had hardly died down when the new commander in chief flew to Camp Lejeune in North Carolina to announce his withdrawal plan for Iraq in front of thousands of camouflage-clad US Marines. Obama's timetable called for most of the 142,000 troops then in Iraq to be redeployed from the largely stabilized Persian Gulf country by August 2010. Those 35,000–50,000 "transitional forces" remaining were scheduled to leave by December 2011. The pull-out accorded with the president's intention to shift troops and resources from a stabilized Iraq to an increasingly volatile Afghanistan.[9]

Afghanistan: Searching for an Exit

Another of the administration's most momentous decisions came early in its tenure. The deteriorating war in Afghanistan cried out for a lifeline. Ironically, the Obama campaign had leveled most of its criticisms against George W. Bush for the Iraq War and on Senator John McCain, the Republican presidential candidate, for mimicking George W. Bush's Iraq policy. Iraq, in this sense, eclipsed Afghanistan as the foremost foreign policy issue at the start of the new government. But the fighting in Iraq had dramatically fallen off by this time. Soon after the election, the campaign's winners were compelled to look again at Afghanistan, not Iraq. A month before President-elect Obama's inauguration, Afghanistan notably re-entered the nation's consciousness. A senior Defense Department official conveyed the sense of urgency when he called for a "tourniquet of some kind" to staunch the swelling violence and the Taliban advances in the South-Central Asian nation.[10]

Days after taking the oath of office, President Obama declared his intention to deploy as many as 30,000 additional combat and support troops to Afghanistan over the spring and summer to strengthen the already 36,000 US personnel in the strife-torn country. Counting NATO and other foreign militaries in the ISAF, the new total was to reach 90,000 soldiers by late August. Additionally, Washington committed to a 50 percent growth in civilian officials, reaching over 900 to administer nation-building and administrative functions. In all, this upsurge in personnel led to a further Americanization of the counterinsurgency effort.[11] Plans were also laid to expand the Afghan army, police, and border guards to 400,000 over the next three years at an estimated cost of $12 billion. Obama officials spoke of a narrowed goal that differed from their predecessors. Even though the still-nascent administration beefed up US troops in Afghanistan, its representatives expressed reduced ambitions for American goals. They articulated a shift toward targeting al Qaeda rather than what they termed the lofty nation-building and democracy-enhancing endeavors of the Bush administration. Standing up Afghanistan's own defense capability was so the United States could concentrate on the terrorist threat.[12] Preparing for an American exit necessitated a buildup of the Afghan National Army, police force, and border guards.[13] Before the US drawdown date arrived, Obama wanted to zero in on al Qaeda, but the Taliban pressed their attacks, requiring a US counteroffensive to save Afghanistan from falling to them. Public opinion polls still favored an active engagement in the landlocked country. A Washington Post-ABC poll indicated that 56 percent believed that "Afghanistan was worth fighting for," while 41 percent held it "was not worth" the fight (only 3 percent had no opinion).[14] These sentiments made Obama's job easier, at least in the near term. But before long, the US citizens tired of this war too.

Also early on in his administration, the president ordered a step up in drone (unmanned aerial vehicles) air strikes on Taliban targets inside Pakistan. In time, the prolific use of drone bombardments inside Pakistan and elsewhere turned into a controversial aspect of Obama's counterterrorism campaign.[15] Together with increased drone strikes, the president called for a regionwide diplomatic strategy encompassing Pakistan as well as Afghanistan, for which Richard Holbrooke, of Dayton glory, assumed the job as special envoy. The veteran diplomat also actively reviewed what fresh initiatives to Iran and Russia would be useful to the United States. Holbrooke's remit included moving Pakistan closer to America's policy for ending the conflict in Afghanistan and for improving US relations with the Greater Middle East. The energetic Holbrooke made some progress before his untimely death. But generally the famed interlocutor ran into personal and political opposition from Obama's inner circle, which impaired his mission.[16] After Holbrooke's death, the Obama administration never again paid Pakistan the same level of attention.

Other policy departures from the preceding administration soon followed. President Obama set a widely different course for American counterterrorism than Bush had. Signaling the new direction, administration officials backed away from George Bush's routinely uttered phrase the "global war on terror." In an e-mailed memo, the Obama's Pentagon requested the use of "overseas contingency operations" rather than the signature expression of the former president, which implied an expansive global conflict rather than specific military actions.[17]

The Middle East, Russia, and Iran

While the fledgling Obama presidency was laying the foundation for a comprehensive battle plan for Afghanistan, it reached out to the Muslim world just five months into office. Traveling to Egypt and speaking at Cairo University, Barack Obama extended an olive branch to the Islamic world for reconciliation with the West. Even though he mentioned American themes of promoting democracy, religious freedom, and women's rights in the Middle East, he noted failings in America's pursuit of its own ideals, particularly in Iraq. He made the point that the United States desired to withdraw its military presence from Iraq and then Afghanistan, once it was assured that the latter country no longer harbored terrorists bent on killing Americans. In a line that drew applause, he avowed: "America is not—and never will be—at war with Islam." Obama tapped into a popular regional cause when he labeled the plight of the Palestinians as "intolerable" after 60 years of statelessness and "dislocation." The president stated that "the United States does not accept the legitimacy of continued Israeli settlements" in West Bank areas. Despite directing his bluntest comments at Israel, the president made it clear that America shared an "unbreakable" bond with the Jewish state.[18]

To his critics, President Obama's moral equivalence detracted from America's resounding message of liberty and democracy in the Middle East.[19] His speech set a different tone toward the Middle East from other presidents. It proved to be a harbinger of strained relations with Israel, of America's withdrawal first from Iraq and then largely from Afghanistan, and of Washington's eager engagement of Iran in the years to come. At a news conference in April 2010, the president advanced the notion that resolving the Israeli-Palestinian dispute was "a vital national security interest of the United States," more than implying that this Middle East standoff deepened the hostile environment in the region for America.[20] These and other such statements became the thin end of an ever-widening wedge that divided Barack Obama and his counterpart Benjamin Netanyahu, the Israeli prime minister, over the US president's tenure.

The Obama administration initiated the opening of a new chapter with Russia to restore the harmony of the early 1990s. Dubbed the "reset," this overture envisioned turning back bilateral relations to before they soured under the Clinton administration. The Kremlin especially resented the Clinton-initiated Kosovo bombing and the NATO expansion into the Czech Republic, Bulgaria, Poland, Hungary, Slovakia, Slovenia, and Albania. The Bush administration raised Russian fears and resentment in 2002 when it abandoned the Anti-Ballistic Treaty with Moscow, because it felt the 1972 treaty restricted American missile defense of European allies from Iran. Five years later, the Bush White House announced plans to install ten anti-missile interceptors in Poland and a battle-management system in the Czech Republic to counter Iranian long-range missiles. The Russians perceived these installations as a direct threat to their ICBMs, which served as a strategic deterrent against the United States.[21] For its part, Moscow considered its 2008 military actions against Georgia as retribution for America's wrongs. By that date, the Kremlin's hectoring of Ukraine and Georgia were harbingers of its neo-imperialist impulses.[22]

Taking Kremlin grievances into account, President Obama displayed an eagerness for a rapprochement with Russia. He dispatched Robert Gates to Russia with a proposal for Russo-American collaboration on East European missile defense. Moscow rejected the defense secretary's proposal unless the United States first scrapped elements of the anti-missile system. Gates even suggested jointly operating a missile facility on Russian territory.[23] Moscow's opposition led the United States to scrub the Bush missile strategy and replace it with a naval anti-missile defense. These short-range, ship-based interceptors posed no threat to Russia's ICBMs. This revamped defensive program also called for a future installation of land-based missiles in Romania and Poland, plus a radar coordination facility in Turkey. Ankara declared in late 2011 that it was going forward with the planned radar system as part of the multilayered NATO shield against Iran's escalating nuclear and missile dangers.[24] The administration's concessions laid the foundation for a Russian-American strategic weapons agreement later and for Moscow's backing economic sanctions against Iran.

The new Washington administration attained one of its short-term goals with Moscow. It revived nuclear arms-control negotiations with Russia and hammered out an agreement, which was signed by President Obama and President Dimiti Medvedev in the majestic gilded hall of the Prague Castle in the Czech Republic's capital city on April 8, 2010. The New START treaty reduced by a proclaimed 30 percent the number of nuclear warheads and launchers from previous the START, which George H.W. Bush entered into with the Soviet Union.[25] It had expired in December 2009. New START, after ratification by the US Senate and the Federal Assembly in Russia, went into force in 2011. It pared down the number of deployed warheads to 1500 from 2200.[26] The Obama administration, nonetheless, rejected a request to remove US tactical nuclear weapons from Europe despite pressure from some NATO allies unless Russia reciprocated, something Moscow refused to entertain.[27] To secure ratification of the New START treaty, the White House went on record supporting missile defense in a manner not previously stated and committed over $80 billion to modernizing the US nuclear arsenal.[28]

Accompanying the rollout of the new arms reduction treaty was the Obama administration's "Nuclear Posture Review." The Defense Department's 50-page document proposed to address the post-Cold War threats posed by "by suicidal terrorist and unfriendly regimes seeking nuclear weapons."[29] It granted nonnuclear nations a form of immunity from any atomic-weapons retaliation from the United States. But "outliers" (the Obama administration's term for rogue states), such as Iran and North Korea, would not be de-targeted by the United States. Robert Gates, the defense secretary, elaborated at a press conference that the review contained "a message for Iran and North Korea." Referring to the two so-called outliers, he added: "if you're not going to play by the rules..., then all options are on the table in terms of how we deal with you."[30] The ostensibly threatening nuclear declaration served as a stepping-stone to an agreement with Iran.

The Islamic Republic of Iran figured prominently in Barack Obama's thinking from his first summer in the White House, when large Iranian crowds took to the streets to protest what they regarded as a fraudulent reelection of President Mahmoud Ahmadinejad on June 12. Rather than loudly condemning the Iranian government's harsh crackdown on demonstrators, journalists, and democracy champions, Washington adopted a near-silent stance, opening itself to charges of breaking faith with freedom advocates. Unlike the EU or both the US Senate and House, which passed nonbinding resolutions condemning Tehran's bloody suppression of its opponents in the urban thoroughfares, the Obama government held back from venting condemnatory statements. Its spokesmen argued that full-throated backing of the protestors would play into the hands of the Iranian regime, which would accuse them of being American puppets.[31]

Be that as it may, Obama's handling evinced a penchant for stage-setting for future nuclear talks with Iran. American foreign policy mandarins looked beyond democracy rioters in the city squares to a time when Iranian and US diplomats would sit down to discuss Iran's nuclear weapons programs. They cynically calculated that the Ahmadinejad regime would prevail over the public demonstrations.[32] Their bet proved sound and subsequently they engaged Iran on nuclear and other issues. In late September, the administration accepted Tehran's offer to hold direct talks between the two parties, together with China, Britain, France, Germany, and Russia. So began, the meetings that in time led to the sustained P5 plus 1 (P5+1) negotiations on Iranian nuclear activities, which loomed large during Obama's second term. Prior to American-Iranian rapprochement, Washington's pursuit of Iran cracked open a rift with Israel that prevailed to the end of Obama's second term.

The Afghanistan Reckoning

As summer 2009 drew to a close, the Obama administration's attention again returned to the failing war in Afghanistan and a resurgent Taliban. The insurgents operated in or held sway in some 30 percent of the country, up sharply from the beginning of the year. The Afghan political scene also offered little optimism, for the August reelection of Hamid Karzai to the presidency was mired in accusation of fraudulent voting practices. This harmed Karzai's legitimacy and by extension Washington's stake in the country. Two factors pushed the White House to confront the realities of the Afghan conflict. First and most importantly, the depressing news from the faraway country required policy changes and resources to freeze the Taliban advances.

Second, when General Stanley McChrystal was appointed as the new commander of American forces and the NATO-led ISAF in May, he was tasked by Secretary Gates to produce a strategic assessment for the Afghan theater by September. The new commander recommended fighting a classic counterinsurgency whereby foreign and Afghan military and police forces would concentrate on winning over the population to their side and to fostering loyalty between the people and central government in Kabul. Killing the enemy dropped in importance to winning hearts and minds. The new four-star general also advocated augmenting and improving the Afghan military and police units over a period of years. To act as "bridge" until the local troops and police were ready, he wanted 40,000 additional troops, most of them US soldiers for ISAF.[33]

The necessity to reverse the floundering, US military campaign took place against a backdrop of declining American interest in Afghanistan's fate. A majority of Americans, according to a Washington Post-ABC News poll in late 2009, held that the "war is not worth fighting." Fifty-one percent of those polled held that view, while 47 percent still thought "the war is worth the costs." Only 24 percent endorsed the idea of sending additional troops to the mountainous country, while nearly twice as many, 45 percent, wanted a decrease in the number of military forces. The public expressed confidence in the US military but they lost faith in the Afghans to govern themselves with an honest and competent government.[34] As such, Americans signaled deepening sentiments for international disengagement, a noticeable factor in Barack Obama's election to the presidency.

Speaking to the Veterans of Foreign Wars Convention in Phoenix, Arizona in mid-August, Obama was cognizant of his retired military audience, when he broached his timetable for withdrawal from Iraq by balancing it with a short-term boost in the Afghan War. He noted the Coalition's turnover of control of all cities and towns to Iraq's security forces in June. He laid out a timetable for the removal of combat brigades and then all US troops from Iraq by the end of 2011. By contrast, he recalled that the insurgency in Afghanistan "is not a war of choice. This is a war of necessity." Not checking the Taliban insurgency "will mean an even larger safe haven from which al Qaeda would plot to kill more Americans."[35] This Afghan-first policy, however, witnessed moderation in its execution.

Before moving on General McChrystal's request for additional military forces, the Obama administration insisted on its own strategic review of the Afghan campaign that took months.[36] Unhurried, the commander-in-chief met and pondered throughout the fall with the Pentagon's top brass, cabinet secretaries, Congressional leaders, and a plethora of advisers to chart a new course in Afghanistan. The officials pored over McChrystal's 66-page assessment and the general officer's proposed posting of 40,000 additional troops for a classic counterinsurgency operation to protect the local population from insurgents and expand their self-defense forces to hundreds of thousands.[37]

That lengthy presidential review kicked off a wide-ranging debate about the correct option to pursue in Afghanistan. This policy tug-of-war involved members of the Obama administration and outside experts. Its importance lies in the fact that the discussions helped define Washington's approach to terrorist networks beyond the Afghan-Pakistan theaters, which took root in Yemen, Syria, Somalia, Libya, and again in Iraq. The dispute centered on three military courses. The first entertained a classic counterterrorism model by which the United States fixed on eliminating al Qaeda by use of drone (unmanned aircraft) airstrikes and commando raids by SOF. These minimalist tactics relied on few military forces and even fewer bases of operation. These half-in operations spared US casualties and large financial expenditures, while still bringing to bear considerable hard power against terrorist adversaries. The reduced-scale tactics were in keeping with Barack Obama's emerging policy of retrenchment, restraint, and cautious projection of armed might. Early on, Vice President Joe Biden backed it as a way to avoid a second Vietnam, which saw America slide down a slippery slope into a big land-war quagmire.[38]

The second strategy looked to scaling up the number and proficiency of the Afghan security forces. A bigger and better trained local army and police force stood as the only way to keep al Qaeda from re-basing itself in the country and re-launching terrorist attacks against the West. Defeating or at least tying down the Taliban offered the only means to stop them from granting safe sanctuaries to al Qaeda cadres. Besides, allowing the Taliban to prevail seemed to ensure that more of Pakistan would fall to its own Taliban insurgency. Almost all the experts and pundits agreed that it behooved the United States to ratchet up the size and performance of the Afghan military and police.

The third option called for pursuing classical counterinsurgency. This tack urged placing the protection of the population over the goal of just killing insurgents. It is often misunderstood as just "winning the hearts and the minds" of the people. Many military units can do this effectively by ensuring the local civilians' safety and well-being with minimal government services, such as providing basic medical treatment and access to water and food supplies. The crucial dimension is linking the villagers' trust to the central government to build a nation from disparate factions and provinces. This is a painstaking and time intensive enterprise. ISAF troops (US and other Coalition personnel) were required until the foreign military could stand up a large and competent Afghan army and police force. Nearly simultaneously, Afghan government and civic functions needed to be greatly enlarged while displaying conspicuous integrity and fairness.

Generals Petraeus and McChrystal favored the fully resourced counterinsurgency, calling for billions of dollars for reconstruction and institution building as well as thousands of additional troops. Proponents of a broader military presence, including the secretaries of state and defense, worried that Afghanistan stood on the brink of being lost. Hillary Clinton held that reinforcements were "the only way to get governance changes" to stabilize Afghanistan. Robert Gates believed upping the number of US forces allowed for training a stand-alone Afghan army in "three to five years is reasonable."[39] The principal holdout against deploying additional ground forces was the president. Obama pushed back against a ten-year counterinsurgency (the average length of such endeavors), a long-term commitment to nation-building, and the expenditure of a trillion dollars.[40] McChrystal took the standard counterinsurgency figure of 20 security force members for every 1000 people as his yardstick. Calculating that Afghanistan had about 24 million inhabitants, he speculated that because of the severity of the insurgency the anti-insurgency effort needed at least a total of 400,000 security personnel.[41]

One strategy session, therefore, followed another in an extended search for the correct American prescription for an insurgency in a distant land. Money was an important consideration but troop numbers and casualties mattered more to President Obama and the American public, who recoiled at the lengthening casualty lists in Iraq and Afghanistan.[42] At last, Obama announced his decision in a speech at the US Military Academy on December 1.

The president granted the Pentagon its requested manpower surge but to only 30,000 troops, not the preferred 40,000. Still, there was a pivotal catch in his offer; the personnel deployments came with deadlines. Rather than a date based on military progress on the ground, Barack Obama arbitrarily etched July 2011 in stone for the time that military forces would begin to redeploy from Afghanistan, despite the fact that the reinforcements would not completely arrive until summer of 2010. In his address to the West Point cadets, he established that by the end of 2014

US combat operations were scheduled to cease (this was later modified). Republicans led by Senator John McCain, who ran against Obama for president, noisily opposed setting an arbitrary timetable, which permitted the insurgents to wait out the expiration date. Members of the president's Democratic Party breathed a sigh of relief with the exit dates established.

The Pentagon and McChrystal stoically soldiered on with smaller numbers and a tighter timetable than desired to battle the insurgents. As it turned out, McChrystal's downfall preceded the withdrawal date. The four-star Army officer was forced to resign in mid-2010 because of indiscreet remarks about Obama and Biden attributed to him and some of his staff officers by a reporter from *Rolling Stone* magazine.[43] General Petraeus moved from CENTCOM to replace him in the Afghan command. Along with the military personnel deployments, there came vast cash transfers to Afghanistan. Annually, the United States expended about $100 billion going forward on infrastructure projects, state-building efforts, and raising as well as equipping security forces nearly from scratch.

As a consequence of bad news and rising US casualties in Afghanistan, Americans lost heart in the Afghan conflict, much as had happened earlier in the Iraq War. Sixty-two percent of Americans believed the war was going badly according to a CBS News poll in July 2010, up from 49 percent two months earlier. The same poll recorded that respondents were divided about the president's handling of the war. Forty-four percent stated disapproval of the Obama's war management, whereas 43 percent approved.[44] Public opinion of President Obama's handling of the war continued to fall over time. Whereas in February, 48 percent of poll respondents endorsed the president's war policy, Americans in August gave him only a 36 percent approval in a USA Today/Gallup Poll.[45] The sinking poll numbers only fed the Obama administration's keenness to hasten American's departure from Afghanistan and to stay clear of future ground wars. Retrenchment was firmly in place in Washington.

Drones and Policy Deficit?

A startling dimension of President Obama's evolving international policy came rapidly into sharp relief. The new White House resident adopted wholesale the drone airstrikes from the Bush administration. Obama differed from his predecessor only in the greater frequency that he wielded drone-launched missiles against al Qaeda chieftains in Pakistan and elsewhere. In the first 13 months of Obama's presidency, he had ordered the firing of lethal airstrikes more times than George W. Bush had during his entire eight years in office. By fall 2012, Obama had carried out 283 drone strikes inside Pakistan, which amounted to six times more than Bush's two terms.[46] Barack Obama's drone strikes played into his retrenchment strategy, for offensive air bombardments permitted—and gave political cover to—the president to reduce ground forces while keeping terrorist networks off balance by killing their leadership.

The CIA-run drone program notched a number of kills. Among the most prominent deaths were the Pakistani Taliban leader Baitullah Mehsud, his replacement at the helm of Tehrik-i-Taliban Pakistan, Hakimullah Mehsud, and Abu Laith al-Libi, a senior al Qaeda leader.[47] Obama interjected himself into the assassination program by carefully reviewing and personally passing on the CIA-vetted lists of potential targets. Both Obama and the anti-terror weapon came under criticism mainly from the president's traditionally ardent loyalists.[48]

Undeterred, the commander-in-chief persevered with what became his weapon of choice against terrorist figures. President Obama, however, did calibrate the missile firings when either domestic disapproval grew too loud or Pakistani street protests endangered that country's rulers, who winked and nodded their permission for the attacks. The drone program did afford the president a measure of political protection from accusations of leading an American retreat from world challenges. When accused of being too soft in his anti-terrorism posture, Obama replied sharply that critics could ask the al Qaeda figures he took off the battlefield if he were too easy on them.[49] Weary and wary of sending off their youth to Iraq and Afghanistan, Americans—Democrats and Republicans—were overwhelmingly in favor of Obama's drone-centric alternative to troop-intensive land wars. One 2012 poll found 77 percent of respondents backed the president's aerial counterterrorism strategy.[50]

Iraq Abandoned

Before considering Barack Obama's signature Iraq policy, it is necessary to mention briefly the implementation of his earlier actions in Afghanistan. The two conflicts were linked; thus the rollback of Taliban gains in Afghanistan eased the decision and the military withdrawal itself from Iraq. At the start of 2010, American Marines and Army soldiers moved into Afghanistan to push back Taliban advances, especially in southern localities. As in the Iraq "surge," the reinforcements and a comprehensive counterinsurgency blueprint led to a wind down of Taliban attacks by 2011. Hard fighting fell to Marine and Army infantry especially in the districts ringing Kandahar, the country's second largest city and the spiritual home of the Taliban. American and Afghan casualties mounted. The US ground units applied the clear, hold, build strategy over much of the contested, southern terrain. But American forces lacked sufficient troops to execute a "clear and hold" strategy in the eastern stretches of the country, let alone the north. This approach entailed clearing Taliban fighters from the land, holding it against insurgent influence, and building the economy and governance-related endeavors to establish legitimacy between local rule and central authority. The Taliban insurgents lost their connection to the population, becoming irrelevant and defeated, at least for a time. Meanwhile, the foreign forces redoubled their efforts to stand up a local army and police so that United States and its ISAF partners could leave the country in the not-too-distant future.

Like all else in Afghanistan, standing up and readying security forces ran into myriad problems. Most Afghan recruits could neither read nor write. These were educational handicaps, especially for the police, who had to be able to takedown license plate numbers or draft reports. Since most Taliban insurgents hailed from the Pashtun ethnic community in the southern tier, the recruits for the Afghan security units, ipso facto, originated from the northern communities of Tajiks, Hazaras, and Uzbeks. Together with their basic military training, ISAF instructors and advisers combined literacy programs and Afghan-tailored affirmative-action programs to form integrated units from disparate ethnic makings. Progress was slow and undone particularly by the sky-high desertion rates among Afghan soldiers and police, sometimes reaching 30 percent of the forces over a six-month period.[51]

Headway was made in spite of all the challenges. The American and NATO reinforcements checked the advance of the Taliban insurgency. Assaults went down. Insurgent strongholds fell and Taliban influence decreased. Before these gains, US combat deaths zoomed upward from 155 in 2008 to 499 in 2010 before descending. The Taliban, however, endured, striking back with spectacular suicide attacks inside Kabul and Kandahar from time to time. The gradual stabilizing by the American-commanded ISAF allowed Washington to re-focus on the American withdrawal from Iraq.

By the time of Barack Obama settled into the White House, Iraq had been retrieved from the brink of civil war due to three factors, noted previously. The Bush administration's surge of 28,500 more combat troops starting in 2007, the implementation of proper counterinsurgency tactics, and, mostly, the switch by the several Sunni tribes from adversaries to partners with the US military forces—all facilitated the transformation of Iraq's phantasmagoria of bloodshed to a much calmer land. Bombings and shootings still happened but nowhere near the peak two years before Obama stepped into Oval Office. By summer 2008, violence had dwindled to the lowest level since the 2003 invasion. Sectarian murders dropped more than 95 percent from their peak in 2006, when interethnic killings nearly ripped apart the country. Prime Minister Nouri al Maliki overcame some of his early difficulties to appear on the surface as a capable and confident leader. By November 2008, the turnaround in Iraq enabled George Bush to agree to a timetable for moving out US troops by late 2011.[52] Iraq's ongoing stability let President Obama stick to his predecessor's withdrawal deadline.

In his first State of the Union address, President Obama said little about foreign issues as he emphasized domestic programs and priorities for the recession economy. Nonetheless, he returned to his campaign pledge, when he stated: "I promised that I would end this war [Iraq], and that is what I am doing as president."[53] Following his January 2010 address, Obama and his top aides often reiterated the electioneering vow in speeches and media interviews. To jump ahead to January 2011, Obama's second State of the Union address also amplified domestic themes to the expense of the Afghan war, which played so large a part in his winning the Democratic Party's nomination and then the presidency. The president mentioned "jobs" 30 times. The Afghan war, on the other hand, warranted only seven mentions. The stricken American economy dominated thinking of both the president and his fellow citizens. Days before his second union address, a Quinnipiac University poll found that public support for the Afghan conflict had fallen to 41 percent, the lowest level since Barack Obama stepped into office.[54]

Reflecting public opinion, the president's lowed-visibility Afghanistan stance became a cornerstone in his administration's foreign policy. But by the time of Obama's second address about the state of the American union, fierce winds of change were howling across the Middle East, a momentous series of events to be described in the next chapter. Despite those revolutionary changes occurring from Libya to Syria, it should be noted here, the White House stuck to its Iraqi pullout timetable.

As a presidential candidate, the Illinois Senator had pledged to pull out all American combat forces from Iraq within 16 months after moving into 1600 Pennsylvania. As president, Barack Obama pushed the deadline back by just two months, to August 2010, and decided on a phased withdrawal of all ground combat units by the end of 2011. As if to underline the discharge of his promise, Obama designated Vice President Biden as the point man on Iraq to oversee the US military departure, allowing the president to move on to other issues. Iraq, in Obama's mind, was a settled question. He stayed disengaged, even aloof, from negotiations surrounding the troop extraction.[55]

Prior to the US retreat from Iraq, much of the exit discussion centered on a Status of Forces Agreement (SOFA) for the contingent that might remain after the withdrawal deadline of December 31, 2011. A SOFA is a document outlining the terms of operation and legal immunities for foreign forces if charged with a crime in the host country. The George W. Bush administration secured a SOFA with Prime Minister Nouri al-Maliki in 2008, when it also established the US quit date for American forces to leave. In mid-2011, Maliki offered to sign another SOFA directly with the Obama administration for a small contingent of residual forces. These units were to be employed in training and mentoring activities for the Iraqi army, while an even smaller number were to pursue counterterrorist operations against the dwindling remnants of the al Qaeda in Iraq network.

This time, Washington refused an agreement just with President Maliki. The Obama administration demanded that any SOFA must also be ratified by the Iraqi parliament. Such a requirement from a hostile parliament was seen as impossible, if not a deliberate step to scuttle any prospect of a renewed SOFA. From the Iraqi point of view, the American conditions seemed disproportionate to the tiny US military contingent offered by Obama officials. Baghdad asked for nearly 20,000 US troops to remain in the country to prolong its stabilization. The Obama administration offered 3500 and a force of 1500 that would regularly rotate through the country for restricted training missions. In the words of one respected study, "Washington was asking a lot and offering only a little."[56] With Iraq's fate sealed, President Obama kept his campaign vow to vacate Iraq. The story did not have a happy ending, however, as will be noted in the next chapter.

Rather than making a public case for retention of a military presence to stabilize and guide a post-American Iraq, the Obama presidency moved lock-step for the exits. There were compelling historical precedents for maintaining US armed forces in once occupied lands, such as Germany,

Japan, and Korea, which contributed to economic growth and democratic development. As administration detractors later argued, American boots on the ground might have steeled the Iraqi army to check the invasion of violent extremists in 2014 as well as guided Baghdad toward multi-sectarian democratic governance to ethnic loyalty among its constituent ethnic communities, as will also be noted in the next chapter. Instead, Washington went along with the tide of popular opinion and washed its hands of Iraq. One month before all US combat troops left Iraq, 75 percent of Americans polled by Gallup approved of Barack Obama's decision to withdraw US military forces by the end of 2011.[57] America's disengagement tide hard reached flood stage.

The president and the American people wanted to put the Iraq War behind them. The war claimed more than 4400 US military lives and killed between 150,000 and 500,000 Iraqi civilians since the 2003 invasion. The United States expended 2 trillion dollars with little to show for it. Iraq did not become a staunch, strategic, and lucrative trading partner as did postwar Germany, Japan, or, even the ROK after the 1950–1953 Korean War. It failed to join the ranks of functioning democracies that might even have served as a model for other countries in the Arab Middle East. Iraq, as a result, never became a regional lynchpin whose values and security concerns aligned with the United States like Germany, Japan, Israel, or Taiwan.

The presidential re-focus on other issues coincided with the slippage in the media's coverage of Iraq. Whereas the Iraq War had been in 2008 "the seventh most covered story, with the three [television] networks devoting 228 minutes to reports about the war," the nightly newscasts on the Persian Gulf country "dropped off the top ten list in 2009, with just 80 minutes of coverage."[58] When the mid-term elections took place for Senate and House seats in November 2010, the wars in Iraq and Afghanistan barely registered a blip on voters' radar. The stalled economy eclipsed American concerns about fighting in far-off lands. A month before the elections, a nationwide New York Times/CBS News poll found that 60 percent of the respondents ranked the poor economy and joblessness as the most important problems facing the nation. A mere 3 percent mentioned the Afghan War.

This transformed orientation contrasted markedly with the 2006 mid-term elections when the Iraq War and terrorism trumped other issues. That election ushered in Democratic majorities in both Congressional houses as American registered their displeasure with George W. Bush's war in Iraq. In 2010, the electorate returned to its usual economic worries, plus President Obama's domestic priority of health care reform.[59] The Republicans gained control of the House but not Senate. The polls and election demonstrated that country and its president had moved on to matters other than fighting wars and international concerns, as America cycled toward disengagement.

As the national sentiment recalibrated after nearly a decade of fighting two wars, President Obama's thinking reflected as well as shaped America's disengagement mood. His foreign policies, indeed, were in accord with the country's changed perceptions. From first setting foot in the White House, he moved to execute policies distinct from his predecessor. As time went on, he put forth policies in Libya and Syria, along with Iraq and Afghanistan, which reflected his disassociation from the muscular actions of the prior administration. In late May 2010, he spelled out his thoughts in the administration's National Security Strategy, a declaration required by Congress of every White House. In the 52-page statement, the president struck themes that were defining his policies. He expressed in his introduction that the "burdens of a young century cannot fall on American shoulders alone. Indeed, our adversaries would like to see America sap our strength by overextending our power." Burden sharing as envisioned within the strategic document came to define Washington's handling of future crises in Libya, Yemen, Syria, and Ukraine. The planned extraction of combat forces from Afghanistan and Iraq aligned with Obama's strategy to sideline American military power and forego its wide application.[60]

President Obama's security blueprint contrasted sharply with that of George W. Bush's strategic review. The sitting commander-in-chief ruled out making counterterrorism the organizing principle of his security policy. He viewed America's interaction with the world in a broader context than anti-terrorism. Nor did he champion democracy promotion around the world in the unabashed way his predecessor did. Obama reserved the right for the "United States to act unilaterally if necessary," but his phrasing shied away from the stridency of Bush aides, who refused to seek a "permission slip" to defend American interests. Obama did track rhetorically at least with Bush in his insistence on maintaining the "military superior that has secured our country, and underpinned global security for decades."[61] But in reality, the White House and Congress enacted funding cutbacks to defense and non-defense programs, known as the Sequester, which went into effect in early 2013.

On most topics, Obama engaged in "self-conscious rejection of the Bush era."[62] Reflecting the president's thoughts about the need for "nation-building at home," his strategy paper departed from previous ones by noting the security imperative of "affordable health care" and "redeveloping our infrastructure." It was not unusual for national security reviews to assert the economic foundations of America's defensive capacity. Thus a thriving economy meant a strong military. Alone, the Obama security strategy set forth a domestic welfare agenda as well.

The Pivot to Asia: Real or Imaginary?

In a bold speech before Australia's parliament in 2011, Barack Obama unveiled a strategy to "pivot" America's diplomatic, economic, and, indeed, military attention to Asia. President Obama admitted that his renewed concentration on Asia "reflects a broader shift" for America from the Middle East. He pronounced the decade-long fighting over when he declared: "the tide of war is receding and America is looking forward to the future." He expressed his decision in authoritative language: "as president, I have, therefore, made a deliberate and strategic decision—as a Pacific nation, the United States will play a larger and long-term role in shaping this region." His warnings to a muscle-flexing China were hardly veiled: "We will allocate the resources necessary to maintain our strong military presence in this region." The president spoke as commander-in-chief: "We are already modernizing America's defense posture across the Asia Pacific." He noted Washington's wide-ranging alliance system in achieving his aims: "And our posture will be more sustainable, by helping allies and partners build their capacity, with training and exercises."[63] The announcement of a pivot toward Asia and, by implication, away from the Middle East evinced a sense of fatigue with the intractable troubles in that region.

President Obama's foreign policy aides explained the new policy of "pivoting," or as they phrased it "rebalancing," away from the concluding but messy wars in Iraq and Afghanistan to the booming economies of the Far East. Thus, the strategic shift was presented as a positive step, not a defensive maneuver against an increasingly assertive China. Obama's officials reiterated the president's disclaimer that America's new rebalance toward Asia was not to contain or isolate China. But the administration's gestures spoke louder than words. The president followed up his forceful speech in the Parliament House with little more than a commitment of 2500 US Marines to be based over time in Darwin, Australia.

When the American leader toured Asian countries to rollout the pivot policy, he made it plain that his government was not solely focusing militarily on the Pacific. Nor was terrorism his main focus as in the George W. Bush era. He omitted any reference to the conflict with Islamic terrorism. Indeed, Obama in his Australian parliament speech, seven months after Osama bin Laden's death at the hands of Navy SEALs, said al Qaeda is "on the path to defeat." The United States, therefore, was switching gears to Asia's fast-growing economies to spur domestic prosperity—a topic much on the minds of American voters as the 2012 presidential elections neared.[64]

Washington's policy of strategic patience (meaning limited high-level diplomatic contact) toward North Korea remained unaffected by the fresh tack toward eastern Asia. Pyongyang used the respite from American scrutiny to perfect its nuclear weapons and long-range missile capability.[65] It tested three nuclear devices during the Obama years (2009, 2013, and 2016), which drew the administration's censure but little else, even though Pyongyang claimed the latter test set off a hydrogen bomb. US delegations visited Beijing—to little avail—so as to enlist China's help in reining its unruly partner. Although the DPRK depended on hefty Chinese aid, it was a prickly ally for the People's Republic of China. For Beijing, North Korea was a useful lever to keep the Americans off balance with warlike posturing. But its antics could also be wearisome. The PRC genuinely feared the collapse of its fraternal communist ally, which could place a South Korean-inspired democratic country on its border.

Two-and-a-half years after the launch of the new Asia strategy, Washington entered into an agreement with the Philippines. Manila granted US ships and planes the most extensive access to bases in the island nation since America had been politically forced by an anti-US government to relinquish its sprawling military installations at Clark Air Base and Subic Bay in 1992. Rattled by Chinese island-grabbing and outcropping-reclamation projects in the South China Sea, the Philippine government welcomed the return of America's geopolitical interest in the Western Pacific. It resolved to strengthen ties with the United States, as did Japan, South Korea, Indonesia, and Taiwan.

For its part, China wanted to recast the Pax Americana dominance in its sphere since 1945 by returning to the bygone era of Chinese centrality in East Asia. Over the past two decades, China's economic and military strength had accelerated. By the time Barack Obama entered the Oval Office, the PRC mounted a challenge to the American-imposed status quo. Beijing gave short shrift to Obama's pivot speech, except for scattered hostile comments. Instead, the PRC redoubled its efforts to establish internationally recognized jurisdiction over its claimed territorial waters. It imposed an Air Defense Identification Zone (ADIZ) above the East China Sea in late 2013. The ADIZ required overflying aircraft to identify themselves to Chinese authorities, a stipulation protested by the United States and Japan. To the south, the PRC undertook island reclamation within the Spratly archipelago. Chinese ships dredged sand from the sea and pumped it onto seven outcroppings to enlarge them for the construction of airfields, harbors, and bases for long-range radars and missile systems. China also modernized its air, naval, and ground units. Additionally, it introduced a variety of anti-access/area denial (known as A2/AD in Pentagon circles) capabilities into its armed forces, including anti-ship ballistic missiles. Cyber warfare and hacking attacks became a familiar weapon brazenly directed at American government agencies and private companies. In short, the US proclaimed rebalance to Asia deterred Beijing not a whit from its restorative mission of Chinese hegemony.[66]

By the time Chuck Hagel visited Beijing in 2014 to meet with Chinese Defense Minister Chang Wanquan, the American secretary of defense got an earful from his counterpart. In fact, the two traded barbed comments. The Pentagon chief argued that "the American rebalance to Asia Pacific, our strategic interests, is not to contain China." General Chang shot back: China "can never be contained."[67] Their near-acrimonious news conference indicated a different Sino-American relationship than the half-century of the US-dominated security architecture in the Pacific Basin.

A refocused policy on the Asia-Pacific region seemingly bespoke of US international engagement, which would run counter to Obama's generalized, disengaged reflex. On the surface, it was classic balance-of-power policy. The pivots implementation, however, lacked coherence, follow-through, and the matching of words with reality. As such, it reflected America's international retrenchment, anti-interventionism, and domestic priorities. The president's frequent call for nation-building at home generated confusion and concern about Washington's genuine commitments in East Asia. The administration's flaccid responses from the Russian takeover of the Crimea and destabilization of eastern Ukraine to the Islamic State's proliferation of terrorism in the Middle East and North Africa all telegraphed a less than vigorous internationalism than the West Wing's rhetoric about America's military superiority. The Asian counterbalance also encountered the reality that the US government reduced the size of the Navy—its main Pacific military instrument—by not building new ships to replace those decommissioned for age and costly repairs.

One study by the London-based International Institute for Strategic Studies pointed up the shortfall in pledged warship transfers to the Pacific fleet by Obama's Pentagon:

> Panetta said that "the navy will reposture its forces from today's roughly 50/50 split between the Pacific and the Atlantic to about a 60/40 split between those oceans." But when examined in detail, the only addition to capacity in East Asia will be the four Littoral Combat Ships to be deployed to Singapore, with three amphibious vessels rotated through the region and two Joint High-Speed Vessels (JHSVs) deployed there.[68]

The explanation makes plain that only small warships, with moderate-to-limited firepower, went to the Pacific as part of the rebalance strategy. The naval component, therefore, came up short of the inflated rhetoric from the administration about a counterweight calculus. In late 2015, the US Marines, a vital part of the Navy, announced that it planned on moving 15 percent of its force to the Pacific in such bases as Guam, Hawaii, and Japan's Okinawa. During World War II, the Marine Corps had predominately fought in the Pacific theater. So, the Marine's small presence today could hardly be seen as evidence of genuine resolve to balance China's assertiveness.

It was during President Obama's Asian trip that he answered questions about the impact of his policies on "reducing America's historical role in global security," given regional concerns about China's quickening militarization and expansive maritime claims in the South China Sea. His reply was to the point: "Why is it that everybody is so eager to use military force after we've just gone a decade of war at enormous costs?" Presidential aides framed the White House rebuttal in a simple phrase: "Don't do stupid stuff," as a mantra to contrast Obama's measured approach to the military assertiveness of George W. Bush.[69]

With slightly more than a year to go in his presidency, Barack Obama completed a major free-trade pact known as the Trans-Pacific Partnership (TPP) with 11 other Asia-Pacific powers, which was almost a decade in the making. When fully implemented over many years, the TPP will eliminate thousands of taxes, tariffs, and non-tariff barriers (such as quotas) to open new markets to American businesses and agriculture products. Because the TPP excluded China from the trade zone, the agreement lent itself to interpretations of decreasing the dependence of the signatories on the roaring China market. Administration officials contended that the TPP contributed to the White House's much-touted Asian pivot.[70] Two years after President Obama inaugurated the "pivot," Beijing countered by establishment of the Asian Infrastructure Investment Bank (AIIB) to compete with Western development institutions. In reaction, the Obama presidency picked up its marbles and refused to join the AIIB.

Not content with this venture, the PRC, as noted above, challenged the military and political status quo by creating and militarizing artificial islands in the South China Sea. China, accordingly, extended its maritime claims over the riches of undersea natural resources and consolidated its sovereignty over one of the world's busiest trade corridors. Through these vital waterways sailed half of the global ship-borne trade, some $5 trillion annually in oil, goods, and products.

A large question mark hung over the adequacy of the Obama administration's response to China's hegemonic and provocative assertions. Two additional questions await the judgment of history as well: first, how much will the TPP really counteract China's deepening economic ties with almost all the states in Asia; and, second, will the US Congress ratify the trade liberalizing pact? Ratification did not occur while President Obama was in office, leaving it unfinished business for the next administration. A judgment not awaiting the future is that China's ambitions will require more than favorable trade openings for US goods and services.

The American pirouette toward the Asia-Pacific has been matched to date by China's extravagant actions off its littoral in the South China Sea that flaunted international law. Beijing notified other nations that they must obtain its permission before flying or sailing within 12 nautical miles the reclaimed shoals in the Spratly Islands. Chinese suzerainty over these micro-islets, on which China dredged sand to enlarge into artificial islands, was disputed by the Philippines, Vietnam, and Taiwan. Other claimants for these former reefs did not deter the PRC from militarizing them while proclaiming peaceful intentions. The occupation of the island chain permitted China to stake out its hegemony over wide swaths of the South China Sea through which 30 percent of the world's annual maritime trade travels, including $1.2 trillion in vessel-borne commerce destined for the United States. China, moreover, matched its oceanic claims with an enormous military buildup of new warships, submarines, anti-ship missiles, and warplanes based along the Chinese coast.[71] China's assertiveness posed a direct confrontation to President Obama's "Pivot to Asia" policy, which remained inadequately addressed.

So, US engagement, or re-engagement, in Asia shaded toward the symbolic rather substantive. As such, the Asian pivot is of a piece with Obama responses to Russian belligerency in Eastern Europe and terrorist militancy in the Middle East and North Africa. This strategy of retrenchment and accommodation, not isolationism, enabled the Obama presidency "focus on progressive policy legacies at home."[72] These included health care reform, financial regulation, gun control, and homosexual rights. Rather than pivoting to Asia, Barack Obama pivoted to domestic affairs. In foreign policy, the White House offset perceptions of an international withdrawal by an unflinching campaign of drone strikes, special-operations raids, small numbers of US advisers in war zones, and surveillance of suspected terrorist communications at home.

Notes

1. Elisabeth Bumiller, "Cast of 300 Advises Obama on Foreign Policy," *New York Times*, July 18, 2008, p. A 1.
2. Jaime Fuller, "How Obama talked about Iraq, from 2002 to 2014," *Washington Post*, June 19, 2014. Downloaded from http://www.washingtonpost.com/blogs/the-fix/wp/2014/06/19/how-obama-talks-about-iraq-before-and-after/. Accessed July 20, 2016.
3. Barack Obama, "My Plan For Iraq," *New York Times*, July 14, 2008, p. A 21.
4. Barack Obama's Acceptance Speech at the Democratic Convention, August 28, 2008. Downloaded from http://elections.nytimes.com/2008/president/conventions/videos/20080828_OBAMA_SPEECH.html. Accessed July 20, 2016.
5. Barack Obama, "Renewing American Leadership," *Foreign Affairs*, 86, no. 4 (July/August 2007), 10 and 14.
6. Adam Nagourney and Marjorie Connelly, "Poll Finds Faith in Obama, Mixed With Patience," *New York Times*, January 17, 2009. Downloaded from http://www.nytimes.com/2009/01/18/us/politics/18poll.html?pagewanted=all&module=Search&mabReward=relbias%3Ar%2C%7B%221%22%3A%22RI%3A7%22%7D. Accessed July 20, 2016.

7. Richard Miniter, *Leading From Behind: The Reluctant President and the Advisors Who Decide for Him* (New York: St. Martin's Griffin, 2012), pp. 116–117.
8. Mark Mazzetti and Carl Hulse, "Panetta Chosen As C.I.A. Chief In Surprise Step," *New York Times*, January 6, 2009, p. A 1.
9. Peter Baker, "In Announcing Withdrawal Plan, Obama Marks Beginning of Iraq War's End," *New York Times*, February 28, 2009, p. A 6.
10. Julian E. Barnes, "Agencies Prep Obama for 'Tourniquet' On Afghanistan," *Los Angeles Times*, December 23, 2008, p. A 1.
11. Karen DeYoung and Rajiv Chandrasekaran, "In Afghan War, U.S. Dominance Increasing," *Washington Post*, March 26, 2009, p. A 16.
12. Helene Cooper and Eric Schmitt, "Obama Afghanistan Plan Would Narrow War Goals," *New York Time*s, March 28, 2009, p. A 1.
13. Thom Shanker and Eric Schmitt, "Obama Seeks Vastly Expanded Afghan Security Forces to Help Stabilize The Nation," *New York Times*, March 19, 2009, p. A 1.
14. The Washington Post-ABC News Poll, "Divisions On Afghanistan Progress, Policy," *Washington Post*, April, 1, 2009, p. A 10.
15. Brian Glyn Williams, *Predators: The CIA's Drone War on al Qaeda* (Washington, DC: Potomac Books, 2013), pp. 142–158 and 180–189.
16. Vali Nasr, *The Dispensable Nation: American Foreign Policy in Retreat* (New York: Doubleday, 2013), pp. 36–40, 49–50, and 74–75.
17. Scott Wilson and Al Kamen, "'Global War On Terror' Is Given New Name," *Washington Post*, March 25, 2009, p. A 4.
18. "Text: Obama's Speech in Cairo," *New York Times*, June 5, 2009, p. A 8.
19. Jeff Zeleny and Alan Cowell, "Addressing Muslims, Obama Pushes Mideast Peace," *New York Times*, June 5, 2009, p. A 1.
20. Mark Landler and Helene Cooper, "Obama Speech Signals a U.S. Shift on Middle East," *New York Times*, April 14, 2010, p. A 1.
21. Karen DeYoung, "Obama Team Seeks To Redefine Russia Ties," *Washington Post*, March 4, 2009, p. A 11.
22. Ronald Asmus, *A Little War That Shook The World* (New York: Palgrave Macmillan, 2010), pp. 170 and 190.

23. Ellen Barry, "Russia Rejects The Notion Of A Joint Missile System in Europe," *New York Times*, June 12, 2009, p. A 10.
24. Rich Gladstone, "Turkey to Install U.S.-Designed Radar, in a Move Seen as Blunting Iran's Missiles," *New York Times*, September 3, 2011, p. A 7.
25. For tough-minded analysis of the New START, see Keith B. Payne, "Evaluating The U.S.-Russia Nuclear Deal," *Wall Street Journal*, April 8, 2010, p. A 21.
26. New START, Department of State. Downloaded from http://www.state.gov/t/avc/newstart/index.htm. Accessed July 20, 2016.
27. Mark Lander, "U.S. Resists Push by Allies for Tactical Nuclear Cuts," *New York Times*, April 22, 2010, p. A 1.
28. Robert Kagan, "The Hard Work After START," *Washington Post*, December 23, 2010, p. A 15.
29. Nuclear Posture Review, Department of Defense, April 6, 2010. Downloaded from http://www.defense.gov/npr/. Accessed July 20, 2016.
30. David E. Sanger and Thom Shanker, "Obama's Nuclear Strategy Intended As A Message," *New York Times*, April 7, 2010, p. A 6.
31. Mark Landler, "Obama Resists Tougher Stand," *New York Times*, June 6, 2009, p. A 1.
32. Glenn Kessler, "U.S. Struggling For Right Response To Iran," *Washington Post*, June 18, 2009, p. A 1.
33. COMISAF, Initial Assessment (Unclassified) September 9, 2009. Downloaded from http://www.washingtonpost.com/wp-dyn/content/article/2009/09/21/AR2009092100110.html. Accessed July 20, 2016.
34. Jennifer Agiesta and Jon Cohen, "Public Opinon In U.S. Turns Against The War," *Washington Post*, August 20, 2009, p. A 9.
35. The White House, "Remarks by the President at the Veterans of Foreign Wars Convention," August 17, 2009, pp. 3–4.
36. Bob Woodward, "McChrystal: More Forces or 'Mission Failure,'" *Washington Post*, September 21, 2009, p. A 1.
37. Peter Baker and Eric Schmitt, "Several Afghan Strategies, None A Clear Choice," *New York Times*, October 1, p. A 1 and Scott Wilson and Ann E. Kornblut, "White House Eying Narrower War Effort," *Washington Post*, October 2, 2009, p. A 1.
38. Peter Baker, "A Biden Challenge to Clinton Would Expose a Policy Split," *New York Times*, October 10, 2015, p. A 1.

39. Bob Woodward, *Obama's Wars* (New York: Simon & Schuster, 2010), p. 223.
40. Jim Mann, *The Obamians: The Struggle Inside the White How to Define American Power* (New York: Viking, 2012), pp. 123–128.
41. Stanley McChrystal, *My Share of the Task: A Memoir* (New York: Penguin Group, 2013), p. 345.
42. Trudy Rubin, "Obama Can't Delay Decision On Afghan Strategy Any Longer," *Philadelphia Inquirer*, September 20, 2009, p. 15.
43. Michael Hastings, *The Operators: The Wild and Terrifying Inside Story of America's War in Afghanistan* (New York: Plume, 2012), pp. 14 and 33–34.
44. Dalia Sussman. "Poll Finds Pessimism On The War," *New York Times*, July 14, 2010, p. A 9.
45. Richard Wolf, "Support Wanes for Obama, War Plan," *USA Today*, August 3, 2010, p. A 1.
46. Brian Glyn Williams, *Predators: The CIA's Drone War on al Qaeda* (Washington, DC: Potomac Books, 2013), p. 90.
47. Spiegel Online Staff, "Drones Are Lynchpin Of Obama's War On Terror," Spiegel Online International, March 12, 2010. Downloaded from http://www.spiegel.de/international/world/killer-app-drones-are-lynchpin-of-obama-s-war-on-terror-a-682612.html. Accessed July 20, 2016.
48. Anthony D. Romero and Vincent Warren, "Sentenced To Death Without Trial," *Washington Post*, September 3, 2010, p. A 19 and Scott Shane, "Rights Groups Sue U.S. On Effort to Kill Cleric," *New York Times*, August 31, 2010, p. A 6.
49. The White House, "Remarks by the President at the National Defense University," May 13, 2013. Downloaded from https://www.whitehouse.gov/the-press-office/2013/05/23/remarks-president-national-defense-university. Accessed July 20, 2016.
50. Scott Wilson and Jon Cohen, "Poll Finds Broad Support for Obama's Counterterrorism Policies," *Washington Post*, February 7, 2012, p. A 1.
51. Joshua Partlow, "More Afghan soldiers deserting the army, NATO statistics show," *Washington Post*, September 3, 2011, p. A 17.
52. George W. Bush, *Decision Points* (New York: Crown Publishers, 2010), pp. 389–390.
53. Helene Cooper, "In Speech, Little Time Spent on National Security," *New York Times*, January 28, 2010, p. A 1.

54. Yochi J. Dreazen, "National Security: War of Few Words," *National Journal*, January 25, 2011. Downloaded from http://www.nationaljournal.com/national-security-a-war-of-few-words-20110125. Accessed July 20, 2016 and Al Neuharth, "How Could Obama Ignore Afghanistan," *USA Today*, January 28, 2011, p. 11.
55. Roy Gutman, "Obama Aloof as Iraqi Talks Faltered," *Miami Herald*, October 26, 2011, p. 1 A.
56. Michael R. Gordon and Bernard E. Trainor, *The Endgame: The Inside Story of the Struggle for Iraq, from George W. Bush to Barack Obama* (New York: Pantheon Books, 2012), p. 670.
57. Jeffery Jones, "Three In Four Americans Back Obama On Iraq Withdrawal," Gallup.com, November 2, 2011. Downloaded from http://www.gallup.com/poll/150497/Three-Four-Americans-Back-Obama-Iraq-Withdrawal.aspx?utm_source=Three%20In%20Four%20Americans%20Back%20Obama%20On%20Iraq%20Withdra&utm_medium=search&utm_campaign=tiles. Accessed October 15, 2015.
58. Joseph Curl, "For Obama And Press, Iraq Falls Off Radar," *Washington Times*, March 4, 2010, p. 1.
59. Dailia Sussman and Megan Thee-Brenan, "For Midterm Voters, War Is Off The Radar," *New York Times*, October 15, 2010, p. A 10.
60. White House, National Security Strategy, May 2010. Downloaded from http://www.whitehouse.gov/sites/default/files/rss_viewer/national_security_strategy.pdf. Accessed July 20, 2016.
61. Ibid.
62. David E. Sanger and Peter Baker, "New U.S. Strategy Focuses On Managing Threats," *New York Times*, May 28, 2010, p. A 8.
63. Remarks By President Obama to the Australian Parliament, Parliament House, Canberra, Australia, November 17, 2011. Downloaded from https://www.whitehouse.gov/the-press-office/2011/11/17/remarks-president-obama-australian-parliament. Accessed July 20, 2016.
64. Peter Nicholas and Christi Parsons, "In Asia, Obama Keeps Focus Off Terrorism," *Los Angeles Times*, November 20, 2011, p. A 1.
65. Missy Ryan, "Missile launch underscores N. Korean threat, U.S. defense secretary says," *Washington Post*, April 9, 2015, p. A 1.
66. Michael Pillsbury, *The Hundred-Year Marathon: China's Secret Strategy to Replace America as the Global Superpower* (New York: Henry Holt and Company, 2015), pp. 25–41.

67. Dion Nissenbaum, "U.S., China Defense Chiefs Trade Barbs Over Regional Ambitions," *Wall Street Journal*, April 8, 2014, p. A 1.
68. International Institute for Strategic Studies, *The Military Balance 2013* (London: Routledge, 2013), p. 54. This was cited first by Colin Dueck in *The Obama Doctrine*, p. 98.
69. Christi Parsons, Kathleen Hennessey, and Paul Richter, "Obama argues against use of force to solve global conflicts," *Los Angeles Times*, April 29, 2014, p. A 1.
70. Jane Perlez, "U.S. Allies See Trade Deal as Check on China," *New York Times*, October 8, 2015, p. A 14.
71. Derek Watkins, "What China Has Been Building in Contested Waters," *New York Times*, August 2, 2015, p. A 8.
72. Dueck, *The Obama Doctrine*, p. 101.

CHAPTER 9

Barack Obama: A Foreign Policy of Disengagement

"What has been will be again, what has been done will be done again; there is nothing new under the sun." —Ecclesiastes

"The further backward you look the further forward you can see." —Winston Churchill

Virtually, every American administration since Theodore Roosevelt and the Spanish-American War has encountered at least one strategic surprise. Each drastically altered Washington's plans and indeed the course of history. For William Howard Taft, the strategic shock came from the Mexican Revolution. For Woodrow Wilson, the strategically unexpected arose with German submarine attacks on transatlantic shipping. For Herbert Hoover, Japan's military invasion of Manchuria astonished America. For Franklin Roosevelt, the Pearl Harbor attack stunned him and the nation. For John Kennedy, the Cuban missile crisis brought the country face to face with a nuclear war with the Soviet Union. And for, George W. Bush, the September 11 terrorist attack tossed America into agony, anger, and disbelief. History did not spare Barack Obama from this recurring pattern.

While the Obama administration went about winding down what it termed as Bush's wars, it ran up against a cataclysmic revolt in the Middle East in early 2011. Spreading like a prairie fire from its start in Tunisia, it leapt across Libya, Egypt, and Yemen to Syria in the Levant. Long-suppressed populations rose up against their autocratic rulers in a

T.H. Henriksen, *Cycles in US Foreign Policy since the Cold War*,
DOI 10.1007/978-3-319-48640-6_9

momentous political upheaval, which became known as the Arab Spring. The desperate calls from the region beckoned to the United States either to restore order or to nurture democratic governance. But there was no need, as Ulysses had done, to lash US foreign policy to a mast to resist the Homeric sirens. By and large, the appeals for American intervention ran counter to Barack Obama's strategic detachment. One former diplomat later reflected that the Obama administration mounted no "strategy for capitalizing on the opportunity that the Arab Spring presented." Nor did "it adequately prepare for the potential fallout in the form of regional rivalry" or sectarian conflicts and economically rooted crises. The approach "to unfolding events," as assessed by that diplomat, "has been wholly reactive."[1]

The powerful tides pulling for US intervention in the Middle East mostly came to naught, although they divided the Obama administration, pitting the White House insiders against the Obama cabinet secretaries and national security figures. The president and his West Wing staffers dismissed the more hawkish consul from Hillary Clinton at the State Department, Robert Gates and then Leon Panetta at the Department of Defense, plus David Petraeus at the CIA. Later, the short-termed Chuck Hagel crossed swords with Obama's inner circle over Syria, Guantánamo Bay detainee transfers, and other differences with the tightknit White House national security team, costing the defense secretary his job.[2] Decision-making was dominated by Denis McDonough, the White House chief of staff, Susan Rice, the national security adviser, and Ben Rhodes, speech writer and assistant national security adviser.[3] Vice President Biden most often stood with the national security circle and against Secretary Clinton.[4] The insiders not only outmaneuvered government opponents but also overcentralized foreign and defense policy-making while micromanaging the Pentagon, according to former officials.[5] Defense secretary Gates later wrote: "The controlling nature of the Obama White House and the NSS staff took micromanagement and operational meddling to a new level."[6]

The Arab Spring and US Disassociation

The Arab Spring touched off internal instability following the popular revolts and fall of several strongmen in Tunisia, Libya, Egypt, and Yemen. Only on the island country of Bahrain did the Sunni monarchy prevail against the Shiite majority who staged large protests in Manama's Pearl

Square. Out of fear that the government's severe crackdown on Shiite crowds might be exploited by radical groups with ties to Iran, the Obama administration leaned on Bahrain to exercise restraint. Bahrain's Sunni-led government pulled back its security forces and started a dialogue with the main Shiite opposition movement that brought calm to the streets.[7] In other countries, the demonstrators ousted the military-backed tyrants. The upheavals played out nearly simultaneously within nations, between states, and among religious and ethnic communities. The Arab Spring ended up re-entrenching autocratic rule and socioeconomic stratification amid ruined economies.

The origins of these revolts will likely be debated for years. Joining that debate now was Kanan Makiya, the renowned Iraqi author of *Republic of Fear*, who argued the Arab Spring had an American provenance with the US ouster of Saddam Hussein. Makiya noted that George W. Bush's democracy agenda for a post-Hussein Iraq was "why support from Arab monarchies was not forthcoming in [the] 2003" invasion. They feared the fall of the first domino. Once US-led forces chased Hussein from power, Washington set about establishing election procedures, political parties, and parliamentary rules for democratic governance. Makiya blamed the Iraqi elites for fighting each other rather than grasping the opportunity for progress.[8] Two well-regarded military historians also make the case in *Moment of Battle: The Twenty Clashes That Changed the World* that the removal of Saddam Hussein served "as a catalyst" for the Arab Spring.[9] Whatever the precise spark, the uprisings developed from deep frustrations over arbitrary rule and economic hardships.[10]

Egypt quickly followed Tunisia, the Arab Spring's birthplace. As the Middle East's most consequential Arab power, Egypt ranked at the top of America's regionwide alliance structure. Hosni Mubarak's expulsion from the presidency caught Washington off guard. Mubarak, a former army general, ascended to the presidency in 1981 after Anwar al Sadat's assassination. He kept Egypt in the historic Camp David agreements with Israel, which his predecessor signed. His security forces relentlessly pursued the terroristic Islamic Group and the Egyptian Islamic Jihad, while he kept the Muslim Brotherhood on a tight leash. Yet, nearly 20 percent unemployment, skewed income inequality toward the wealthy, 45 percent illiteracy, nearly non-existent health care for the masses, and endemic corruption—all made Egypt ripe for unrest. Once lit, the rebellion was fueled by the Internet and social media, which served to connect and excite demonstrators in Cairo and other cities.

Washington underestimated the force of the political conflagration consuming Egypt. Determined anti-government protestors in Tahrir Square upended early assessments. When the handwriting on the wall could no longer be ignored, the Obama administration decided on public and private initiatives to nudge Mubarak from office to secure a transition and free elections.[11] Next, Washington publically approved of the Muslim Brotherhood as the new Egyptian government after its election victory, despite its disavowal of the 1978 Camp David Accords that led to peace between Egypt and Israel. The White House's acceptance of the Muslim Brotherhood—a political movement advocating adherence to strict Islamic laws—departed from previous US policy. This about-face was noted by America's dynastic allies in the Arabian Peninsula, who were wary of the Muslim Brotherhood's anti-monarchical declarations.[12] The Obama administration soon backtracked when a military coup displaced the Muslim Brotherhood.

Libya—Leading from Behind

The Arab Spring convulsions soon tossed Libya into turmoil. Like Egypt and Tunisia, Libya had long been ruled by a dictatorial regime. The North African country had only recently moved from outright pariah status to a marginally acceptable regime by the West. After Colonel Muammar al Qaddafi seized power in 1969 from the monarchy, he turned the former Italian colony into a sponsor of terrorism and a procurer of WMD. Libya's oil wealth helped insulate the Mediterranean nation from American-orchestrated UN sanctions. Qaddafi retaliated in ways similar to other rogue states against UN embargoes and censure. He allied with Moscow from which Libyan military forces gained access to up-to-date weapons. He offered sanctuaries and funds for such notorious terrorists as Abu Nidal.

Colonel Qaddafi's provocative actions and pursuit of chemical and nuclear weapons almost foreordained that he would cross swords with the United States.[13] But he also collided with the US Navy over Libya's exclusive claims to the Gulf of Sidra off the Libyan coast during Ronald Reagan's presidency. President Reagan countered, and US warplanes shot down two of the Libyan jets in 1981. The Reagan White House also ordered an airstrike that nearly killed Qaddafi in retaliation for a Libyan-instigated bombing in a Berlin disco.

Later, during President George H.W. Bush's tenure, Qaddafi struck back by blowing up Pan Am flight 103 over the Scottish village of

Lockerbie in December 1989. The New York City-bound plane exploded after leaving London, killing all 259 persons on board and 11 villagers on the ground. Bush replied with a series of UN economic and travel sanctions against Libya when Tripoli refused to hand over two Libyan agents who were indicted in American and British courts. Next, Qaddafi chased after chemical arms, which he used in a conflict with Chad. Finally, he acquired nuclear weapons components by relying on the notorious A.Q. Khan's Pakistani black market network. Economic sanctions, political isolation, and, perhaps, the fear that he might suffer the same fate as Saddam Hussein after the George W. Bush invasion of Iraq, prompted Qaddafi to have second thoughts. Unique among rogue states, Libya mended its ways as it groped for a way out of the political cold. Washington and other governments oversaw the dismantling of Qaddafi's WMD facilities in the early 2000s. In time, the international community eased its sanction regime, allowing for greater Tripoli oil sales.

None of Qaddafi's accommodations saved his murderous and corrupt rule from the Arab Spring revolt. Qaddafi, his villainous sons, and their henchmen fought back fiercely against their opponents.[14] The Hobbesian conflict descended into a shooting civil war pitting militias, regions, and tribes against one another. Outsiders intruded into the Libyan fighting, unlike their hands-off behavior during the popular revolts in Tunisia and Egypt. Qatar aided the rebels by providing arms and training. The British committed military and intelligence officials to help the opposition fighters with organizational and logistical tasks. France and Britain, in addition, called for international intercession to safeguard the Libyan population against the massacring dictatorship.[15] Prominent figures from both major American political parties clamored for action against Colonel Qaddafi.

America's role in Libya was hesitant and circumscribed from the beginning of the anti-Qaddafi revolt. President Obama was cool to talk of military intervention, although some of his closest aides, such as Hillary Clinton, felt a need to intervene "to protect civilians and prevent a massacre."[16] Robert Gates, the Republican holdover as secretary of defense, adamantly opposed no-fly zones over Libya as a means to protect the rebels.[17] He viewed them as just the first steps toward greater involvement.[18] Thus, Secretary Gates stoutly resisted any incursions.[19] The main impediment to any form of intervention, nonetheless, came from the commander-in-chief himself. His spokesmen took pains to explain that entering a third conflict in the Middle East was not in the country's best interests. He feared that air exclusionary spheres would drag America deeper into the Libyan imbroglio so as to retrieve an inconclusive venture.[20] In early March, the president did voice demands that the embattled Libyan leader "step down from power and leave" otherwise the United States would review options to end the bloodshed.[21]

Along with calls for involvement from major NATO allies, there came an unusual request from an unexpected quarter. The Arab League asked the UN Security Council to impose a no-flight zone over Libya in hopes of preventing Qaddafi's savagery against his own people. The 22-nation Arab League usually decried Western interference in the Middle East. The regional bloc's invitation refuted Russian and Chinese objections to an American-led intervention. Obama officials dismissed the Arab League's endorsement without its active participation in some tangible form.[22]

The United States and other major powers could invoke the 2005 UN doctrine, which conferred the right and obligation to take up a protective mantle for at-risk populations. That concept outlined as the "responsibility to protect," nicknamed R2P, loomed in the background as Libya descended into the abyss. This humanitarian doctrine dated from the delayed Bosnian intervention and, more so, the Clinton administration's washing its hands during the Rwandan genocide, when America and other countries stood aside in 1994 as the Hutu community massacred the Tutsi people. The Obama government was loath to enter a third regional fight, whatever the stipulations of R2P.[23]

Bowing finally to the reality of a human tragedy in Libya, Washington reluctantly joined nine other governments in the passage of UN Resolution 1973 which authorized all necessary measures to protect civilians as well as a no-fly zone over the country. The parties invoked "the responsibility to protect" to justify their decision. Even while voting for the authorizing resolution, the United States assumed none of its typical leadership in the implementation. Indeed, President Obama speaking in the White House's East room depicted American tasks as merely "shaping" and "enabling operations." He made it plain that the "United States is not going to deploy ground troops in Libya." Obama officials added that the US actions included airstrikes to take down Libyan air defenses along with American command-and-control functions to enable bombing flights by NATO partners and United Arab Emirates aircraft.[24] By spring 2011, Qaddafi's relentless siege of the rebel's stronghold in Benghazi appeared unstoppable, signaling an impending bloodbath for its defenders.

These realties on the ground redefined Obama administration's calculations. Its foreign policy team now pushed for the UN to authorize military action to repel Qaddafi's tank-led advances on the rebel's Benghazi bastion.[25] Washington's urgings carried the day in the Security Council, when on March 17 it authorized member nations to take "all necessary measures" (meaning military operations) to protect Libyan civilians. Once again, the principle opponents—Russia, China, and Germany—abstained, which enabled the resolution to pass. Later when allied bombing shifted from noncombatant protection to regime change, Moscow denounced this new mission as unwarranted and perfidious American behavior. Afterward, Vladimir Putin expressed his lack of trust in Washington's official word. The Russian president was "horrified by the death of Muammar al Qaddafi and considered Russia betrayed."[26] Years later, Russian officials circled back to their UN abstention on Libya. They regarded themselves duped by the Libyan incident and resolved to never again be snookered by Washington.[27]

American leadership and martial power seemed abundantly forthcoming at the start of Operation Odyssey Dawn. US ships unleashed salvos of Tomahawk missiles to take down the Libyan air defenses. Then, other NATO countries joined the fray with aerial bombing runs against forces loyal to Qaddafi. Qatar, Jordan, and the United Arab Emirates contributed aircraft to the patrolling mission. Toward the end of March, nevertheless, the United States announced a subordinate role to NATO's armed patrols in the Libyan skies. The Atlantic alliance agreed to lead the aerial operation five days after it commenced.[28] Speaking at the National Defense University, Obama informed the American people: "the United States will play a supporting role" in NATO's mission to protect the Libyan people from Qaddafi. He spelled out these support roles as "including intelligence, logistical support, search-and-rescue assistance, and capabilities to jam regime communications."[29]

The handoff fell well short of eliminating all American assistance such as airborne refueling tankers, surveillance planes, and other advance logistical services. But officially, America was not leading. In his national address, Obama outlined his strategy only to end the Libyan dictator's deadly attack on Benghazi, not a regime-change mission. He warned that "if we try to overthrow Qaddafi by force.... We would likely have to put U.S. troops on the ground." The president went on to outline his foreign policy philosophy that governed his decision: "We went down that road in Iraq." He added: "regime change there [Iraq] took eight years, thousands of American and Iraqi lives, and nearly a trillion dollars." In his judgment, this was not a prescription that America could afford again.[30]

"Leading from behind" was how a staffer on Obama's National Security Council memorably characterized the limited US role in the Libyan military intervention.[31] Rather than challenging this often-mocked phrase, Barack Obama amplified the three-word depiction of his handling of the Libyan crisis. He explained: "Real leadership creates the conditions and coalitions for others to step up as well."[32] NATO's Allied Joint Forces Command in Naples took over management of the no-fly zone and air operations to protect Libyan citizens under the renamed Operation United Protector on March 25, 2011.

What accounts for the sudden step back by the United States during the UN's Libyan incursion? In reality, the plan for the cutback in America's commitment existed before the onset of Odyssey Dawn. President Obama went along with the British and French military proposal with strings attached. Once the air campaign was up and running, the White House insisted on a turnover of leadership unless the aerial operation required some unique American capability. The United States did handle about 75 percent of the refueling of allied aircraft, provided most of the reconnaissance, and exceeded others in the number of sorties. America also supplied munitions and drones to European states when they depleted their inventories. Yet, the impetus for the Libyan enterprise came from Paris and London. Before a European audience, Hillary Clinton correctly summed up the administration's handling of Libya: "We did not lead this."[33]

Perceptions of Obama's reluctance to engage wholeheartedly in armed enterprises dropped off the screen of his political opponents in light of Osama bin Laden's death in Pakistan at the hands of US Navy SEALs on May 2. Taking the arch-terrorist off the battlefield, by a risky helicopter raid, recast President Obama's image as bold commander-in-chief, just as detractors decried his "passivity in the Middle East" during the Arab Spring.[34] The assault on bin Laden's terrorist lair in Abbottabad gave the president a boost in the polls. Days after the dramatic SEAL operation, his job approval rating shot to 57 percent, up from 46 percent a month earlier.[35]

Bin Laden's death masked the fact that even the White House's part in this spectacular operation had been marked by its characteristic hesitation and reluctance. One account noted the president's "paralyzing indecision, political calculation" prior to authorizing the mission. According to officials directly involved, "the president canceled the mission three times in 2011 alone and delayed it throughout 2010."[36] Part of this indecision can be explained by Barack Obama's own deeply held retrenchment policy.[37] Another part of the explanation stems from the knowledge that influenced all White House occupants since Jimmy Carter's failed hostage-rescue raid to free 52 American diplomats held by Iranian "students" after the takeover of the US Embassy in Tehran. That doomed effort contributed to Carter's lost reelection bid in 1980.

The master terrorist's death contributed to the narrative that the al Qaeda network was now on the ropes—a view which the administration promoted as the national election neared. A year after the SEAL operation, the president spoke from Bagram Air Base in Afghanistan. Too prematurely, the commander-in-chief perceived the end of the terrorist threat, when he proclaimed: "The goal that I set—to defeat al Qaeda and deny it a chance to rebuild—is now within our reach."[38] Al Qaeda enjoyed something of a second life, albeit through a splinter movement in the Levant two years after the president spoke of its near-defeat, as will be subsequently related.

Washington conducted the Libyan mission in a manner to spare the United States dollars and casualties. It had much less to do with enhancing the Arab Spring prospects for the birth of democracies.[39] The administrations desired to maintain sound relations with its NATO allies, particularly France and Britain—the leading lights of the anti-Qaddafi attack. After Qaddafi's shooting death, the United Protector campaign lingered on until October 31, the date agreed upon by the Security Council to terminate the mandate for NATO's military action. Standing up a democratic government enjoyed only moderate patronage from the Obama government.[40] The 19-nation intervention accomplished its regime-change goal without allied casualties. As such, Washington touted it as a "model intervention."[41]

The Post-Qaddafi Legacy

Post-Qaddafi Libya, in fact, held up two cautionary tales for US foreign policy. First, Americans could still be killed by terrorist-inspired assaults outside declared war zones. In the eastern city of Benghazi, the US ambassador to the country, Christopher Stevens, and three other Americans died in a terrorist-instigated storming of the US Consulate on September 11, 2012. The orchestrated attack ignited a fierce and protracted controversy within the American body politic, which generated heated arguments for years over the veracity of the administration's public statements about the consulate attack as well as its failure to rescue the besieged victims. The White House portrayed the machinegun and rocket siege of the Benghazi consulate as a spontaneous consequence of an anti-Muslim video briefly shown in the United States. Contradicting this view, a former deputy director of the CIA wrote that the agency "analysts never said the video was a factor in the Benghazi attacks."[42] Political opponents and skeptics of the administration's interpretation—and there were legions of them—argued that Obama appointees simply conformed to the 2012 preelection campaign line that terrorism was on the wane. The uproar over the incident even spawned a Select Committee on Benghazi in the US House of Representatives to investigate the role of government officials before, during, and after the attack.[43] Despite the passionate accusations hurled at the White House's narrative, the arguments cut little ice overall, as Barack Obama handily won a second term in November.

For Washington, the second Libyan lesson was how it came to reinforce the president's reluctance to intervene in Syria's playout of the Arab Spring. Without Colonel Qaddafi, Libya tumbled into a multisided militia war. A political vacuum developed into which rushed scores of rival bands of armed men, who confronted the shaky National Transitional Council. The lawlessness also made Libya a security threat to its neighbors, as arms from its opened arsenals found their way into the hands of Islamist extremists in Mali, Boko Haram in Nigeria, and even Syria militants. Using Libyan arms, the semi-nomadic Tuareg peoples within Mali temporarily ousted their government. For the first time in its history, the Atlantic alliance left no stabilization force to ensure order in Libya as it had in Bosnia and Kosovo. Instead, it turned to a tiny UN mission, which lacked resources and executive authority to coordinate a trickle of international support. Three years after the aerial bombardment ended, the Obama administration tardily planned to train some 8000 soldiers for the fragile central government. By this time, dangerous conditions and a dysfunctional government retarded its execution.[44]

Barack Obama's reaction to the intervention differed from former president Bill Clinton, who dragged his feet before entering the Bosnian slaughterhouse in the 1990s. Afterward, the Clinton presidency acted with more confidence on the world stage. But after the NATO air intervention into Libya, the differences between the two presidents quickly came into sharp relief. As one scholar of presidential foreign policies wrote: "But far from giving him [Obama] a new direction, intervention against Gadhafi in Libya—and even more, the raid against Osama bin Laden six weeks later—appeared to strengthen the president's commitment to retrenchment."[45] Following his reluctant approval of the US participation in the Libyan air war, President Obama soured even more on American interventions.[46] Obama stayed wedded to his standoffish and hesitant posture as Syria, Iraq, and Yemen succumbed to the Arab Spring's reverberations.

The Syrian Sidestep

The principles outlined by President Obama at his George Washington University address about Libya in late March 2011 seemingly laid out a model for intervention into Syria. Described by some as an Obama doctrine, the president's speech maintained that America bore a responsibility to put the brakes on a bloodbath that hung over the Qaddafi-besieged city of Benghazi. Taking up the humanitarian gauntlet, nevertheless, depended on other nations joining with America. The similarities between Libya and Syria, notwithstanding, Obama's foreign policy advisers repudiated the universality of the Libyan involvement as a model for other countries. They sized up differences between Libya and, say, Syria.[47]

Obama officials had long perceived Syria a less straightforward trouble spot than Libya. To start with, the Obama presidency reached out to the young, Western-educated Syrian dictator before the Arab Spring enveloped his regime, while it aided democracy advocates who worked against the dictatorship.[48] Its foreign policy team hoped to promote reform within Syria, to peel Damascus away from its primary backer, Iran, and to entice Syria into peace talks with Israel. In 2010, the United States appointed Robert Ford as ambassador to Syria, the first time it filled the post since 2005. This gambit came to naught. Once the Arab Spring political storm beset Syria, Washington had to recalibrate its Syrian stance.

For one thing, there were geopolitical concerns to take into account. The Obama administration harbored strong strategic reasons to hold its fire in Syria's growing humanitarian nightmare, lest it endanger a nuclear accord with Tehran. The United States together with other world powers had been engaged in nuclear talks with Iran since 2006. While difficulties lay ahead before Washington struck an accord with Iran in 2015, the Obama administration warmed to the notion of arms control and re-integration of the Islamic Republic into the international system. The Obama presidency cringed at the specter of an unremittingly hostile and estranged Iran, made worse over a US intervention into the Syrian civil war against Assad, Iran's staunch partner in fighting the West.

For another thing, there were dreadful complexities of Syria's bloody fragmentation. The dismal outcome of the Libyan case gave the president and his closest White House advisors pause about entering the worsening Syrian battleground.[49] Whereas Muammar Qaddafi stood virtually ally-less against the United States and its partners, Bashar al-Assad in Damascus enjoyed staunch diplomatic and material backing from Iran, Russia, and, to a lesser extent, China. During the Soviet era, the Kremlin opened naval and air bases in Syria and supplied military hardware to the Syrian dictatorship. In the post-Cold War years, Moscow ran diplomatic interference in the Security Council for Damascus, while still supplying the Syrian military with arms and training.

The Islamic Republic of Iran was aligned even closer to the authoritarian ruler in Damascus, which relied heavily on the Alawite sect, an offshoot of Iran's Shiite branch of Islam. Politically, both states stood together against the West in general and the United States in particular, which they resented for its support of Israel, their sworn enemy.[50] Tehran, moreover, depended on the "land bridge" across Syria for resupply and contact with its co-religious brethren in Lebanon. There, the Lebanese Shiite community formed Hezbollah (the "Party of God"), a militant party and highly trained militia army, which received extensive military and subversive instruction from Iran's Islamic Revolutionary Guard Corps. Hezbollah protected the Shia and Iranian interests in multi-confessional Lebanon and opened an Iranian gateway to the Mediterranean Sea. In time, Hezbollah fighters crossed into Syria and waged a fierce defense of the Assad regime. Thus, Damascus and Tehran had formed a co-dependency relationship.[51]

When the Arab Spring revolt struck Syria, it ran up against a much more intransient adversary than the pro-democracy protestors faced in Tunisia, Egypt, and Yemen, each of which ushered out their long-term dictators. Bashar al Assad, on the other hand, ruthlessly clung to power by the most barbaric methods imaginable, including the use of chemical weapons, widespread torture and summary executions, and shrapnel-filled barrel bombs dropped on civilians. Like Hafez al Assad, his dictatorial father from whom he inherited power, Bashar al Assad hailed from the minority Alawites in a country where over three-quarters of the people belonged to the Sunni branch. At 12 percent of the population, the Alawite sect benefited enormously from having their hands on the levers of military and commercial power. As such, they could be counted on to defend furiously the House of Assad against the much larger Sunni constituency.

Syrian quiescence gave way to small, peaceful demonstrations in several urban centers but particularly in the southern city of Deraa during the second week of March 2011. One keen expert hinted the plausibility that

Bashar al-Assad, who was trained in the West as an ophthalmologist and regarded as a reformer, missed an opportunity to make timely concessions to nip the revolt in the bud before the street movement took on martyrs and radicalism.[52] Alas, moderate reform was not to be, and Syria's version of the Arab Spring turned out to be the most protracted, bloody, and nightmarishly violent.

Reacting to Assad's heavy-handed clampdown, a National Security Council member offered an empty censure: "the Syrian government must address the legitimate aspirations of their people."[53] Other Washington officials also expressed concerns about a destabilized Syria, because violence, refugees, and a militant Sunni government in Assad's place would spell major troubles for neighboring Lebanon, Iraq, Turkey, and Israel.[54] Four months after the onset of violent retaliation on his restive population, Assad drew little but anodyne rebukes from Washington officials. Speaking after pro-government demonstrators stormed the US Embassy in Damascus while the Syrian police stood aside, Hillary Clinton declared: "From our perspective, he has lost legitimacy."[55] Washington put its faith in trying to bring together various moderate, exiled factions, which ultimately went nowhere to end the Assad reign of terror.

By summer 2011, a disturbing pattern arose that would define the Syrian rebellion; this factor was the mounting bloody clashes between Alawite and Sunni communities in the city of Homs and beyond. The anti-regime opposition going forward broke down along sectarian lines rather than simple, pro- and anti-government factions. In time, this sectarian divide gave way to Islamist ultra-extremism within the Sunni community, as militias embraced Islam in greater or lesser degrees, further fracturing the Sunni rebels among extremists, moderates, and secular groupings. In time, radicalization bred two, competing networks among the fanatical fringe. The ISIS (also known as Islamic State of Iraq and the Levant, or ISIL, and ultimately as just the Islamic State) resurrected itself from the decimated ranks of al-Qaeda in Iraq after the death of its pathological head, Abu Musab al-Zarqawi. Led by another mass murderer, Abu Bakr al-Baghdadi, ISIS engaged in brutal combat against moderate Islamic rebels and hacked out enclaves within Syria before it rampaged southward into Iraq in mid-2014. Months earlier, it broke with al Qaeda central and its Syrian affiliate, Jabhat al-Nusra, which was also an extremist outfit. Atrocities begat counter atrocities in the spiraling sectarian violence.

As the carnage ground on, the United States assumed the position of bystander as the Syrian tragedy consumed hundreds of thousands of lives. It produced millions of refugees in neighboring countries and Europe, while fighting displaced even more people within the country. The Obama administration neither promoted humanitarian "safe zones" along the country's borders with Turkey nor supplied adequate weapons to the Syrian rebels locked in a life-and-death struggle with Assad's security forces. Instead, Washington looked vainly for a resolution by the UN, where Moscow held veto power in the Security Council to block any threat to Damascus. Seeing Russian and even Chinese opposition within the Security Council to any forward policy, Washington expressed its lack of legal authority to take a more active part and mainly folded its hands. It did endorse efforts by UN envoys, such as Kofi Annan and Lakhdar Brahimi, to bring together the fragmented Syrian opposition and negotiate a political settlement with Assad—thankless and fruitless endeavors—which led to both resigning in frustration.

For years, the United States hesitated in training Syrian volunteers to fight the Assad regime, lest American instruction, arms, and equipment eventually benefit radical Islamists. When Hillary Clinton championed the arming of moderate units, the secretary of state lost the debate to her boss in summer 2012.[56] The president saw little utility in aiding the Syrian insurgency. The administration based its decision on a widely touted, classified, CIA review of the Agency's record of failures in equipping and instructing anti-regime fighters in its 67-year history.[57] The Obama administration at first furnished only non-lethal military equipment through the Western-leaning Free Syrian Army's Supreme Military Council. Under pressure from its Gulf allies, the president authorized a covert CIA program to muster a moderate Syrian armed unit capable of fighting but not defeating the Assad regime.

When in June 2013 the White House announced its intention of arming Syrian rebels, the plan touched off bipartisan debates within the House and Senate intelligence committees over its wisdom, lest the arms wind up in the hands of Sunni Islamic extremists. The CIA dispersal of weaponry usually amounted to less than 20 percent of what the opposition fighters requested at that.[58] The training of opposition fighters also fared poorly. Recruits numbering in the low hundreds from the Free Syrian Army underwent military instruction by Saudi Arabian and American personnel from the start of 2013 in CIA camps inside Jordan.[59] The CIA-trained troops, moreover, disconcerted the Agency by battling forces loyal to Assad instead of taking on the Islamist militants. The CIA trainees also numbered too few to change the tide of war. Two years after its start, the CIA program was sputtering, as the heavily vetted "trusted commanders" complained about the paucity of anti-tank weapons and air defense missiles. Complicating matters, Washington redirected its focus from going after Assad's army to attacking the Islamic State. This switch made it tougher to attract rebel recruits, who eyed the Damascus regime as their chief enemy.[60]

Congress approved funds for the arming and training programs the previous September, just prior to the 2014 mid-term elections, with solid majorities. Its votes, though, masked ambivalence over entering another Middle East war and apprehensions about arms falling into the wrong hands.[61] When the US military instruction project got underway, only 60 rebel fighters graduated from the first round of training. The goal was to instruct about 5000 trainees a year, a far cry from tiny numbers actually turned out.[62] This small number raised doubts on the utility of the entire effort.

Another key US objective—to drive a wedge between the moderate rebel militias and the Islamist networks—crashed on the rocks of Syrian realities. Rather than fighting each other, the two wings of the anti-Assad front coordinated offensives to capture government positions. At the risk of losing their American and European aid, the Western-supported factions downplayed their cooperation with the Islamists.[63]

Chemical Weapons and Red Lines

At first blush, America's posture toward Syria appeared to toughen with Assad's increasing use of chemical weapons against his rebellious population. Based on outside reportage, the trajectory of Syrian sarin gas attacks shot upward in 2013 over the previous year. The United States did stiffen its public pronouncements on the topic. President Obama uttered his now-famous "red line" marker on August 20, 2012. Answering a journalist's question about whether he envisioned "using the U.S. military" for the "safe keeping of chemical weapons" within Syria, Obama replied: "a red line for us is we start seeing a whole bunch of chemical weapons moving around or being utilized. That would change my calculus."[64] After the president's "red line" utterance, a White House official in a conference call held later with reporters said: "We go on to reaffirm that the President has set a clear red line as it relates to the United States that the use of chemical weapons or the transfer of chemical weapons to terrorists groups is a red line."[65]

Then in late August 2013, information came to light that exploding rockets carried a toxic sarin gas from which a reported 1429 people died in East Ghouta near Damascus. Washington and West European capitals condemned the attack but no government was eager to become enmeshed in the messy, sectarian civil war raging throughout most of Syria. Taking the side of the radicalized Islamists or even the so-called moderate Syrian opposition held little appeal for outside powers.[66]

Already on record with its red-line saber-rattling, the White House seemed poised to strike Syria. Instead, it passed the buck to a divided Congress. By early September, President Obama reversed course at a news conference in Stockholm: "I didn't set a red line. The world set a red line."[67] Faced with the real prospect of militarily striking Syria, President Obama laid the decision on a surprised Congress, which had played no previous role in the administration's airstrikes on targets in Pakistan, Yemen, or Somalia. Rather than acting on his own, the US commander-in-chief asked Congress for a formal military authorization to attack Syria.

Such a request struck former officials and political opponents at first as bewildering, since the president made no such request before launching military strikes against Qaddafi in March 2011. At that time, the White House contented that the limited air campaign envisioned no ground troops. Therefore, it informed Congress that the decision was consistent with the 1973 War Powers Resolution that mandated legislative approval solely after a 60-day ground intervention. In the Syria case, Obama requested Congressional authorization ahead of military operations on which he placed further restrictions—the strikes could not alter the course of the war, nor could they target the regime's leadership. In fact, the president clarified that his intention was merely a "shot across the bow" to the Assad regime. This shot-across-the-bow phrase received much derisive commentary as little more than a blank cartridge.[68]

Former CIA director and Secretary of Defense Leon Panetta wrote in his memoir that President Obama "vacillated" at first and then by submitting the matter to Congress he knew it was an "almost certain way to scotch any action." Panetta concluded that Obama's handling of the red line controversy resulted in "a blow to American credibility" by "failing to respond, it [Obama administration] sent the wrong message to the world."[69] The Oval Office was unable to escape totally unscathed from criticism for its failure to hold Damascus to account for crossing over its own red line. From the start of the Syrian conflict, President Obama "wanted to keep his distance, and at that—in the most dismal fashion—

he succeeded," according to one foreign policy expert, who concluded: "Looking weak and foolish was perhaps an acceptable cost."[70]

Meanwhile Secretary of State John F. Kerry and other officials succeeded, nevertheless, in lining up allied endorsements for a possible retaliatory action against Syria. But those for and against bombing wanted to await the UN investigators' confirmation of a chemical attack.[71] The White House also took note of the public polls, which reflected surging opposition to American airstrikes on Syria. By more than 2 to 1 (63 percent to 28 percent), those canvased by a USA Today/Pew Research Center Poll opposed bombing Syria for gassing its own civilians.[72] These public surveys reinforced the Obama administration's predisposition for retrenchment.

The Oval Office's one-and-done-attack formula aroused little enthusiasm even from Congressional hawks who questioned the strategic value of such a limited riposte to the Syrian people or to America's larger interests. Democratic lawmakers were even more resistant than their Republican counterparts, as both understood the public's aversion to yet another American-led conflict in the Middle East. The president's Congressional request for authorizing a military operation was headed for an almost certain rejection, when out of the blue, Vladimir Putin snatched a presidential victory from an impending legislative defeat. Ironically, the way out of Obama's dilemma was broached first by John Kerry, who suggested offhandedly that by turning over its chemical weapons to the international community the Syrian regime might avert an attack. The Russian president seized on the idea and urged Damascus to accept the offer. The Assad regime welcomed the proposal, and so did many in the US Congress. President Obama embraced the Russian offer in a scheduled speech to the nation in mid-September. Furthermore, he requested that Congress postpone its vote on authorizing aerial strikes, thereby escaping a bipartisan, Congressional defeat.[73]

The upshot of the president's maneuvers and the Russians' diplomatic initiative was a deal between Washington and Moscow to bring Syrian chemical weapons, which Assad finally acknowledged possessing, under international control for their destruction. Acting in compliance with the UN resolution, the Syrian regime disclosed many locations of poison gas storage and production sites. The UN dispatched the Organization for the Prohibition of Chemical Weapons (OPCW) to ferret out and to oversee the demolition of the toxic substance.[74] An advance party of OPCW inspectors traveled to Syria in early October to take up the task of dismantling Assad's chemical stockpiles. Over the next eight months, the OPCW busied itself in supervising the search and the destruction of the toxic stockpiles.

Even after OPCW's announcement in June 2014 that it had taken possession of the last Syrian chemical arms for destruction at sea, the fears lingered about the Assad regime's total compliance.[75] In fact, the OPCW refused to state categorically that Syria had been stripped of all chemical arms. The United States formally accused the Syrian regime of dropping chlorine-filled barrels on residential areas in May 2015.[76] But Damascus suffered no punishment for its violations of the UN stipulations.

As the chemical destruction process played out, US policy toward Syria drifted onto the backburner until mid-2014. Its support, therefore, was calibrated just to sustain the moderate rebels rather than furnish sufficient arms and trained fighters for them to triumph over their militant adversaries. Saudi Arabia stepped into the breach by supplying modest quantities of anti-tank missiles to the Syrian rebels, who remained frustrated by insufficient firepower.[77] The CIA also sent paramilitary teams to Jordan in order to train forces for the Supreme Military Council, an umbrella organization run by former Syrian generals that received the most American support.[78] Technically secret, the CIA program trained and funded so-called moderate rebels, who fought against Assad. In time, this training operation turned out several thousand troops. This effort was separate from the failed Pentagon undertaking, which concentrated on producing fighters to combat only ISIS. Sometimes, the fighters battled more against each other to shore up their micro-states than they fought the Syrian security forces. By the end of 2013, Syria resembled a checkerboard of political mini-states as militant groups violently partitioned the country.

The close of that year marked no real change in America's non-involvement stance in Syria as it spiraled deeper into violence and balkanization. Not least, it was devoid of any strategy to remove Assad, who inched toward the status of a de facto ally because the United States aimed most bombs at ISIS. The Turkish government complained that the United States bombed Islamist rebels more than the Assad regime.[79] America's aloofness flowed from its president's perceptions of the world. In an interview with a journalist, Barack Obama defended America's disengagement from the Syrian imbroglio; "It is very difficult to imagine a scenario in which our involvement in Syria would have led to a better outcome." He fell back on his pre-presidential views about the consequences of the Iraq and Afghan wars he inherited by stating: "I am not haunted by my decision not to engage in another Middle Eastern war."[80]

Syria, Iraq, and the Islamic State Network

At the start of 2014, American officials took temporary comfort from the deadly infighting between the two leading extremist movements. Jahbat al-Nusra and the Islamic State of Iraq and Syria clashed in northern Syria. Exacerbated by ISIS's grisly displays of atrocities, Al-Qaeda central broke ties with the Islamic State after repeated warnings to its Syrian affiliate to eschew excessive cruelties that the Western media captured on film.[81] Any prospect that a rebellion-within-a-rebellion would provide a respite to Washington proved illusory. ISIS militants rapidly made inroads in the swath of territory spanning southern Syria and northern Iraq.[82] Agencies outside the executive residence warned about the gathering danger from ISIS conquests but their warnings went unheeded in the Oval Office.[83]

Almost overnight, ISIS crossed back over the Syrian border and swiftly marched on the Iraqi cities of Mosul, Tikrit, and Fallujah. Many Iraqi Sunnis viewed the Islamic State as deliverers from the detested Shiite-controlled government in Baghdad. Taken by surprise, Washington presented no immediate counterforce to advance of the black-flagged jihadi militias.

Speechmaking at West Point's commencement, just as ISIS pushed deeper into Iraq, President Obama delivered his perspective on America's detachment from the Middle East. He professed to the military cadets that it was time to end what he called "a long season of war" and to forgo seeing every problem solvable by America's armed forces. Instead of US boots on the ground, he favored leaving the fighting to others. He, therefore, called on Congress for $5 billion for a new Counterterrorism Partnerships Fund in order "to train, build capacity, and facilitate partner countries on the front lines," such as Yemen, Somalia, Libya, and for "French operations in Mali." He re-expressed his preference for a disengagement policy, when he asserted: "Since World War II, some of our most costly mistakes came not from our restraint, but from our willingness to rush into military adventures without thinking through the consequences." In the future, Obama argued that when the United States is not directly threatened "the threshold for military action must be higher."[84]

His detractors sprang with their usual charge that the president was once again retreating from America's post-World War II dominance, leaving political vacuums to be filled by adversaries. One critic of presidential restraint, historian Robert Kagan, argued that the Military Academy speech articulated a common critique that the president held "a more narrow definition of our national interest than the post-World War II tradition."[85] Another detractor, a former George W. Bush official, argued that Obama's tardy assistance to the moderate Syrian opposition "comes about three years after such training might actually have made a difference."[86] The commander-in-chief's speech before the graduating US Army cadets outlined no winning strategy on how he planned to lead in the final years of his presidency.[87]

Just as the terrorist tsunami struck into central Iraq, President Obama answered Congressional opponents' demands for legislation authorizing military actions against ISIS. The White House sent Congress a draft proposal for a new AUMF, which would show "our resolve to counter the threat posed by ISIL."[88] The proposed authorization sought presidential approval for actions against the Islamic State he deemed necessary. Obama's requested authority would repeal George W. Bush's 2002 AUMF and would terminate three years after enactment.[89] The Congressional response to the president's requested legislation was underwhelming. The two houses fell into disarray. Some Democratic members thought the authorization was too hawkish; some Republican lawmakers believed it was too dovish. Still others wanted sentences removed or added to constrict or expand the president's actions. As a consequence, legislative action stalled, and the executive branch turned to the unfolding drama in the Middle East without a congressional mandate for fighting.

The US Minimalist Counter

The White House embarked on a limited political as well as military counterstrategy to the ISIS offensive. Politically, American officials pushed for peaceful regime change in Baghdad against Prime Minister Nuri Kamal al-Maliki, whose sectarian policies alienated the Sunni minority. Obama's new view represented a reversal on Maliki. After the inconclusive Iraqi elections in 2010, the US Ambassador to Iraq, Christopher R. Hill, threw America's political weight behind Maliki and pooh-pooed Sunni complaints—and those US military advisors who backed them—about the Shiite-biased Maliki regime. Experienced mainly in Asian affairs and backed by Hillary Clinton, then secretary of state, Hill paid little attention to the advice from long-term Iraqi hands.[90] By persecuting Sunnis,

Maliki's policies forfeited the pluralistic gains won by the US occupation and its high price in lives and money. Without a political change at the top, military operations alone would not prevail. Obama officials, therefore, helped force out al-Maliki for Haider al-Abadi who they considered a moderate Shiite politician.

Washington made other political adjustments to the new reality in the Middle East. John Kerry signaled that the United States was ready to mend relations with Egypt's Abdel Fattah al-Sisi, the general who led the 2013 military ouster of the democratically elected President Mohamed Morsi after the fall of Hosni Mubarak. Now, the United States abandoned Morsi's cause and backed al-Sisi. The White House needed Mideast partners to confront the marauding ISIS bands. The secretary of state traveled to Cairo to reaffirm America's "historic partnership" and to pledge restoration of the military aid package.[91]

In addition, the Pentagon warily sent a small training contingent back into the Iraqi theater in mid-2014. Numbering "up to 300" Special Forces advisers, the tiny force was supposed to reverse the ISIS gains and stop the insurgents from taking Baghdad. Before long, concerns about ISIS prompted the Pentagon to deploy more troops. Each time the president upped the size of the small US footprint in Iraq, he reassured the American people that he would not recommit American "combat forces" to the fractured nation. The danger posed to Baghdad and Erbil, the Kurdish capital, by the onrushing ISIS offensive forced President Obama's hand, compelling him to authorize airstrikes on the swift-moving militants in August 2014. In approving limited aerial attacks, the American leader insisted that they did not amount to a re-invasion into the Persian Gulf nation: "As commander in chief, I will not allow the United States to be dragged into another war in Iraq."[92]

This reluctant reversal of his withdrawal policy revealed Obama's preference for disengagement, which ISIS upset. His political opponents seized on Obama's minimization of the threat posed by the Islamic State when he characterized it as "a jayvee team" in an Oval Office interview six months earlier.[93] Congress went along with the president's military decisions; no groundswell of opposition erupted as happened a year before when the White House broached the striking of Syria over its use of chemical weapons. In fact, the president's Republican opposition called for a more vigorous counteraction. John McCain contented that air attacks too narrowly focused on protecting Americans working in Iraq from the Islamic State rather than wiping out the terrorist network. The Republican senator from Arizona perceived the Islamic State as "a threat to America" and thus warranting a bigger US counterstrike.[94]

Despite the very limited intervention, the Pentagon grandly dubbed it "Operation Inherent Resolve." In September, the president announced a further deployment of 450 troops. In an address at the White House, he pledged: "We will degrade and ultimately destroy ISIL." He reassured his audience "how this effort will be different from the wars in Iraq and Afghanistan," because "it will not involve American combat troops." Rather, his new effort will center on US airpower along with SOF and CIA operatives assisting local "partner forces on the ground." The American president compared his counterterrorism strategy to Yemen and Somalia "as one that we have successfully pursued…for years."[95] Reality in Iraq quickly outstripped the hesitant US countermeasures, however. The Islamic State replenished its ranks with hundreds of recruits from abroad arriving each month to take up arms. Nor did events in Yemen lend comfort to the presidential battle plan, for that nation tumbled into a multisided civil war, which necessitated the temporary evacuation of US security personnel six months after the White House speech on Iraq.

Meanwhile in Iraq, the US ground force grew to more than 3500 personnel after several months, but their initial guidelines prohibited them from accompanying their partners into battle. In the final months of his presidency, President Obama upped the official number to nearly 5000, excluding special forces and rotational personnel. Small in number though they might be, the US armed forces required a SOFA to cover the US military personnel in a foreign country over issues of domestic law and service members' behavior. This time the Obama administration accepted a similar type of legal immunity agreement for US troops that it turned down in 2011. Iraq's government provided assurances in a diplomatic note, without its parliament's approval, which exempted US personnel from Iraqi laws. Three years earlier, Washington had demanded parliamentary ratification of immunity, effectively killing any hope for a SOFA. Even with al-Maliki's assurances, the Obama White House still pulled out all American forces in 2011. This time the legal niceties were bypassed so as to retrieve US interests in a disintegrating Iraq.[96]

From air bases in the region, American and allied aircraft pummeled ISIS columns and fortifications. These counterattacks broke the ISIS advance on Baghdad. Midway through August, the Pentagon provided air support to the Kurd's ground assault of Mosul Dam. Then it ordered aerial strikes to other Kurdish counteroffenses in the months ahead. The

Iraqi Kurds earned the reputation as Washington's best local forces against the Islamic State peril. But the Kurds' aspirations for sovereignty complicated the Obama administration's relations with Turkey and Iraq, which resisted moves to accommodate Kurdish statehood.

After three-and-a-half years of US opposition to overt and direct military action in Syria's civil war, President Obama finally did order airstrikes against ISIS militants as means to check their offensive deep into Iraq. Initially, he kept a tight rein on the Syrian airstrikes and restricted bombing in Iraq. In Syria, Obama demanded that the Pentagon get White House's sign-off for aerial strikes. By these controls, the president ensured that the US armed forces conformed to his guidelines to degrade the Islamic State without falling into a wider war or another occupation of Iraq. He also reined in the scope of bombing to avert any resemblance to a "shock and awe" campaign, which might lead to another ground invasion.[97]

On the ground, the Obama administration sought to replicate Bush junior's victory by rallying Sunni sheiks against the terrorist al Qaeda in Iraq network (discussed in Chap. 7). But this time, Baghdad's Shiite-run government complicated matters. The Sunnis hated Baghdad's reliance on the feared and loathed Popular Mobilization Forces, since these Shiite militias were often armed and trained by Iran's secretive Quds Force of the Islamic Revolutionary Guards Corps. This close Baghdad-Tehran collaboration disconcerted American plans for a multi-sectarian government in Baghdad. In reality, the presence of the Islamic State militants and the Shiite militias furthered the balkanization of Iraq into three de facto subnations—Shiastan, Sunnistan, and Kurdistan.

Other anomalies materialized. By both attacking ISIS in Iraq and Syria, the United States and Iran wound up as nearly de facto allies. More to the point, the president's anti-ISIS campaign seemed calibrated to the administration's pursuit of a nuclear arms control agreement with the Islamic Republic of Iran. Domestic opponents of Obama and some Iraq's Sunnis contended that the president would sell out Iraq to conclude a nuclear deal with Tehran.[98] After the conclusion of the agreement in 2015, the Washington did step up its military campaigns in Iraq and Syria but adhered to its pre-deal focus on Islamic State rather than Damascus's forces.[99]

For much of 2015, the United States minimized its involvement in Iraq by relying on Kurdish forces, airpower, Shiite militias, and a handful of Iraqi regular soldiers. Despite Washington's banking on the Kurds, it hesitated in transferring weapons directly to Kurdistan's pesh merga fighters out of concern that it signaled a willingness to encourage Kurdish independence from Baghdad. The Kurdish leadership favored direct delivery for that very reason—America's recognition of their separateness from Baghdad.[100]

President Obama kept regular "boots on the ground" out of the fight against the Islamic State so as to avoid retreating on his 2008 campaign pledges to end America's wars. Instead, he turned to SOF, whose secretive silhouette obscured their combat missions in Iraq and Syria. As a pair of journalists wrote, US officials often resorted to "linguistic contortions to mask the forces' combat role."[101] America's commander-in-chief viewed the elite troops and clandestine operations as an alternative to the large occupation wars he inherited from George W. Bush.

This "fierce minimalist" course of action, as expounded by one commentator, held that Obama "only unsheathes his sword against people he thinks might kill Americans."[102] But the president did not really unsheathe the nation's sword against terrorist networks expanding in Iraq and Syria. From mid-2014 onward, the self-proclaimed Islamic State made wide gains in Iraq and Syria, while beheading Western hostages and exporting terrorism abroad. In Iraq, the fall of Ramadi, a northern city, in May 2015 to ISIS, raised further questions about the administration's incremental strategy for containing the radical Islamists.[103] Even after the retaking Ramadi by Iraqi security forces later in the same year, the pace of the anti-ISIS campaign stayed plodding against Mosul and Fallujah. Obama wanted no part of a "shock and awe" assault so celebrated by his immediate predecessor.

Diplomatically, the United States did pull together a sizeable international coalition against the Islamic State. Numbering more than 60 nations, the US-led Global Coalition to Degrade and Defeat ISIL included participants with varying levels of engagement.[104] Most participated in name only, whereas a dozen furnished warplanes for airstrikes, supplied arms to the Kurds, or opened their territory (Jordan, Turkey, Saudi Arabia) for training programs calling for moderate Syrian fighters. At his sixth address to the UN General Assembly in 2014, President Obama implored world leaders to join the anti-Islamic State front "to dismantle this network of death."[105] These policies were at a piece with Washington's goal of avoiding direct combat involvement in the Syrian cauldron.

At home, Obama's poll numbers temporarily nosedived over his international inaction and non-interventionist leadership amid growing fears of terrorist attacks. The Islamic State's territorial advances and Internetbroadcasted beheadings rattled the general public. In one New York Times/CBS News poll, 58 percent of Americans disapproved of the president's handling of foreign affairs in 2014.[106] But the poll responders were conflicted in their opinions. They held no appetite for a large US intrusion into the boiling crises in Ukraine, Iraq, or Syria. On specifics, the public's mood matched the White House's restrained policy. These conflicting perceptions frustrated presidential aides, who believed that Obama deserved higher numbers for carrying out the people's wishes.[107]

President Obama's tentative strategy in Syria and Iraq was upended by Vladimir Putin's unexpected military intrusion into Syria in September 2015. The Russian Federation's president deployed ground-attack warplanes, troops, armored tanks, and air defense systems to bases near Latakia and Tartus. Russia's armed forces now bolstered Moscow's pro-Assad stance, as the strongman's army was flagging at that moment. Russian planes mostly struck non-Islamic State insurgents whose ground conquests threatened the Damascus regime's Alawite community in northwestern Syria. To administration critics, the Russian deployments provided proof that the White House's inaction in Syria had ceded the initiative in the Levantine country to the Kremlin.[108]

Iraq's Implications for Afghanistan and Yemen

The third American conflict in Iraq, however much smaller than the preceding two, held implications for the US withdrawal from the Middle East and Afghanistan. Since his circumscribed US forces build-up in Afghanistan was announced in late 2009, President Obama planned on a phased pullout of US Army and Marine troops beginning by mid-2011 from the Central Asian nation. But the Islamic State's unexpected terrorist rampage deep into Iraq, in part, delayed the US pullout from Afghanistan. In May 2014, the president called for substantial withdrawals of US regular forces and an end to combat operations by the end of the year within the Afghan theater. Afterward, the remaining American military forces would switch to training and mentoring missions, except for counterterrorism operations. The Pentagon mapped out a reduction in the US footprint to just 9800 troops by the end of 2014; some 5500 by the end of 2015; and only a standard embassy staff (plus a small, an extra security detail) as President Obama left office in early 2017. Thus, the United States would have zero regular combat units stationed within the country as a new American leader stepped into Oval office.

The deteriorating state of affairs in Iraq caused the White House to backtrack on its withdrawal schedule from Afghanistan. The Pentagon convinced its commander-in-chief to reverse course or face an emerging terrorist state *á la* Iraq. Afghanistan's new president, Ashraf Ghani, also requested the White House to reverse its withdrawal plans.[109] Thus, the prospect of a similar Iraqi fate befalling the Central Asian nation modified the Oval Office's abrupt plans for total exfiltration, especially as the Taliban mounted attacks in areas heretofore peaceful. But the American president never bought into the general's recommendations to leave 20,000 or more military personnel in the distraught country. At the tail end of his presidency, Obama announced that he would leave 8400 troops in the Afghan warzone after he left office. His July 2016 decision was recognition of Taliban gains in the embattled country.

Yemen also felt political tremors from the violent upheavals in Iraq and Syria. On the bottom tip of the Arabian Peninsula, Yemen had drawn US concern even before the Arab Spring ignited the Islamic State scourge. Western apprehensions mounted after the founding of Al-Qaeda in the Arabian Peninsula (AQAP) out of splinter jihadi groups in 2009. AQAP aroused concern mainly from the incendiary preaching of American-born Anwar al-Awlaki whose charismatic appeals motivated US Army Major Nidal Hasan to kill 13 people in Fort Hood and Umar Farouk Abdulmutallab to try to blow up a Detroit-bound airliner with a bomb in his underwear. Even after the Obama administration killed al-Awlaki with drone-fired missiles in 2012, it continued its involvement in the increasingly chaotic Yemen.

Not long after the formation of AQAP, Washington reinforced its ties to President Ali Abdullah Saleh, a former Yemeni army general, to combat the shadowy terrorist network before it struck American targets. The Pentagon assigned SOF to help train Yemen's security forces. But the American train and equip program stumbled in fending off both AQAP and a rebellious faction known as the Houthis. The Houthis took their name from their onetime leader, Hussein al-Houthi. Comprised mainly from the Zaidi sect, an offshoot of Shiite Islam, the Houthis started an Iranian-backed insurgency in 2004 against the central government for greater autonomy in their northern homeland. Washington took aim at the al-Qaeda branch rather than Saleh's other enemies. The CIA, operating from a secret air base in Saudi Arabia, launched deadly drone airstrikes on several AQAP leaders as part of the American counterterrorism strategy.

Yemen fell into nationwide turmoil with the onset of the Arab Spring. Its strongman, Ali Abdullah Saleh, succumbed to the chaos and mayhem perpetrated by the Houthi rebels and AQAP after ruling the impoverished country for three decades. Sana'a's army and police, no matter how much US mentoring they received, were unable to cope with the double threat posed by the Houthis and AQAP fighters. Trying to calm his rebellious countrymen, Saleh picked his vice president to succeed him when he vacated the presidency in 2012. But Abed Rabbo Mansour Hadi fared no better. Indeed, Saleh executed an abrupt U-turn and made common cause with the Houthis against Hadi in a desperate comeback bid as the new president fled to Saudi Arabia.

So chaotic had Yemen become that Washington yanked out its embassy staff and even the Special Forces contingent, together with the CIA field operatives in spring 2015 (small military teams were re-inserted in 2016). The Arabian Peninsula country's debacle cast doubt on President Obama's counterterrorism tactics of kinetic drone operations and Special Forces to professionalize indigenous security forces. Since its application failed in Yemen, how could it be used proficiently in Iraq, Syria, Somalia, or elsewhere?[110] The tentative answer came with the realization that the White House offered no alternative solution.

Given its deep aversion to sliding into another Mideast war, the Obama presidency stuck to its overall disengagement policy. Getting governments in Riyadh, Baghdad, Erbil, Tripoli, or Kabul to pull the laboring oar in their own defense, by Obama's reckoning, spelled success for the United States. Skeptics assessed the US detachment as an abdication of leadership and a diminution of American power, influence, and prestige. They also perceived the wages of Washington's policies as a welter of future challenges as radical Islamist movements made territorial advances, sparked a spate of deadly terrorist attacks, and refugees flooded Europe. The unraveling of nations in the Middle East, nevertheless, was not the only active crisis begging for Washington's strategic attention.

Ukraine, Unconventional Warfare, and Unbridled Russia

Although lying within the heart of Europe, Ukraine also got little US backing when it fell prey to Russia's revanchist designs. Ukraine's plight worsened after the Russian Federation's abrupt annexation of its Crimean Peninsula with all the surprise of a black swan event. Russia's recovery of this former, imperial land called to mind the Novorossiya (New Russia) of the czarist past. America's focus momentarily shifted from the Syrian-Iraqi arena to Russia's swallowing the Crimea in March 2014 and then Moscow's subverting eastern Ukraine. Washington's attention snapped back to the Middle East with ISIS's lightning thrust deep into the bosom of Iraq and the capture of Mosul, the country's second largest city.

The two crises were connected despite their different circumstances. Moscow's takeover of Crimea impacted the Syrian conflict. The Kremlin's land grab of the Black Sea peninsula deepened Russia's rift with the West, almost guaranteeing its bolstering of President Assad's belligerency against the West. Indeed, the bonds between the two anti-Western states strengthened in the face of what they perceived as a battle against America's post-Cold War unilateralism, regime-change intrusions, and meddling in the affairs of other states. This bonding went beyond the foreign chancelleries to ordinary people, culture exchanges, and research institutes in the two nations.[111] For Damascus, Russian succor was only surpassed by the regime-saving resources from Iran, which included financing, military instruction, arms, and Hezbollah fighters from Lebanon.

Washington's reaction to Russian revanchist seizures first in Crimea and then Ukraine fell short of the magnitude of the threat posed to the post-Cold War order and stable boundaries within Eastern Europe. True to form, the United States reacted in a measured manner. Guided by the United States, the West Europeans pursued conferences, dialogue, and limited sanctions in response. Because of the Russian Federation's atomic arsenal, the West shrank from pressuring Moscow too hard. Negotiating parties on each side of the Ukrainian divide signed a string of accords and statements to bring about a cease-fire in the strife-ridden borderlands. But all the agreements ended with the resumption of gunfire and the death of over 10,000 people by the start of 2016. Instigated and aided by the Russian military, the Ukrainian separatists resumed their attacks on the central government's hapless army. Labeled "hybrid warfare," the Kremlin's slow-motion aggression relied on local insurgents who denied the presence of their powerful Russian benefactor. The Federation likewise denied involvement in Ukrainian fighting. The United States and its NATO partners offered meager military assistance. Despite bipartisan pleas from Congress to arm the Ukrainians with defensive weapons, the Obama administration dragged its feet, putting its faith in every targeted sanctions and verbal condemnations against Russian encroachments.

Against the Russian-orchestrated hybrid war, the United States first consulted with its NATO allies. Germany, Western Europe's lynchpin, proved to be preternaturally circumspect about defending Ukraine's territorial integrity. Angela Merkel stated that the eventual collapse of the Berlin Wall justified a stoic but pacifist stance toward Russia's thinly veiled invasion into eastern Ukraine. In the longer run of history, this Russian aggression, the German chancellor argued, would not prevail any more than had Soviet occupation of Eastern Europe. Thus, no military counteroffense should be mounted by the West. Still, the West took up its favorite weapon against Russia's hostile intervention; it adopted economic sanctions against Putin officials and cronies, prohibiting them from traveling and investing in the West. It also booted Russia from membership in the Group of eight major economic powers. These measures failed to convince Moscow to withhold aid to the Ukrainian separatists, although the Russian economy shrank.

Washington's direct assistance to Ukraine also faltered. Over the next several months, the United States offered $23 million in non-lethal assistance, including body armor, communications equipment, night-vision goggles, and food. Wags commented that America's lame answer to military aggression was MREs—Meals Ready to Eat—the unpalatable, prepared food for US troops in the field. The Pentagon withheld more powerful weapons, including much-desired anti-tank missiles.[112] Hoping to isolate Russia, Washington confronted Putin's further aggressiveness in eastern Ukraine in mid-2014 with additional sanctions on its own, since the West Europeans balked at hurting their lucrative economic ties with Moscow. The fresh economic punishments expanded the targets from wealthy oligarchs within Putin's ruling circle to the Federation's financial, defense, and energy giants. The Obama administration denied specific corporations, such as Rosneft (the largest oil producer), access to American capital markets, which impacted their ability to gain loans for business development.

France, Germany, and Russia made it clear that United States was not welcome at their negotiating table with Ukraine. They formed the Normandy format after a meeting on June 6, 2014, in France to commemorate the 70th anniversary of Operation Overlord on Normandy's beaches. The negotiators reached a peace agreement in February 2015 in Minsk, Belarus, that curbed the worst violence between Kiev's army and the Russian-aided separatist operating in southeastern Ukraine. This Minsk II accord passed a test in late June 2015 when the 28-member EU re-approved the economic sanctions, in spite of doubts about Moscow's future intentions.[113]

The different approaches adopted by the United States and Europe led to initial disharmony within the transatlantic alliance.[114] In time, the EC, which defines the EU's political directions, demanded that the European Investment Bank curtail financing for Federation projects. Gradually, Europe suspended other Russian investments. The Euro-American confluence on a common sanction regime eased their former taut relations regarding policy toward Russian aggrandizement.

The Russian Federation did not accept the West's economic warfare lying down. Moscow violated the 1987 landmark arms control accord between the two countries. By testing intermediate-range (from 300 to 3400 miles), ground-launched missiles, Moscow breached the treaty. The Russians broke the Intermediate-range Nuclear Forces Treaty (INF Treaty) by test-firing cruise missiles. The State Department raised further concerns about the Federation's violations of the Open Skies Treaty which allowed for observation flights by unarmed aircraft. It also called Moscow to account for its transgressing the Vienna Document which required notification to European governments when Russian forces massed in Central Europe, as they did along the Ukrainian border starting in 2014. The Kremlin countered that the US Aegis missile defense system being installed in Eastern Europe constituted a danger. Aimed at Iran's growing missile threat, Washington replied that the Aegis possessed only defensive, not offensive, capabilities; therefore it was permitted by the INF Treaty.[115]

Worries about Moscow's possible intervention into Poland and the Baltic States also brought together Americans and Europeans to address Russia's aggressive intentions. At the NATO summit in Wales in early September 2014, President Obama vowed to defend the Baltic nations' independence. The American leader urged his transatlantic partners to bolster Ukraine's security by leveling additional economic sanctions against Russia and by upping their defense spending to the agreed-upon 2 percent of their GDP.[116] Like its fellow NATO members, the United States stopped well short of granting Ukraine's pleas for armaments, especially short-range missiles and anti-tank weapons. Once again, European nations pledged to up their defense spending at the summer 2016 NATO summit, while the United States pledged a battalion for defense.

Continued Russian backing of the Ukrainian separatists' attacks prompted modest US countermeasures after months of dithering. The Pentagon dispatched 300 US Army paratroopers to train Ukrainian

National Guardsmen in April 2015. The six-month Fearless Guardian exercise was strictly restricted to training alone. At about the same time, the Defense Department also airlifted American paratroopers to the Republic of Georgia for a five-day, joint military exercise to train Georgian soldiers to participate in the NATO Response Force. Both US deployments elicited Moscow's condemnation for treading in its sphere. In the next year, the Pentagon planned to station a battalion in Poland to reassure a jittery Warsaw of US backing.

In the Middle East, President Obama's twin decision to—recommit troops and aircraft to Iraq and retain small numbers of US troops in Afghanistan—undercut his promise to end the wars he inherited but only slowed America's insular drift. Neither detour amounted to a full-fledged re-commitment of real US military power to address adequately terrorist scourge. In this minimalist stake, the president's actions resembled the boldly announced Asian pivot, a policy declaration with minimum political or military heft. Taken together with anemic countermeasures in Afghanistan, Libya, Iraq, and Syria, it signaled another step backward toward disengagement. Not strong-pointing the US presence in terrorist-embattled nations just invited and enabled jihadi attacks in the West.

The US-Iran Nuclear Deal

As the Obama presidency neared its conclusion, the United States struck a landmark nuclear weapons agreement with the Islamic Republic of Iran whereby Tehran pledged that its nuclear energy program would remain peaceful. The accord represented the culmination of fraught and prolonged negotiations over several years in which five major powers joined with Washington and Tehran for what were known as the P5+1 (this term refers to the Security Council's five permanent members, namely the United States, China, Britain, France, and Russia, plus Germany) talks with the Islamic Republic.

Concluded on July 14, 2015, the Joint Comprehensive Plan of Action (JCPOA) set forth the terms for Iran and the main world powers. In return for lifting seven separate sets of international sanctions imposed since 2006, mainly by the EU through the UN (American firms did little business with Iran at that point) on its economy, Iran agreed to suspend specific nuclear activities and to forgo the pursuit, development, or acquisition of nuclear arms for a minimum of ten years. Among the pared-back capabilities was Iran's reduction from 19,000 centrifuges, used for uranium enrichment to bomb-grade levels, to 6000. It consented to shipping more than 12 tons of low-enriched nuclear fuel—98 percent of Iran's total stockpile—out of the country. The Iranian regime accept other cuts in the production of uranium, including no construction of new enrichment facilities for 15 years and no use of its Fordow facility for enriching uranium, also for 15 years.

At the 11th hour, the JCPOA's inspection capacity was watered down. Up through April, just ten weeks prior to the deal's signing, the Obama administration touted tough-minded safeguards against the possibility of Iranian cheating. Washington officials claimed the agreement guaranteed inspections anytime and anywhere inside Iran. But this fail-safe stipulation was dropped from the final draft to win Tehran's acceptance, leaving observers fearful of a potential Iranian "sneakout" from the nuclear pact.

Additional provisions appeared to rein in Iran's decade-long quest for atomic weapons. Yet, the deal left Iran as a nuclear-threshold state with a relatively short breakout period for nuclear weapons. The breakout timeline—the time necessary to acquire enough fissile material for one nuclear warhead—rose to one year from the assessed 2–3 months at the time of the signing, according to US negotiators. The Vienna-signed agreement also called for the suspension of conventional arms and ballistic missile embargoes on Iran for five and eight years, respectively. Iran's acceptance of the JCPOA terms provided it roughly $100 in impounded money, mostly from past oil sales. Critics argued that these monies were destined to fund Iran's regional subversive and hegemonic activities through proxies like Hezbollah, Hamas, and related militias in Iraq and Afghanistan. The Obama government insisted that it would react sternly to the expansion of Iranian imperialism or revolutionary Shiite Islam into nearby countries.

The agreement, which the White House never called a treaty, touched off a firestorm of opposition from Republican and some Democratic opponents as well as not a few US-based, pro-Israel lobbyists. Israel itself, under Prime Minister Benjamin Netanyahu, also embarked on a high-profile, anti-agreement campaign at the UN and in the United States.[117] The skeptics, who despised and distrusted the mullah-headed Iranian regime, doggedly fought acceptance. They noted the long-standing and deep trust deficit with Iranian rulers, a few of whom had been party to the 1979 takeover of the US Embassy in Tehran, the 1983 truck-bombing deaths of 241 American servicemen in Beirut, or the killing of nearly 200 US soldiers and Marines by the so-called special groups in eastern Iraq during the American occupation. These opponents were distrustful because the agreement outsourced responsibility for nuclear inspections inside Iran to the International Atomic Energy Agency. The anti-agreement voices raised many serious flaws in the 159-page document.[118] But their arguments came to naught.

The Obama administration easily outmaneuvered the opposition, although its Congressional opponents played with a weak hand from the beginning because the White House refused to deem the formal agreement as a treaty, which required two-thirds approval in the US Senate. It handled the nuclear deal as an executive agreement, which is usually reserved for minor or temporary matters rather than significant international obligations. Moreover, the political opponents lacked enough votes in the Senate and House for veto-proof majorities to prevail against the executive branch's proposed sanction relief for Iran.

The Oval Office played a clever game. From the start, it insisted that either the US entered into the accord or war with Iran was certain. The opponents, therefore, were placed in the position of being pro-war. As for tactics, the administration went first to the Security Council where it easily secured a unanimous endorsement of the accord less than a week after the foreign ministers signed it in the Austrian capital. Days later, European companies began entering into business deals with their Iranian counterparts. Iranian and European firms hastened to conclude their own business deals before the JCPOA became law in the United States. Once opened, these commercial dams posed little prospect of ever being closed down again. The consummation of the nuclear deal, therefore, became inevitable. Congress did vote but the outcome was a forgone certainty that the agreement would enter into force. What is far from a forgone conclusion is whether Iran, a pariah nation for decades, will dutifully abide by the provisions of the accord. Only history will reveal the answer to that question.

For the White House, the over-arching purpose of the nuclear agreement always lay well beyond only curbing Iran's nuclear arms capacity. Its ambitions were greater than just détente with Iran. The accord entailed a larger, geopolitical transformation in the Persian Gulf. It encompassed the goal of re-integrating Iran into the global comity of nations as a peaceful power. Since taking the keys to the Oval Office, Barack Obama wanted détente with Iran. His striving for a historic rapprochement with the Islamic Republic signified another form of his retrenchment of American power, although detractors interpreted it as merely crass legacy building.

One close observer of the Mideast scene suggested that the administration desire for the Iran deal "stems from fatigue at the prospect of confronting another enemy in a region that seems to confound us."[119]

Still more important to President Obama was the US retrenchment that the agreement afforded him to initiate from an epicenter of turbulence and bloodshed. One of the chief White House architects of the Iran accord allowed that the primary rationale for the deal centered on disentangling the United States from alliances with Saudi Arabia, Israel, Turkey, and Egypt to pave the way for wholesale disengagement from the Middle East.[120] Such re-alignment would be truly historic and transformative for the United States.

Can the United States walk away from the expanse stretching from Casablanca to Kabul via the Iran nuclear deal? It seems unlikely at this point. Commenting on the Iran agreement, two elder statesmen wrote: "Some advocates have suggested that the agreement can serve as a way to dissociate America from Middle East conflicts, culminating in the military retreat from the region initiated by the current administration." The former top officials went on to speculate: "rather than enabling American disengagement from the Middle East, the nuclear framework is more likely to necessitate deepening involvement there—on complex new terms."[121] That speculation hovered over the far-reaching agreement which went into force on the so-called Implementation Day in mid-January 2016. It was accompanied by prisoner swaps between the United States and Iran and the return of ten American sailors whose two small boats inadvertently strayed into Iranian waters.

How permanent or how successful Barack Obama's policy of disengagement and retrenchment will be remains to be seen. The future always evaluates the past, just as the future remembers the past in fashioning response to present circumstances. An interim judgment notes the significance of Obama's half-retreat from projecting US military power overseas. He departed from previous administrations in seeing American exceptionalism as but a license for messianic illusions justifying military interventions. In reality, President Obama's pivot was not toward Asia but toward domestic issues. History may interpret Obama's pullbacks as opening vacuums and signaling weakness to aggressive powers ready to fill political voids or to take advantage of hesitancy in their adversaries. Or, history might smile on Obama's judgments at the right decision at the right time to spare America needless, bloody wars and costly financial drains in desert sands. Only time will tell.

Notes

1. Vali Nasr, *The Dispensable Nation: American Foreign Policy in Retreat* (New York: Doubleday, 2013), p. 159.
2. Helene Cooper, "Hagel Resigns Under Pressure as Global Crises Test Pentagon," *New York Times*, November 24, 2014, p. A 1.
3. David J. Rothkopf, *National Insecurity: American Leadership in an Age of Fear* (New York: Public Affairs, 2014), pp. 206, 275.
4. Peter Baker, "A Biden Challenge to Clinton Would Expose a Policy Split," *New York Times*, October 10, 2015, p. A 1.
5. Leon Panetta, *Worthy Fights: A Memoir of Leadership in War and Peace* (New York: Penguin Press, 2014), pp. 231–232 and 448–450.
6. Robert M. Gates, *Duty: Memoirs of A Secretary at War* (New York: Alfred A. Knopf, 2014), p. 587.
7. Joby Warrick, "U.S. Leaned on Bahrain To Show Restraint," *Washington Post*, February 20, 2011, p. A 15.
8. Kana Makiya, "The Arab Spring Started in Iraq," Sunday Review, *New York Times*, April 7, 2013, p. SR 7.
9. James Lacey and Williamson Murray, *Moment of Battle: The Twenty Clashes that Changed the World* (New York: Bantam, 2013), p. 407.
10. Paul Danahar, *The New Middle East: The World after the Arab Spring* (London: Bloomsbury, 2013), pp. 21–31.
11. Karen DeYoung, "U.S. Now Hopes For Earlier Exit By Mubarak," *Washington Post*, February 1, 2011, p. A 1.
12. Paul Richter and Peter Nicholas, "U.S. Open To A Role For Islamists," *Los Angeles Times*, February 1, 2011, p. A 1.
13. Thomas H. Henriksen, *America and the Rogue States* (New York: Palgrave, 2012), pp. 146–154.
14. For article disputing the conventional view of Qaddafi's heavy-handed reaction to civil strife, see Alan J. Kuperman, "A Model Humanitarian Intervention?: Reassessing NATO's Libya Campaign," *International Security*, 38, no. 1 (Summer 2013), pp. 105–136.
15. David D. Kirkpatrick, "Qaddafi Brutalizes Foes, Armed Or Defenseless," *New York Times*, March 5, 2011, p. A 11.
16. Hillary Rodham Clinton, *Hard Choices* (New York: Simon & Schuster, 2014), p. 370.
17. David E. Sanger and Thom Shanker, "Gates Warns of Risks Of A No-Flight Zone," *New York Times*, March 3, 2011, p. A 1.

18. Greg Jaffe, "In One Final Address to Army, Gates Describes Vision for Military's Future," *Washington Post*, February 26, 2011, p. A 1.
19. Robert M. Gates, *Duty: Memoirs of a Secretary of State at War* (New York: Alfred A. Knopf, 2014), pp. 514–516.
20. David E. Sanger, *Confront and Conceal: Obama's Secret War and Surprising Use of American Power* (New York: Crown Publishers, 2012), pp. 339–40 and 342–344.
21. Mark Landler, "Obama Tells Qaddafi To Quit And Authorizes Refugee Airlifts," *New York Times*, March 4, 2011, p. A 11.
22. Richard Leiby and Scott Wilson, "Arab League's Backing Of No-Fly Zone Over Libya Ramps Up Pressure On West," *Washington Post*, March 13, 2011, p. A 1.
23. Luke Glanville, *Sovereignty and the Responsibility to Protect* (Chicago: University of Chicago Press, 2014), pp. 108, 209, 178–189, and 205–211.
24. Karen DeYoung, "U.S. Takes On Support Role As Allies Mobilize For No-Fly Zone," *Washington Post*, March 19, 2011, p. A. 11.
25. Peter Nicholas, "U.S. Urges Tough Libya Action," *Los Angeles Times*, March 17, 2011, p. A 1.
26. Kathy Lally and Will Englund, "What Lies Behind Putin's Anti-American Turnabout," *Washington Post*, September 15, 2013, p. A 9.
27. Somini Sengupta, "Russia Has Reservations On Push for Naval Action," *New York Times*, September 16, 2016, p. A 6.
28. Elisabeth Bumiller and David D. Kirkpatrick, "NATO Agrees To Take Command Of No-Fly Zone in Libya," *New York Times*, March 25, 2011, p. A 9.
29. The White House, "Remarks by the President in Address to the Nation on Libya," March 28, 2011. Downloaded from https://www.whitehouse.gov/the-press-office/2011/03/28/remarks-president-address-nation-libya. Accessed July 20, 2016.
30. Helen Cooper, "Obama Cites Limits Of U.S. Role in Libya," *New York Times*, March 29, 2011, p. A 1.
31. Ryan Lizza, "Leading From Behind," *New Yorker*, April 26, 2011, p. 26.
32. James Mann, *The Obamians: The Struggle Inside the White House to Redefine American Power* (New York: Viking, 2012), p. 294.
33. Stephen Sestanovitch, *Maximalist: America in the World From Truman To Obama* (New York: Alfred A. Knopf, 2014), p. 317.

34. See the editorial, "A Strategy of Slowness?" *Washington Post*, May 1, 2011, p. A 22.
35. James Dao and Dalia Sussman, "Bin Laden Raid gives President Big Lift In Poll," *New York Times*, May 5, 2011, p. A 1.
36. Richard Miniter, *Leading From Behind* (New York: St. Martin's Griffen, 2013), p. 116.
37. For a flattering picture of Barack Obama's handling of the Osama bin Laden mission, see Mark Bowden, *The Finish: The Killing of Osama bin Laden* (New York: Atlantic Monthly Press, 2012), pp. 198–208.
38. Remarks by President Obama in Address to the Nation from Afghanistan, May 1, 2012. Downloaded from https://www.whitehouse.gov/the-press-office/2012/05/01/remarks-president-obama-address-nation-afghanistan. Accessed July 20, 2016.
39. Mann, *The Obamians*, pp. 293–294.
40. Christopher S. Chivvis, *Toppling Qaddafi: Libya and the Limits of Intervention* (New York: Cambridge University Press, 2014), pp. 173–178.
41. Ibid., pp. 299–301.
42. Michael Morell, *The Great War Of Our Time: The CIA's Fight Against Terrorism—From al Qa'ida to ISIS* (New York: Hachette Book Group, 2015), p. 206.
43. Select Committee on Benghazi, U.S. House of Representatives. Downloaded from https://benghazi.house.gov/. Accessed July 20, 2016.
44. Paul Richter and Christi Parsons, "U.S. intervention in Libya now seen as cautionary tale," *Los Angeles Times*, June 27, 2014, p. A 1.
45. Sestanovitch, *Maximalist*, p. 317.
46. Peter Baker, "A Biden Challenge to Clinton Would Expose a Policy Split," *New York Times*, October 10, 2015, p. A 1.
47. Helene Cooper and Steven Lee Myers, "U.S. Tactics In Libya May Be A Model For Other Efforts," *New York Times*, August 29, 2011, p. A 9.
48. James Glanz and John Markoff, "Internet Detour around Censors," *New York Times*, June 12, 2011, p. A 1.
49. Fouad Ajami, *The Syrian Rebellion* (Stanford, CA: Hoover Institution Press, 2012), pp. 153–155.
50. Henriksen, *America and the Rogue States*, pp. 169–171.

51. Amir Taheri, *The Persian Night: Iran Under the Khomeinist Revolution* (New York: Encounter Books, 2009), pp. 245–251.
52. Ajami, *The Syrian Rebellion*, p. 76.
53. Mark Landler, "Unrest in Syria And Jordan Poses New Test For U.S. Policy," *New York Times*, March 27, 2011, p. A 1.
54. Mark Landler, "U.S. Takes Cautious Steps Over Crackdown by Syria," *New York Times*, April 30, 2011, p. A 1.
55. Liz Sly and Joby Warrick, "U.S. Assails Assad, Says He Has Lost 'Legitimacy,'" *Washington Post*, July 12, 2011, p. A 1.
56. Clinton, *Hard Choices*, pp. 463–464.
57. Mark Mazzetti, "C.I.A. Study of Covert Aid Fueled Skepticism About Helping Syrian Rebels," *New York Times*, October 14, 2014, p. A 1.
58. Jim Michaels and Oren Dorell, "U.S. Aid Helping Wrong Side," *U.S.A. Today*, July 11, 2013, p. A 1.
59. Adam Entous, Nour Malas, and Margaret Coker, "A Veteran Saudi Power Player Works To Build Support To Topple Assad," *Wall Street Journal*, August 26, 2013, p. A 1.
60. Adam Entous, "Covert CIA Mission to Arm Syrian Rebels Goes Awry," *Wall Street Journal*, January 27, 2015, p. A 1.
61. Siobhan Hughes, "House Backs Aid to Fight Islamic State," *Wall Street Journal*, September 18, 2014, p. A 4 and Jonathan Weisman and Jeremy W. Peters, "Congress Gives Final Approval to Aid rebels in Fight With ISIS," *New York Times*, September 18, 2014, p. A 1.
62. Matthew Rosenberg, "U.S. Trains Syrian Rebels in Jordan to Fight ISIS," *New York Times*, May 7, 2015, p. A 8.
63. Raja Abdulrahm, "Rebels in Syria Coordinate to Capture Base," *Wall Street Journal*, April 28, 2015, p. A 11.
64. For a clear dissection of President Obama's "red line" statements and later his retraction, see Glenn Kessler, "President Obama and the 'red line' on Syria's chemical weapons," *Washington Post*, September 6, 2013, p. A 19.
65. Ibid.
66. C.J. Chivers, "Rebel Brutality in Syria Posing Dilemma in West," *New York Times*, September 5, 2013, p. A 1.
67. Kessler, "President Obama and the 'red line' on Syria's chemical weapons," p. A 19.
68. Stephen F. Hayes, "The Hawk's Case Against Obama On Syria," *Wall Street Journal*, September 5, 2013, p. A 15.

69. Leon Panetta, *Worthy Fights* (New York: Penguin Press, 2014), p. 450.
70. Sestanovich, *Maximalist*, p. 319.
71. Karen De Young, "Kerry: Saudis Support Strike," *Washington Post*, September 9, 2013, p. A 1.
72. Susan Page, "Public Opposition To Airstrikes Surges," *USA Today*, September 10, 2013, p. 1.
73. Zachary A. Goldfarb and David Nakamura, "Obama Takes Syria Case To People," *Washington Post*, September 11, 2015, p. A 1.
74. Ben Hubbard, "Second Team of Weapons Experts to Head to Syria," *New York Times*, October 8, 2013, p. A 8.
75. William Branigin, "Agency: Last of Syria's chemical weapons handed over destruction," *Washington Post*, June 23, 2014, p. A 8.
76. Naftali Bendavid, "U.S. Accuses Syria of New Uses of Chemical Arms," *Wall Street Journal*, May 9, 2014, p. A 5.
77. Anne Barnard, "Syrian Rebels Say Saudi Arabia Is Stepping Up Weapons," *New York Times*, September 13, 2013, p. A 11.
78. Greg Miller, "CIA ramping up covert training program for moderate Syrian rebels," *Washington Post*, October 2, 2013, p. A 10.
79. Maria Abi-Habib, "Europeans Spies Reach Out to Syria," *Wall Street Journal*, January 14, 2014, p. A 9.
80. Max Fisher, "Obama explains his thinking on Syria and it is profoundly conservative," *Washington Post*, January 21, 2014, p. A 10.
81. For an examination of the rivalry, see Michael Weiss and Hassan Hassan, *ISIS: Inside the Army of Terror* (New York: Regan Arts, 2015), pp. 179–197.
82. Ellen Knickmeyer, "Syrian Rebels Press Fight Against al Qaeda," *Wall Street Journal*, January 7, 2014, p. A 7.
83. Rothkopf, *National Insecurity*, pp. 305–306, Yasir Ghazi and Christine Hauser, "Violence In Iraq Swells At Year's End Leaving At Least 3 Dozen Dead," *New York Times*, January 1, 2013, p. A 8, and Editorial, "U.S. Inaction in Syria Could Be Far More Costly Than Intervention," *Washington Post*, December 17, 2013, p. A 27.
84. Barack Obama, "Remarks by the President at the United States Military Academy Commencement Ceremony," May 28, 2014. Downloaded from http://search.tb.ask.com/search/GGmain.jhtml?searchfor=Remarks+by+the+President+at+the+United+States+Military+Academy+Commencement+Ceremony&tpr=hpsb&p2=

%5EUX%5Exdm423%5ES11476%5Eus&n=780CEAFE&st=hp&qs=&ptb=7ED50CF6-EE87-4BD1-89BE-00B315831DBE&si=250652_Map-Display-PC-FF-IE. Accessed July 20, 2016.
85. Cited in Peter Baker, "Rebutting Critics, Obama Seeks Higher Bar for Military Action," *New York Times*, May 29, 2014, p. A 8.
86. John Bolton, "Doubling Down on a Muddled Foreign Policy," *Wall Street Journal*, May 29, 2014, p. A 15.
87. Editorial, "President Obama misses a chance on foreign affairs," *New York Times*, May 29, 2014, p. A 30.
88. President Barack Obama, Letter from the President—Authorization for the Use of United States Armed Forces in connection with the Islamic State of Iraq and the Levant, February 11, 2015. Downloaded from https://www.whitehouse.gov/the-press-office/2015/02/11/letter-president-authorization-use-united-states-armed-forces-connection. Accessed July 20, 2016.
89. Matthew C. Weed, A New Authorization for Use of Military Force Against the Islamic State: Issues and Current Proposals in Brief, Congressional Research Service, February 20, 2015. Downloaded from https://www.fas.org/sgp/crs/natsec/R43760.pdf. Accessed July 20, 2016.
90. Emma Sky, *The Unraveling: High Hopes and Missed Opportunities in Iraq* (New York: Public Affairs, 2015), pp. 311–13, 317–318, and 322.
91. David D. Kirkpatrick and Michael R. Gordon, "Kerry Says Administration Is Ready to Renew Ties With Egypt, a Year After Takeover," *New York Times*, June 23, 2014, p. A 6.
92. Helene Cooper, "Obama Allows Limited Airstrikes on ISIS," *New York Times*, August 7, 2014, p. A 1.
93. David Remnick, "Going the Distance: On and off the road with Barack Obama," *New Yorker*, January 27, 2014, p. 43.
94. Jonathan Weisman, "McCain Says Limited U.S. Strikes on Militants in Iraq Are Not Enough," *New York Times*, August 9, 2014, p. A 11.
95. Barack Obama, Statement from the White House, September 10, 2014. Downloaded from https://www.whitehouse.gov/the-press-office/2014/09/10/statement-president-isil-1. Accessed July 20, 2016.
96. Peter Baker, "Diplomatic Note Promises Immunity From Iraqi Law for U.S. Advisory Troops," *New York Times*, June 26, 2014, p. A 10.

97. Julian E. Barnes and Carol E. Lee, "Obama Tightens Grip on Strikes," *Wall Street Journal*, September 18, 2014, p. A 1.
98. Tim Arango and Thomas Erdbrink, "U.S. and Iran Both Attack ISIS, But Try Not to Look Like Allies," *New York Times*, December 4, 2014, p. A 1.
99. Anne Barnard and Somini Sengupta, "U.S. Signals Shift On How To End Syrian Civil War," *New York Times*, January 20, 2015, p. A 1.
100. Michael R. Gordon, "Kurdish Leader Agrees to Accept Arms on U.S. Terms in Fight Against ISIS," *New York Times*, May 9, 2015, p. A 8.
101. Mark Mazzetti and Eric Schmitt, "Obama's 'Boots on the Ground': U.S. Special Forces Are Sent to Tackle Global Threats," *New York Times*, December 27, 2015, p. A 1.
102. Peter Beinart, "Actually, Obama Does Have a Strategy in the Middle East," *The Atlantic*, August 28, 2014. Downloaded from http://www.theatlantic.com/international/archive/2014/08/actually-obama-does-have-a-strategy-in-the-middle-east/379368. Accessed July 20, 2016.
103. Karen DeYoung and Missy Ryan, "Fall of Ramadi raises new questions about U.S. strategy in Iraq," *Washington Post*, May 19, 2015, p. A 1.
104. "Global Coalition to Degrade and Defeat ISIL," Department of State site. Downloaded from http://search.state.gov/search?q=Global+Coalition+to+Degrade+and+Defeat+ISIL&site=state_en_stategov&client=state_en_stategov&output=xml:no_dtd&proxystylesheet=state_en_stategov&filter=0&entqr=3&lr=lang_en&oe=utf8&ie=utf8&getfields=*&search-button=Search. Accessed July 20, 2016.
105. Carol E. Lee, "U.S. Presses for World to Act," *Wall Street Journal*, September 25, 2014, p. A 1.
106. Peter Baker, "As World Boils, Fingers Point Obama's Way," *New York Times*, August 15, 2014, p. A 1.
107. Janet Hook and Carol E. Lee, "WSJ/NBC Poll: Almost Two-Thirds Back Attacking Militants," *Wall Street Journal*, September 10, 2014, p. A 6.
108. Michael R. Gordon and Eric Scmitt, "Former U.S. Commander Sharply Criticizes Syria Policy," *New York Times*, September 23, 2015, p. A 4.

109. Mark Mazzetti and Eric Schmitt, "In Secret, Obama Extends U.S. Role in Afghan Combat," *New York Times*, November 22, 2014, p. A 1.
110. Maria Abi-Habib, "Yemen Exposes Difficulties in U.S. Strategy," *Wall Street Journal*, December 4, 2014, p. A 13.
111. Anne Barnard, "Russian Defiance Is Seen as a Confidence Builder for Syria's Government," *New York Times*, March 21, 2014, p. A 8.
112. David M. Herszenhorn, "Ukraine Military Fids Its Footing Against Pro-Russian Rebels," *New York Times*, July 6, 2014, p. A 8.
113. Neil MacFarquhar, "American Envoy to Hold Talks With Russians on Peace Deal for Ukraine," *New York Times*, May 18, 2015, p. A 8.
114. Peter Baker and James Kanter, "Raising Stakes On Russia, U.S. Adds Sanctions," *New York Times*, July 16, 2014, p. A 1.
115. Michael R. Gordon, "U.S. Says Russia Fails to Correct Violation of Landmark 1987 Arms Control Deal," *New York Times*, June 6, 2015, p. A 6.
116. Colleen McCain Nelson, "U.S. Vows NATO Defense of Baltics," *Wall Street Journal*, September 4, 2014, p. A 8.
117. Laurence Norman and Kristina Peterson, "Iran Deal Ignites Fierce Fight," *Wall Street Journal*, July 15, 2015, p. A 1.
118. Bret Stephens, "The Iran Deal's Collapsing Rationale," *Wall Street Journal*, July 21, 2015, p. A 11 and David B. Rivkin Jr. and Lee A. Casey, "The Lawless Underpinnings of the Iran Nuclear Deal," *Wall Street Journal*, July 27, 2015, p. A 13.
119. Neil Rogachevsky, "Agents of Their Own Destiny," *Wall Street Journal*, September 25, 2015, p. A 15.
120. David Samuel's "The Aspiring Novelist Who Became Obama's Foreign-Policy Guru," *New York Times Magazine*, May 5, 2016, p. 14.
121. Henry Kissinger and George Shultz, "The Iran Deal and Its Consequences," *Wall Street Journal*, April 8, 2015, p. A 13.

CHAPTER 10

Observations on the Cycles in US Foreign Policy

"History repeats itself, but only in outline and in the large" —Will and Ariel Durant, The Lessons of History

"By liberalizing the mind, by deepening the sympathies, by fortifying the will, history enables us to control not society but ourselves—a much more important thing, it prepares us to live more humanely in the present and to meet rather than foretell the future." —Carl Becker, American historian

The conclusion reached in this volume is that the US foreign policy pendulum's yawing between cycles of interventionism and retrenchment generally conformed to a president's tenure in office. Each president came into office determined to zig where his predecessor zagged. Each strove to avoid the pitfalls of the preceding White House occupant. All these factors, and more, go a long way to explain the ebbs and flows in America's internationalism. Little wonder, then, that US foreign policy went through the cycles described in this work as alternating pendulum-like between intervention and retrenchment.

Each president, in fact, campaigned for office with a set of foreign policy prescriptions. They can be as simple as to do the opposite of his predecessor. Certainly, Barack Obama stepped into the Oval Office determined to be the un-Bush president.[1] The same observation could be written about the incoming George W. Bush administration, which set about to be different from the Bill Clinton government.[2] But there are deeper

T.H. Henriksen, *Cycles in US Foreign Policy since the Cold War*,
DOI 10.1007/978-3-319-48640-6_10

reasons than just the personal considerations of the commanders-in-chief to implement differing policies from their predecessors. The political parties, which each president headed, greatly contributed to the philosophies embraced by American leaders.

These factors underline the importance of the presidential political party, the president's own foreign policy views, and the sentiments of the voting coalition assembled to win the White House.

Politics and party ideology predisposed presidents to adopt a particular international course. American political parties have agendas and ideology upon which their candidates run for office. Once elected, presidents can make—and have made—decisions contrary to their party's political platform or against the preferences of its core voters for a variety of reasons. They are not rigidly bound by party statements or even campaign pledges. International circumstances might demand recalibration of earlier positions. Thus, White House residents can modify or refute their own international bearings or their party's orthodoxy. In this volume, these directional changes and their rationale have been described for each of the four post-Cold War presidencies.

The two major US political parties hold dissimilar, even conflicting, visions for American foreign policy, as was noted in the Introduction. During the post-Cold War years, the Democratic Party attracted voters due to its "trademark focus on economic and social problems at home."[3] Antiwar voters flocked to the Democratic Party also. In fact, self-identified Democrats turned out for antiwar demonstrations because they vehemently opposed the Iraq War and loathed President George W. Bush for starting it. When President Obama took office and assumed direction for the wars in Iraq and Afghanistan, Democratic voters followed the party's lead "away from the issue of war and toward other highly salient agenda items, such as health care."[4] Barack Obama's disengagement and retrenchment more or less jived with the feelings of mainline Democrats and antiwar constituents, while incurring steady Republican objections for his tepidness. Only the American president's widespread use of drone strikes outside the war zones in the Middle East raised anemic opposition among a segment of his party's members.

For the Republican Party, the Vietnam era was a watershed for its outlook and prospective policies. Some Republicans considered the Democratic Party as "unpatriotic and prone to treason" for its leaving a generation of young Americans face down in the Vietnamese mud.[5] While the Republicans did not hold the White House until 1969, they took over the patriotic mantle when so many Democratic voices denounced American involvement in the war. Since Vietnam, the Republicans could be counted on to invest more funds in defense for advanced ships and planes than their political opponents. The Reagan administration spent abundantly on the Pentagon, the weaponry from which handily won the conventional phases in the Persian Gulf, Afghanistan, and Iraq wars while suffering relatively minor casualties.

The perceptions of the two major parties exerted an outsized influence on the respective presidencies, at least as each came into office. Subsequent events and public sentiments at home can serve to reverse the initial course. When the electorate judged both Bush senior and junior as spending a disproportionate amount of American resources on overseas military interventions, they signaled their displeasure in opinion polls, protests, and elections. Both the Clinton and the Obama political campaigns benefited from voters' disenchantment with the international focus of the incumbents. The worsening economies under the two Bush administrations also played a part in their low end-of-term poll numbers. In a case of supreme irony, Bush campaigned against the Clinton-Gore overuse of US military forces in Somalia, Haiti, Bosnia, and Kosovo for humanitarian purposes. Obviously, as president, Bush greatly changed his mind when he championed military policies against Iraq as well as Afghanistan.

The White House residents were not doctrinally bound by their campaign pledges or post-campaign statements. Presidents have long enjoyed more latitude in making foreign policy than in legislating change in domestic affairs. When trying to pass and implement domestic policies, presidents face legislative roadblocks requiring compromises and dealmaking with House and Senate members in time-consuming and complex ways unnecessary in many foreign initiatives. A president does have to rely on the US Senate to ratify treaties; but the executive branch can bypass the legislative branch and enter into mere agreements with foreign nations, as Bill Clinton did with North Korea on its nuclear program and as Barack Obama did with Iran over its nuclear weapons ambitions. Congress alone can declare war, and it must also pass legislation to fund wars. But presidents have committed troops and circumvented constraints in the Constitution and the War Powers Act, which attempted to restrain presidential military ventures in the post-Vietnam era.[6] In short, presidents enjoy greater freedom in the international domain than in domestic policy, opening the way for cycler foreign policies.

Historical Predictor?

Politicians and other observers are nearly united in seeing benefits derived from historical knowledge. Some admiringly quote George Santayana's famous admonition—"those who do not remember the past are condemned to repeat it."[7] That said, professional historians—almost down to the lowliest lecturer—are dubious over any proposition espousing the replication of historical events. Rather, they argue that each historical incident is unique. They see no universal laws of history as there are laws of physics. Revolutions, wars, or flourishing empires may experience similar elements. For instance, Crane Brinton identified in his *Anatomy of Revolution* the life cycle of revolutions from the fever of radicalism to a Thermidorian period of some moderation. The English, French, American, and Russian revolutions might share "uniformities" while retaining their respective distinctiveness.[8] This acknowledgment of similarities, however, stands light years away from the kind of exactness that permits prediction or much less prophesies of future historical courses.

Some historians scoff at the notion of history teaching humankind anything. One well-regarded historian wrote: "history, whatever its value in educating the judgment, teaches no 'lessons,' and professional historians will be as skeptical of those who claim that it does as professional doctors are of their colleagues who peddle patent medicines guaranteeing instant cures. Historians may claim to teach lessons, and often they teach very wisely. But 'history' as such does not."[9]

Each major historical event has so many dissimilarities to ever be a carbon copy of other notable incidents. So, when this author writes of circular ebbs and flows of American's engagement of and disengagement from world affairs, he adopts the broadest notion about pendulum swings. Engagement, intervention, and even international entanglements are broadly descriptive of overseas activism, characterized by military action or focused diplomatic pressure directed at another power. Something similar can be written about disengagement, withdrawal, and disentanglement from foreign affairs, which are typified by routine economic and normal political intercourse.

Besides, some American foreign policy is far too complex to arbitrarily assign every action into category of either engagement or disengagement. In short, some individual action will defy the general classification of a particular administration. For example, the Clinton administration, while generally conflict-averse, still managed to send military forces to Bosnia and Kosovo to alleviate suffering and restore order. The George W. Bush government, for that matter, went to war easily in Afghanistan and Iraq but held back on military action against Iran or to counter Russia's armed attacks against the Republic of Georgia. Thus, the overall predisposition of an administration's policies form the basis for seeing it prone either to intervene or to retrench internationally despite a few exceptions to the main trend.

Back to the Future?

In his foreword, Frank Klingberg wrote that cyclical trends "appear to guide and limit policy-makers."[10] This is more than a reasonable assumption, since presidents and their administrations take into account previous governments' policies when they formulate their plans. Klingberg also thought that policy cyclicity "should present an additional element in the interpretation of past events." Otherwise put, historians, students, or policy makers should factor into their understanding of what has gone before the concept of rotational alterations in history or human actions. No harm is done by considering the ebb and flow of historical actions when contemplating new initiatives. Finally, Klingberg boldly concluded that cycles are an important element in "the prediction of likely directions for the future."[11] This hardly seems an outlandish predisposition to greet a new Washington administration. It will, after all, be judged by the media, pundits, and eventually historians against what its immediate predecessor did overseas.

It seems likely—but hardly foreordained—that the next presidential administration will tilt toward greater international engagement than Barack Obama's policies. There is no iron law determining such a forecast, and there can be no evidence produced justifying the claim or to disprove it. But the high probability exists that a future American government will find it necessary to reverse President Obama's decided retrenchment. Indeed, Obama's last year in office has already witnessed a reversal of his earlier desire to withdraw all US military forces from Afghanistan and Iraq. He has also re-committed a small, armed presence to Iraq, retained slightly less than 10,000 military personnel in Afghanistan, and even committed "less than 50" SOF to the Syrian conflict. These decisions flowed from necessity. Had he stuck rigidly to his campaign pledges, it is safe to state that these countries would have seen even greater gains by Islamist or Taliban insurgents. The White House's less than initially robust countermoves to the radical Islamist inroads may necessitate the next administration to pick up the defense in Iraq and especially Afghanistan. At this junction, it appears that the conflict with violent extremist groups will persist for decades and that Russia and China will continue to clash, if not war, with the United States over contending interests.

What remains unknown at this moment is how vigorous US counterterrorism will be and whether it and American foreign policy in general toward Moscow and Beijing will alternate toward greater engagement or disengagement. So long as the United States remains a great power, the strong possibility exists that future governments will find themselves engaging and disengaging the world at fairly regular turns to match circumstances and capabilities. Yet it is wise to conclude that Clio, history's muse, is full of the unexpected and scornful of predictions.[12]

Notes

1. Mann, *The Obamians*, pp. 337–338.
2. Mann, *Rise Of The Vulcans*, p. 293.
3. Witcover, *Party of the People*, p. 732.
4. Michael T. Heaney and Fabio Rojas, *Party in the Street: The Antiwar Movement and the Democratic Party after 9/11* (New York: Cambridge University Press, 2015), p. 128.
5. Lewis L. Gould, *The Republicans: A History of the Grand Old Party* (New York: Oxford University Press, 2014), p. 259.
6. Mariah Zeisburg, *War Powers: The Politics of Constitutional Authority* (Princeton, NJ: Princeton University Press, 2013), pp. 222–260 and Louis Fisher, *Presidential War Power* (Lawrence, KS: University of Kansas, 3rd rev ed., 2013), pp. 306–312.
7. George Santayana, *The Life of Reason: Reason in Commonsense* (New York: Scribner, 1954), p. 284.
8. Crane Brinton, *The Anatomy of Revolution* (New York: Vintage, 1965), pp. 270–274.
9. Michael Howard, *The Lessons of History* (New Haven, CT: Yale University Press, 1881), p. 11.
10. Klingberg, *Trends in American Foreign Policy Moods*, p. 15.
11. Ibid., p. xiii
12. Franklin L. Ford, *Political Murder: From Tyrannicide to Terrorism* (Cambridge, MA: Harvard University Press, 1985), p. 180.

Bibliography

The 9/11 Commission Report: Final Report of the National Commission on Terrorist Attacks Upon The United States. New York: W.W. Norton, 2004.

Ajami, Fouad. *The Syrian Rebellion.* Stanford, CA: Hoover Institution Press, 2012.

Albright, Madeleine. *Madam Secretary.* New York: Miramax Books, 2003.

Allawi, Ali A. *Faisal I of Iraq.* New Haven, CT: Yale University Press, 2014.

———. *The Occupation of Iraq: Winning the War, Losing the Peace.* New Haven, CT: Yale University Press, 2007.

Allison, Graham, and Philip Zelikow. *Essence of Decision: Explaining the Cuban Missile Crisis.* New York: Longman, 1999.

Asmus, Ronald D. *A Little War That Shook The World.* New York: Palgrave Macmillan, 2010.

Atkinson, Rick. *Crusade: The Untold Story of the Persian Gulf War.* Boston: Houghton Mifflin, 1993.

Bacevich, Andrew. *The Limits of Power: The End of American Exceptionalism.* New York: Metropolitan Books, 2008.

Baker, James A., III. *The Politics of Diplomacy: Revolution, War, and Peace, 1989–1992.* New York: G.P. Putnam's Sons, 1995.

Barfield, Thomas. *Afghanistan: A Cultural and Political History.* Princeton, NJ: Princeton University Press, 2010.

Barnett, Michael. *Eyewitness to a Genocide: The United Nations and Rwanda.* Ithaca, NY: Cornell University Press, 2002.

Benjamin, Daniel, and Steven Simon. *The Age of Sacred Terror.* New York: Random House, 2002.

T.H. Henriksen, *Cycles in US Foreign Policy since the Cold War,*
DOI 10.1007/978-3-319-48640-6

Bergen, Peter L. *Man Hunt: The Ten-Year Search for Bin Laden from 9/11 to Abbottabad*. New York: Crown Publishers, 2012.

Blix, Hans. *Disarming Iraq*. New York: Pantheon Books, 2004.

Blumenthal, Sidney. *The Clinton Wars*. New York: Farrar, Straus and Giroux, 2003.

Bowden, Mark. *Black Hawk Down: A Story of Modern Warfare*. New York: New American Library, 1999.

Bremer, L. Paul, III. *My Year In Iraq: The Struggle To Build A Future of Hope*. New York: Simon & Schuster, 2006.

Brinton, Crane. *The Anatomy of Revolution*. New York: Vintage, 1965.

Buchanan, Patrick J. *A Republic, Not An Empire*. Washington, DC: Regnery Publishing, 2001.

van Buren, Peter. *We Meant Well: How I Helped Lose the Battle for the Hearts and Minds of the Iraqi People*. New York: Metropolitan, 2011.

Bush, George W. *Decision Points*. New York: Crown Publishers, 2010.

Bush, George H.W., and Brent Scowcroft. *A World Transformed*. New York: Vintage Books, 1999.

Butler, Richard. *The Greatest Threat: Iraq, Weapons of Mass Destruction, and the Crisis of Global Security*. New York: Public Affairs, 2000.

Butterfield, Herbert. *The Origins of History*. London: Eyre Methuen, 1981.

Cha, Victor. *Impossible State: North Korea, Past and Future*. New York: Harper Collins, 2012.

Cha, Victor, and David C. Kang. *Nuclear North Korea: A Debate on Engagement Strategies*. New York: Columbia University Press, 2003.

Chayes, Sarah. *The Punishment of Virtue: Inside Afghanistan After the Taliban*. New York: Penguin Press, 2006.

Cheney, Dick. *In My Time: A Personal and Political Memoir*. New York: Threshold Editions, 2011.

Chivvis, Christopher S. *Toppling Qaddafi: Libya and the Limits of Intervention*. New York: Cambridge University Press, 2014.

Churchill, Winston. *The Gathering Storm*. New York: Houghton Mifflin Company, 1948.

Clark, Wesley. *Waging Modern War*. New York: Public Affairs, 2001.

Clarke, Richard A. *Against All Enemies: Inside America's War on Terror*. New York: Free Press, 2004.

Cleveland, William L. *A History of the Modern Middle East*. Boulder, CO: Westview Press, 2000.

Clinton, Hillary Rodham. *Hard Choices*. New York: Simon & Schuster, 2014.

Clinton, Bill. *My Life*. New York: Alfred A. Knopf, 2004.

Cohen, Warren I. *The Cambridge History of American Foreign Relations, Volume IV, America in the Age of Soviet Power, 1945–1991*. New York: Cambridge, 1993.

Cordesman, Anthony H. *The Iraq War: Strategy, Tactics, and Military Lessons.* Washington, DC: CSIS Press, 2004.

Corera, Gordon. *Shopping for Bombs: Nuclear Proliferation, Global Insecurity, and the Rise and Fall of the A.Q. Khan Network.* New York: Oxford University Press, 2006.

Crabb, Cecil V., Jr. *The Doctrines of American Foreign Policy: Their Meaning, Role, and Future.* Baton Rouge, LA: Louisiana State University Press, 1982.

Crowell, Lorenzo. The Anatomy of Just Cause: The Forces Involved, the Adequacy of Intelligence, and Its Success as a Joint Operation. In *Operation Just Cause: The U.S. Intervention in Panama*, ed. Bruce W. Watson and Peter G. Tsouras. Boulder, CO: Westview Press, 1991.

Crozier, Brian. *The Rise and Fall of the Soviet Empire.* Rocklin, CA: Prima, 1999.

Daalder, Ivo H., and Michael E. O'Hanlon. *Winning Ugly: NATO's War to Save Kosovo.* Washington, DC: Brookings Institution Press, 2000.

Danahar, Paul. *The New Middle East: The World after the Arab Spring.* London: Bloomsbury, 2013.

Dobbins, James, John G. McGinn, Keith Crane, Seth G. Jones, Rollie Lal, Andrew Rathmell, Rachel Swanger, and Anga Timilsina. *America's Role in Nation-Building: From Germany to Iraq.* Santa Monica, CA: Rand, 2003.

Donnelly, Thomas, Margaret Roth, and Caleb Baker. *Operation Just Cause: The Storming of Panama.* New York: Lexington Books, 1991.

Drew, Elizabeth. *On the Edge: The Clinton Presidency.* New York: Simon and Schuster, 1994.

Dueck, Colin. *Hard Line: The Republican Party and U.S. Foreign Policy since World War II.* Princeton, NJ: Princeton University Press, 2010.

———. *The Obama Doctrine: American Grand Strategy Today.* New York: Oxford University Press, 2015.

Ehrenfeld, Rachel. *Funding Evil: How Terrorism is Financed—and How to Stop It.* Chicago: Bonus Books, 2005.

Fatton, Robert, Jr. *Haiti's Predatory Republic: The Unending Transition to Democracy.* Boulder, CO: Lynne Rienner, 2002.

Fisher, Louis. *Presidential War Power.* Lawrence, KS: University Press of Kansas, 2013.

Flint, Julie, and Alex de Waal. *Darfur: A New History of a Long War.* London: Zed Books, 2008.

Ford, Franklin L. *Political Murder: From Tyrannicide to Terrorism.* Cambridge, MA: Harvard University Press, 1985.

French, Paul. *North Korea: State of Paranoia.* London: Zed Books, 2014.

Gaddis, John Lewis. *Surprise, Security and the American Experience.* Cambridge, MA: Harvard University Press, 2004.

———. *The United States and the End of the Cold War: Implications, Reconsiderations, Provocations.* New York: Oxford University Press, 1992.

Gates, Robert M. *Duty: Memoirs of a Secretary of State*. New York: Alfred A. Knopf, 2014.

Gellman, Barton. *Angler: The Cheney Vice Presidency*. New York: Penguin, 2008.

Glanville, Luke. *Sovereignty and the Responsibility to Protect*. Chicago: University of Chicago Press, 2014.

Gorbachev, Mikhail. *Memoirs*. New York: Doubleday, 1995.

Gordon, Michael R., and Bernard E. Trainor. *The Endgame: The Inside Story of the Struggle for Iraq, From George W. Bush to Barack Obama*. New York: Pantheon Books, 2013.

———. *The Generals War: The Inside Story of the Conflict in the Gulf*. New York: Little, Brown, 1995.

Gould, Lewis L. *The Republicans: A History of the Grand Old Party*. New York: Oxford University Press, 2014.

Graebner, Norman. *Foundations of American Foreign Policy: A Realist Appraisal from Franklin to McKinley*. Wilmington, DE: Scholarly Resources, 1985.

Graham, Bob. *Intelligence Matters*. New York: Random House, 2004.

Halper, Stefan, and Jonathan Clarke. *America Alone: The Neo-Conservatives and the Global Order*. New York: Cambridge University Press, 2004.

Harding, Robert C. *The History of Panama*. Westport, CT: Greenwood Press, 2006.

Hastings, Michael. *The Operators: The Wild and Terrifying Inside Story of America's War in Afghanistan*. New York: Plume, 2012.

Heaney, Michael T., and Fabio Rojas. *Party in the Street: The Antiwar Movement and the Democratic Party after 9/11*. New York: Cambridge University Press, 2015.

Heilbrunn, Jacob. *They Knew They Were Right: The Rise of the Neocons*. New York: Doubleday, 2008.

Hemmer, Christopher. *American Pendulum: Recurring Debates in U.S. Grand Strategy*. Ithaca, NY: Cornell University Press, 2015.

Henriksen, Thomas H. *America and the Rogue States*. New York: Palgrave Macmillan, 2012.

Hill, Christopher R. *Outpost: Life on the Frontlines of American Diplomacy*. New York: Simon and Schuster, 2014.

Hiro, Dilip. *Desert Shield to Desert Storm: The Second Gulf War*. New York: Author's Choice Books, 2003.

———. *Neighbors, Not Friends: Iraq and Iran After the Gulf Wars*. London: Routlege, 2001.

Holbrooke, Richard. *To End a War*. New York: Random House, 1998.

Howard, Michael. *The Lessons of History*. New Haven, CT: Yale University Press, 1881.

Hyland, William G. *Clinton's World: Remaking American Foreign Policy*. Westport, CT: Praeger, 1999.

The Iraq Study Group Report: The Way Forward—A New Approach. New York: Vintage Books, 2006.

Johnson, Chalmers. *Blowback: The Costs and Consequences of American Empire.* New York: Henry Holt, 2000.

Judah, Tim. *Kosovo: War and Revenge.* New Haven, CT: Yale University, 2002.

Kagan, Robert. *Of Paradise and Power: America and Europe in the New World Order.* New York: Alfred A. Knopf, 2003.

Kagan, Kimberly. *The Surge: A Military History.* New York: Encounter Books, 2009.

Kennedy, David M. *Freedom from Fear: The American People in Depression and War, 1929–1945.* New York: Oxford University Press, 1999.

Klingberg, Frank L. *Cyclical Trends in American Foreign Policy Moods.* Lanham, MD: University Press of America, 1983.

Koster, R.M., and Guillermo Sanchez Borbon. *In The Time of Tyrants.* London: Secker & Warburg, 1990.

Lacey, James, and Williamson Murray. *Moment of Battle: The Twenty Clashes that Changed the World.* New York: Bantam, 2013.

Lagon, Mark P. *The Reagan Doctrine: Sources of American Conduct in the Cold War's Last Chapter.* Westport, CT: Preager, 1994.

Lambeth, Benjamin S. *NATO's Air War for Kosovo: A Strategic and Operational Assessment.* Santa Monica, CA: RAND, 2001.

———. *Transformation of American Air Power.* Ithaca, NY: Cornell University Press, 2000.

Litwak, Robert S. *Regime Change: U.S. Strategy through the Prism of 9/11.* Washington, DC: Woodrow Wilson Center Press, 2007.

Lucas, Edward. *The New Cold War.* New York: Palgrave Macmillan, 2014.

Machiavelli, Niccolò. *Discourses on Livy.* Trans. Harvey C. Mansfield and Nathan Tarcov. Chicago: University of Chicago Press, 1996.

Malcolm, Noel. *Kosovo: A Short History.* New York: New York University Press, 1998.

Malone, David. *Decision-Making in the UN Security Council: The Case of Haiti.* New York: Oxford University Press, 1998.

Mann, James. *George W. Bush.* New York: Times Books, 2015.

———. *The Obamians: The Struggle Inside the White How to Define American Power.* New York: Viking, 2012.

———. *Rise of the Vulcans: The History of Bush's War Cabinet.* New York: Viking, 2004.

Mansoor, Peter R. *Surge: My Journey with General David Petraeus and the Remaking of the Iraq War.* New Haven, CT: Yale University Press, 2013.

Marker, Jamsheed. *East Timor: A Memoir of the Negotiations for Independence.* Jefferson, NC: McFarland, 2003.

Mattson, Kevin. *What the Heck Are You Up To, Mr. President?: Jimmy Carter, America's "Malaise," and the Speech that Should Have Changed the Country.* New York: Bloombury, 2010.

Mazarr, Michael J. *North Korea and the Bomb: A Case Study in Nonproliferation*. New York: St. Martin's Press, 1995.

Mazzetti, Mark. *The Way of the Knife*. New York: Penguin Press, 2013.

McChrystal, Stanley. *My Share of the Task: A Memoir*. New York: Penguin Group, 2013.

McDougall, Walter A. *Promised Land, Crusader State*. New York: Houghton Mifflin Company, 1997.

McGing, Brian. *Polybius' Histories*. New York: Oxford University Press, 2010.

Meacham, Jon. *Destiny and Power: The American Odyssey of George Herbert Walker Bush*. New York: Random House, 2015.

Melvern, L.R. *A People Betrayed: The Role of the West in Rwanda's Genocide*. London: Zed Books, 2000.

Michaels, Jim. *A Chance in Hell: the Men Who Triumphed over Iraq's Deadliest City and Turned the Tide of War*. New York: St. Martin's Press, 2010.

Miller, Judith. *The Story: A Reporter's Journey*. New York: Simon & Schuster, 2015.

Miniter, Richard. *Leading From Behind: The Reluctant President and the Advisors Who Decide for Him*. New York: St. Martin's Griffin, 2012.

Morell, Michael. *The Great War Of Our Time: The CIA's Fight Against Terrorism—From al Qa'ida to ISIS*. New York: Hachette, 2015.

Nasr, Vali. *The Dispensable Nation: American Foreign Policy in Retreat*. New York: Doubleday, 2013.

———. *The Shia Revival: How Conflicts within Islam Will Shape the Future*. New York: W.W. Norton, 2006.

Nau, Henry R. 2013. *Conservative Internationalism: Armed Diplomacy Under Jefferson, Polk, Truman, and Reagan*. Princetion, NJ: Princeton University Press.

Owen, David. *Balkan Odyssey*. New York: Harcourt Brace, 1995.

Owen, Robert C., ed. *Deliberate Force: A Case Study in Effective Air Campaign*. Montgomery, AL: Air University Press, 2000.

Paine, S.C.M. *The Wars for Asia, 1911–1949*. New York: Cambridge University Press, 2012.

Panetta, Leon. *Worthy Fights: A Memoir of Leadership in War and Peace*. New York: Penguin Press, 2014.

Pillar, Paul. *Intelligence and U.S. Foreign Policy: Iraq, 9/11, and Misguided Reform*. New York: Columbia University Press, 2011.

Pillsbury, Michael. *The Hundred-Year Marathon: China's Secret Strategy to Replace America as the Global Superpower*. New York: Henry Holt and Company, 2015.

Powell, Colin. *My American Journey*. New York: Random House, 1995.

Power, Samantha. *A Problem from Hell: America and the Age of Genocide*. New York: Basic Books, 2002.

Priest, Dana, and William M. Arkin. *Top Secret America: The Rise of the New American Security State*. New York: Little, Brown and Company, 2011.

Reid, T.R. *The United States of Europe: The New Superpower and The End of American Supremacy*. New York: Penguin, 2005.

Reiss, Mitchell. *Bridled Ambition: Why Countries Constrain Their Nuclear Capabilities*. Washington, DC: Woodrow Wilson Center Press, 1995.

Rice, Condoleezza. *No Higher Honor: A Memoir of My Years in Washington*. New York: Broadway Books, 2011.

Ricks, Thomas E. *Fiasco: The American Military Adventure in Iraq*. New York: Penguin Press, 2006.

Riddell, Peter. *Hug Them Close: Blair, Clinton, Bush, and the 'Special Relationship,'*. London: Politico's Publishing, 2003.

Rieff, David. *Slaughterhouse: Bosnia and the Failure of the West*. New York: Simon & Schuster, 1995.

Roosevelt, Theodore. *American Problems*. New York: The Outlook Company, 1910.

Rothkopf, David J. *National Insecurity: American Leadership in an Age of Fear*. New York: Public Affairs, 2014.

———. *Running the World: The Inside Story of the National Security Council and the Architects of American Power*. New York: Public Affairs, 2005.

Rumsfeld, Donald. *Known and Unknown: A Memoir*. New York: Sentinel, 2011.

Sammon, Bill. *Fighting Back: The War on Terrorism—Inside the Bush White House*. Washington, DC: Regnery Publishing, 2002.

Sanger, David E. *Confront and Conceal: Obama's Secret War and Surprising Use of American Power*. New York: Crown Publishers, 2012.

Santayana, George. *The Life of Reason: Reason in Common Sense*. New York: Scribner, 1958.

Sarotte, Mary Elise. *The Collapse: The Accidental Opening of the Berlin Wall*. New York: Basic Books, 2014.

Schlesinger, Arthur M., Jr. *The Cycles of American Politics*. Boston: Houghton Mifflin, 1986.

———. *War and the American Presidency*. New York: W.W. Norton, 2004.

Schmitt, Eric, and Thom Shanker. *Counterstrike: Untold Story of America's Secret Campaign Against Al Qaeda*. New York: Time Books, 2011.

Schroen, Gary C. *First In: An Insider's Account of How the CIA Spearheaded the War on Terror in Afghanistan*. New York: Ballentine Books, 2005.

Sestanovitch, Stephen. *Maximalist: America in the World From Truman To Obama*. New York: Alfred A. Knopf, 2014.

Sifry, Micah L., and Christopher Cerf, eds. *The Gulf War Reader: History, Documents, Opinion*. New York: Random House, 1991.

Silber, Laura, and Allan Little. *Yugoslavia: Death of a Nation*. New York: Penguin Books, 1995.

Singer, P.W. *Corporate Warriors: the Rise of the Privatized Military Industry*. Ithaca, NY: Cornell University Press, 2003.

Sky, Emma. *The Unraveling: High Hopes and Missed Opportunities in Iraq*. New York: Public Affairs, 2015.

Snow, Richard. *I Invented the Modern Age: The Rise of Henry Ford.* New York: Scribner, 2013.

Spence, Michael. *The Next Convergence: The Future of Economic Growth in a Multispeed World.* New York: Farrar, Straus, and Giroux, 2011.

Stephens, Philip. *Tony Blair: The Making of a World Leader.* New York: Viking, 2004.

Stimson, James A. *Tides of Consent: How Public Opinion Shapes American Politics.* Cambridge, MA: Cambridge University Press, 2004.

Sultan, Khaled bin, General. *Desert Warrior: A Personal View of the Gulf War by the Joint Forces Commander.* New York: Harper Collins, 1995.

Sushko, Oleksandr, and Olena Prystayko. Western Influence. In *Revolution in Orange: The Origins of Ukraine's Democratic Breakthrough*, ed. Anders Aslund and Michael McFaul. Washington, DC: Carnegie Endowment for Peace, 2006.

Taheri, Amir. *The Persian Night: Iran Under the Khomeinist Revolution.* New York: Encounter Books, 2009.

Talbott, Strobe. *The Russia Hand: A Memoir of Presidential Diplomacy.* New York: Random House, 2002.

Tanner, Stephan. *Afghanistan: A Military History from Alexander the Great to the Fall of the Taliban.* New York: Da Capo Press, 2002.

Taylor, Frederick. *The Berlin Wall: 13 August 1961–9 November 1989.* London: Bloomsbury, 2004.

Tenet, George. *At the Center of the Storm: My Years at the CIA.* New York: Harper Collins, 2007.

Thatcher, Margaret. *The Downing Street Years.* New York: Harper Collins, 1993.

Thucydides. *History of the Peloponnesian War.* Trans. Richard Crawley. London: J.M. Dent & Sons, 1910.

Tripp, Charles. *A History of Iraq.* New York: Cambridge University Press, 2002.

Trompf, G.W. *The Idea of Historical Recurrence in Western Thought: From Antiquity to the Reformation.* Berkeley, CA: University of California Press, 1979.

Vico, Giambattista. *The New Science.* Trans. Thomas Goddard Bergin and Max Harold Fisch. Ithaca, NY: Cornell University Press, 1961.

Weiss, Michael, and Hassan Hassan. *ISIS: Inside the Army of Terror.* New York: Regan Arts, 2015.

Williams, Brian Glyn. *Predators: The CIA's Drone War on al Qaeda.* Washington, DC: Potomac Books, 2013.

Williams, William Appleman. *The Tragedy of American Diplomacy.* New York: W. W. Norton, 1972.

Wilson, Joseph C. *The Politics of Truth.* New York: Carroll & Graf, 2004.

Wit, Joel S., Daniel B. Poneman, and Robert L. Gallucci. *Going Critical: The First North Korean Crisis.* Washington, DC: Brookings Institution Press, 2004.

Witcover, Jules. *Party of the People: A History of the Democrats.* New York: Random House, 2004.

Woodward, Bob. *The Agenda: Inside the Clinton White House.* New York: Simon & Schuster, 1994.

———. *Bush at War.* New York: Simon & Schuster, 2002.

———. *Obama's Wars.* New York: Simon & Schuster, 2010.

———. *Plan of Attack.* New York: Simon and Schuster, 2004.

Wurmser, David. *Tyranny's Ally: America's Failure to Defeat Saddam Hussein.* Washington, DC: American Enterprise Institute, 1999.

Zeisburg, Mariah. *War Powers: The Politics of Constitutional Authority.* Princeton, NJ: Princeton University Press, 2013.

Zelikow, Philip, and Condoleezza Rice. *Germany United and Europe Transformed: A Study in Statecraft.* Cambridge, MA: Harvard University Press, 1995.

Index

Note: Page numbers followed by 'n' denote notes.

T.H. Henriksen, *Cycles in US Foreign Policy since the Cold War*,
DOI 10.1007/978-3-319-48640-6

F

G

H

CPSIA information can be obtained
at www.ICGtesting.com
Printed in the USA
LVHW051946040221
678392LV00010B/209